Freethinkers and Labor Leaders

Confluencias

SERIES EDITORS

Susie S. Porter
University of Utah

María L. O. Muñoz
Susquehanna University

Diana Montaño
Washington University in St. Louis

Freethinkers and Labor Leaders

Women, Social Change, and Politics in Modern Mexico

MARÍA TERESA FERNÁNDEZ ACEVES

Translated by
TANYA HUNTINGTON

University of Nebraska Press
LINCOLN

© 2025 by the Board of Regents of the University of Nebraska
All rights reserved

Acknowledgments for the use of copyrighted material appear on page xii, which constitutes an extension of the copyright page.

The University of Nebraska Press is part of a land-grant institution with campuses and programs on the past, present, and future homelands of the Pawnee, Ponca, Otoe-Missouria, Omaha, Dakota, Lakota, Kaw, Cheyenne, and Arapaho Peoples, as well as those of the relocated Ho-Chunk, Sac and Fox, and Iowa Peoples.

For customers in the EU with safety/GPSR concerns, contact:
gpsr@mare-nostrum.co.uk
Mare Nostrum Group BV
Mauritskade 21D
1091 GC Amsterdam
The Netherlands

Library of Congress Cataloging-in-Publication Data
Names: Fernández Aceves, María Teresa, author.
Title: Freethinkers and labor leaders: women, social change, and politics in modern Mexico / María Teresa Fernández Aceves; translated by Tanya Huntington.
Other titles: Mujeres en el cambio social en el siglo XX mexicano. English
Description: Lincoln: University of Nebraska Press, 2025. | Series: Confluencias | Includes bibliographical references and index.
Identifiers: LCCN 2024033089
ISBN 9781496231277 (hardcover)
ISBN 9781496243171 (paperback)
ISBN 9781496243614 (epub)
ISBN 9781496243621 (pdf)
Subjects: LCSH: Women—Political activity—Mexico—History—20th century. | Social change—Mexico—History—20th century. | Women social reformers—Mexico—Biography. | Women political activists—Mexico—Biography. | Mexico—History—Revolution, 1910–1920—Women. | Mexico—Politics and government—20th century. | Mexico—Social conditions—20th century.
Classification: LCC HQ1236.5.M6 F4713 2025 |
DDC 972.08092/52—dc23/eng/20250210
LC record available at https://lccn.loc.gov/2024033089

Set in Minion Pro by Scribe Inc.

For Graciela A., Abel, Rodrigo, and Diego
For Mary Kay Vaughan

CONTENTS

List of Illustrations	ix
Acknowledgments	xi
List of Abbreviations	xiii
Introduction	1
1. The "Modern Woman," Politics, and the Mexican Revolution in Guadalajara, 1910–17	20
2. Belén de Sárraga Hernández: Anticlericalism, Freethinkers, and the Mexican Revolution	46
3. Atala Apodaca Anaya: Anticlericalism, Civic Education, Progressive Forces, and the Mexican Revolution	82
4. María Arcelia Díaz: Labor and Women's Politics within the Context of the Construction of the Postrevolutionary State of Guadalajara	120
5. María Guadalupe Martínez Villanueva: The Mobilization of Women and Corporatist Politics	153
6. María Guadalupe Urzúa Flores: Advocate and Modernizer of Jalisco Rural Politics	181
Epilogue	209
Appendix: Mexico's Population Ages Ten Years and Older According to Literacy, Illiteracy, and Sex in Mexico, 1895–2000	215
Notes	217
Bibliography	265
Index	291

ILLUSTRATIONS

Figures

1. Laura Apodaca Anaya, 1902 — 22
2. General Manuel M. Diéguez, 1917 — 29
3. Parade commemorating Carranza's visit to Guadalajara, 1917 — 33
4. Front page of *Boletín militar*'s first anniversary issue — 38
5. Cover of *El clericalismo en América* — 54
6. Belén de Sárraga in Montevideo, 1914 — 55
7. Francisco I. Madero, 1910 — 58
8. Belén de Sárraga giving a speech in Mexico City, 1912 — 60
9. Belén de Sárraga at a gathering in Mexico City, 1912 — 61
10. Sisters Laura and Atala Apodaca, 1915 — 85
11. Atala Apodaca Anaya, ca. 1914 — 92
12. Andrés and Atala Apodaca Anaya, ca. 1914 — 92
13. Atala Apodaca Anaya with two Constitutionalists, ca. 1914 — 113
14. President Venustiano Carranza, 1917 — 115
15. Atala Apodaca Anaya, ca. 1946 — 117
16. Unión Obrera de La Experiencia board of directors, 1922 — 131
17. María A. Díaz and Círculo Feminista de Occidente members, 1936 — 137
18. María A. Díaz's Círculo Feminista de Occidente letterhead — 138
19. María A. Díaz's death anniversary pamphlet — 143

20.	Mural at Federación de Trabajadores de Jalisco	145
21.	"The Motherland" depicted in Federación de Trabajadores de Jalisco mural	146
22.	Title page of *Some Passages from the Life of María Arcelia Díaz*	147
23.	Mural at the Labor Department of the State of Jalisco	150
24.	*Effective Suffrage, No Reelection* tableaux vivant, 1912	157
25.	Círculo Feminista de Occidente board of directors	160
26.	Heliodoro Hernández Loza and María Guadalupe Martínez	163
27.	The CIRFO female basketball team, 1937	172
28.	The CIRFO basketball team, including Guadalupe Martínez, 1943	173
29.	Flores Monroy family	187
30.	María Guadalupe Urzúa Flores in her youth	189
31.	Hospital construction at San Martín Hidalgo, Jalisco	192
32.	María Guadalupe Urzúa surrounded by peasant women	199
33.	Freyer cartoon depicting the first federal congresswomen (1955)	203

Tables

1.	Labor force distribution in Jalisco by sector and by sex, 1921	128
2.	Textile industry workers in the Guadalajara region, 1906–35	129
3.	Mexico's population ages ten years and older according to literacy, illiteracy, and sex in Mexico, 1895–2000	215

ACKNOWLEDGMENTS

This book required many years of research and dedication. Questions that arose during my research but had no explanation at the time were the ones I attempted to answer after joining Centro de Investigaciones y Estudios Superiores en Antropología Social (CIESAS) Occidente as a researcher in 2001. During my course of inquiry, I ran into a few other very interesting women and themes that motivated me to embark on a path that was long and sinuous but undeniably fascinating.

Various institutions have contributed to this work through grants, such as the Fulbright García Robles Scholarship (1993–95); the Ford-MacArthur Fellowship (1993–95); the Consejo Nacional de Ciencia y Tecnología (CONACYT), which gave a complementary grant to support my studies (1995–2000); the Spencer Fellowship (1998–99); and the Woodrow Wilson Women's Studies Fellowship (1998). I also received the support of CONACYT for my project entitled "Mujeres, madres, trabajadoras y ciudadanas en Guadalajara: La lucha del Círculo Feminista de Occidente por la ciudadanía, 1940–1955," which was financed under the auspices of the REF 137755-H program for installation projects. CIESAS has always supported me with the per diems needed to visit various archives and libraries in the United States and Mexico.

During this time many people generously heard me out, recommended readings, patiently read different versions of the manuscript, made pertinent comments, and exchanged materials with me. In Mexico, I have held passionate conversations regarding women's history, labor history, and Catholicism with Carmen Castañeda García (RI), Carmen Ramos Escandón, Alma Dorantes, Julia Preciado, Dawn Keremitsis, Susan Street, Claudia Rivas Jiménez, Elisa Cárdenas, Cande Ochoa, Mílada Bazant, Alicia Civera, Laurie Schaffner, Anayanci Fregoso, Alejandra Aguilar, Teresa Orozco, Enriqueta Tuñón Pablos, María Dolores Ramos, Romina Martínez (RI), Robert Curley, José

Alfredo Gómez Estrada (RI), and Yolanda Padilla. My students Laura Zapién, Ileana Gómez Ortega, Susana Gutiérrez Portillo, Marcela López Arellano, Ana Isabel Enríquez, Isabel Juárez, Christian Osnaya, Gonzalo Miramontes Fausto, Kenia Torres, Milagros Cruz Guerrero, Rosy Villarreal, and Tania Aguilar have also heard or generously read various sections of this book.

In the United States, I would like to thank the following people for their time, friendship, and generosity: Mary Kay Vaughan, Heather Fowler-Salamini, Susie S. Porter, Francie Chassen-López, Silvia Arrom, Ana María Kapelusz-Poppi, Margaret Power, Nilda Flores González, Dawn Deaton, Kristina Boylan, Sarah Buck, Sasha Schell, Nikki Sanders, Victor Macías-González, Chris Boyer, and Susan Gauss.

I thank all my sisters and my brother, who have always provided me with their solidarity and ample support. My husband, Abel Mercado, and our sons, Rodrigo and Diego, have suffered my absence during the many hours dedicated to bringing this book to light. I enormously appreciate their patience, enthusiasm, words of encouragement, and above all, unconditional love.

Previously published sections of these chapters have been substantially expanded and modified. Part of chapter 1 appeared as "'La mujer moderna' y la Revolución Mexicana en Guadalajara, 1910–1920," in *Independencia y revolución: Reflexiones en torno al bicentenario y el centenario*, vol. 3, edited by Jaime Olveda, 265–304 (Guadalajara: El Colegio de Jalisco, 2010). Part of chapter 3 appeared as "Educación secular: El caso de Atala Apodaca," in *Cátedras y catedráticos en la historia de las universidades en México*, edited by María de Lourdes Alvarado and Leticia Pérez Puente, 1–15 (Mexico: IISUE-UNAM, 2008). Part of chapter 4 appeared as "María Arcelia Díaz, la política laboral y de mujeres en Guadalajara, 1896–1939," in *Siete historias de vida: Mujeres jaliscienses del siglo XX*, compiled by Anayanci Fregoso, 15–39 (Guadalajara: Universidad de Guadalajara, 2006). Part of chapter 5 appeared as "Engendering Caciquismo: Guadalupe Martínez and Heliodoro Hernández Loza and the Politics of Organized Labor in Jalisco," in *Caciquismo in Twentieth-Century Mexico*, edited by Alan Knight and Wil G. Pansters, 201–24 (London: ILAS, 2005).

ABBREVIATIONS

ADCG	Asociación de Damas Católicas de Guadalajara (Catholic ladies association of Guadalajara)
ACJM	Asociación Católica de la Juventud Mexicana (Mexican youth Catholic association)
CAOLJ	Confederación de Agrupaciones Obreras Libertarias de Jalisco (Jalisco confederation of libertarian labor associations)
CCT	Confederación Católica del Trabajo (Catholic labor confederation)
CEM	Centro Evolucionista de Mujeres (Women's evolutionist center)
CFALV	Club Femenil Antireeleccionista Leona Vicario (Leona Vicario Femenine antireelectionist club)
CFO	Círculo Feminista de Occidente (Western feminist circle)
CFOMAD	Círculo Feminista de Occidente María Arcelia Díaz (María Arcelia Díaz Western feminist circle)
CLJOD	Círculo Liberal Josefa Ortiz de Domínguez (Josefa Ortiz de Domínguez liberal circle)
CNC	Confederación Nacional Campesina (National peasants' confederation)
CNCT	Confederación Nacional Católica del Trabajo (National Catholic labor confederation)
CNOP	Confederación Nacional de Organizaciones Populares (People's national confederation of organizations)
COJ	Confederación Obrera de Jalisco (Jalisco labor confederation)
COM	Casa del Obrero Mundial (Worldwide house for workers)
CPLJ	Confederación de Partidos Liberales de Jalisco (Jalisco confederation of liberal parties)
CRF	Centro Radical Femenino (Women's radical center)

CROC	Confederación Revolucionaria Obrera y Campesina (Revolutionary confederation of workers and peasants)
CROM	Confederación Regional Obrera Mexicana (Mexican regional labor confederation)
CFM	Consejo Feminista Mexicano (Mexican feminist council)
CTM	Confederación de Trabajadores de México (Workers' confederation of Mexico)
FAM	Federación Anticlerical Mexicana (Mexican anticlerical federation)
FAOJ	Federación de Agrupaciones Obreras de Jalisco (Jalisco federation of workers' associations)
FMSO	Federación Malagueña de Sociedades Obreras (Málaga federation of workers' societies)
FTJ	Federación de Trabajadores de Jalisco (Jalisco federation of workers)
FUPDM	Frente Único Pro Derechos de la Mujer (United front for the rights of women)
JDACS	Junta Diocesana de Acción Católica Social (Catholic social action diocese board)
LAP	Liga Amigos del Pueblo (Friends of the people league)
LNDLR	Liga Nacional Defensora de la Libertad Religiosa (National defense of religious freedom league)
LPO	Liga Protectora de la Obrera (Women workers' protective league)
PCM	Partido Comunista Mexicano (Mexican Communist Party)
PCN	Partido Católico Nacional (National Catholic Party)
PCP	Partido Constitucional Progresista (Constitutional progressive party).
PRI	Partido Revolucionario Institucional (Institutional revolutionary party)
PRM	Partido de la Revolución Mexicana (Party of the Mexican Revolution)
PNR	Partido Nacional Revolucionario (National revolutionary party)
PP	Partido Popular (People's Party)
SEP	Secretaría de Educación Pública (Secretariat of public education)
STMNS	Sindicato de Trabajadores de Molinos de Nixtamal y Similares (Union of cornmeal mill and similar workers)
SUTAJ	Sindicato Único de Trabajadores Automovilistas de Jalisco (Sole labor union of the automobile workers of Jalisco)
UOLE	Unión Obrera de La Experiencia (La experiencia labor union)

Freethinkers and Labor Leaders

Introduction

On January 12, 1923, wearing a work suit still full of cotton dust, the feminist María Arcelia Díaz, a textile worker and general secretary of the Unión Obrera de La Experiencia, delivered an eloquent speech advocating for labor rights at Guadalajara's main theater, the Degollado Theater. Many workers applauded Díaz's articulate discourse, which drew on the experience of textile workers and highlighted the grievances of artisans, workers, and laborers during the Mexican Revolution and the ensuing conflict between the Catholic Church and the new postrevolutionary state. This speech was part of the program of the conference featuring Belén de Sárraga Hernández as the main speaker.[1] Sárraga, an anticlerical and freethinking Spanish feminist, had engaged in and promoted transnational political work with the International Federation of Freethinkers of Brussels to combat what they considered the primary obstacle to progress in the Americas: clericalism.

This event marked the first and only meeting between Díaz and Sárraga. Although they championed common causes, they did not maintain communication. Nevertheless, both continued to fight for the emancipation of women and for broader women's rights—civic, economic, labor, political, and social—beyond mere women's suffrage, an effort Katherine M. Marino refers to as *feminismo americano*.[2] Sárraga pursued these goals primarily at the transnational level, while Díaz focused on the local, regional, and national spheres. Their political biographies illustrate how the battle for women's rights intersects at the local, regional, national, and transnational realms.

This work uses biographical, local, regional, and national perspectives to explore the diaspora and transnational movements advocating for women's rights. It examines the lives, political careers, and involvement in the public sphere of five militant feminist women who fought for these rights. Through this analysis, I explain why, how, and when the participation of women became more evident in res publica at the start of the twentieth century, not only in Guadalajara and Mexico, but also in other parts of the world, such as Spain and Latin America. These cases delve into subjective, practical experiences as well as representations and cultural memories of women with strong ties to the Mexican State. Throughout the book, I develop the following arguments: (1) these five women, through their political careers and changing discourses, aided the creation of a "modern" culture in the revolutionary and postrevolutionary eras in Mexico and, in some ways, Latin America as a whole; (2) historical conditions and different processes influenced their personal experiences from the 1870s to the 2000s and, in turn, contributed to the formation of their own identities as activists and feminists who struggled for a more just society; (3) their lives are a patent demonstration of the ways social change and the Mexican Revolution (1910–17) constructed gender and how, in turn, gender molded the revolution and social change; (4) likewise, these women transformed the social configurations of femininity, masculinity, politics, and citizenship in twentieth-century Mexico.

Belén de Sárraga Hernández (1872–1950), Atala Apodaca Anaya (1884–1977), María Arcelia Díaz (1896–1939), María Guadalupe Martínez Villanueva (1906–2002), and María Guadalupe Urzúa Flores (1912–2004) formed part of two cultural generations that interacted with each other. Both generations contributed to the consolidation of state cooperative institutions and the antiestablishment and dissident politics that evolved in the late 1940s.[3] Each of these women shared the anticlerical views of certain revolutionary leaders, such as Francisco I. Madero, Manuel M. Diéguez, Álvaro Obregón, Plutarco Elías Calles, and José Guadalupe Zuno Hernández. These women drew on different liberal traditions (both Spanish and Mexican) that were gradually enriched and transformed by various trends of thought (anticlericalism, anarcho-syndicalism, and freethinking). Sárraga, Apodaca, Díaz, Martínez, and Urzúa conceived of the means necessary to secure the emancipation of women; they expressed what the position of women in society ought to be; they argued in favor of the role played by women as citizens in education and in politics. By doing so, they transformed the social constructs associated with citizenship, femininity, masculinity, and politics. They confronted a liberal system that reinforced and legitimized female subordination and negotiated new spaces, practices, and representations for women.

This book starts from a long-term perspective of social processes and social configurations integrated by "individuals who together form societies" to examine further, as Joan Scott would say, how women's participation constructed gender and how politics determined their contributions.[4] I draw from the theoretical-methodological proposals of Norbert Elias regarding the long view, which is based on a multicausal, procedural, and relational analysis—one that distances itself from determinisms and linear causalities in order to examine the lengthy process of social change. According to Elias, this perspective "helps resolve ... the ... problem of connection among individual psychological structures, that is to say, of so-called personality structures and the compositions that constitute many interdependent individuals, i.e., social structures. Both structures [are] shifting, like interdependent components of the same long-term development."[5] These configurations convey complex and changing balances of power between interdependent figures and are formed and transformed over the course of social processes. The changing balance of power "allows for the conceptualization of various levels and shades of meaning in the existing power disparities between groups of human beings."[6] The changes in individual structures and social structures are tracked in different discourses, practices, and representations of gender, education, citizenship, and politics. In the five cases selected here, I examine how long-term processes had repercussions (within local, regional, national, and transnational arenas) on diachronic and synchronic temporalities.

Although the five women studied here were exceptional, they were by no means unique to their time. Postrevisionist historiographies dedicated to the Mexican Revolution of 1910, the formation of the new state, and the conflict between the Catholic Church and the state have salvaged records of the political participation of women.[7] But what relates these women to one another? What social processes converge in them? What similarities did they share? Utilizing microhistorical and transnational approaches, these women highlight the circulation of ideas about women's rights and their interconnected roles in relation to anticlericalism, women's emancipation, and political participation.[8] Each one advocated for the civic or modern woman during the early decades of the twentieth century and for the rights of the masses; access to jobs and education; the gradual increase in educational, philanthropic, labor, political, and social organizations led by women; and greater access to a culture of capitalist consumption.

Sárraga developed her career and thought by drawing on Spanish anticlerical, Spiritist, freethinking, Masonic, and Republican ideals. She completed four propaganda tours across Hispanic America and visited Guadalajara in 1912, 1922, and 1923. Apodaca, Díaz, and Martínez seized the opportunity to hear her speak on these occasions. These points of contact and encounters between Apodaca, Díaz, Martínez, and Sárraga were crucial to their dissemination of the anticlerical policies of the 1910 Mexican Revolution and the new revolutionary state, which stemmed from everyday life and their own subjective experiences. These convergences and encounters reinforced their convictions and commitment to viewing the modern woman as a citizen with economic, labor, political, and social rights.

In order to better understand the dissemination of these ideas, I draw on the explanation provided by literary critic Mary Louise Pratt regarding modernity and its "other": women. Pratt holds that within "the conflictive and destabilizing status of women as the internal Other of modernity . . . are intersected three contradictory imperatives of modernity: . . . its need to fix 'others' in order to define itself, its need to produce modern subjects, and its need to modernize those same Others through assimilation."[9] Pratt states that modernity in Latin America has interacted "with imported or imposed trends and the profound and heterogeneous traditions of popular culture."[10] She and other scholars of popular culture have identified the need to reflect more deeply on how this dissemination functions in the Americas. She rejects "most emphatically the centralist assumption that one dissemination substitutes the previous one," specifying "that even that which is imposed has to enter through that which is already there, and modernity enters through all social sectors, not only the elite."[11]

In order to go beyond both exceptionalism and a vision of women as victimized or subordinated, my analysis of Sárraga, Apodaca, Díaz, Martínez, and Urzúa Flores combines proposals of new cultural history; new biography; postrevisionist and gender studies of the Mexican Revolution and the revolutionary process of new state formation; women's mobilizations regarding gender, power, politics, and citizenship; and transnational feminism.

From New Cultural History to New Biography
New cultural history grants me the tools necessary to analyze the discourses, practices, representations, power relations, and negotiations that all five

women featured in *Freethinkers and Labor Leaders* carried out. The narrative of their experiences serves as a vehicle to set up a dialogue between primary sources and theoretical discussions regarding discourse, experience, gender, memory, narrative, and subjectivity. Such interlocution arose in the field of history because of the impact of new cultural history in the late 1980s. This perspective was influenced by cultural anthropology, inviting historians to examine sociocultural formations as texts and to pay close attention to the uses of language in their analyses of discourse; it promoted an approach to anthropology and stimulated historians to consider cultural artifacts as performative rather than as mere expressions. New cultural history was also receptive to feminist proposals that sensitized the linkages between public and private life, subjectivities, and fictions and ideologies. Likewise, new cultural history approached literary studies to examine concepts such as intertextuality (one story always alludes to another story) and the reception of readers.[12] New cultural history also placed emphasis on power relations to examine "from below" how marginalized groups excluded from hegemonic power resisted or negotiated with it.

By the 2000s, some cultural historians had embraced a "turn to new biography," a shift that Mary Kay Vaughan explains as a response to the limitations of poststructuralism.[13] According to Vaughan, biography allows historians to move beyond confining subjects within social discourse, restoring individual agency and the capacity for personal and social change. She argues that the use of biography "can bring to light a surprising heterogeneity of discourses (dominant, residual, marginal, and spatially circumscribed) that an individual encounters; the complicated ways in which he/she combines them to constitute subjectivity; and the conditions through which new, often subversive discourses emerge to become dominant, to join the polyphony, or to be relegated to the margins."[14]

Like Vaughan, Mílada Bazant argues that employing cultural history, microhistory, and the history of emotions can enhance biographical studies by examining how "the link of a life with the different contexts it illuminates can explain a plurality of times and views of a historical process that was believed to be more coherent and unitary."[15] Similarly, Francie Chassen-López employs several methodologies—including feminist methodologies (gender analysis), the biographical turn, and microhistory—to reveal what macrohistory and grand narratives have obscured for centuries. In her biography *Mujer y poder en el siglo XIX: La vida extraordinaria de Juana Catarina Romero, cacica de Tehuantepec,* Chassen-López demonstrates "how the case of a Oaxacan provincial woman clarifies not only how great processes were carried out in practice, but also how it is possible to capture and glimpse the performance of women in those processes."[16] She argues that "it is necessary to continue the revolutionary work in biography, finding and developing the appropriate methodologies and theories to rescue and explain stories that until now have gone unnoticed and obscured, to make the invisible visible."[17] Therefore, feminist biography reflects on rethinking the gender order as a social structure that systematically produces relations of identity, power, hierarchy, inequity, and inequality. These dynamics are intertwined in all dimensions of social life. It is not limited to the traditional roles assigned to men and women; gender order is a broader and more complex relational structure that affects all social interactions.

The proposals of new biography are complemented by the gender perspective proposed by Joan Scott, who states that biographies can act as opportunities to examine in detail the multiple and complete discursive contents—cultural and political—that create a historic figure.[18] The biographic gaze allows us to elucidate how some women have negotiated and transformed gender roles not only in a specific society but also in their daily lives.[19] According to Jean Franco, through biography, it is possible to scrutinize the discourses and representations of women in the history of Mexico. She specifies that these discursive positions have been characterized by a series of discontinuities, violence, and clashes.[20] The five women whose stories are revealed here provide a fine example of this throughout much of the Mexican twentieth century.

Gender Studies on the Mexican Revolution

I rely on postrevisionist and gender studies on the Mexican Revolution (1910–17) and the revolutionary process of new state formation (1917–40) in order to contextualize how popular sectors gained voice and political space through cultural and social processes, public policies, and corporate state organizations.[21] The contributions of these historiographies show that subaltern groups were integrated under new parameters of domination by the new Mexican State following constant and contentious negotiation and resistance. This gaze refutes the revisionist vision of a Mexican Revolution that, according to Vaughan, "seemed to have produced an all-powerful, single-party state that promoted capitalist growth at the expense of social welfare" and "questioned the popular and democratic nature of the revolution, casting the central state as the revolution's principal actor and as an effective manipulator of the masses in the interest of a bourgeois project."[22] The postrevisionism of scholars in the United States offers a variation on cultural history that emphasizes participation, inclusion, and resistance, adopting a perspective "from below."[23] This extensive historiography analyzes the role of peasants, Catholics, revolutionary leaders, women, and workers.[24]

According to Heather Fowler-Salamini in her comparison of the revisionist and postrevisionist visions of gender in historic studies from the twentieth century, the "analysis of gender helps us to better understand the inclusion or marginalization of women in revolutionary processes that took place between 1900 and 1930."[25] As stated by this author, over the past two decades the use of the category of gender has generated two major interpretations. Whereas some studies highlight the ideas and norms that signal continuity of the feminist ideas and norms of the Porfirian regime, others concentrate on the armed struggle and on how it allowed the participation of women "to bring about changes in the status of women and gender relations."[26] In this book, I intertwine both interpretations and contribute to connecting their analyses.

Regarding the agency of women in postrevisionist analyses and the history of women and gender in Mexico, the interpretation of the revisionist historiography of the Mexican Revolution, which focused primarily on revolutionary leaders, was radically transformed. If women happened to be mentioned by the revisionists, they appeared only as symbols, not as social agents. However, the role of the Adelitas, the Cristeras, the Hijas del Anáhuac, and the women of the Ácrata Group has been well documented.[27] These women not only struggled at the front during military combats or acted as propagandists, like Sárraga and Apodaca; they were also major social figures in the formation of the new Mexican State in the education sector, the organized labor movement, agrarian reform, feminist movements, the formation of political parties, and electoral processes. The five women featured in this book shed light on the ways in which they collaborated in these processes.

Various historians have written about women and the revolution from a revisionist perspective.[28] For example, Ilene O'Malley pointed out that the armed struggle was a patriarchal movement that destroyed the dictatorship of Porfirio Díaz and established a new Mexican State as of 1917.[29] The revolutionary leaders of different social classes and regions were homogenized through masculine symbols.[30] Carmen Ramos Escandón and Sandra McGee Deutsch were pioneers in incorporating a gender perspective into their historical analyses of women as social figures.[31] McGee Deutsch made progress in gender analysis by indicating how revolutionary leaders, between 1910 and 1924, delimited the private and public spheres. The public sphere was reserved for men, who were identified as virile, authoritarian figures; the domestic realm was for women, who were perceived as wives, mothers, and "fearful of men."[32]

Vaughan and Fowler-Salamini complicated the historic analysis of gender by examining the changing relationships between gender and the agrarian policies of the Mexican Revolution between 1910 and 1940.[33] In the introduction to their anthology *Women of the Countryside*, they broke away from the image of women as submissive or invisible in rural areas. They argued that these new policies generated changes within the patriarchal family and contributed to eroding its power. Women and young people took on new roles thanks to a developmental policy that focused on family, which permitted their mobilization and empowerment. Bourgeois revolutionary leaders expanded the definition of domesticity because of the modernization of the patriarchal family and, as a result, diminished gender inequality. According to Vaughan, the modernization of the patriarchy was linked to the rationalization of domesticity, to public policies that incorporated the private sphere and rural women as a means of realizing the interests of the state, and to the restricted definition of citizenship for women under male domination in a patriarchal state. Women continued to be second-class citizens, subject to male domination; however, traditional roles such as motherhood took on an expanded meaning. The state, and women as mothers in a modernizing process, collaborated in the areas of education, health, morality, and child welfare.[34] The case of Urzúa, discussed in this book, is particularly enlightening regarding the role of rural women and provides plenty of intriguing clues to advance our understanding of the interconnections between gender, power, and politics in twentieth-century Mexico.

The cases of Sárraga, Apodaca, Díaz, and Martínez contribute to historiographies dedicated to the role schoolteachers played in the organized labor movement and women's mobilizations. They also shed light on the alliance between female teachers and workers. Historiographies regarding education and the organized labor movement have failed to consider the political participation of female schoolteachers, even though education was significantly feminized. Most studies regarding education in Mexico in the twentieth century have highlighted the role of schools in state formation through, for example, the promotion of certain behaviors, loyalties, and skills that would contribute to national integration and modernization.[35] A coalition emerged between female schoolteachers and workers because of the strong Catholic social action movement and the significant participation of Catholic women. During the 1920s and 1930s, teachers represented and organized workers. However, in the 1930s they were forced to concentrate their demands on the improvement of teaching conditions. By doing so, they shaped nationalist politics and joined national organizations; the teachers were thus separated from the workers. In the end, this weakened teachers and workers alike.[36]

Catholic Church versus Revolutionary State

In the early twentieth century, Mexico experienced significant ideological conflict between the Catholic Church and the state, each attempting to mold society's views, particularly regarding the roles of women. The church pursued a re-Christianization that rekindled political anticlericalism, while the state promoted an image of women as bourgeois and apolitical, contrary to the male image rooted in military, labor, and civic duties.[37] The church offered mixed messages to women, ranging from the passive Virgin Mary to proactive figures like Joan of Arc and Sor Juana Inés de la Cruz.

During this time, a variety of cultural representations of women circulated with diverse or contradictory messages, such as "the mother," "the angel of the home," "the saint," "the modern woman," "the modern girl," "the victimized and exploited working woman," "the fallen woman," "the political militant," "the caller on the poor," and "the female soldier." These were produced by transnational ideas and representations through the press, literature, cinema, and political discourse, although not all of them had the same cultural meanings. These representations and transnational cultural products acted to open up new possibilities in the field of self-reflection, self-creation, and self-evaluation.[38] They were used as symbols to motivate social and political reform, or rather to resist said transformations. Some of these symbols and discourses influenced the cultural constructs of the policies contained in legislation (for example, the Constitution of 1917 and civil, penal, labor, and electoral legislation), institutions (state and Catholic), the press, and welfare, feminist, educational, labor, and political organizations. The practices of women show that they did not stick to these representations but rather modified them and tailored them to their own subjective experience.

The ideological conflict between the Catholic Church and the state in Mexico was crystallized in a strong debate regarding the role of women in education, labor, and politics, just as it was in the United States, France, England, Chile, Argentina, and Brazil.[39] Representatives of each institution spoke out in favor of women receiving education and employment, if and when they were controlled and supervised, so that they did not prejudice the family order or undermine male authority. According to both the church and state, women's education ought to contribute to reinforcing their primordial role as mothers, and yet they accepted that there was room for a "modernization of the patriarchy."[40] Indeed, the participation of women in politics was a crucial and polemic theme—not only in Guadalajara and Mexico but also in Latin America, Europe, and the United States.[41]

The book details the political engagements of figures like Sárraga, Apodaca, Díaz, Martínez Villanueva, and Urzúa Flores during certain key political and social processes in twentieth-century Mexican history. These women leveraged and transformed transnational symbols like "the mother," "the angel of the home," "the modern woman," and "the modern girl" to fit their own experiences and, in doing so, reshaped public perceptions and the societal roles of women. Their actions paved the way for the gradual transformation of the role of women in society, politics, and the workforce. As Maxine Molyneux argues for Latin America more broadly, "female activism ensured that some account was taken of women's interest. Yet concessions from governments were piecemeal, usually minimal, and the arenas of decision-making power remained largely impermeable to female accession until the century's close."[42]

From Caciquismo to Women's Political Power

The cases of Díaz, Martínez, and Urzúa discussed in my book are strongly linked to *cacique* political praxis in twentieth-century Mexico.[43] Abundant historiography regarding caciquismo characterizes the cacique as a strongman whose authority stems from informal sources, someone who holds personal and arbitrary political power in a region or location because he has succeeded in mediating with political, economic, social, and cultural structures as well as his own base.[44] Sometimes he wields power through violence in order to dominate others; sometimes he employs more paternalist, clientelist means. The cacique succeeds in controlling wealth, honor, political positions, and political power.[45] He is upheld by clientelist relations that include networks of family, friends, and dependents. Likewise, he has been seen as a political and cultural intermediary who acts as a go-between for his superiors and his subordinates because he succeeds in articulating different political cultures and creating connections despite myriad differences.[46] He must show his superiors obedience and political support, while his subordinates are expected to be loyal and faithful, fulfilling any obligations or tasks they are assigned.[47] These characteristics are mentioned above all to explain how caciquismo has been an integral part of the Mexican political system. Most studies on caciquismo give the impression that women, apparently, could not fulfill any of these roles.

Both the masculine origin of the word *cacique* and the reflections of those who have studied the topic have centered their focus mainly on the role of men. However, feminist historians have taken into account women as part of cacique power.[48] The historian Raymond Buve points out that the majority of studies regarding caciques have centered on the nineteenth and twentieth centuries and have therefore neglected to mention that in the colonial era, there were also Indigenous women who inherited and exercised their role as caciques.[49] Nicolás Cárdenas García and Enrique Guerra Manzo suggested a more balanced analysis "in order to interpret the postrevolutionary State and its ties to local powers, proposing that the use of the integrated and marginalized categories allows us to rethink the way in which some actors, in a shifting context, perceived the political system."[50] Despite these nuances, the perspective regarding caciquismo tends to maintain and reproduce a "natural" distinction between the different traditional roles of men (identified with the public and political sphere) and those of women (related to domesticity and the private sector) in society.[51] Although no study has explicitly expressed why women go unmentioned, it seems evident that they do not appear because they did not do "politics"—understood as a field exclusive to men. As Joan Scott accurately argues, "The terms of exclusion repeatedly produce 'sexual difference' as a fixed, natural boundary between the political and the domestic, or the self-representing and the represented, or the autonomous and the dependent."[52]

Studies of citizenship, gender, politics, and power in twentieth-century Latin America show that with the emergence of women's movements, women demanded equality in civil, labor, and agrarian codes and the vote. However, states sought to regulate gender relations with a variety of laws, and thus women slowly but surely increased their numbers in state bureaucracy and in official organizations. According to Elizabeth Dore and Maxine Molyneux, the historiography about women's activism in Latin America in politics has shown the contributions of middle-class women, but the struggles of Indigenous, peasant, and working-class women are now being recovered as well.[53]

In her work on citizenship in postrevolution Mexico (1917–34), Jocelyn Olcott argues that citizenship was constructed as masculine and based in a liberal rhetoric of suffrage, traditional forms of clientelism, and the revolutionary promise of collective action. The Constitution of 1917 incorporated a notion of citizenship that implied that three activities were traditionally male: military service, civic participation, and labor force participation. The participation of women in such activities (gendered as male) triggered strong reactions that showed the instability of gender roles. This semantic and cultural fluctuation illustrated the changing notions and practices of gender and of citizenship. Olcott argues that women activists, upon reclaiming revolutionary citizenship, softened the accusations of disloyal "malinchistas" and adjusted to the prevailing male ideology to appropriate and change it. She also argues that women, instead of negotiating revolutionary citizenship by means of demands based on gender differences, employed a more common strategy of destabilizing exclusively male nature from three cornerstones, military service, paid labor, and civic commitment. The five women in this book at some point used these three forms and thereby complicate a historical analysis of the construction of citizenship as masculine.[54]

In analyses of citizenship, gender, politics, and power, other theoretical tools are employed in order to locate women in politics and expand the concept of politics through categories such as empowerment—the process by which the oppressed control their lives through the development of activities and structures in order to increase their participation in issues that affect them directly—female awareness, gender issues, and motherhood.[55] In her study on women in Barcelona in the early twentieth century, Temma Kaplan developed the concept of female consciousness in order to explain the social and political mobilization of women workers. For them, "female consciousness centers upon the rights of gender, on social concerns, on survival. Those with female consciousness accept the gender system of their society; indeed, such consciousness emerges from the division of labor by sex, which assigns women the responsibility of preserving life."[56] Kaplan's concept is useful in order to gain an understanding of the political actions of women, but her perspective has been complemented and enriched by the studies of Maxine Molyneux regarding the socialist state in Nicaragua and of Sonia Alvarez regarding the fall of the dictatorship in Brazil. In these analyses, Alvarez and Molyneux describe two similar patterns of politicization. According to Alvarez, women can participate in either reactive or proactive movements, whereas according to Molyneux, the political movements of women can procure practical or strategic gender interests. On one hand, in reactive social movements or practical gender interests, women accept and reinforce traditional divisions of labor. These collective actions are a response to their immediate needs and are formulated by the women themselves. On the other hand, proactive movements or those with strategic gender interests mobilize women to radically change gender roles.[57]

The motherhood perspective, for example, takes aim at recounting the contribution of middle-class women in the emergence of welfare states (1890–1940) with different competing discourses—regarding citizenship, class relations, gender differences, and national identity.[58] This rich historiography shows that women have often mobilized as mothers and caretakers of the community. In these collective actions, they have drawn on traditional discourses centered on domesticity and maternity, and they have taken motherhood into the public sphere, showing us just how powerful maternity can be as a political identity. Through these actions, women have transformed the discursive and spatial limits of the public and private spheres and, indeed, have changed the nature of politics. Some feminist historians have defined motherhood as an argument made so that women could claim political voice and be taken seriously, in keeping with what has been called "motherwork."[59] The debate regarding maternalism in the early twentieth century in the United States, Europe, and Latin America operated as a discourse on two levels: it extolled the virtues of domesticity, and at the same time it legitimized women's role in the public sphere. Feminist academics have argued that women politicize any movement they participate in.

This book also contributes to the discussion regarding citizenship and gender. The detailed revision of different social and political constructions of citizenship by the state, liberals, Catholics, and women shows how they defined their citizenship as members of a community. Each group held different ideas regarding laws and rights. One used and favored principally the rights granted by the modern revolutionary state. The Catholics went beyond this limited concept and based their rights on natural law, placing them before the state. Most studies regarding the revolutionary period in Mexico have looked to liberal and radical organizations but without considering the Catholic notions of citizenship.

Transnational Feminism

Recently, the historiography of citizenship and women's mobilizations have expanded these topics by using a transnational perspective. I draw on transnationalism in a broad sense to refer to how feminist organizations worked across and beyond the boundaries of the nation-state (as Megan Threlkeld, Jocelyn Olcott, Katherine M. Marino, and Sonia Hernández use the term).[60] Threlkeld, Olcott, and Marino discuss and distinguish two distinct terms: *international* and *transnational* networks of U.S. and Latin American feminists who worked at the national and across international boundaries.

While Marino focuses on six well-known international feminists—Paulina Luisi from Uruguay, Bertha Lutz from Brazil, Clara González from Panama, Ofelia Domínguez Navarro from Cuba, Doris Stevens from the United States, and Marta Vergara from Chile—I examine other women: one notable from Spain who naturalized as Mexican in late 1920s, and four nonprivileged from Jalisco. The only well known internationally was Sárraga Hernández. The rest—Apodaca Anaya, Díaz, Martínez Villanueva, and Urzúa Flores—were known locally, regional, and nationally but had transnational connections. One of their contacts was Sárraga. As I already mentioned, Díaz gave a labor speech when Sárraga Hernández visited Guadalajara and campaigned in favor of anticlericalism, while the schoolteacher Apodaca became known as "the Sárraga from Guadalajara" for her anticlerical discourses. Sárraga, Apodaca Anaya, Díaz, Martínez Villanueva, and Urzúa Flores all developed and transformed their ideas and discourses regarding women's rights. I place special attention on the project of emancipating women from the control of the Catholic Church, parting from the gaze of anticlerical women themselves. This is a significant contribution, given that I contextualize how revolutionary this proposal was—one that sought to provide the necessary tools for women, and citizens in general, to become autonomous, thinking beings to achieve their own liberation. At the time, it was transformational, and it continues to be revolutionary today.

Hernández examines transnational feminism through several working-class anarchist women, like Caritina Piña Montalvo, who fought for labor rights both from within the region of the Gulf of Mexico and transnationally. Like Hernández, this book contributes to the history of feminist movements in Latin America from a biographical and regional perspective. Through sharing the lives of five feminist women—de Sárraga Hernández, Apodaca Anaya, Díaz, Martínez Villanueva, and Urzúa Flores—I shed light on how and when women were involved in different feminist movements from local, regional, national, and transnational perspectives and had an impact on different social movements (feminist, labor, and peasant) and social policies during the emergence of welfare states (1880–1940).

The five women in this volume, with their conflictive and destabilizing status within modernity, were born in different places (Sárraga in Spain and the other four in Jalisco, Mexico), yet they possessed considerable spatial, political, and social mobility. The roles they played over the course of their lives were not exclusive to any geographic location. However, there are contrasts among these five women in terms of their individual geographic mobility. For example, Sárraga, like other great feminist, literary, and political figures of her time (Gabriela Mistral, Tina Modotti, Margaret Sanger, and Alexandra Kollontai), led a wandering, transatlantic existence.[61] In contrast, Martínez's political work was concentrated in the region of Guadalajara, specifically the world of working women in Jalisco and Mexico City. Apodaca Anaya, Díaz, and Urzúa Flores advocated for change not only in Jalisco but in other states as well. Their status as single, divorced, or widowed women at certain stages of their lives granted all five women autonomy and facilitated their spatial and political mobility.

One of the marks they left was the increased visibility of women. This was intertwined with various processes: the political mobilizations mediated by the Mexican Revolution of 1910 and the formation of a new state, the conflict between the Catholic Church and the state, the emergence of social movements (labor, feminist, and Catholic), changes in the labor force, the increase in the rates of female literacy and schooling, and the new forms of corporate power that emerged during much of the twentieth century.[62] These women were active social protagonists in these processes, and their participation expanded their social, economic, and political rights. Throughout the twentieth century, women participated in the process of changing constructs of citizenship in all its connotations—economic, political, and social. The opening of new spaces and discourses in favor of women expanded, albeit still under male domination.

Organization of Chapters

In the first chapter, "'The Modern Woman,' Politics, and the Mexican Revolution in Guadalajara, 1910–17," I examine the context of a struggle that opened the doors for women to an active role in civic society. Through these mobilizations, the participation of women in the public sphere redefined cultural and social constructions of what a "man" or "woman" ought to be—that is, femininity and masculinity. I show that women who were politicized prioritized women's increased access to education and expanded political and social rights. Through their activism, they changed discourses regarding "the new woman," "the civic woman," or "the modern, politicized woman." Women were objects and subjects of discourse in social reforms; some of them configured new gender relations that resisted both male patriarchal power and that of the Catholic Church in their discursive forms, as their desires and discontents spawned new discursive systems that gave rise to agency.

In chapter 2, "Belén de Sárraga Hernández: Anticlericalism, Freethinkers, and the Mexican Revolution," I examine Sárraga's transnational propaganda campaigns in favor of free thought and her visits to and residences in Mexico (1912, 1922–1927), which coincided with different stages of the Mexican Revolution and the revolutionary process of new state formation (1920–40). Sárraga's anticlerical and freethinking identities aligned with the patriarchal politics of a revolutionary state that sought to destroy the power of the Catholic Church while securing the emancipation of women from the influence of the clergy. Sárraga and Mexican revolutionary leaders agreed that this was the path to modernity and progress. Within this secular trend, Mexicans who elaborated public policies considered the modernization of "la raza" (the race), the patriarchy, and women to be decisive in the transformation of Mexico into a competitive, modern nation in a capitalist world.

In chapter 3, "Atala Apodaca Anaya: Anticlericalism, Civic Education, Progressive Forces, and the Mexican Revolution," I analyze Apodaca's lengthy political career in the antireelectionist campaign of Francisco I. Madero (1909–10), her actions and discourses against the dictatorship of General Victoriano Huerta and the Catholic Church, and the way she wove together anticlericalism and Constitutionalism. I describe in detail how Apodaca and the women of the Centro Radical Femenino (CRF) went from anticlericalism to a Jacobin stance with antireligious overtones in mid-1918, following massive Catholic resistance to the implementation of anticlerical policies restricting the number of priests and Catholic temples. Apodaca's case is quite enlightening for those who wish to gain an understanding of the radicalization and politicization of ideas and liberal, nineteenth-century values with regards to the fatherland, citizenship, and education as understood and used by various subaltern groups. Her case also sheds light on how historical actors sought to condemn the feminine in politics during the revolutionary process.

In chapter 4, "María Arcelia Díaz: Labor and Women's Politics within the Context of the Construction of the Postrevolutionary State of Guadalajara," I reconstruct the labor and political career of a *trocilera*, or textile worker. I identify the different stages of Díaz's politicization and examine how she progressed from an agenda of workers' rights to one focused on women's issues. The reconstruction of Díaz's political career and life involves delving into the debate regarding "speaking for others" and returning to the question posed by Gayatri Chakravorty Spivak: Can the subaltern speak? Like Sárraga and Apodaca, Díaz collaborated with students, teachers, and female workers to expand the unionization of said workers through the Círculo Feminista de Occidente (CFO), a center for literacy and the politicization of women within the organized labor movement. Women of the CFO constructed and reproduced a cultural memorial following the death of Díaz in 1939. They carried out different activities and funereal ceremonies from 1939 to 2001 to maintain unity in her group and to recall how they had gained a political foothold in the organized labor movement.

In chapter 5, "María Guadalupe Martínez Villanueva: The Mobilization of Women and Corporatist Politics," I reconstruct the long life and political career of Martínez, as well as her ties to Apodaca and Díaz. I explore her different stages of politicization (the Casa del Obrero Mundial [COM], the CFO, the CFO-FTJ alliance, and the public offices she occupied). I examine her changing conceptualization of citizenship, women, and the history of Mexico. As an integral part of that perfect duo of union bosses, the CFO-FTJ, Martínez designed educational, labor, political, and social policies for men and women within her political group.

In chapter 6, "María Guadalupe Urzúa Flores: Advocate and Modernizer of Jalisco Rural Politics," I delve into the concept of advocate and distinguish it from our conceptualization of the cacique. I explore how Urzúa's personal experience in rural Mexico was related to broader processes associated with the postrevolutionary process of state formation (1917–40) and the emergence of the "Mexican miracle" (1940–70). I identify the elements that politicized Urzúa Flores and trace how she emerged as a rural leader who enjoyed a lengthy political career in public office. She became a cultural and political intermediary representing farmers and women to local, state, and federal political entities. Over the course of her career, Urzúa constantly confronted the changing balances of power between caciques, peasants, politicians, representatives of government agencies, state political parties, opposition political parties, and women.

In summary, these specific cases help us register the history of the presence of women in the public sphere and identify different stages in their political participation: their visibility in the public arena in the early twentieth century; their collaboration in the creation of organizations (civic, educational, feminist, liberal, labor, and political) linked to the emergence of feminist and labor movements in order to struggle for the expansion of civil, political, and social rights for women; their support of political parties at the director's table as well as through women's rural and labor sections; their participation in electoral processes; their nomination and ultimately their election to political offices; and their performance as antiestablishment or administrative *cacicas*.

Freethinkers and Labor Leaders enriches the transnational discussion regarding the impact of organized women in social movements and social policy during the emergence of welfare states (1880–1940). Some of these women's activism (Sárraga, Apodaca, Díaz) parts from a transnational lens and helps reveal new forms of activism, new modes of identity, and ideas about citizenship. Grounded in a biographical, local, and regional perspective, this book elevates the everyday life, labor struggles, and demands articulated by these women: equal pay for equal work and the extension of labor legislation to rural and domestic workers.

1

The "Modern Woman," Politics, and the Mexican Revolution in Guadalajara, 1910–17

On July 8, 1914, the Constitutionalist army took Guadalajara with two objectives: first, to advance in their military campaign toward Mexico City against General Victoriano Huerta's usurping government and the federal army, and second, to reduce the power of the Catholic Church, which had allied with Huerta after his coup d'état (February 23, 1913). In October 1914, two people took the podium at the Degollado Teatro to defend the Constitutionalist cause. On October 1, a young student named Daniel Galindo, from the prestigious Boys' Lyceum (Liceo de Varones), made a speech to criticize Catholic education (Jesuit) and to extol the virtues of Constitutionalists' program of public education that would contribute to the construction of a new social order, one that drew on Eurocentric and male ideas of Francis Bacon, René Descartes, Auguste Comte, Voltaire, Jacques Rousseau, Molière, Jacques-Henri Bernardin de Saint Pierre, Charles Perrault, and Mexican politician, philosopher, and writer Justo Sierra. These thinkers stimulated the modern scientific thought and method that would contribute to the discussion on the importance of liberty and rationalist, humanist, and scientific notions of education. For Galindo, these ideas ultimately would build the common good, the soul of the fatherland (*patria*) and of race (*raza*). Women did not figure in Galindo's vision. On October 25, Laura Apodaca, director of the Jalisco Normal School for Women, took the stage at the Degollado Theater and made a public speech advocating for women's education for modern life and the role of the "modern woman" in society.[1] Apodaca's actions were audacious—both her taking to the stage and the contents of her speech—for as Mary Louise Pratt argues, "modern women expressed their inconstant identity as citizens in an increasingly disconcerting fashion."[2] As a modern woman herself and aware of the advancements of the feminist movements in Europe and the United States, Apodaca drew on the male European classical canon (Plutarco,

Ciceron, Virgilio, Homero, René Descartes, François Fénelon, Montesquieu, and Victor Hugo) and on a strong legacy of nineteenth-century liberalism to refute the gender norms propagated by the Catholic Church. Her speech countered the image of women as conservative Catholics who represented an impediment to the construction of a new, revolutionary society. Apodaca argued that a woman can fulfill the same job as a man, only in a different way. The two speeches, both in support of the Constitutionalist cause, serve to demonstrate the gendered nature of revolutionary rhetoric in the 1910s.

Political divisions in 1910s Mexico have been characterized as a split between the Catholic Right and the revolutionary Left; however, the political effervescence of the era was more complex than dichotomies can communicate. Anarchists, Catholics, liberals, socialists, and those between the various revolutionary factions—Villistas, Zapatistas, and Constitutionalists—debated about the role and representation of women and men during the armed movement and their role in the new state and in the future modern society. All discussed possible educational projects for women, and the function of modern women, but within a context of radically accelerated cultural, political, and social change. And yet with all these different trends, both social Catholicism and the Constitutionalists shared the idea that women should be prepared for modern life. However, both had different conceptions of the role of women. Whereas Catholics sought an active role of Catholic women defending the motto "Everything is restored in Christ," Constitutionalists encouraged women to be active participants in a new society that could campaign against the power of the Catholic Church and in favor of temperance, hygiene, and education. What were the gender policies, and what were the social and political programs of Catholic social action versus those of the revolutionary leaders or *caudillos* for both men and women? What was the perspective of women themselves expressed in periodicals regarding the purpose of women in modern society? My argument is along these lines. Both the Catholic Church and Constitutionalists constructed women as active participants but limited their role in defense of their own political and social programs.

Catholic Social Action
The Constitutionalists sought to counteract the robust Catholic social action movement in Jalisco, led by Archbishop Francisco Orozco y Jiménez since 1913. This movement in Mexico originated in the social doctrine of the

FIG. 1. Laura Apodaca Anaya in 1902. Courtesy of Colección Independencia y Revolución en la Memoria Ciudadana, file 44 (Atala Apodaca Anaya), BCCG-CO-CIRMC.

Catholic Church and the international movement of so-called Catholic social action that preached a solution for social issues.[3] The Catholic Church had built a social and political platform with a generation of Mexican bishops, trained at Collegio Pio-Latino-Americano Pontificio at the Vatican, in keeping with the postulates of the encyclical *Rerum Novarum* (1891). The economic and social conditions that prevailed in Mexico in the early twentieth century matched the call made by Pope Leo XIII in said encyclical to diminish the excesses of industrial capitalism, to resolve social issues through protection of the home as the foundation of social order, and to struggle against socialism.[4] The dissemination of this encyclical and its implementation were delayed because the bishops and archbishops were not in agreement as to how to "follow the teachings of Leo XIII regarding the social question."[5]

In general terms, Mexican bishops carried out clerical reform, practiced a Catholicism that was intolerant of the state, and strongly criticized the conciliatory policy that existed between the church and the liberal Porfirian State.[6] In Jalisco, "the civil and ecclesiastical authorities developed a modus vivendi that was characterized by non-aggression and cordiality."[7] The bishops indicated that the Porfirian State had permitted the enrichment of large hacienda owners, industrialists, and national and foreign entrepreneurs while social conditions deteriorated for the masses. Under the circumstances and in response to the proposals of this encyclical, the bishops promoted social reform to improve working conditions and living standards among peasants and workers. Catholics established lay organizations engaged in charity toward the poor, especially during the political vacuum created by the rural and popular armed movement of the Mexican Revolution that destroyed the Porfirian State. They pursued a new social order: a hierarchical society in which different social classes would live in harmony for the common good, all the while linked by charity. They believed that through these actions, they would restore the power of the church. In 1902, the Catholics of Guadalajara established their first labor organization: the Catholic Workers' Society of the Holy Family and Our Lady of Guadalupe (Sociedad de Obreros Católicos de la Sagrada Familia y Nuestra Señora de Guadalupe).[8] During various national congresses held between 1903 and 1909, Catholics debated how to remedy peasant debt and the need for agrarian and labor reform.[9] Catholic social action was implemented in the Jalisco countryside. Its backers were above all priests, Jesuits, and militant Catholics. Some of them were locals, others from other regions of the country or even Europe.

The Partido Católico Nacional (PCN) emerged from the most belligerent and political sector of the movement. In 1911, lay Catholics founded the PCN to lay the foundation for a Catholic platform that would enable them to gain access to parliamentary government.[10] This group was not born directly out of the nineteenth-century Mexican conservatism that promoted the establishment of the empire of Maximilian (1864–67). On the contrary, it was a trend linked to transnational tendencies that sought to resolve social issues and participate politically through Christian democracy. The Catholic social action movement experienced internal divisions, and there were differences regarding the political alliances forged during the democratic opening created by Maderismo (on a national and local scale) and following the assassinations of Madero and Pino Suárez. The Guadalupan Workers Organization (Operarios Guadalupanos), which had formed between the Third National Catholic Congress (Guadalajara, 1906) and the fourth (Oaxaca, 1909), broke away from the Porfirista political game that blocked open, confessional political participation.[11] This association was one of the most solid and perhaps most structured pillars of the PCN.[12] They made Jalisco their laboratory for change and, for a time, dominated their own organization on a national scale. The decline of Porfirio Díaz's dictatorship and the start of the Mexican Revolution allowed Catholics to disseminate their reformist project and become one of the major social and political forces during this period.¹³

In Jalisco, the PCN garnered enough support from the economic and religious elite and from Catholic militants in different parts of the state to secure the governorship in October 1912 and to control the legislature from February 1912 to June 1914. The PCN faced resistance from the Partido Liberal (PL), which won federal deputy seats in June 1912. The PL in Jalisco was linked to the Partido Nacional Liberal (PNL), which brought together former Porfiristas. In the national arena, the PNL formed an alliance with the Partido Constitucional Progresista (PCP, created by Madero), but in Jalisco, the PL and the PCP were enemies.¹⁴ It is worthwhile to note that the PCP represented a minority in Jalisco and was not in power during the Madero administration (1911–13). During this period, different Jalisco political forces such as anarcho-syndicalists, former Reyistas, Spiritists, liberal-conservatives, Maderistas, Masons, and anticlericals did not form a compact political bloc capable of counteracting the advance of militant Catholics. The three elections held in Jalisco in 1912 (state and federal deputies, plus the governorship) were not a dichotomic struggle between liberals and conservatives but rather a political effervescence that made way for a dynamic political process.

The PCN won the governorship in October of 1912 because it forged a coalition with independent Catholic-liberal organizations. The PCN perceived liberals as their political enemies because they were anticlerical.¹⁵ Catholic legislators in Jalisco passed laws that followed the guidelines of the encyclical of Leo XIII—that is to say, they legislated for freedom of education, family welfare, a Raiffeisen model of credit and savings cooperatives (Caja Raiffeisen), and professional unions.¹⁶ Mexican Catholics incorporated a new element into their program: municipal independence as a way to counteract the centralist policies of state and federal governments. In 1913, the Jesuit Alfredo Méndez Medina, "a central figure in the debate over confessionalism in Mexico," set into motion a national program for Catholics, published as *La cuestión social en México*, and called the second meeting of the National Confederation of Catholic Worker Organizations (Confederación Nacional de Círculos Católicos de Obreros) in Zamora, Michoacán.¹⁷

The designation of Francisco Orozco y Jiménez (1913–36) as Archbishop of Guadalajara in February of 1913 strengthened the social Catholic movement.¹⁸

An energetic leader, Orozco y Jiménez was known for his phrase "Everything is restored in Christ." The archbishop wielded his influence beyond religious affairs. The PCN dominated the legislative and executive branches, favoring the archbishop's influential policies. The archbishop laid out how Catholics would transform themselves into militant defenders of the church and its properties. This included norms of conduct in the private and public spheres. The liberal press objected to him for trying to impose Catholic ideals.[19] Orozco y Jiménez prohibited his congregation from reading the impious press and explicitly forbade them from supporting the PCN, causing the liberal press to criticize his authoritarian politics and his Catholic social action program. The confrontation between the different groups that composed the factions of Catholics and liberals in the press continued and became increasingly heated. Orozco y Jiménez demanded that Governor José López Portillo y Rojas (1912–14) provide him with protection from liberal, Jacobin, and Masonic critics, but the governor remained silent and did not intervene.[20]

Upper-class Catholic women played a fundamental role in the re-Christianization of society. In 1913, Archbishop Orozco y Jiménez established the Junta Diocesana de Acción Católica Social (JDACS) as a lay organization. The JDACS intervened successfully in the structure, organization, and activities of labor organizations to preserve their confessional character.[21] He also organized the lay Catholics and established the Asociación de Damas Católicas de Guadalajara (ADCG) and the Círculo de Estudios Sociales León XIII.[22]

The archbishop supervised the ADCG and designated a priest as his assistant director.[23] The ADCG became a very important Catholic organization because it sought to expand the mobilization of Catholic women in support of the church and worked in favor of female Catholic social action.[24] The ADCG carried out campaigns against what it considered to be immoral cinema and pornography; it also lobbied to close commercial establishments during certain religious holidays.[25] In the beginning, only upper-class women had the right to form part of the ADCG. But after the archbishop was sent into exile in May 1914 under allegations of seditious behavior, the ADCG coordinated the organization of other women as well, in keeping with their social class, occupation, generation, and municipality. Thus, associations were formed for teachers, employees, servants, and workers. However, only the ladies and priests occupied positions of leadership.

The case of the women of Guadalajara is similar to what Laura O'Dogherty found in Mexico City, given that they shared "with the Catholic clergy the idea of a hierarchical society, divided into social classes that collaborate[d] in the procurement of the common good and linked by the bonds of charity. In this society, the lower classes had to be aware of the limitations of their condition, and the upper classes had to remember their responsibility of charity toward the dispossessed."[26] Organized Catholic women sought to create a new social order in which drastic conditions would be remedied and harmonious social relations established—but without social equality. According to historian Patience Schell, the programs of Catholic women responded to urban issues of poverty, illiteracy, and industrialization but without erasing hierarchical differences. They promoted the active participation of women in the social debate.[27]

The ADCG established and administrated two kinds of Catholic schools: parish—equivalent to elementary or grammar schools—and Sunday. In these, girls and women workers learned about religion, catechism, and certain skills related to sewing and accounting. Likewise, the ADCG attempted to maintain a representative association in each of the parishes of Guadalajara and throughout the Archdiocese of Guadalajara. The ladies founded study circles for the teaching of catechism and to give conferences. They created the Ropero de los Pobres (Poor people's wardrobe) to distribute used clothing to the dispossessed as well as a public soup kitchen for the poor.[28]

Through the study circles, Luis Navarro, Assistant Director of the ADCG and canon, sought to purge women of Masonic liberalism, the corruption that such ideologies conveyed, and the manipulation of liberal men. Canon Navarro advocated for a righteous social reconstruction of the fatherland to confront the threats the church faced from liberal politicians and revolutionaries. Navarro perceived liberal women as beings manipulated by men after losing their judgment due to the influence of "evil passions."[29] This canon urged Catholic women to work constantly for a righteous social reconstruction of the fatherland, but always through abnegation because the threat against the church from liberal politicians and revolutionaries was very pronounced.[30]

The invitation for a more active participation of the women of the ADCG also resounded among the men and their parallel Catholic organizations, such as the Asociación Católica de la Juventud Mexicana (ACJM), created in August 1913. Both had to resist the laws that prohibited a major public presence of the church as well as attacks against the institution. Hence in January 1914, Governor López Portillo y Rojas banned political and religious demonstrations, refusing to allow the crowning of the image of the Sacred Heart of Jesus. For Catholic militants, this crowning symbolized the consecration of the Mexican republic to said image.[31] Despite this restriction, women and children were led by the archbishop in a religious procession on January 11, 1914. Orozco y Jiménez addressed over three thousand people and spoke against liberal anticlericals and Benito Juárez (1858–72), the liberal president of the nineteenth century who facilitated the separation of church and state through social, educational, and economic reforms. To avoid bloodshed, Governor López Portillo y Rojas did not repress this religious demonstration. The press criticized him for being a weak governor who had failed to contain the archbishop.[32] After this religious ceremony, the liberal newspaper *El correo de Jalisco* published that the Partido Liberal had been gravely wounded and that it was shameful how the laws of reform had not been obeyed. *El correo de Jalisco* called liberals to join the Partido Liberal in confronting anticlerical insubordination.[33] However, the arrival of the Constitutionalists in July 1914 accelerated the rupture of the alliance between the legislature controlled by the PCN, the divided PCN, the church hierarchy, and the weak governor, López Portillo.[34]

The Arrival of the Constitutionalists in Jalisco

In June 1914, the Constitucionalista army defeated the Huertista troops near Guadalajara. On July 8, 1914, General Manuel M. Diéguez (1874–1924) arrived in Guadalajara at the command of the Constitucionalista forces. In this victorious and decisive moment, the Constitucionalistas did not fail to recall that the Catholic Church had established an alliance with General Victoriano Huerta, who had seized power by means of a coup d'état, and that they had not protested the assassination of President Francisco I. Madero on February 22, 1913. Like nineteenth-century liberals, the Constitucionalistas (although they were not unified in their anticlerical and reformist politics) had sought to destroy the power that the church had over society, revive the ideals of the War of Reform (1857–61) by means of the confiscation of church properties, and expand secular public education. In addition, the new

Constitutionalists promoted the improvement of living and labor conditions of urban and rural workers.

The anticlerical, educational, and labor policies of Diéguez were the product not only of his individual experiences in Tequila, Guadalajara, and Cananea but also of the collective experiences of rural teachers, Masons, Magonistas, and miners in those same places. Diéguez came from a Catholic family in Tequila that had suffered a loss of fortune during the Porfiriato. His father, Crisanto Diéguez, was a modest scribe and small-scale merchant. His mother, Juana Lara, was also a Catholic. The Diéguez Lara family produced ten children, of whom Manuel was the eldest; he was a rural teacher and municipal employee. Through these careers, he became familiar with the scarcities suffered by teachers and the lack of mobility in the Porfirista administration. In 1898, he migrated north, reaching Cananea in 1902. There he observed firsthand the stark contrasts between U.S. Americans and poor Mexican miners, as he himself worked as a peon in a gold mine. Once he had learned English, he was hired as a supervisor and became an intermediary between the Cananea Copper Company and the miners. In addition to acting as a cultural and political intermediary, the great exploitation of the miners and the racial discrimination they suffered led him to organize the Unión Liberal Humanidad, which followed the ideological program of the Partido Liberal Mexicano and the Magonistas, anarchists, and libertarians who opposed the Díaz regime in their struggle for an economic and political revolution.

In 1906, Diéguez was one of the leaders of the Cananea strike, which was brutally repressed. Its leaders were jailed in San Juan de Ulúa until 1912, when the Maderista administration freed them. After his release, Diéguez returned to Cananea and ran for the post of municipal president. He won the election. Following the Madero assassination on February 23, 1913, he rose up in arms in Cananea together with six hundred miners to demand the reestablishment of the rule of law and respect for the Constitution of 1857. These events left an indelible mark on Diéguez and informed his anticlericalism, nationalism, and laicism.[35] Both the individual and collective experiences of Diéguez and his public policies signaled that he conceptualized a civic, benefactor state that promoted social reforms in favor of the dispossessed. According to Mario Aldana Rendón, he considered strong authority necessary to establish civil order and prevent militarism from prevailing.[36]

FIG. 2. General Manuel M. Diéguez, June 26, 1917. Courtesy of Colección Independencia y Revolución en la Memoria Ciudadana, file 44 (Atala Apodaca Anaya), BCCG-CO-CIRMC.

Immediately after Diéguez seized control of Guadalajara and was named governor of Jalisco, he ordered the exile of all foreign bishops and priests, persecuted the clergy, shut down the Catholic newspapers, shot or imprisoned several Huerta supporters, and confiscated many holdings of the church and oligarchy. The ADCG found itself obliged to meet in private quarters.[37] According to Friedrich Katz, the cost was very high: "Diéguez's massive confiscations of the property of the rich, which did not benefit the poor in any way, his persecution of the clergy, and the arbitrariness of his soldiers—'wherever the soldiers are located they take whatever they want without paying'—created a rare unity between the upper and lower classes of society."[38]

When the Villistas reached Guadalajara in December 1914, the Catholics, the rich, and the masses all welcomed them. Francisco Villa had a more tolerant attitude toward the Catholic Church. His troops were seen as liberators from the reign of terror of Diéguez.[39] However, Villa lost their support when he imposed a forced loan on the rich, announced the drafting of agrarian reform, and ordered several executions. Despite all this, Villa was preferred by the popular classes and teachers of Guadalajara.[40] The polarization between Constitucionalistas and Villistas also affected the participation of women. In February 1915, the sisters Atala and Laura Apodaca supported the Constitucionalistas in their battle against Villistas at Cuesta Sayula, Sinaloa.[41]

Diéguez assigned a fundamental role to the state so that it would promote secular, popular, and modern education. This vision entailed an expansion of the activities of women. Despite economic, political, and social instability, the Constitucionalistas passed laws to transform the educational system and create a more interventionist, anticlerical state.[42] Counteracting Archbishop Orozco y Jiménez, Diéguez ordered all bureaucrats to renounce their Catholicism.[43] The general converted the Cathedral of Guadalajara and various former convents into military headquarters and closed the Catholic Normal School (Normal Católica, 1902–14).[44] This building formed part of the Jalisco Normal School and the Teacher Training Annex (Escuela Normal para Profesores and the Escuela Práctica Anexa).[45]

Within the field of education, Diéguez laid the foundations for a public educational system. According to Irene Robledo, a teacher who lived through the revolutionary period, Diéguez was the first to carry out educational reform. He helped the teachers and conceptualized education for the masses.[46] Together with teachers and principals of elementary schools, Diéguez established a breakfast program in Guadalajara schools. The teachers sent poor children to have breakfast and took advantage of the opportunity to supervise their general hygiene. As Robledo described it, "Diéguez would get milk and bread from producers at a low price. School breakfasts consisted of a glass of milk, a plate of beans, tortillas, bread, and fruit."[47] This kind of state policy in England and France from the late nineteenth to the early twentieth centuries has been examined by the historian Susan Pedersen. According to her, the introduction of school breakfasts formed part of an incipient state policy, so that the morning meal would not have an adverse effect on family income. This policy attempted to create new independent benefits for children.[48] From the point of view of revolutionary leaders like Diéguez, the responsibility of maintaining children fell not only to their parents but also to the state. And so it was. This policy marked the beginning of a new social sphere for women that combined both the public and private, and although it was significant, it was not the first of its kind. In early 1913, the Catholic ladies had founded a soup kitchen for the poor as a manifestation of their charitable duty that did not seek to destroy social class structure or the autonomy of the working family. In contrast, the revolutionary state perceived its role as a responsibility that ought to guide the poor, illiterate masses. Despite this obligation, revolutionary leaders, like the Catholic Church, held prejudices against workers because they saw them as lazy, alcoholic, and undisciplined. Through their modernizing impulses and dreams, the Constitucionalistas believed that they could transform them into a disciplined and responsible workforce.[49]

On August 15, 1914, Diéguez passed the Ley Protectora del Obrero Mexicano (Protective law of the Mexican Worker), which granted the right to earn a minimum wage, regulated the workday, and banned company stores. These laws were limited because no Labor Department or regulatory laws were created. The institutionalization of this labor policy would not take place until the 1920s. Afterward, Diéguez approved legislation in favor of a free municipal area. Sisters Laura and Atala Apodaca, both teachers, collaborated in this broad program of social reform. Together with political and labor leaders, they helped carry out social programs and disseminate revolutionary ideals, as illustrated in chapter 3 of this book, dedicated to Atala Apodaca.

Diéguez passed labor laws that had the intention of granting protection and rights to all workers, but there were unforeseen consequences. The Constitucionalista labor policy created "from above" did not consider the real needs of workers in keeping with their occupations and gender. Some workers, such as lunch counter owners, butchers, and sandal makers did not approve of this legislation because by closing markets on Sundays, as the Diéguez decree ordained, or on civic holidays, their economic income was adversely affected.[50] Based on principles of equity and justice, these workers asked the governor to revoke said decree. They argued that their economic conditions were already precarious and that failing to open the market on Sunday would only aggravate their situation.[51] This legislation was designed to help industrial workers and peasants who had very long workdays and fixed salaries. But most of all, it sought to protect the individual rights of workers and pacify unrest at industrial factories. In contrast, other female workers, particularly tortilla makers and lunch counter owners, relied on the quantity of goods or food they sold rather than the number of products they produced. Hence if they could sell on Sundays, they benefited more than from a day of rest. The women maintained that they too were heads of family who had to bring food home for their children and who had no partner to maintain them. They underscored that they were on their own and sought only means for survival.

The owners of textile factories also protested the law because they opposed paying the minimum wage to women who worked at textile factories. The owners based their argument on the fact that in Europe, workers received different salaries according to gender. Workers had the right to receive a family salary, the owners sustained, but female workers should not receive a salary equal to that of men because they were considered unskilled laborers. The owners also complained that they could not pay the female workers more money because they faced strong competition from home-based workshops where production was sold at very low prices. In the old textile factories in the region of Guadalajara, 72 percent to 77 percent of the workers were women, whereas in the modern factories, only 9 percent were women.[52] The owners added that unstable conditions and scarcity of raw materials for production had affected them considerably.[53]

Many textile workers demanded the payment of a minimum wage to cover the needs of their families and asked that the workday be regulated.[54] For many workers, male and female, who were independent or organized in unions, this legislation, like the Constitution of 1917, "was met with consent where collective rights were honored and met with resistance where they were not."[55]

The Revolution Constructs Gender; Gender Constructs the Revolution

The church and the state structured similar programs, but their main dispute centered on the role to be held by the church in the public sphere. During the armed struggle, factions from different regions fought for diverse interests, including agrarian reform, destruction of the hacienda system, municipal autonomy, and the integrity of the electoral vote. By 1915 the Constitucionalista faction had prevailed politically. By the end of the decade and into the early 1920s, the Constitucionalistas had initiated the process of constructing a new Mexican State.

FIG. 3. To commemorate the visit Venustiano Carranza paid to Guadalajara in 1917, the townspeople showed their admiration and affection by holding a parade in which two thousand young ladies took part, dressed in their nursing uniforms. Archivo Fotográfico Jesús Hermenegildo Abitia Garcés, AFJHAG.

Different revolutionary leaders, journalists, feminists, political and Catholic leaders from various social classes, political perspectives, religious beliefs, and occupations created diverse representations of the "male" and the "female." In the case of women, their presence in the armed struggle was very diverse. *Campesinas* and *Adelitas* were the female foundation of the rural armed movement; they cooked, cared for wounded soldiers, and participated in battles on the front.[56] Likewise, the nurses of the Ácrata group, affiliated with the Casa del Obrero Mundial (COM), joined the health division of the Red Battalions (Batallones Rojos).[57]

While revolutionary leaders relied on the labor of these women, those same leaders continued to portray such women as challenging traditional gender norms. The women of the middle and upper classes were also deemed untraditional and problematic when they mobilized for their rights. The five women of *Freethinkers and Labor Leaders* illustrate how women lobbied to change the civil code and obtain recognition of women's rights. These women mobilized on a large scale and included women like the Apodaca sisters, who, while in the minority, were important because they did not subscribe to the preordained construct of a "woman" in Guadalajara: Catholic, submissive, and passive.

Despite this female participation, the political planning of the Mexican Revolution was a movement led by middle- and upper-class men who possessed a male perspective and who were uninterested in the emancipation of women. Like the revolutionary leaders, revolutionary women also sought to modernize and secularize the country by means of the destruction of the power of the Catholic Church and of traditional practices—such as fanaticism, religion, ignorance, and superstition—in order to create a more competitive nation in a capitalist world.[58] Like other social and political revolutions of the world, a cultural, gender, political, and social revolution was generated to create "modern" citizens, bound to national values, who would transform the fatherland by means of a rational education and work ethic.[59] These social changes affected both men and women, but how were masculinity and femininity reconfigured in this armed struggle?

According to the editorials and military bios published in the *Boletín militar*, revolutionary leaders that represented the new state were "active," "combative," "frank," "trail-blazing," "honorable," "just," "liberal," "noble," "rational," "patriots," "productive," "protective," "triumphant," "valiant," and "virile."[60] They identified the old political elite (*científicos*), Porfirista military officers, Catholic women, and the Catholic Church as their enemies.[61] Of these, the Catholic Church was their principal adversary, characterized as an old, fanatical, highly superstitious, and unproductive woman.[62] According to the Constitucionalistas, the Catholic Church had a negative influence on both men and women. The revolutionary leaders sought to diminish the control of the church over women, whom they perceived as a conservative bloc. With regards to the authority of the church over men, the *Boletín militar* described "the underhanded and audacious clericalism that takes advantage of religious feeling and the confessional to extract idiotic oaths and mocks the consciences of men, transforming them into puppets of the clergy [sic]."[63]

It was within this context of gendered conceptions of civic engagement that Laura Apodaca entered the stage. When Laura Apodaca made her speech at Degollado Theater in mid-1914, she advocated for women to be independent and engaged. She criticized those young women who were preparing to be no more than housewives, no matter what their level of education. If young women desired to become only mothers and wives, Apodaca sustained, they still ought to acquire a broad cultural education so that they would have very clear general notions about all aspects of daily life. Young women ought to educate themselves in the ways of modern life to achieve a physical and mental equilibrium. Apodaca recommended reading anthologies within the male European classical canon and believed the reading of novels should be prohibited because it "did not serve to form the intelligence, nor the heart of the young women." At the same time, she advised daily hygiene and practicing at least one sport. She approved of following the dictates of fashion but only when adjusted to the convenience of each person. She proposed loving the modern and "retain[ing] affection for our national past," stating that "the traditions worth being preserved should be those recognized for their beauty, their nobility, and their profoundly national character."[64] Adopting an anticlerical position, Apodaca criticized the Catholic Church for failing to offer useful teachings to women and for opposing their entry into universities and professional training programs. Apodaca's rhetoric contained shades of a liberal feminism because she held that a woman could do the same work as a man, only in a different manner. She praised women who were modern and educated, who would enroll in university, work outside of the home, and become free and independent.

Although Apodaca did not specify where she got her ideas about women's education and home economics, what she proposed was part of a broader transnational debate about women's education in the modern world. Based on these discussions, she considered that an educated woman should know "national language (Spanish), mathematics, languages, natural sciences, sewing, what relates to the management of the house, a craft, history of art, architectural styles, furniture, decor, the organization of the city and the modern State, and hygiene." Reflecting on these events of the Mexican Revolution (1910–17), Apodaca stated that young women had witnessed the struggle against oppression, acquiring awareness of their strengths, their rights, and their future.[65] As a Constitucionalista, she praised the labor and social policies of General Manuel M. Diéguez (1914–18) because he concerned himself with the plight of the working class. She asked young women to show compassion for workers because they were harshly exploited, for children and families who were poor and oppressed, and "for the fatherland that slowly bleeds." She suggested that it was necessary to advocate concordance (*concordia*) so that the country would be able to progress.

Like Apodaca at the conference, Daniel Galindo, a student at the Liceo de Varones (Boys' lyceum), also recognized the positive changes offered by Constitutionalism but with a masculine gaze. Galindo construed the Constitutionalists as a national saving grace.[66] Among the actions of said revolution, he noted the expulsion of priests, Jesuits, and the expropriation of the Instituto San José (Saint Joseph institute). For Galindo, Jesuit education neglected attention to civic duties and encouraged egotism. The Constitucionalistas, he argued, incorporated civic values in public education to form character as well as love for both the fatherland and humankind. Freed now from the Jesuit subjugation, Galindo stated that there would be a return to the reason of Voltaire, Rousseau, and science. A "temple to the positive truth" would be built.[67] In the words of this student, "the study that we have to make of that science whose modern progress was initiated by Bacon and Descartes, has been facilitated by the State Government, separating it into faculties and completing it with the magisterial crown of the series of abstract sciences that Auguste Comte has named: Sociology."[68] The theoretical and philosophical proposals of Comte to resolve the chaos occasioned by the French Revolution (1789–99) were incorporated into the Escuela Nacional Preparatoria (National preparatory school) by Gabino

Barreda in 1868 in order to foment order and progress under the regime of Porfirio Díaz.[69] Perhaps the importance of positivism shows the continuation of these Porfirista ideas in the process of modernization, whereas the return to French and Juarista Jacobinism was notable among progressive military commanders. All these ideas formed part of a new Constitucionalista pedagogy in high schools. During the ascent of Constitutionalism in 1914, the student Galindo interwove scientific ideas of Comte with French Jacobin concepts to resolve the issues of society, annul the power of the Catholic Church, and construct a nation with civic values that would promote a love for science and the fatherland.

The speeches of Apodaca and Daniel Galindo were given in October 1914 to support the Constitucionalista cause, yet they contained different representations of gender. According to Galindo, wholesome, honorable, secular men sought to reinitiate science, liberty, and reason to instill patriotism and love for the Mexican race. With a vision that blended evolutionist, modern, and positivist ideas, Constitucionalista masculinity was constructed through participation in the revolution and the foundation of a new nation. Women did not figure in his vision. Apodaca, by contrast, countered the image of women as reactionary and with little capacity for academic and public activities and argued for the importance of preparing them for modern life. Education for women, especially at the university level, and exposure to a broad range of readings would open new horizons, transforming them into modern women trained to perform in the domestic, national, and public arenas. With this new role, they would topple the constructions of femininity during the Porfiriato, when they were seen as the weaker sex.

The propagandists for Constitutionalism (women and men) agreed that the "salvation of the people" would be achieved through the program for action of Venustiano Carranza, who favored democracy, honor, and patriotism.[70] With an apologetic perspective that reproduced patriarchal viewpoints, the teacher Antonia Ortiz sustained that men who had participated in combat on the battlefield "would return to their suffering, awaiting mothers who would save them," protect them, and put them at the disposition of the leadership of Carranza for the regeneration of Mexican life.[71] In the *Boletín militar* it was very significant that they allowed anticlerical women, such as teachers Antonia Ortiz and Atala Apodaca, to publish their writing. The speech by Ortiz shows the continuation of the representation of the suffering

FIG. 4. "Our First Anniversary." *Boletín militar* 3, no. 214 (July 15, 1915), FE/BPE.

women of the nineteenth century, while Apodaca lobbied for more active, modern women who were capable of transforming society. These two discourses illustrate the diverse social constructs that existed among Jalisco teachers regarding the role of women. The Constitucionalista propagandists, men and women alike, affirmed that authentic revolutionaries should solely support Constitutionalism. From a Constitucionalista perspective, Villismo and Zapatismo had betrayed Carranza because they had protected the Catholic religion.[72]

These speeches also generated visual images, as illustrated by the collage of pictorial representations published in the *Boletín militar* to celebrate the first anniversary of said bulletin and the arrival of the Constitucionalistas in Guadalajara.[73] This includes caricatures, drawings, and portraits in which generals Victoriano Huerta and Francisco Villa were ridiculed and satirized. From the Constitucionalista perspective, the fact that these two figures are found in the lower section of the collage is because they were regarded as enemies. They symbolize the amoral underworld, where betrayal reigns. Huerta is depicted as a serpent. His face displays a hard, tense expression. Villa is represented as a beast alongside Huerta; his body language is that of a worn-out, beaten-down animal. Both contrast with the photographs featured of Constitucionalista military officers. The collage marks a clear difference between enemies (the beast and the serpent) and the Constitucionalista political group. Moreover, there is also a marked difference between the images of animals and those of civilized and militarized masculine figures, boasting of their victories in western Mexico. At the center is Carranza, surrounded by Obregón, Diéguez, and other colonels. The cities are shown where the Constitucionalistas overcame the Villistas (Celaya, Lagos, León, and Tuxpan). In the upper section an image of a woman appears. She personifies the "angel of the home," not the modern woman who follows the latest dictates of fashion and consumerism. The revolutionary leaders conceived of the role of women as a moralizing force in the modernization of Mexican society, within the family environment. They thought that women should not be prominent in politics because politics were dirty and corrupt. This moralization allowed the participation of women in a new social sphere somewhere between the public and private, but it was not considered to be political.

During the decades of 1910 and 1920 in Guadalajara and nationally, anticlerical women joined the revolution as propagandists who opposed the

Porfirista State. Women established female political organizations or mixed-sex political and social associations that promoted revolutionary ideas in the struggle against the Catholic social action movement. In response, Catholic women defended their Catholicism. Guadalajara experienced one of the most dynamic mobilizations of women, both Catholic and anticlerical. The latter, together with teachers and workers, joined the incipient anticlerical state in support of the masses. The influence of the revolutionary state to counteract the strong Catholic movement empowered campesinos, women, and workers. The state required anticlerical women in its struggle against the Catholics. On the other hand, Catholics resisted the anticlerical measures through mobilization. In this uprising, Catholic women were very important due to their participation in the struggle and their resistance.

In an initial assessment of the activism of Catholic and anticlerical women, it would seem that the Catholics organized earlier on—since the 1870s—because the Catholic Church sought to recover the terrain lost after the War of Reform while following the guidelines of the encyclical *Rerum Novarum* to resolve the social question. Although the politicization of women in literary salons, Masonic lodges, liberal clubs, and labor associations and in the non-Catholic press has already begun to be reconstructed, there is still a need to evaluate in a more nuanced fashion the trends of activism in both groups. Recent historical investigations have shed light on the fact that the organizations of Catholic women were very well structured in rural and urban areas and that perhaps they comprised the majority, while liberal associations of women were a minority.[74]

Women Teachers and the Revolution in Guadalajara

The coming into power of the Constitucionalistas allowed liberal women teachers (sustained with values that centered on civic education, justice, and respect for the constitution) to join the revolutionary government. Among these were the sisters Laura and Atala Apodaca, Irene Robledo García (1990–88), and the women teachers who founded the CRF in 1918. The Apodacas and Robledo had supported different political and social movements as teachers, such as Reyismo (1909) by wearing a red carnation during their classes; they had read the newspapers of the Flores Magón brothers and had attended or given speeches at political meetings during the Madero presidential campaign. The case of these women teachers shows that teacher's colleges were incubators for the mobilization of men and women during both the antireelectionist movement and the armed struggle.[75] In the words of Irene Robledo, "At the Normal, support for the Reyista movement was absolute. It seemed to us that he would be a good President; besides, we were supporters of the ideas of the Flores Magón brothers; that is to say, we were with both groups."[76]

Due to their liberal heritage, the Apodaca sisters and Robledo supported the revolutionary forces (Constitucionalista or Villista) even before the arrival of the Constitucionalistas in July of 1914. Atala Apodaca in particular, by means of the Liga Amigos del Pueblo (LAP) and the Círculo Liberal Josefa Ortiz de Domínguez (CLJOD), organized revolutionary and labor associations in favor of the Constitucionalista cause.[77] Even when the PCN controlled the executive branch and the legislature and the Catholic social action movement was strong, Atala waged an intense anticlerical campaign. According to Irene Robledo, "Atala was one of the initiators in Guadalajara of the labor and revolutionary groups. Public conferences were held, preferably on Sundays, at the Teatro Principal located on Juárez street. The objective was to politicize people and intellectuals."[78]

A lot of women teachers attended the conferences without being members of any group. Atala extended the invitation to one and all, including her students at the Escuela Práctica de la Normal. She was not repressed by the Catholic authorities. Apodaca and the CLJOD were opposed to the Catholic Church because they held it responsible for the backwardness of Mexico. According to Irene Robledo, at Apodaca's conferences people listened to her, but no one debated because they were afraid to, due to the tense political situation.

During the statewide administration of Diéguez, Atala held the position of General Inspector of Schools in Guadalajara. She also presided over the Comisión de Estudios y Propaganda Nacionalista and edited the magazine *Argos*. Through this commission, Atala and Laura Apodaca were active in the Constitucionalista cause. Laura was director of the Jalisco Normal School and Irene Robledo was named principal of a school in Guadalajara. Each one took advantage of these new arenas to promote change in the quality of education and the role of the "modern woman" in revolutionary times and to mobilize other women in the defense of revolutionary ideals.

Discursive and Visual Representations of the "Modern Woman"

For Constitucionalista men, the modern woman was necessarily an agent who defended Carrancismo and its moralizing social revolution. The vision female Constitucionalistas held of the modern woman was somewhat broader. According to them, the modern woman had to possess habits of hygiene and reading. She could follow fashion cautiously, and it was recommended that she attend university, have a job, and practice at least one sport. These characteristics are akin to those of the prerevolutionary modern woman who was also supposed to have a taste for reading and the mandates of fashion. Whereas the postrevolutionary modern woman not only consumed transnational perishable goods but also worked and demanded to exercise her rights (civil, political, and social) in addition to being a moralizing agent.

The proposals of Laura Apodaca regarding the role of the modern women in her 1914 conference and the attempt of the CRF to forge a "new woman" beg the question: Where is the revolutionary aspect of the "modern woman"? The use of gender categories to analyze the different revolutions and processes inside the Mexican Revolution allows us to move beyond the vision that suggests women did not play a crucial role in the military battles of the armed struggle of 1910. Both gender perspective and the history of daily life help us understand the radical and rapid changes experienced over that decade by both men and women "of flesh and blood." As I have argued from the outset, the debate surrounding the "modern woman" was not only cultural but political as well. Laura Apodaca articulated brilliantly, as the U.S. American historian Joan Scott would say, how "politics constructs gender and gender constructs politics."[79]

After Apodaca's speech in Guadalajara about the "modern woman" in October 1914, the feminist private secretary of the Constitucionalista leader Venustiano Carranza, Hermila Galindo, launched the *Semanario ilustrado la mujer moderna* in September 1915. Like Apodaca, in this publication, she considered a better education for women to be an urgent matter and granted new meaning to the role of women inside the home. In subsequent issues, Galindo argued in favor of female suffrage to improve conditions for women. Galindo sought the politicization of maternal functions; mothers had to educate their sons and instill them with civil responsibilities. She looked for leaving "in the past timid, nervous, modest, demure women to give rise to *modern* women: participative, non-fanatical, hard-working, free to make their own choices in life, filled with love for the fatherland."[80]

Apodaca, Galindo, Salomé Carranza, and other writers argued that education would bring them independence and the capacity to express their demands and desires. Over the next few years, works were published such as *La Enciclopedia Católica* (1907–15), *La mujer moderna y su papel en la evolución actual del mundo* (1919) by Amado Nervo, *La mujer en la vida moderna* (1920) by Ricardo Delgado Capeans, and *Mujer antigua y mujer moderna* (1920) by Antonio Pavissich.[81] Based on a reading of these publications, I infer that perhaps the transnational debate regarding the "modern woman" in the early decades of the twentieth century within the context of modern Hispanic America (Spain, Argentina, and other countries) versed more on this subject than on the direction the Mexican Revolution should take.

Outstanding among these editions was *La Enciclopedia Católica*, consisting of fifteen volumes and over twelve thousand articles written by different authors of various nationalities. The *Enciclopedia* synthesized the scientific, philosophical, and intellectual contributions of the role of women from the perspective of the Catholic Church, as well as the "feminine question," the movement for the emancipation of women, and the itemization of women's rights and obligations in the early twentieth century; moreover, it illustrated the modern position of the Catholic Church. From a Eurocentric, essentialist, and modern perspective, Agustine Rössler and William H. W. Fanning approached in their article "Mujer" human nature, the history of women, the modern question of womankind and women and canonical law. Rössler and Fanning recognized the right of women to enjoy full, complete lives. Explicitly, they favored equality between men and women and rejected the definition of the male sex "as solely and absolutely perfect or as an assessment of the other."[82] But this equality was not absolute because the female sex did show differences with regard to the male counterpart in body and soul; moreover, women had qualities that men were lacking. They declared themselves to be in favor of a moral equality between the sexes; thus, the moral law for men and women ought to be the same.

From an essentialist perspective, the differences between men and women were not only found in the body; they were also physiological, psychological, and vocational. The distinctions increased or diminished because of education or customs. Humanity was derived from social union and the organization of men and women. The male sex was only half of humanity; the female sex represented the other half. Between the two of them there should be harmonious cooperation, but the man was the leader. The creator had designated him as such in his corporeal and intellectual structure. The woman was subordinate, but supposedly she would not lose her autonomy or her rights. Rössler and Fanning's argumentation was interwoven with the concepts of difference and equality, a central part of the feminist discussion in the nineteenth century.[83] With regard to the position of the woman in modern life in the twentieth century, they stated that her influence ought to reach beyond the home and extend to church and state. They recognized that the debate about the modern woman in European countries such as Germany, France, Belgium, and England was related to their conditions of life, education, and legal standing. They identified three great positions regarding the social question of the "modern woman": radical emancipation (social democrat), the moderate path (liberal), and the way of the Catholic Church. For Rössler and Fanning, the solution to the female question lay in the reorganization of modern conditions—the restoration of Christianity in society, which would contribute to reestablishing natural relations between men and women. Therefore, modern times demanded the direct participation of women in the public sphere, given their influence in the home and at the workplace. The debate, which was already found in transnational, national, regional, and local spheres, continued over the decade of 1910 and those that followed.

In addition to this transnational debate, different daily newspapers with state and national circulation debated the role of women, the "modern woman," her body, her education, the products she should consume and use, and whether she should have braids or go about "bobbed." It is difficult to evaluate how public opinion received these debates, but in this book, I reconstruct how new discursive systems gave rise to agency—that is to say, the median point between discourses and experiences that broke away from a determinist vision. I identify how discourses changed with regard to "the new woman," "the civic woman," or the "modern politicized woman." Women were both the object and subject of discourse in social reforms, and certain women configured new gender relations that resisted masculine patriarchal power and the Catholic Church in their discursive forms, their desires and discontents triggering new systems.

Women like Laura Apodaca and Hermila Galindo initiated processes that feminist historians have characterized as a rationalization of domesticity and a modernization of the patriarchy.[84] Like some feminists and liberal women of the nineteenth century, the Apodaca sisters and Robledo García ascribed greater importance to a secular education than to suffrage. In this they differed from women like Galindo. This posture could be liberating because it empowered subjects and allowed them to make independent decisions. The idea was revolutionary and remains so today. But the gendered construction of revolutionary politics resulted in the eclipse of their proposals. It was assumed that Diéguez's anticlerical, revolutionary programs were "natural" and fitting, simply because he was a man. In contrast, the women teachers who supported him and transgressed the gender order—the social structure that systematically produces gender relations of identity, power, hierarchy, inequality, and inequity across all dimensions of social life—were characterized as "making a lot of racket." They were compensated less and did not receive the same recognition. As for Catholic women, their clericalism served as a means for social engagement. They appeared as visible, collective figures. Within the context of massive, successful Catholic mobilization from 1918 to 1919 to repeal the decrees numbered 1913 and 1927, these women formed part of the public memory and were preserved as a latent conservative power that could explode at any moment, preventing the modernization of the nation.

2

Belén de Sárraga Hernández
Anticlericalism, Freethinkers, and the Mexican Revolution

In August 1912, during her first visit to Mexico, Belén de Sárraga Hernández (1872–1950)—a labor rights activist, pacifist, and antifascist from Spain—stated that she was not a suffragette in the English manner, nor was she akin to feminists from the United States.[1] She did not identify herself as a feminist who would "wish women to become men in petticoats."[2] Sárraga was a Mason and Spiritist, anticlerical, feminist, and a freethinker. Her motto was "For the liberty of free thought and the emancipation of humanity."[3] In an interview with a reporter from the *Mexican Herald*, Sárraga stated that she believed in the equality of the sexes in all spheres, including politics. Regarding female suffrage, she believed no country would flourish until its women had taken a genuine interest in the affairs of the nation. For Sárraga, "woman's suffrage is at best a side issue, when brains are taken at their worth."[4] As a freethinker and a Mason, she believed that women had rights and responsibilities not just as women but as thinking human beings. "Intelligence has no sex," she wrote. "Whether a great mind is in a masculine or feminine body will, [in the future, not] be given a thought."[5] In her conversation with a journalist from the *Mexican Herald*, Sárraga held the Catholic Church responsible for the conditions the country was suffering. The kind of education it provided did not permit freedom of thought. The clergy merely encouraged mass fanaticism and enslaved women.

Sárraga's statements to the press provide clues as to how she conceived of sexual difference. She inquired about the ways in which basic differentiations between men and women were articulated, questioning the idea that women had little or no capacity for discernment. According to Sárraga, arguments about differences between the sexes generated inequality. Women were at a disadvantage and excluded where they ought to be emancipated. Once equality between men and women was achieved, sexual differences would become inconsequential. Through her many activities, Sárraga constructed and displayed her understanding of gender order through anticlerical, freethinking, Masonic thought and Republican politics. She questioned gender stereotypes and destabilized the masculine construction of liberal and Republican politics. For many, her brilliant writing, her great eloquence, and her extraordinary intelligence were not considered typical of her sex. In the early twentieth century, it was inconceivable that a woman was able to inspire such an ecstatic response from her audience.

Scholars have often identified female emancipation with liberal thought. Sárraga, however, nourished herself with anarchist, anticlerical, Spiritist, freethinking, Republican, and theosophist trends that gave rise to a secular feminism in fin de siècle Spain. Sárraga and other Spanish anticlerical feminists from the late nineteenth century sought to find solutions through associations, Athenaeum, protests, meetings, and newspapers in hopes of achieving a legitimate public arena for women. They established associations, libraries, and schools. They participated in lodges, political parties, and the written press. As Joan Scott suggests in her analysis of French feminists who debated the categories of equality and difference from the late eighteenth century up until 1940, Sárraga's discourse ought to be understood considering the theories it invoked and the changes it generated in political structures in both Spain and Latin America at the time.

But who was Belén de Sárraga Hernández? What were her cultural understandings of politics and gender? How was each constructed? How and why did a young middle-class woman engage in practices that upset the social order and gender identities that perceived her as a "'rebellious woman' straddling Spain and America in the first third of the 20th century"? What theories did she invoke? What political changes did she engage in? How and why did she sustain this vision of the Mexican Revolution of 1910?[6] In order to answer these questions, I look to her first visit to Mexico in 1912 as part of a tour across Hispanic America to speak out against clericalism and in favor of free thought. During this initial phase (1893–1909) Sárraga participated in conferences, meetings, and the press in southern Spain. In the second phase (1909–31) she began her transnational political work in association with the International Federation of Freethinkers of Brussels to eradicate what they considered the main obstacle to progress in the Americas: clericalism. During the third phase (1931–39) Sárraga returned to Spain to collaborate with the Second Republic. During a fourth phase (1939–50), while in exile, she continued to collaborate with antifascist women's organizations in France and in Mexico; however, she left behind the anticlerical campaign she had waged in the decades of 1910 and 1920.

Life and Legacy (1872–1950)

Born in Valladolid, Spain, in 1872, Sárraga was raised in a family that held liberal values and was committed to fighting for them.[7] Her father, Vicente de Sárraga, was a Republican Mason and liberal colonel who belonged to a bourgeois Puerto Rican family and who was sentenced to death for his failure to accept the restoration of the Bourbon monarchy. In the end, he was not executed but rather sent into exile on the coast of Africa and later transferred to Puerto Rico, his place of birth.[8] Her mother was Felisa Hernández, who came from a modest family from Valladolid. The Sárraga Hernández marriage produced two children, Belén and Rafael, and in 1880 the family moved to Puerto Rico. There, Belén Sárraga studied at the teacher's college directed by her grandfather, Fernando Ascensión de Sárraga y Aguayo. She received an enlightened, liberal education and began her studies in medicine.[9] Eight years later (1888), the Sárraga Hernández family returned to Spain.

In her youth, Sárraga encountered the freethinking ideas that radicalized her liberal cultural politics. Around the age of twenty-one, in 1893, she joined the Centro Instructivo Obrero Republicano de Madrid (Republican workers' educational center of Madrid), a center frequented by anarchists. There she became familiar with the rights of workers, rationalist education, and the struggle against capitalism. During her university studies, she took classes from distinguished Republican professors such as philosopher and legal expert Francisco Pi y Margall (1824–1901) and oceanographer Odón de Buen (1863–1945). As leaders of Masonic freethinking, they had a more open, positive stance regarding the role of women in the republic they hoped to build.[10] They aligned with anarchist and Republican ideals in their search for a solution to the battle of the sexes.[11] This position was corroborated by the educated middle-class women who frequented Republican circles and contributed to the anticlerical and liberal press, as well as to political mobilizations.[12] Sárraga considered herself to be a disciple of Odón de Buen, who favored the early vindication of women. This scientist contributed to *Las dominicales del librepensamiento*, a freethinking weekly newspaper, and participated as a lecturer at Francisco Ferrer Guardia's Escuela Moderna on themes of natural history. He was stripped of his tenure because his texts described the functions of reproduction and because he defended the transmutation and evolution of species.[13] Sárraga and other students protested this measure, which reaffirmed her inner desire for a Republican, freethinking Spain.[14]

According to historian María Dolores Ramos, freethinking facilitated the Republican action that attracted socialists and anarchists. The convergence of these contributed to cross-class relations between the bourgeoisie and the working class. Socialists and anarchists utilized speeches and representations as well as agnostic, atheist, liberal, Masonic, and Republican rituals.[15] In the case of freethinking Spanish women, they joined forces to express what they thought beyond the orthodoxy.[16] For Sárraga, "freethought" "is not a religion, given that it is not exclusivist. Freethought seeks that women and men investigate the truth by means of their own thinking, free of prejudice and by means of personal reasoning. . . . The only enemy of freethought is, thus, religious dogma, characterized by mysteries that are considered to be inscrutable to reason."[17]

Krausism also played an important role in Sárraga's thought. Named after the German philosopher Karl Christian Friedrich Krause (1781–1832), Krausism advocated for doctrinal tolerance and academic freedom from dogma; it also emphasized the importance of scientific understanding in the service of greater human liberties. For the Krausists, education was an instrument that would help the country and national morality bounce back. With the Institución Libre de Enseñanza (Free institution of teaching, 1876), educational innovations were implemented that admitted women into higher education and favored an active, public participation of intellectuals. Adherents hoped thus to win over the opinion of the elites.[18]

At the age of twenty-two, in 1894, Sárraga married Emilio Ferrero Balaguer, a private sector employee, freethinker, and Republican.[19] The couple had three children: Libertad, Demófilo Danton, and Víctor Volney.[20] The names of Sárraga's children speak to the influence the French Revolution and Masonry had on her. When she married Emilio, her liberal and Republican political perspective expanded to include Spiritism. Belén and Emilio regularly attended the Spiritist center La Buena Nueva. Her involvement with Spiritism significantly marked her political work. In 1895, Sárraga published a text entitled "To Kardec," in which she described her admiration for the founder of Spiritism, the French pedagogue Hippolyte Léon Dénizard Rivail (1804–95), known under the pseudonym Allan Kardec during the third French Republic.[21] Kardec developed the Spiritist doctrine in *The Book of Spirits* (1857) as well as other works that were sold with great success in his day. According to historian Warne Monroe, Kardec attained broad acceptance because he reconciled science with religion during a moment of tension between the two. He based his philosophy on empirical evidence of the phenomena of spirits and promoted practices and values to improve social interaction.[22] Kardec's doctrine presented a particular idea of the afterlife and introduced a new way to experience the sacred. Mediums provided believers with a means of communication with spirits, including deceased relatives, and thus provided a powerful, tangible validation of the philosophical principles they followed.[23] The "rational foundation" of Spiritism and its positivist explanation represented the most perfect example of the Republican system because they provided a basis for social morality without a Catholic perspective.[24]

Spiritism attracted more women because they embraced the private and homey atmosphere of the séances. Judith Walkowitz states that "the séance reversed the usual sexual hierarchy of knowledge and power: it shifted attention away from men and focused it on the female medium, the center of spiritual knowledge and insight."[25] For Spiritists, women were suitable as mediums because "they were weak in the masculine attributes of will and intelligence, but strong in the feminine qualities of passivity, chastity, and impressionability."[26] As mediums, they became "guides" to these qualities in the other world. While channeling, they would act as masculine entities. According to Walkowitz, this "reflected the contradictory dynamic operating around gender in spiritualist circles: women could authoritatively 'speak spirit' if they were controlled by others, notably men; their access to male authority was accomplished through the fragmentation of their own personality."[27] Spiritism situated women as guides and redeemers of humanity, to emancipate them from the power of the church.

Spiritism also proposed to transform the traditional gender hierarchy.[28] Insisting that women were the "sovereigns of the conjugal bed,"[29] it challenged dominant gender values, critiqued patriarchal sexual power within marriage, and allowed the proposal in public arenas of demands that had already been elaborated in the private sphere. The Spiritists called for the vindication of women in three areas: it proposed an education that would encourage them to become emancipated and achieve progress, fought for the presence of women in the labor market and in functions beyond marriage and the convent, and favored reforms to the legal codes in order to diminish the legal inequality of women.

In subsequent years Sárraga intertwined Spiritism with other political trends of the day that sought emancipation, liberty, justice, and fraternity. In the mid-1890s, Sárraga upheld her liberal values of democracy and liberty to support the independence of Cuba and the Philippines. In 1895, with an advanced pregnancy, she published a journalistic article in which she defended the right of Cuba to independence. The Spanish monarchy considered this to be a seditious act. That same year, she contributed to *La conciencia libre* (1896–1907), a leading international freethinking publication and one of the most important newspapers of Spanish lay feminism.[30]

Sárraga collaborated with Amalia Domingo Soler (1835–1909), the most important Spiritist of her time, and Ángeles López de Ayala (1856–1926), one of the most outstanding secular feminists and writers of the nineteenth century. Sárraga also participated in the reconstruction of the freethinking movement and aided the establishment of the Asociación Librepensadora de Mujeres en Gracia.[31] The authorities arrested Sárraga when she presented the statutes of said association.[32] In 1896, she joined the Severidad lodge, where she learned the values of fraternity, justice, and reason.[33] *La antorcha valenciana*, the press organ of the Puritan lodge of Valencia that staunchly defended freethinking theories, depicted her as "a lively woman, an illustrious writer, and the heroine who will give days of glory and triumphs to masonry," and in the welcome speech she was charged with "attracting womankind and emancipating her conscience, imprisoned today by preoccupations that sterilize the conquests that men obtain in their struggle against fanaticism and ignorance"—a task to which Sárraga declared herself to be "fully disposed."[34]

Sárraga's ideas about the world and women's place in it were also informed by her being a Mason. Masonry concerned itself with themes such as education in general and instruction for women, both issues that formed part of the public debate between freethinkers, Krausists, and Masons. The Spanish Masonry of the nineteenth century shared the gender discourse that constructed women as the mothers and educators of their children.[35]

According to Ramos, Masons exhorted novices to outline "new horizons."[36] Sárraga participated in the rites and tasks of masculine lodges outside the usual framework of feminine Masonry and backed the creation of a mixed Masonry to which other freethinking Catalonian and Andalusian women contributed.[37] She became affiliated with the Mixed Masonic Order known as El Derecho Humano. This lodge did not restrict the admission of women and favored equality between the sexes. The founders of this order (which was a pioneer of women's rights in France), Marie Deraismes (1828–94) and doctor and politician Georges Martin (1844–1916), were Spiritists, feminists, and ardent Republicans.[38]

In 1896, Sárraga protested the shooting of José Rizal (1861–96), leader of the independence movement in the Philippines.[39] That same year, she participated in women's protests of the war in Cuba and was jailed. According to Luz Sanfeliú Giménez, at the time mothers and other women "habitually led protests in various Spanish cities against the war in Cuba."[40] The following year (1897), Sárraga and Ana Carvia founded the Asociación General Femenina in Valencia (General women's association). Sárraga argued that women were a crucial element in the advancement of societies yet were held captive by ignorance; she emphasized the urgency of rescuing them from fanaticism through education.[41]

Sárraga and other anticlerical feminists inherited the ideas of Charles Fourier (1772–1837) about utopian socialism and Masonry. For them, the model was the "woman as guide" or "social teacher" who would promote fraternity in order to educate, moralize, and secularize.[42] They created new arenas, constructed networks of women, and changed their places of residence in order to form secular associations.[43] According to Ramos, the anticlerical feminists sought to "spread Republican and rationalist ideals among their members, making way for the educated, modern woman distanced from clerical rites, a circumstance that, in the long run, would facilitate a major change in feminine identities."[44] They established social spaces for women: commemorations, educational conferences, group readings, civic rituals, meetings, and cultural evenings. In particular, the Asociación General Femenina of Andalusia, Catalonia, and other communities founded secular schools, libraries, and newspapers for women in Málaga, Barcelona, Valencia, and Córdoba. Its members held that "the 'common good' does not exist without the 'good of women.'"[45] They favored the inclusion of women in liberal politics and its practice and in secular teachings. This was the common ground between feminists, freethinkers, Masons, and Republicans. They did not fight for women's suffrage, but they did fight for the institution of secular education, something quite revolutionary for their time.

At the age of twenty-five, in 1897, Sárraga arrived with her family in Málaga and contributed to the organization of the Federación Malagueña de Sociedades Obreras (FMSO), which included freethinkers, Republicans, and socialists. The actions of the FMSO aligned with the position taken by the weekly *Conciencia libre*: anticlerical, prolabor, and Republican. The Ferrero Sárraga family resided in Málaga from 1897 to 1907, during which time Sárraga engaged in the mobilization of masses, confrontations in the street, and securing the backing for labor organizations.[46] From 1899 to 1906, the FMSO demanded the separation of church and state, including the termination of the state budget for worship and clergy. Sárraga was placed in charge of a boycott of the Corazón de Jesús religious procession and of demonstrations against the Cristo de las Cabrillas pilgrimage during Holy Week in 1904, during which the cheer "Long live Christ our King!" was answered by "Long live Doña Belén!" In 1906, Sárraga and the members of the FMSO established an anticlerical league with a secular program, emphasizing that the anticlerical agenda took precedence over the struggle of improving the labor and social conditions of the working class.

In 1899, Belén and Emilio traveled to Almería, where they succeeded in attracting over two thousand followers in Andalusia. In 1900, Sárraga's public presence and oratory transcended contemporary limits on women's engagement in politics. Her great success led her to be the first woman to form part of the national council of the Federal Republican Party during the leadership of Pi y Margall.[47] In 1902 Belén, Emilio, and other Spanish freethinkers attended the Universal Congress of Freethinkers in Geneva. Their propaganda work, protests, and conferences inciting workers to action and for the expulsion of Jesuits resulted in the incarceration of Sárraga on several occasions—not only in Barcelona but in Málaga, Murcia, and Valencia as well.[48]

Sárraga then embarked on an international phase of her activism. Over the course of her lifetime, Sárraga established seven women's organizations, four in Spain and three in Latin America—Argentina, Uruguay, and

FIG. 5. Cover of Belén de Sárraga's *El clericalismo en América a través de un continente* (Lisboa: Editorial Lux, 1914).

FIG. 6. Belén de Sárraga in Montevideo in 1914. From Belén de Sárraga, *El clericalismo en América a través de un continente* (Lisboa: Editorial Lux, 1914).

Ecuador. She attended four international freethinking congresses—Geneva (1902), Rome (1904), Buenos Aires (1906), and Lisbon (1909)—and she edited the weekly *La conciencia libre*, which circulated in Barcelona, Valencia, and Málaga; the newspaper *El liberal* in Montevideo, Uruguay; and the monthly magazine *Rumbos nuevos* in Mexico (1925–27). She lived in Lisbon, Montevideo (1909–15), Buenos Aires (1915–21), and Mexico City (1922–23, 1926–31, 1939–50); she went on four speaking tours that extended from the Caribbean to Tierra del Fuego (1912–13, 1915, 1918, and 1930), and she was a close collaborator with four presidents (three from Mexico and one from Uruguay).[49] In 1926, she became a naturalized Mexican citizen.[50]

When Belén and Emilio attended the First Congress of Freethinkers in Buenos Aires in 1906, she realized that "the new continent" was a land of promise for political and social change.[51] At the age of thirty-seven, in Lisbon, she collaborated with the organization of the First Congress of Freethinkers and the Republican League of Portuguese Women (1909) and relocated to Portugal when the republic triumphed there in 1910.[52] The Ferrero Sárraga family moved from Barcelona to Montevideo, Uruguay, in 1909.[53] From there she began her travels to Argentina, Cuba, Mexico, Chile, Costa Rica, and Venezuela. During these tours, Sárraga expanded her political actions supporting anticlericalism, freethinking, and Republicanism to a transnational cause. She became the defender of "a new continent" of liberty that would promote liberal policies in different arenas.

El clericalismo en América (1914)

In 1914, Sárraga published *El clericalismo en América a través de un continente* (*Clericalism in America*).[54] The cover of *El clericalismo en América* represents the main idea Sárraga conveys in her book: that clericalism impedes the advance of modernity. The priest with his black cassock expresses an attitude of "nervousness and fear"—perhaps because of the spread of progressive and radical ideas across the American continent. Part of his body is hidden, and his hands are positioned over the hemisphere, suggesting an attempt to control it. The illustration is completely opposite to the image the Catholic Church sought to present regarding love, benevolence, charity, and serenity.

In this book, which she wrote in Montevideo and published in Lisbon in 1914, Sárraga explains how she cooperated with liberal governments and organizations, as well as the International Federation of Freethinkers, to create a secularizing campaign in Latin America. The objectives were to diminish the vigor of the Catholic Church, to prevent its popular acceptance, and to struggle against its considerable power. For Sárraga, clericalism was the most negative force in Latin America. She emphasized that her love for humanity led her to work for the salvation of "this America," which she perceived "as a promised land for the destinies of the world."[55] She claimed that America "is nothing of what the European imagines, and yet it is everything. Neither wonderland, nor Indian mob, nor market, nor penitentiary. It is the center of human activity where the races can break away from atavistic traditions."[56]

Based on a dichotomous perspective of backwardness-progress and tradition-modernity, Sárraga described over the course of twelve chapters her points of view on Latin American culture, education, history, intellectual progress, psychology, and religion.[57] Sárraga argued that since the (Spanish and Portuguese) conquest, the Catholic religion and the monarchy had formed an alliance to block the progress of liberal, modern ideas. These institutions had vehemently opposed the independence movements and liberal reforms of the nineteenth century. Clericalism used women as a weapon against progress and to enforce tradition.[58] Sárraga also pointed to the religious mercantilism hidden within Catholic charitable institutions.

The asylums and schools for the poor were nothing more than sweatshops where the church turned a profit, where poor people, young and old, produced the merchandise for the financial benefit of the church.[59] To eradicate the negative influence of clericalism, Sárraga supported the elaboration of secular educational policies. She called on Masons, young workers, and of course, the "new civic woman" to build an egalitarian, free, and modern society. She recognized that workers were a force capable of changing tradition, given that they did not always follow religious dogma. On the contrary, through their organizations and political parties, they could display belligerent attitudes.[60] In the case of women, she admitted that there had been some advances thanks to secular education but thought that women should demand still more instruction and independence.[61] Since then, the Catholic Church had challenged any attempt to put into practice liberal policies and allied itself with dictator Porfirio Díaz (1877–1911). She sustained that the democratic revolution of Francisco I. Madero (1911–13) faced a coup d'état produced by a coalition between old Porfirians and the church. Villistas and Zapatistas facilitated its fall because they fueled chaos, destruction, and revolution. According to Sárraga, the Zapatistas were like a furious hurricane that spared only the clergy.[62] These arguments were presented in the following terms: "The fanatically Catholic nature of those indigenous insurrections became increasingly evident. . . . Zapatismo, which in its terrible feats respected neither persons nor interests, would respectfully stand down before the clergy. There can be no doubt that a religious spirit presided over the rebel bands. . . . Who took advantage of this?"[63]

Sárraga finished writing this book, but she did not perceive its legacy, nor did she understand the popular, radical, and rural ideal of the Zapatistas and Villistas: agrarian reform. She failed to consider the incorporation of the anarchist motto "Land and liberty" in Zapatismo. From Sárraga's perspective, their fanaticism was not compatible with a liberal, modern revolution. To her, this was central to the Mexican Revolution.

Sárraga, Catholic Social Action, Spiritism, and the Mexican Revolution
On August 15, 1912, Belén de Sárraga, now divorced, forty years old, and a recognized public speaker and freethinking author, visited Mexico for the first time. President Madero (a freethinker and Spiritist), the Masons, and other liberal organizations called on her to undermine the strength of the

FIG. 7. Francisco I. Madero, 1910. Courtesy of Colección Independencia y Revolución en la Memoria Ciudadana, Biblioteca Carmen Castañeda García, CIESAS Occidente.

Partido Católico Nacional (PCN) through an attack on the Catholic Church and religion.[64] Madero concurred with many of her ideas and, through Sárraga's conferences, sought to secure his own presence in the Partido PCP and disseminate Spiritist principles.[65]

Madero disguised these ideas behind an anticlerical, freethinking, and Masonic stance.[66] As a Spiritist, he carried out sessions to invoke the spirits. Soaking up this philosophical proposal, he wrote that "Spiritism has developed a social project focused on attaining the well-being of the most needy population," while at the same time attempting to spread the moralizing doctrine of Spiritism.[67] According to Yolia Tortolero, Spiritism "was the underlying reason that impelled him to struggle beyond other circumstances he experienced so that there would be a political, democratic, and educational change in Mexico in the early 20th century."[68] As historian Mary Kay Vaughan puts it, "Utopian visions surged in the heat and hope of revolution."[69]

When Sárraga arrived in Mexico, there was a political vacuum created by the popular and rural armed movement of the Mexican Revolution (1910–17), while at the same time, Catholics were also mobilizing for social reform according to their own understandings.[70] In 1911, secular Catholics established the PCN to provide the means to create a Catholic platform in the parliamentarian government. From August to September 1912, Sárraga gave a series of conferences at the Teatro Xicoténcatl in Mexico City. On the stage she addressed the president of Mexico, members of the presidential cabinet and their families, Spiritists, intellectuals, Masons, women, politicians, and workers. Nearly everyone attended the event in formal dress. In her speech, which the press described as eloquent, she addressed the evolution of human thought, religious congregations, women as human beings, education, progress, tradition, and morality.[71]

The reactions to Sárraga's conferences show that public opinion was not uniform. On the contrary, it was composed of multiple audiences: anticlericalists, Spaniards residing in Mexico (anarchists, freethinkers, and monarchists), Spiritists, freethinkers, liberals, politicians, ministers (Catholics, Methodists, Presbyterians), workers, and women.[72] The Spiritists and liberals—represented by *Helios*, a Spiritist publication, and *Nueva era*, the organ of the Partido Constitucional Progresivo—applauded Sárraga's declarations: "I believe in a religion of thought, . . . not of faith. For a religion of thought there should be no credo, worship, or ceremony. . . . I am not against Christianity as an

FIG. 8. Belén de Sárraga giving a speech at the Hemicycle to Juárez in Mexico City, 1912. Courtesy of Colección Gustavo Casasola.

ethical system but as an enterprise, such as the Roman Catholic Church has made it, yes."[73] Catholic reactions ranged from publications of articles of protest in daily papers to mobilizing against Sárraga. The Catholic press (*La nación*—an organ of the PCAN) and the conservative press (*El país*) were scandalized by her "extravagant doctrines."[74] *El correo español*, a daily newspaper devoted to the defense of Spain and the Spanish colony in Mexico, was surprised at the harsh criticism launched against Sárraga by *El país*. The newspaper also indicated that the Asturian Spanish community was divided.[75] Against *El correo español*, *La patria* published a letter supporting the Spaniards residing in Orizaba, Veracruz. Men and women were proud of the "enlightened conferences" Sárraga gave, showing the exuberance and vigor of Spanish freethinking as developed and popularized by Amalia Domingo Soler, Pi y Margall, Ramón Chíes, Fernando Lozano, Ramón Verea, Joaquín Costa, Doctor Esquerdo, Blasco Ibáñez, José Ñaques, Pérez Galdós, and other intellectuals.[76] *El faro*, the official bulletin of the General

FIG. 9. Belén de Sárraga (*seated second from left*) accompanied by Fernando Iglesias Calderón (*left*) at the Hemicycleto Juárez in Mexico City, 1912. Courtesy of Colección Gustavo Casasola.

Synod of the Presbyterian Church in Mexico, argued that there was nothing new in her speeches: "She uses the same phrases, sometimes reckless, used by scientists in her attacks on Christianity."[77] A group of 110 Catholic ladies asked President Madero to use his influence to "avoid these outrages against religion or likewise, the outrages against freedom of thought."[78] Madero promised them that their freedom of thought would be guaranteed.

The strong Catholic response against Sárraga's conferences caused liberals to defend her in public meetings.[79] The Madero administration declared that the government would respect freedom of thought and would not apply Article 33 to Sárraga.[80] (The Constitution of 1857 stipulated that the government had the right to expel pernicious foreigners.)[81] Despite the fact that various protests were staged against Sárraga in Mexico City, she ended her conferences with a speech at the Juárez Monument.[82] *La nación* and *El país* published, over the course of several days, long lists of signatures of Catholic men and women who protested "against the immoral, antisocial, and antipatriotic propaganda of Madam Belén."[83]

Sárraga's public speeches triggered a strong debate about femininity, masculinity, and the role of women in society. During her first conference on August 15, Sárraga stated that "woman was not formed from the rib of man; rather, as God set about forming her, a female monkey snatched the rib from his hands and fled, and so God went after her, but unable to rescue the rib, the only thing he managed to catch hold of was the monkey's tail and from that end, woman was made."[84] These declarations not only challenged and ridiculed the Catholic version of the creation of man and woman, but they also overturned the traditional gender hierarchy. In September 1912, a reporter from *La patria* reflected on the negative representations surrounding the figure of Sárraga as a "male brain" or a "male spirit" and pondered on the outlook of womanhood. The article described the innovations in the female situation, pointing out that women had gone from seclusion in the home, in the *harem*, in the gynoecium, to the action of public contemporary life.[85]

Sárraga was a new woman, one who inspired admiration, debate, and polemics in public opinion. She represented social renewal. In April 1917, Sárraga and Constitucionalista feminist Hermila Galindo were compared in a daily newspaper. It was indicated that first Sárraga, then Hermila had corroborated the changes experienced by women in the new realms of education and politics.[86] Meanwhile, an article in *El mañana* considered that Mexican women had no need for someone to instruct them in order to fulfill the selfless, heroic tasks that the country required.[87] Either way, the debate whether women ought to participate in politics and the public sphere was now on the table.[88]

In addition to her conferences in the capital, Sárraga traveled to Guadalajara, Mérida, Monterrey, San Luis Potosí, and Veracruz.[89] She spent the early days of October in San Luis Potosí. Her arrival was triumphant: "It was as if we found ourselves before a notable leader of the Maderista revolution."[90] The Presbyterian weekly *El faro* reported that three days before the arrival of Sárraga in San Luis Potosí, Catholic priests attempted to generate an unfavorable environment, but the priests forgot that "forbidden fruit is the most desirable."[91] An enormous crowd of all social classes welcomed her to the train station. Sárraga gave three conferences. At the end of the first, "people would not allow the coach hired to drive her to her lodgings to be drawn by horses. They were unharnessed from the coach and then, a crowd of men of all social classes dragged the coach through the main streets of the city."[92] A crowd followed behind, exclaiming, "Long live Madam Sárraga! Long live the redeemer of free thinking! Long live the woman of the 20th century! Death to the cassocked!" During her second speech, Sárraga declared that the confessional had sown dissent among families and had become a place of temptation between women and priests. In her third presentation, Sárraga stated that the cause of the "week of tragedy in Barcelona" was that workers had become sick and tired of the exploitation they suffered at the hands of friars. She asked women not to deliver their sons to the "greedy Jesuits" and demanded that schools instill true patriotism. Although *El faro* and *El abogado cristiano* did not concur with freethinking ideals because they did not support religion, they appreciated Sárraga's anticlericalism, eloquence, extraordinary intelligence, and valor (for a woman).

In every city, Sárraga met with strong Catholic opposition, though Guadalajara stands out. After a conference, shots were fired, and a bomb exploded.[93] Guadalajara paid the price of setting into motion "the democratic laboratory" in elections for federal and state deputies and the governorship.[94] The panorama was confrontational. The Catholics and PCN stood against the liberals, freethinkers, Maderistas, Masons, and former Reyistas. In all three elections of 1912, Catholics actively participated to support the PCN, whereas the "progressives" nearly abstained from voting. The result was an "embarrassing" defeat.[95] By October 1912, the PCN controlled both the executive and legislative branches in Jalisco and decreed legislative reforms based on Catholic social action.[96]

In Guadalajara, four newspapers reported on Sárraga's public speeches. Before the elections for state governor and the arrival of Sárraga in Guadalajara, *El regional* (representing social Catholicism) responded to a campaign against the PCN and the Catholic Church promoted by President Madero, anticlericals, freethinkers, and Masons. The newspaper published editorials against Spiritism, liberalism, freemasonry, socialism, and Sárraga, all of them considered heretical and enemies to family and religion.[97] According to one such editorial, Sárraga held a deformed notion of the Catholic Church. This newspaper argued that she did not know any theologians and failed to prove her arguments, merely offering "her word of honor."[98] According to *El regional*, her audience showed up out of curiosity. The women who attended were not of elite society. This same publication claimed that the

Catholics of Guadalajara were not as ignorant and fanatical as the liberal newspapers supposed. On the contrary, they were tolerant.[99] It highlighted the detonation of dynamite in the sewer system beneath the presses of *El regional* to indicate that Sárraga had vowed she would not disturb the peace of local families, yet her actions were endangering the civil rights, dignity, and lives of Catholics.[100]

By contrast, *El correo de Jalisco* and *La gaceta de Guadalajara*, liberal newspapers close to Governor Emeterio Robles Gil of the Partido Liberal, described the events as festive. At the train station, the assistant secretary to the governor, male city council members, professionals, students, workers, and a commission of ladies of the Alianza society received her with flowers, confetti, and the music of a military band.[101] As in Mexico City and San Luis Potosí, *La gaceta de Guadalajara* described in detail the actions of Jaliscan clericalism to boycott the first conference given by Sárraga on October 14, 1912.[102] At the same time, it recognized her colossal success in Mexico City, having filled theaters with Catholics, the political elite, Spiritists, families, workers, materialists, positivists, and theosophists. This newspaper knew of the attacks of *La nación* and *El país*, daily papers that had called her "corrupting," "bedeviled," "a female of bad customs who has come to pervert our wives and daughters," a "Mason," and a "red virgin." According to *La gaceta de Guadalajara*, Sárraga was a woman with extraordinary intelligence, filled with feeling for the peoples of Latin America, who generated brilliant ideas. Although some might have characterized her as masculine, noting the sharpness of her arguments, *La gaceta de Guadalajara* described her with feminine notions as a woman of science, an abnegated and courageous missionary who predicated fraternity, freethinking, and progress.

Like Mexico City and San Luis Potosí, during her first conference in Guadalajara, Sárraga spoke about human development. She "masterfully" outlined the different phases of the religions of humanity, from primitive times to the modern era. She spoke of the life of Jesus, of the true Christian doctrine, of the fatherland and home. She painted Catholicism in the blackest tones and extolled and glorified freedom of conscience. The officious daily papers and antiestablishment press considered Sárraga's conference to be brilliant, noting that the crowd accompanied her back to her hotel.[103] The second presentation followed nearly the same protocol, plus an artisan read a poem dedicated to Sárraga. In her preamble, Sárraga pardoned the Catholic ladies for their protests because "they know not what they do."[104] She refuted the false idea that women lacked the intellectual capacity for scientific and artistic conceptions; she provided examples of historic cases—such as Cornelia, the famous Roman matron, mother of the Gracchi, and Mademoiselle Roland, soul of the French Revolution—as arguments in favor of the capacity of women.

Sárraga argued that the church had ensnared women and that their minds were atrophied and sick from Catholic education. As she had done in Málaga in 1906 and in San Luis Potosí in October 1912, she attacked the celibacy of priests and the practice of confession. She reproached women who used confession to be unfaithful to their husbands and who were seduced by priests.[105] In Spain, anticlerical Republicans like Pi y Margall and Nakens (editor of the satiric anticlerical weekly *El motín*) regarded this denunciation of the damaged honor of men as proof of Sárraga's virility. This was linked to another problem: the loss of honor of nineteenth-century Spain. According to anticlerical Republicans, Catholic priests controlled and seduced women and, by extension, their entire households. For Nakens, the public accusation by Sárraga that men were not fulfilling their duty to defend the republic must have awakened a sense of shame—because a woman was doing their "manly" duty.[106] Although Sárraga sustained this same argument in Málaga, San Luis Potosí, and Guadalajara, it did not have the same resonance in Mexico. On the contrary, revolutionary strongmen were leading an armed, secular struggle against the Catholic Church that exalted their liberal, masculine, and virile vision. However, the newspaper articles against Catholic women published in the Constitucionalista Jalisco newspaper *Boletín militar* did concur with the sexual anxieties analyzed by historian Enrique Sanabria.[107]

However, immediate responses to Sárraga's conferences on all fronts (Catholic, Episcopal, liberal, freethinking, Mason, and Protestant) showed existing divisions (religious and political). For *La libertad*, Sárraga was sowing more discrepancies at a time when the country required concordance and union due to the revolution it was experiencing.[108] In San Luis Potosí, her host David Berlanga also invited her to the local Normal School and the offices of the General Department of Primary Education. According to a local newspaper, "the distinguished lady was given an affectionate reception, showing herself to be very satisfied with the teaching methods in the first building and the system of educational organization statewide."[109] According to Ramírez Hurtado, Berlanga "fell head over heels in love with her." This was taken advantage of by the poet Ramón López Velarde to mock both Berlanga and Sárraga while denigrating her anticlerical campaign.[110]

The press in Mexico City, Guadalajara, and San Luis Potosí represented Sárraga as both a "male spirit" and a "female apostle."[111] Her public anticlerical actions and performances brought her very close to the practices of men, but she was a woman. She dressed as a bourgeois woman, not as a "modern girl" or flapper. For the public and the Mexican press, she used masculine language with amazing lucidity and solid rhetoric. She was familiar with the political language used mainly in masculine organizations to speak of fraternity, independence, justice, freedom, reason, and freemasonry. Sárraga incited public debate. She disrupted the use of gendered language and the constructions of masculinity and femininity. This had already been the case in Spain. In her native country, they also employed representations of gender to refer to her political work. Pi y Margall dedicated his last book to Sárraga, whom he considered to be a "virile woman" due to her political work.[112] This was seen as part of an exclusively male sphere, thus her leadership transcended what was "appropriate for her sex" and the men of her generation.[113] The Spanish Catholic press, instead of confirming the masculinization of Sárraga, associated her with French anarchist Louise Michel (1830–1905), leader of the Paris Commune (1871), as they both represented the "antiwoman" and the irrational.[114] Like Michel, Sárraga destabilized the hierarchy of gender, both politically and socially. In Mexico, the revolutionary government accepted her anticlerical ideas, but it did not support the transformation of women into autonomous and combatant citizens like Sárraga.

What was the response of non-Catholic women to Sárraga's speeches? Were there meetings between Sárraga and these women? Of what scattered information is available, we know *El diario* announced that Sárraga participated in the silver anniversary celebration of the first Mexican female doctor, Matilde Petra Montoya y Lafragua. This celebration, held at the Teatro Arbeu, was organized by doctors Columba Rivera, Antonia Ursúa, Guadalupe Sánchez, and Soledad de Régules; the pharmacist Luque; the teacher Margarita Kleinhans Wright; the lawyer María Sandoval de Zarco; and the dentist Avilés.[115] Doctor Montoya and Sárraga were, moreover, present at a *tenida blanca* or public Masonic rite at the Pantheon of San Fernando, where Juárez was buried.[116] President Madero and Sárraga led the event from beside Juárez's tomb. In Guadalajara, the Grupo Alianza of liberal women, together with the anticlericals, freethinkers, and Masons, received Sárraga at the train station. Their objectives were unspecified, although it is possible that the teacher Atala Apodaca took part in this association. During her stay in Guadalajara, Soledad Calleja de Echeverría published a poem dedicated to Sárraga that describes her erudition, strength, and drive.[117] We do not know whether any of these contacts continued in later years or whether Sárraga established bonds of friendship with any of the aforementioned women.

From what little information is available to us regarding the meetings between Sárraga and workers in 1912 and the biographic reconstruction of the Federación Anticlerical Mexicana (FAM) in 1928, we do know that a group of railroad workers honored her by founding a school for adults in her name. The FAM book does not specify when and where.[118] Perhaps the school belonged to the Liga de Ferrocarrileros of Yucatán. In April 1918, this league requested the autonomy of their "Belén de Zárraga" school because they were not in agreement with the pedagogical orientation provided by the Secretaría de Educación Pública.[119] It is possible that during her first visit to Mexico in 1912, Sárraga came into contact with the anticlerical general Salvador Alvarado, who was later the governor of Yucatán (1915–18).[120] Like Sárraga, Alvarado also believed that religion was the archenemy of progress and that it was urgent that women be freed from the control of the church. He favored policies and programs of de-fanaticism, such as the first two feminist congresses held in Yucatán in 1916.[121] Sárraga did not attend these meetings because she was not in Mexico at the time.

After Sárraga's propaganda tour was complete, the Methodists made a summary of her message and the results obtained. *El abogado cristiano*, an organ of the Episcopal Methodist Church, recognized that Sárraga had "talent, erudition, an ease with words, culture, penetration, lucidness (ability that some people have to think with great intelligence, speed and clarity) and judgment."[122] This newspaper considered that she attracted a wide audience because she was a woman liberated from the tyrannies of the clergy. This was a novelty that drew many curious onlookers. Moreover, the Partido Constitucional Progresista and the Partido Liberal created a favorable environment and extolled her virtues. It was rumored that the Madero administration had subsidized her speaking tour with Mex$200 a month. Sárraga was a political weapon for anticlericals and Maderistas. But what results did she obtain?

El abogado cristiano did not conclude that the foundations of clericalism had cracked. Liberals were no stronger, women had not been emancipated from religious fanaticism, and there had been no substantial change. One of the results was the creation of clubs for free thought in different areas of the republic. The magazine that was promised to be edited, *El pensamiento libre*, had not been published. The economic benefits were for her alone. Mexico was no more liberal nor any less Catholic—nor was it more freethinking. It concluded that certain merits of hers were recognized, but her achievements were null. Although Sárraga's propaganda was focused against the Catholic Church, this did not do any good to the Presbyterians because "her propaganda is demolishing the Christian principles and indeed, that is why we do not applaud her with such fervor."[123]

What did Madero get out of Sárraga's visit? His administration accentuated its anticlerical position and continued to harshly criticize the PCN. According to Tortolero, although Sárraga did not bring about immediate change, the strong divisions in Mexican society did become evident, as did the absence of inroads for dialogue and negotiation between different groups. Moreover, Madero had left the judicial branch intact, as well as the army. The immediate response of his enemies was to plan a conspiracy: "Archbishop Mora y del Río, Prior Manuel Díaz Santibáñez, Ambassador Henry Lane Wilson, Alberto García Granados, León de la Barra, Victoriano Huerta, and others gathered to plot what would culminate in the *coup d'état* led by General Huerta on February 20, 1913."[124]

On Anticlerical Campaigns and International Propaganda Supporting the Mexican Revolution

When Sárraga returned to Mexico at the age of fifty in 1922, during the Álvaro Obregón presidential administration, the conflict between the church and state was at a different stage. Due to the moderate anticlerical policies of Obregón, the Catholic Church bounced back, creating more organizations and criticizing the political regime from the pulpit. Strong clashes increased during the presidency of Plutarco Elías Calles because the "Jacobins had incorporated strict anticlerical policies into the Constitution of 1917."[125] The Catholic Church was the strongest civil society organization with the capacity to resist the policies of the new, weak revolutionary state in the areas of educational reform, land distribution, and labor.[126] The Catholics challenged the anticlerical policies of the state and sought to restore the supremacy of the church in all areas of society. This set off a strong confrontation in civil society between the non-Catholics—anarcho-syndicalists, communists, socialists, and liberals—and the Catholics in various parts of Mexico, sparking a fiery conflict in many cities across the country.

From 1922 to 1926, Sárraga's conferences acquired greater visibility as she became more vocal and active. She gave lectures for Masons, teachers, military officers, and workers in Aguascalientes, Colima, Chihuahua, Durango, Guadalajara, Morelia, Pachuca, Puebla, Oaxaca, Toluca, Torreón, Tulancingo, Xalapa, and Zacatecas.[127] Sárraga attracted a very broad audience in her talks. In Puebla, she attracted "20,000 workers."[128] In Tampico, the number of people who wanted to attend her conference was so large that she had to change venues.[129] In that city, she joined a labor organization as an honorary member. In Chihuahua, she met with the Tarahumaras and, in Puebla, with the oldest veterans from the 1857 constitution.[130] In Monterrey, a local newspaper indicated that Sárraga was an enlightened woman. She had absolute dominion over rhetoric and electrified her audience with a masterful performance, vast cultural knowledge, and perfect diction.[131]

In June 1922, standing before the Juárez Monument in Mexico City, Sárraga denied the existence of God.[132] In August and December 1922, her conferences at the Teatro Obrero and the Teatro Degollado in Guadalajara were colossal successes.[133] Her second visit to the "Pearl of Jalisco" contrasted significantly with the first occasion in October 1912. This time, shots were fired and a bomb detonated in an environment dominated by strong ideological and political clashes. By 1922, the social and political environment had changed. Basilio Badillo (governor of Jalisco, 1921–22) and José Guadalupe Zuno Hernández (municipal president of Guadalajara, 1922) were radical Obregonist leaders who sought the politicization of workers by way of Marxist and Leninist ideals.[134] Zuno Hernández backed a popular anticlerical movement composed of peasants, teachers, women, and workers through the Confederación de Partidos Liberales de Jalisco (Confederation of liberal parties of Jalisco). Sárraga's talks reinforced the combativeness of "the Reds": electricians, railroad workers, miners, bakers, and textile workers. *El cruzado*, a low-cost Catholic weekly edited by Agustín Yáñez and Francisco Gollaz, continued to ridicule Sárraga along the same lines by which the Catholic press of Mexico City and Guadalajara had done in 1912. It categorized her as "a two-bit woman, like something out of a makeshift nativity scene, who has come to cure all the bile"[135] of the Bolsheviks, Spiritists, liberals, and Masons who dreamed of the destruction of the Catholic Church. *El cruzado* reminded its readers that Sárraga was a vulgar woman. Besides these phrases, they employed others such as "vile witch" and "grotesque display of encyclopedic science."[136] *El cruzado* emphasized its disdain for this woman who had broken away from "biologically" essential and natural femininity. It warned its readers to stay alert because their enemy was approaching. They repudiated Sárraga for being an emancipated, new woman. But this was not the only female representation they condemned. They also rejected the "modern women" who followed the latest fashion trends as women who had forgotten their duties as mothers.[137] *El cruzado* advocated that those women be virtuous mothers and active defenders of the Catholic religion and the family.[138] According to this newspaper, their "evil" enemies were Bolshevism, feminism, liberalism, Masonry, the "modern woman," socialism, the impious press, and Sárraga.[139]

In November 1922, Sárraga's conferences triggered a reaction among the local population, led by Catholic ladies and the ACJM.[140] In January 1923 *El cruzado* (in Guadalajara) remarked on the events in Durango: "How convenient to preach the error of our ways without any danger, surrounded by all today's comforts and applauded by Masons and sidekicks, as is the case of that poor, old woman Madam Belén de Sárraga, brought expressly to combat the Catholic Church by the frauds of liberty . . . and now they bring us a woman who is moreover too old to defend them, enlighten them and encourage them in the battle they have chosen. Are there no longer any men among the Masons and liberals?"[141] Thus *El cruzado* construed the conflict as deeply gendered, questioning the masculinity of anticlerical men who hid behind a female body and voice to further their cause.

On January 11, 1923, "between 50 and 80,000 churchgoers made a pilgrimage to the Cerro del Cubilete in Guanajuato, because they consider it to be the geographic heart of the country."[142] During this symbolic ceremony, the church and all Catholic organizations sought to establish the kingdom of Christ the King. In response to this mass pilgrimage and the furious reactions of anticlericals, the state began to put into practice an anticlerical policy and expelled Vatican representative Monsignor Ernesto Fillipi from Mexico. Immediately, Catholic organizations staged a national protest.

Neither church nor state moderated their discourse and instead became increasingly belligerent.[143]

That year, Sárraga participated in the creation of the FAM to temper the influence of the Catholic clergy—"enemy of home, Fatherland, science, and progress."[144] The tension between the Catholic hierarchy, Catholic organizations, anticlerical associations, and the Obregón administration was escalating. The FAM and Sárraga demanded that President Obregón apply Article 33 because this ceremony had instigated a rebellion against the anticlerical clauses of the Constitution of 1917 and advanced the power of the Catholic Church.[145]

Jesuit priest Alfonso Junco, in his publication *La sra. Belén de Sárraga desfanatizando* (*Madame Sárraga Defanaticizing*), sustained that Sárraga was an extreme antireligious fanatic.[146] According to Junco, Sárraga made no distinctions between the pope and priests. Junco wondered why this exotic lady had come to try to offend what in Mexico was held to be most pure and high: womanhood.[147] Junco did not agree with Sárraga's idea that religion caused ignorance. To him, the church had undertaken the task of education rather than the prevention of knowledge.

From January to May 1923, Sárraga continued her speaking tour in Aguascalientes, Guadalajara, Puebla, and Zacatecas.[148] In May, the Confederación Ferrocarrilera (Railway confederation) in Aguascalientes (the organizing commission sponsored by the Masonic lodge and labor corporations) collected Mex$300 for a propaganda campaign. In June, the news spread that she had been arrested in San Francisco, California. The Mexican Consulate of that city clarified that the "clericals circulated this slanderous rumor confusing her, news has it, with a woman who was accompanying Flores Magón."[149] Her tours had received major backing from Calles as secretary of the interior. In December, as president-elect, Calles communicated to Sárraga that she would receive a monthly stipend of Mex$500. He ordered Mr. Marcos E. Raya of the pro-Calles committee to deliver said sum to Sárraga and specified that the money be taken from his personal account, should the committee lack the necessary funds. In early 1924, Sárraga congratulated him on his electoral triumph and thanked him for his financial support.[150] But what was Sárraga using the money for? Was it destined for the creation of anticlerical leagues in each city she visited across the country? We know that this sum helped her cover transportation, hotel, and food expenses. It was a significant quantity compared to the salary of a schoolteacher—sixty pesos per month—during that same period.[151] These funds were fundamental in allowing her to travel to Laredo in the United States and from there to Havana, Cuba. From March to May 1924, Sárraga became a defender of the Obregón and Calles administrations. In New Orleans and Havana, she extolled the revolutionary policies of these two leaders. In both cities, Sárraga would find Delahuertistas who questioned her defense.[152] In Laredo, the American Consul made her wait for more than twelve hours because a reporter from the *New Orleans Times* announced her as a Bolshevik who would endanger the future of America. Sárraga informed Soledad González, the private secretary to President Calles, that such an accusation was absurd, given that she did not speak English.[153]

During Sárraga's second visit to Cuba in 1924, she organized the Liga Anticlerical. She was accompanied by Cuban communist Julio Antonio Mella, president of the Federación Estudiantil Universitaria (University student federation)—a man who held feminist ideals very dear—and the propagandist Emilio Rodríguez (1882–1962), a labor leader who came to the island in 1906 and was a rationalist, propagandist teacher of anarchism.[154] In May, she gave a conference paying tribute to Felipe Carrillo Puerto in the Teatro Maxim of Havana. She won a standing ovation, inspiring cheers for the Mexican Revolution, and brought together more than five thousand students, intellectuals, and workers.[155] Sárraga commented that it was very hot and that her conference would be brief, in response to which people shouted in protest to ensure she would continue. She referred to Carrillo Puerto as a leader of humble origins and part of the Mexican Revolution, asking herself how such a great task could have been accomplished in relatively little time, overcoming so many forms of resistance. "The brilliant Mexican Revolution," she declared, "has acted like a lighthouse whose beams reach other peoples, illuminating them with light and hope. . . . The cause of Mexico is also that of all those who seek the happiness of the people, which is why we must lend it our moral support and applause, because its triumph will become that of all men of good will."[156] She indicated that in the Delahuertista rebellion, military officers allied with the church had conspired to defeat the revolutionary government; those who joined the revolt were not true revolutionaries like Calles, Carrillo Puerto, Madero, and Obregón. After her conferences on radio and in theaters, Sárraga informed Soledad González,

Calles's private secretary, that the Delahuertistas in Havana were a minority faction of no real significance. She asked for Calles's authorization to travel from Cuba to Guatemala.

In June, there was another tribute to Carrillo Puerto in the city of Mérida. At this ceremony were Julio Antonio Mella, Eusebio Adolfo Hernández, Fernando Sirgo, Leonardo Hernández, and Sárraga herself.[157] That same month, she returned to Veracruz, and in July she arrived in Mexico City, where she congratulated the newspaper *El demócrata* for its educational efforts with the Mexican working class.[158] At the reception were representatives of the FAM and the lodges of Espíritu Juana de Arco, Anáhuac, and Valle de México. Sárraga arrived with her personal secretary, Luis Pardo Bernabé.[159] In November, she responded to Calles that she understood his weariness and his numerous commitments. She indicated to him that in Cuba, the people showed affection for him as a revolutionary and that soon she would visit to personally "express her sentiments of respect and affection."[160] Calles responded that he would be glad to receive her.

In 1924, Sárraga participated in civic rituals to honor Hidalgo, Juárez, and Madero. She marched in a ceremony held at the Monument of Independence to commemorate the relocation of the exhumed remains of the heroes formerly buried at the cathedral.[161] During this period, there were violent confrontations between Catholics and Reds.[162] The labor movement, encompassing different influences and labor organizations (anarchist, anarcho-syndicalist, and communist known as the "Reds"; Catholic identified as the "Whites"; and nationalist or belonging to the state called "Yellows"), brought to the forefront of the national debate different interests that complicated the conflict between them and their relationship with a weak, incipient, revolutionary state. There were violent confrontations between Catholics and Reds during the early 1920s in Michoacán, Jalisco, Puebla, and Yucatán, where the governors were Jacobins and the labor movements were dominated by the Reds.

President Obregón was a moderate who employed a radical discourse. He did not seek to set in motion the anticlerical postulates of the constitution, nor did he approve of the violence that direct action by the Reds would lead to. Despite this, Obregón allowed radical governors like Felipe Carrillo Puerto (1922–24) in Yucatán, José Guadalupe Zuno (1923–26) in Jalisco, and Francisco Mújica (1920–22) in Michoacán to carry out ferocious anticlerical policies against the Catholic Church.[163] Different regions of Mexico "became laboratories of antireligiosity, where caciques experimented with 'defanaticization' campaigns involving anticlerical legislation, rationalist education, religious persecution, and systematic iconoclasm."[164] Carrillo Puerto belonged to the Partido Popular Socialista (Popular socialist party), and like other anticlericals, he was in agreement with Sárraga regarding the need to emancipate women from the power of the Catholic Church. They were also close friends.

In order to defeat the Catholic social action movement, on February 21, 1925, President Calles, through Luis N. Morones, leader of the Confederación Regional Obrera Mexicana (CROM) and secretary of industry, created the Schismatic Apostolic Catholic Church, which did not recognize the Vatican. Priests would be Mexican nationals and not be required to practice celibacy. By means of this church, the state would attempt to promote a more liberal discourse. According to Jean Meyer, the CROM hoped to use its union building to create the new church.[165]

Sárraga "Picks Up the Gauntlet": The Publication of *Rumbos nuevos* (1925–27)

Sárraga resided in Mexico from 1922 to 1927. During that time, she was naturalized as a Mexican citizen. Her petition, filed in November 1926, shows that she lived comfortably. She claimed to be a fifty-four-year-old divorced Spanish woman and author who resided at number 284 Reforma Avenue.[166] In the month of April 1925, the first issue of her monthly magazine *Rumbos nuevos* appeared. The graphic design of the publication blended pre-Hispanic imagery with a woman dressed in the fashion of the twenties—wearing a loose, sleeveless dress and a feathered crown. The woman gazes at a map of the American continent. To one side she has several books, some of them open and some of them closed. The closed books are dedicated to art, science, and religion. In contrast to the nervous, fearful priest who appeared on the cover of her 1914 book *El clericalismo en América*, this image suggests that women are at the center of the construction of the modern nation. Women as builders of the modern nation were a sample of the highly visible transformations that were taking place in the 1920s. It was an attempt to suggest that the clergy had already been displaced, that they were no longer in the foreground.

In the first issue of *Rumbos nuevos*, Sárraga described the purposes of this monthly magazine: to divulge and defend the universal doctrines of freethinking. Through this publication, Sárraga and the FAM sought to put an end to the influence of the adversary over peasants and workers, "warning them of the danger that these Catholic labor associations hold as a Jesuit way to recruit benighted forces, so that they may serve at certain moments as recreation."[167] The main objective was to "assist in the liberation of individual science as the foundation of all social and political liberties. This magazine will unfurl its indoctrinating labor, not once sinking to the level of personal insults."[168] Moreover, it would link the FAM with similar existing organizations across the Americas in order to "constitute a unique front, due to the strength of its numbers and the homogeneity of its purposes, capable of detaining the reactionary wave out of Rome that attempts to invade us on this continent."[169] Therefore, *Rumbos nuevos* would appear before public opinion with a frankly combative attitude. Its banner was one not of transaction but of struggle. It sought the well-being of the people. Sárraga, as director of the magazine, and General Manuel Navarro Angulo, as its copy editor, specified, "To our sincere adversaries, a greeting as loyal combatants, to all hypocrites, our disdain, and to those who struggle for noble causes as we do, a friendly handshake and the cordial embrace of camaraderie."[170]

Rumbos nuevos was published from April 1925 to April 1927 in order to "pick up the gauntlet" thrown down by the Catholic Church in February 1923, following the establishment of the FAM.[171] As in the dueling rituals of eighteenth-century nobility and the defense of masculine honor in the nineteenth century, following this rite of challenge, the *Gaceta eclesiástica potosina* called to Catholics to respond to the offensive attitude of the FAM with a strategy of "picking up the gauntlet." This publication identified Sárraga's return to Mexico in 1922 and the creation of the FAM in 1923 as the beginning of a more bellicose moment characterized by intransigent policy that invaded consciences, schools, homes, families. It warned the churchgoers that the FAM would disseminate its doctrines by means of books, teachings, and newspapers based on calumny and lies. It asked itself what they ought to do in response and whether they ought to take up arms. To take up arms would destroy only bodies, not ideas. The *Gaceta eclesiástica potosina* would follow the trail that the FAM had blazed. It would fall back on the virility of Catholic men to defend their right to freedom of consciousness. It was necessary to bolster the Catholic press so that it might become a "lever to move opinion, to orient it, to provide encouragement, and to raise the spirits of the meek."[172] It gauged that the government and legislature had them by the necks. There was an urgent need for patriotic men to vote in greater numbers than the revolutionaries, to change the laws. The work of Catholics was insufficient unless it was backed legislatively. The editorial ended with a call to action: to be fearless and start "picking up the gauntlet."

On March 9, 1925, different organizations of secular Catholics established the Liga Nacional Defensora de la Libertad Religiosa (LNDLR; National League for the Defense of Religious Freedom) to safeguard their Catholicism and their ties to the Vatican.[173] In a conference at the Teatro Arbeu, Sárraga explained how the clergy had obstructed her work and the schism that had divided the Catholic Church in Mexico. She held that the Liga de Resistencia Católica ought to be punished for attempting to violate the law. She sympathized with the reform the Mexican Church had attempted to make through the creation of a Schismatic Apostolic Catholic Church that rejected the Vatican. For Sárraga, it was better for the priest to compare saints to the heroes of his fatherland "than to those who humiliate it, placing it at the feet of a foreign pope."[174] In this solemn ceremony before the figure of Benito Juárez (prominent liberal and anticlerical president of the nineteenth century during the Reform War and the second French intervention), the FAM and Sárraga publicly picked up the gauntlet. They declared combat, taking up the challenge to renew activities that had been interrupted by the 1924 electoral process.

The FAM planned to hold monthly conferences on current affairs, to create a library that would remain open at night and a night school for adult literacy, to strengthen their ties to anticlerical associations across the continent (Argentina, Brazil, Cuba, Chile, and Paraguay), to promote of civic and labor celebrations, and to launch a campaign against the religious beggars who filled the streets of Mexico City. They announced that the patriotic public ought to subscribe to *Rumbos nuevos*. Businesses ought to advertise in the widely circulated magazine. The magazine described the monthly meetings of the FAM Catholic foundations, and social doctrines were studied and discussed, seeking to put theories into practice. The members of the FAM aspired to form a spiritual, anticlerical family to break away from the customs of the Catholic Church and invited family groups to participate in their activities. With this kind of propaganda, they hoped to attract women and thus facilitate "the labor of female defanaticization, the sole obstacle over which progressive ideas stumble today."[175]

Through parody and ridicule, on April 10, 1925, the FAM organized an event themed around Good Friday—a Christian holy day that remembers the crucifixion of Jesus and his death on Calvary, also known as Black Friday—by hosting a "banquet of promiscuities" to illustrate the FAM's perspective and position. On that day, the Catholic Church was depicted in a comedy of pain to mock the concept of grief. The photographers of the event identified two girls disguised as a priest and a nun who performed the Mexican hat dance. Two hundred guests were in attendance. Although it was no earth-shaking event, it did show a certain influence among approximately forty families. The dinner menu was as follows:

- Schismatic rice
- Goose à la Capistrano
- Picadillo of "Popes" (potatoes)
- Pork à la Cimino
- Refried cassocked beans
- Holier than Thou cucumber salad
- Consecration wine
- Mother Abbess beer
- Desserts
  - Little Priest Heads
  - Sighs of a Nun
- Liquors
  - Anise liqueur from the Roman Monkey
  - Coffee or Tea-Deum
  - Revolutionary cigars

From April to December, the FAM's intense labor of revolutionary propaganda continued in Coahuila, Colima, Durango, Guadalajara, Manzanillo, Morelia, Nuevo Laredo, Saltillo, Yurécuaro, Toluca, Uruapan, and Zamora, where anticlerical or freethinking leagues were established.[176] Four months after its first edition, *Rumbos nuevos* claimed its readers in Mexico and abroad had reached five thousand, a figure few magazines were able to attain at the start of publication. In response to their success, the newspaper *El universal* held the FAM and Sárraga responsible for violence in Guadalajara, presenting Catholics as victims of persecution and anticlericals as promoters of religious intolerance. This daily newspaper blamed Sárraga for the anticlerical measures taken by Governor Zuno, who closed churches and the major Guadalajara seminary, as well as growing Catholic resistance to "the intemperances of the clergy."[177] For *Rumbos nuevos*, it was absurd that any outside influences be ascribed to Zuno. *El universal* failed to consider the strong political conflict between Zuno's regional autonomy and the centralist policies of Calles, who sought to impeach him. Zuno was a fervent anticlerical who agreed on the subject with Calles but had other strong differences with him. For *El universal*, this confrontation between Zuno and Calles was a distraction from the larger goal of presenting Sárraga as an agent of social unrest.

The two papers debated Sárraga's words and actions. *Rumbos nuevos* declared that Sárraga's behavior had been correct.[178] *El universal* criticized "her costly typographical presentation and magnificent paper," sold at low prices and widely distributed in Mexico and abroad, claiming that this was possible only thanks to the support she received from an anticlerical presidential administration. Enthusiastic letters were received from all social classes across Mexico and the Americas.

The main debates Sárraga and, in consequence, *Rumbos nuevos* raised were with the following: the archbishops and bishops of the Catholic Church, for having violated anticlerical laws and challenged the secularity of the postrevolutionary state; José Vasconcelos, for criticizing in *El universal* the change in direction that the Calles administration was using to alter the educational model (according to Vasconcelos, the president was succumbing to a secular education that conveyed an intransigent, anticlerical fanaticism); and the newspaper *Excélsior*, for contrasting Sárraga in an article with the feminist educator and poet Gabriela Mistral (1889–1957), whom they extolled as a model woman.[179] A copywriter from that same daily newspaper insulted Belén de Sárraga for being a foreigner who performed anticlerical work. *Rumbos nuevos* emphasized that everywhere she went, Sárraga carried out the dignified, honorable task of promoting the moral elevation of consciences. The editorial concluded that Sárraga was among the most honorable of Mexican ladies.

Rumbos nuevos reported on the many activities in which Sárraga was engaged. In July 1925, for example, Sárraga found herself in the midst of the dispute between Catholic and non-Catholic feminists at the Congreso de Mujeres de la Raza (Women's congress race) organized by the Liga de Mujeres Ibéricas e Hispanoamericans (League of Ibero-American women).[180] It is worthwhile to clarify here that early issues of the periodical described this clash from a dichotomic perspective, not taking into account the participation of the socialist feminist Elvia Carrillo Puerto (1881–1967), who spoke of the divorce law proposed by her brother, Felipe Carrillo Puerto, when he was governor of Yucatán.[181] *Rumbos nuevos* also reported on resistance to her campaigns in, for example, Colima, where Catholic ladies distributed whistles among their domestic employees to boycott Sárraga's public lecture. After her conference on "the evolution of thought" in the Teatro Hidalgo, she established the Comité Colimense Pro Constitución (Colima committee for constitution), which acted as a base for the governor to restrict "the tolling of bells on Catholic temples during the December festivities of 1925."[182] The edition ended with articles that expressed surprise that in the twentieth century, a "medieval crusade" in defense of the Catholic Church had begun. Sárraga delivered to Calles all the published issues of *Rumbos nuevos* bound in a volume she dedicated to him personally.

In January 1926, the archbishop of Mexico City, José Mora y del Río, orchestrated a public protest over the Constitution of 1917 and published a statement calling on Catholic women to defend their rights. In response, Calles ordered the enforcement of the Regulatory Law of Article 130. Calles asked Congress to immediately reform the penal code and demanded that governors enforce said law. On July 14, 1926, Congress published the Calles Law, which reiterated the anticlerical provisions of Article 130 that allowed for only one priest for every six thousand people and the suspension of religious services. In the wake of the Calles Law, the robust Catholic social action crusade evolved into a rural movement against state anticlerical policies, known as the Cristiada (1926–29).

There is no further information about Sárraga after 1928. Although Sárraga had become a naturalized citizen in 1926, she was still seen as a foreigner who contributed to souring the political environment and as a close collaborator with Calles. As was the case between 1898 and 1906 with the FMSO in Málaga, despite favoring "reasonable" scientific arguments (anticlerical and freethinking) and being in favor of public debate, closed-mindedness prevailed. The FAM published *Belén de Sárraga* in 1928 to honor her work in Mexico. This publication displays a male gaze on her family background and her anticlerical work in Hispanic America. But there is no trace of her to be found from 1928 to 1930. Perhaps Sárraga did not approve of the armed violence of the Cristiada. And with the 1929 accords between the Catholic Church and the state, the conflict with the church was considered over and done with. The Mexican government no longer needed her. Perhaps Sárraga felt that her work in Mexico had concluded and that she should seek new opportunities to spread freethinking. In 1930, she visited Quito. Her presence and speeches triggered a strong confrontation and disturbances there. The government of Ecuador asked her to leave the country.[183]

At the age of fifty-nine, in 1931, Sárraga returned to Spain, where she rejoined the Federal Republican Party.[184] In 1932, the magazine *Crónica* interviewed her about the decision to return to Spain.[185] Sárraga expressed her commitment to fighting for the federal republic and her concerns about the role of women. Sárraga was concerned about how women in Spain might exercise their recently gained right to vote. Women, she feared, tended to be very conservative. The most urgent task at hand was the organization of women in favor of the republic. She was also concerned that men recognize women's contributions. Men and women had to work together for political change. She was not in favor of "masculinisms" (viewpoints only in favor of men) or "feminisms" (stances that only support women); on the contrary, she reiterated her humanism, as she had done since the decade of 1890. In 1933, at the age of sixty-one, she ran and lost an electoral campaign as a candidate to the courts representing Málaga.[186] People identified her with the old Republican Party.

During the Spanish Civil War (1936–39) Sárraga went into exile, first to France and in 1939 to Mexico. She was sixty-seven at the time. Her strong bond with the exiled former president Calles likely hindered her invitation to join the political circle of Lázaro Cárdenas (1934–40). The strong rivalry between Calles and Cárdenas and the atmosphere of World War II contributed to Sárraga gradually losing visibility in her anticlerical and freethinking proposals. The context of the Second World War forced her to redirect her criticism against fascism. In France and in Mexico, she collaborated with antifascist women's associations. At the age of seventy-three, in 1945, she participated in a celebration of Women's Day on March 8, organized by the Comité Coordinador Feminino para la Defensa de la Patria (Women's coordinating committee for the defense of the fatherland) together with Teresa Flores Magón and a Republican writer exiled in Mexico: Margarita Nelken, of the Comité de Mujeres por la Defensa de la Patria.[187] In that celebration the Congress was asked to recognize women's suffrage, a demand Sárraga did not publicly support. She was writing her memoirs when she passed away in Mexico City on September 9, 1950, at the age of seventy-eight.[188]

Sárraga's political work lingered in the cultural memory of Catholics. They remembered her as a loudmouthed old lady who caused a lot of damage to the working class and to certain women, such as, for example, Atala Apodaca, the teacher from Jalisco.[189] Sárraga's anticlericalism and freethinking had dovetailed with the patriarchal revolutionary politics of a state that sought to destroy the power of the Catholic Church. Sárraga had worked closely with anticlerical presidents such as Obregón and Calles and with labor organizations such as the CROM. She also overlapped with revolutionary leaders who considered the Catholic Church the archenemy of modernity. Since her first visit to Mexico in 1912, she had approached workers and encouraged them to rebel against the Catholic Church, but not as actors autonomous from the state.

Questions that require investigation remain. Did Sárraga contact Mexican feminists such as Hermila Galindo and Elvia Carrillo Puerto? The rich historiography regarding feminist congresses in Mexico (1916, 1923, 1925, 1931, 1933, and 1934) does not mention her as a participant in these meetings. Who read her book *El clericalismo* and her articles in the monthly magazine *Rumbos nuevos*? What impact did her conferences, propaganda, and articles have on Masons, workers of both genders, and feminists? How different was her work in Mexico from her transnational work in other countries of Hispanic America? These questions ought to be considered, to honor the career and legacy of this exceptional woman, who contributed to the cause of social justice in Mexico.

3

Atala Apodaca Anaya

Anticlericalism, Civic Education, Progressive Forces, and the Mexican Revolution

> Close the door, Madam,
> Lest you be killed,
> Here come the Carrancistas,
> Brothers of Satan.
> Here come Diéguez and Berlanga
> along with Manzano and Obregón.
> In other words, the choicest selection
> Ever vomited from Hell.
> Here comes Doña Atala as well,
> With her shawl on backwards.
> That elegant cookie who blasphemes
> through the very soles of her feet.
> —Anonymous corrido (ballad)

In December 1914, a conservative corrido narrated the arrival of the Constitucionalistas in Ciudad Guzmán, Jalisco. The Villistas had expelled them from Guadalajara, albeit only for a few months. The ballad called on women to close their doors because the new arrivals were "brothers of Satan."[1] It ridiculed the revolutionary endeavors of the schoolteacher Atala Apodaca Anaya (1884–1977), portraying her as an "elegant dame who blasphemes through the very soles of her feet." Apodaca was a teacher who broke away from the liberal stereotype that viewed Catholic women as passively resisting progress. She promoted a new feminine identity: anticlerical, revolutionary, and political. Her practices and conferences were opposed to the gender policies of the Catholic Church and the revolutionary state. The Catholic Church and the state had points in common: they both believed that women belonged to the domestic sphere, whether as guardians of the home who must emulate the virtues of the Virgin Mary or as persons who ought to fit into the bourgeois model, under which women could only aspire to become mothers and apolitical wives. The Catholic Church and the state accepted that women would carry out activities outside the home when they participated in charitable institutions and welfare campaigns; they approved of having them become their defenders and propagandists. As I argued in chapter 1, the revolutionary state backed its own image as that of a young, radical, productive, and virile man who had to destroy the Catholic Church, his main enemy, represented through the eyes of revolutionary leaders as an old woman who was unproductive, superstitious, and fanatical. The practices of the Apodaca sisters did not conform to what was expected of women according to the traditional conception but rather crossed into what was considered to be a solely masculine field: politics.

In the case of Apodaca, various ideological currents converged—anticlericalism, anarcho-syndicalism, social Catholicism, Spiritism, freethinking, Masonry, and avant-garde thought—alongside protracted struggles, such as the violent confrontations over secularization during the Mexican Revolution and the Cristiada. These dynamics also involved the liberal state's attempts to dismantle colonial-era protective legislation that applied to women and corporations, including the Catholic Church and Indigenous peoples.[2] Moreover, this coincided with a gradual increase in the indices of literacy, schooling, the expansion of practices of written culture and writing, and the editorial work of women. These changes had been taking place since the nineteenth century and continued in the one that followed.

During this turn-of-the-century period, from different tribunals and ideological positions, the social question of women was debated, as was their emancipation from the control of the Catholic Church; moreover, women were increasingly visible as social figures, targets of state social policies, and active promoters of social change. I base my interpretation on the arguments of Elizabeth Dore and Maxine Molyneux in the sense that the liberal politics of the state affected gender relations, and these, in turn, influenced its formation; that secularization had effects (both positive and negative) on the configuration of gender order; and that the activism of women did not always emancipate these effects.[3] On the contrary, it triggered more complex power relations, both vertically and horizontally.[4] The social gender constructions of the legislation of the liberal Mexican State during the nineteenth century and of the new revolutionary state represent different moments in the process of gender differentiation. In this long-term process, gendered differences increased; thus, women were excluded from their rights and obligations as citizens, specifically in agrarian and political affairs, and patriarchal power dominated, meaning women were subordinate to male authority. As sustained by Carmen Ramos Escandón in her study on the civil code of Guadalajara in the nineteenth century, "the law seems to possess different densities and dimensions for diverse social groups, but the main difference in their application and implementation comes from gender difference. Men and women are measured differently in their relationship with the law and power structures that are represented in the legislation."[5] By the twentieth century, revolutionary leaders legally recognized some cultural, social, and labor opportunities for women; however, these were accompanied by limitations and enforcement of traditional roles. Stephanie Smith discusses these social changes and reforms, focusing on those brought about by Salvador Alvarado that touched upon women. She states that Alvarado's transformations sought control over the bodies and actions of women in the areas of family and morality—specifically, in those laws referring to divorce and prostitution.[6] Different groups of women negotiated, contentiously, during the armed struggle and postrevolutionary process for the recognition of some of their rights (civil and labor), but they were recruited into the service of state structures.[7] The analysis of the educational and political career of Apodaca brings us into the possible continuities, the developments and schisms of these doctrines of thought, illustrating the convergences and divergences of these trends and of the changing balance of power in processes on a local, regional, national, and transnational scale, from a long-term perspective in two areas: that of the subject and that of society as a whole.

Shaping Civic Ideals and Progressive Movements in Revolutionary Mexico

Atala Apodaca Anaya and her sister Laura played a pivotal role in the reconfiguration of the public sphere during the revolutionary era, forging strong bonds with the new revolutionary state. They championed the ideal of the "modern woman," a concept advanced by Hermila Galindo (a stenographer and typist who was the private secretary to the Constitucionalista president

FIG. 10. Sisters Laura and Atala Apodaca, both Constitutionalist teachers, in 1915. Courtesy of Colección Independencia y Revolución en la Memoria Ciudadana, file 44 (Atala Apodaca Anaya), BCCG-CO-CIRMC.

Venustiano Carranza), whose feminist ideas were conveyed in her *Semanario ilustrado la mujer moderna*. The Constitucionalista governor Salvador Alvarado also promoted the image of a new woman and supported the two feminist congresses held in 1916 in Mérida, Yucatán, to contribute to the emancipation of women.[8] As illustrated in chapter 1, the concept of the "modern woman" was interpreted in various ways. Constitucionalista men and women with utopian visions regarding modernity and progress agreed that women ought to be secular, not Catholic: that is, emancipated from religious education and the influence of the Catholic Church. But Constitucionalista men believed that the most important task of women in society was to safeguard the home, practice morality, and procreate disciplined and patriotic citizens as part of their duty as wives.[9] Female Constitucionalistas like Apodaca developed a broader, more nuanced concept of womanhood during the armed struggle and the new revolutionary state.

Upon examining the life story and the educational and political career of Apodaca, not only are clashing Catholic and revolutionary processes intertwined, but so is the incipient growth trend in indices of female literacy, levels of education, and professionalization.[10] Very little documentation has been preserved regarding her family background and her educational, political, and social career. Despite these difficulties and "gaps," her life story and determination to work intensely for a secular vision of society in all its spheres shed light on the frictions between different gender ideologies of that time. Among the historical works that reference Apodaca are studies on Catholic social action, the memoirs of political and labor leaders from the Mexican Revolution, historical studies of education in Jalisco, and accounts of women's roles during the revolution.[11]

Apodaca was born in Tapalpa, Jalisco, on April 9, 1884.[12] Her parents were Praxedis Apodaca, a topographical engineering assistant who worked on the construction of roads statewide and who was also a painter, and Julia Anaya de Apodaca. We know nothing of the professional activity of her mother or the political beliefs of either parent.[13] Her family belonged to the rural working class. From the birthplace of the six children of this marriage, we may assume that the family lived in Ciudad Guzmán and Tapalpa, Jalisco. The Apodaca Anaya family probably changed its residence on several occasions; the father perhaps offered his services as a painter and an assistant topographical engineer in rural areas. They had six children: Laura, Atala, Jesús, Mariana (who died during childhood), Andrés, and Rafael. The professions of four of these children—Laura (teacher), Atala (teacher), Andrés (infantry captain), and Rafael (machinist of the Division of the West)—show significant social mobility from the rural working class to the urban middle class or skilled labor class, partly due to the Mexican Revolution and partly due to the opening of new spaces for women and workers in education and politics. Each of them occupied key positions in the state bureaucracy: the educational system, the army, and the national railroad system.

When she was between eleven and fourteen years of age (from 1895 to 1898), Apodaca completed her elementary school studies in Guadalajara. She later entered the Liceo de Niñas (Girls' lyceum). During her adolescence, between the ages of sixteen and nineteen, she was admitted to the Jalisco Normal School, where she studied from 1900 to 1903 with a scholarship from the Jalisco government.[14] Those years were crucial because she learned liberal values related to citizenship, rights, fraternity, liberty, and equality by studying the French Revolution and the history of Mexico and Guadalajara. Moreover, the violent military experience between liberals and conservatives during the War of Reform (1857–61) still lingered in the minds of the residents of that urban area. Throughout the nineteenth century, Catholics and liberals disputed control over the streets of Guadalajara; thus, while the former intended to preserve Catholic and religious traditions in their schools and institutions, the latter attempted to impose a new urban image by changing the nomenclature of streets to commemorate and pay tribute to all those liberals who had fought for the Independence of Mexico and for the liberal agenda.[15] Like other nineteenth-century thinkers and women who were writers, editors, and educators, such as Laureana Wright de Kleinhans (1846–96) and Laura Méndez de Cuenca (1853–1928), Apodaca considered these values to be fundamental to the creation of a new fatherland: secular and modern.

In order to understand Apodaca's process of politicization and to avoid lapsing into a view of this woman as exceptional or unique (while at the same time recognizing her as one of the few emancipated women of her time), I place her within long-term cultural, ideological, and social trends—not only on a local, regional, and national scale but transnationally as well. In the transnational debate, anticlericalism, freethinking, and Masonry confronted the powerful control wielded by the Catholic Church and its detrimental effect on the education of women. Although there are national and regional differences in these lines of thought, in Mexico anticlericalism and Masonry wielded a significant influence over national political development.[16] However, the roles played by women in these debates and their anticlerical and Masonic actions and proposals are not very well known. In-depth studies are still lacking on the practices of women in Masonry in the nineteenth and twentieth centuries in Mexico; whether female Masonry experienced a boom as it did in Argentina, Chile, and Spain;[17] how many lodges of adoption and how many coeds there were; whether these promoted secular schools and instruction for women, how Mexican Masonry conceived of the participation of women as mothers and educators; and how women received the values of fraternity, justice, and reason—all elements vital to their conscious emancipation.[18]

Laura Apodaca, in the conference she presented at the Teatro Degollado in July 1914 (following the arrival of the Constitucionalistas to Guadalajara), quoted French Republican writer Victor Hugo in her invitation to honorable citizens to work on the reconstruction of the country through the Constitucionalista project.[19] Hugo (1802–85) supported women's rights and contributed to development of the idea of a "Republican mother": a woman in the service of the republic who would save other women from a fate determined by their social status, guiding them toward civic and patriotic tasks. From the perspective of nineteenth-century French Republican men, bourgeois women were corrupted by luxury and clericalism, while working-class women lived in poverty. From the male Republican perspective, Republican mothers would train and educate orderly Republican citizens.[20]

From the Normal School to Maderismo

The passage of Apodaca through the Normal School, between the ages of twenty and twenty-nine, was crucial for her not only because she gained years of training as a schoolteacher but also because she became politicized through her affiliation with cultural associations within the context of the collapse of the Porfiriato, the ascent of Maderismo, and the emergence of the PCN. After her graduation from the Normal School on October 28, 1903,[21] Apodaca worked as an assistant teacher at the premiere school for girls in Sayula, Jalisco, from January 13, 1904, to January 12, 1905. After that, she was an assistant teacher at the school for girls in Guadalajara, from January 13, 1905, to August 28, 1913. From August 29, 1913, to July 27, 1914, she was an assistant at the Practical School Annex of the Normal School.[22] The decades of 1900 and 1910 were of incipient politicization during her teaching career in collaboration with liberal schoolteacher Aurelia Guevara (1864–1956) and other liberal teachers like Abel Ayala and Aurelio Ortega, who took charge of the transformation of Porfirian education into the school of the revolution. Apodaca also observed the conditions of poverty and exploitation that the people in the countryside and in the city endured. She also experienced the deficient working conditions of teachers, whose salaries were very low.[23]

Apodaca's liberal nineteenth-century values (citizenship, liberty, justice, and equality) would become radicalized with the antireelectionist movement, the Madero presidential campaign, the strong Catholic movement, the armed movement of the Mexican Revolution, Masonry, and the editorial, propaganda, and pedagogical creation of liberal women. According to Aldana Redón, Apodaca became a Mason, but she does not indicate when and to what lodge she was affiliated.[24] At any rate, she collaborated with many political leaders and generals who were Masons.

Apodaca actively supported the antireelectionist movement and the Madero presidential campaign. In 1909, at a political meeting in downtown

Guadalajara supporting Madero, democracy, and political change, speeches were given by Roque Estrada (attorney, journalist, and politician), students, propagandists from the Club Valentín Gómez Farías (composed of tailors, weavers, workers, and politicians with anarchist, liberal, and socialist ideals), the Club Antireelecionista, and the schoolteacher Apodaca. The Club Valentín Gómez Farías, directed by the tailor Enrique R. Calleros (1870–1950), and its clandestine organization, the Círculo Liberal Fénix (Phoenix liberal circle), promoted the Maderista movement in Jalisco from 1909 to 1911. Its members backed different uprisings in Ahualulco, Atemajac de Brizuela, La Barca, Sayula, Tapalpa, Tecolotlán, Zapotlán, and Zacoalco.[25]

During the rise of the antireelectionist movement, Apodaca was only twenty-five years old.[26] Various leaders of student, labor, and political associations formed a major hub of antireelectionism in Jalisco and organized Madero's first visit to Guadalajara. Among these were Atala Apodaca, Enrique Díaz de León, Miguel Mendoza López Schwerdefeger, Ignacio Ramos Praslow, Francisco del Toro, and the miner Julián Medina, all linked to Roque Estrada. Some were members of the Independent Party, a political organization that encouraged the candidacy of General Bernardo Reyes. All were earnest Maderistas.[27] A few were also members of the Justo Sierra group or of Aurora Social, composed of socialist writers and politicians who contributed to the Liga de las Clases Productoras (League of the working classes). According to Elisa Cárdenas, the clubs linked to Maderismo "were spaces that opened up to new political figures, either because the players responded to a corporatist logic or because they had a definition of gender, like the Maderista women of Club Sara Pérez de Madero, which did not exclude the participation of figures of this kind in other clubs of broader scope."[28]

Apodaca was not the only antireelectionist woman in Guadalajara; there were also women like María Victoria Ordorica or the members of the Club Femenil Antireeleccionista Leona Vicario (CFALV), organized by the schoolteacher Florita Vargas Trejo. This organization contributed money, collaborated with people in favor of political change, and made collections of pecuniary donations for the Maderista uprising in Jalisco, coordinated by the Club Valentín Gómez Farías and the Círculo Liberal Fénix. The CFALV sought "to uplift [the Maderista cause] and therefore, the Mexican woman, a beautiful example to the indifferent who deserve only to remain under the yoke they bear so patiently."[29] The CFALV formed a retinue to welcome Sara

Pérez, Madero's wife, on her visit to Guadalajara in May 1910.[30] They also asked the Club Valentín Gómez Farías for financial support "to make a banner and send it to Mexico on the 29th [of May 1910] to the protest march to be carried out by the independent press" in favor of Maderista candidates.[31] No information is available that allows us to determine whether Apodaca formed part of the CFALV. The teacher Vargas Trejo was a governess to the children of the Collignon family. Likely, the careers of Vargas Trejo (in the home of that family) and of Apodaca (the Escuela de Niñas [Girls' school]) did not lead to their meeting, but if they had it might have been in the sessions held at the Club Valentín Gómez Farías. In addition to the political involvement of Apodaca and Vargas Trejo, the women of the CFALV often enlisted the support of both single and married women to further the antireelectionist cause.[32] Apodaca was in favor of Madero's political ideals, including his anticlericalism and Spiritist practices. Madero favored a greater presence of women in the public sphere, as illustrated by the active and visible participation of Sara Pérez, Madero's wife, who accompanied him on his political marches and during his electoral campaign.[33] Madero accepted the presence of women in the public sphere, albeit from a maternalistic perspective. He sustained that "although women are not conceded the right to meddle in political affairs, they are always ready to instill love for the fatherland and liberty in the hearts of children, who will be the heart of tomorrow."[34] Despite this traditional gender stance, Spiritist, liberal, and radical women like Apodaca joined the revolutionary struggle. Their participation questioned traditional, restricted notions of gender roles.

From 1912 to 1913, Apodaca formed part of the liberal group of intellectuals called the Liga de Amigos del Pueblo (LAP), led by politician Luis Alatorre, who had run for governor in October 1912. Alatorre represented the Great Liberal Convention, which united some of the radical liberals of Jalisco.[35] The LAP gave weekly conferences on agrarian, freethinking, and labor-related themes in neighborhoods and theaters, using plays, oratory, and poetry to combat fanaticism.[36] The LAP sought "to instruct workers and employees in various branches of knowledge and [sustained] various schools in which elementary instruction, commercial coursework and various arts are taught, as are the obligatory classes for all students such as ethics, civics, and hygiene."[37] The freethinking labor ideas of the LAP transcended the local arena, given that they coincided with the transnational campaign of Belén de Sárraga and her visit to Guadalajara in October 1912.

Alatorre introduced Apodaca to José Guadalupe Zuno Hernández and the young progressives of the Centro Bohemio (Bohemian Center), which he led.[38] The Centro Bohemio was part of the avant-garde and sought cultural innovation in order to replace "tradition with new forms of language capable of expressing the world as well as the infinite scope of art."[39] According to Arturo Camacho, the Bohemios possessed an audacious creativity: "Their works compile the gestures of experimentation with visual materials, a definitive break from academicism and a strong social content, sheathed in the sarcasm of the caricatures practiced by some of its members."[40] According to David Alfaro Siqueiros, at meetings of the Centro Bohemio, "soldier artists" developed ideas for murals and visual art in general.[41] Men and women of the Centro Bohemio and the LAP overlapped in their search for social and cultural renewal, which implied transforming the status quo of gender and politics. Moreover, some of the members of both associations would eventually collaborate in conferences.[42] Members of the LAP Florencio Luna and J. Concepción Cortés introduced Apodaca to Manuel M. Diéguez, who was left captivated by her intelligence, conviction, and vitality.[43]

From Antihuertista Resistance to Constitucionalismo

From 1912 to 1914, Catholics controlled the legislature, and organizations of Catholic social action increased. Due to this significant growth, liberal groups condemned Catholic expansion and the regime of General Victoriano Huerta (1913–14), which was responsible for the assassinations of Madero and Pino Suárez on February 22, 1913. That year, different political forces initiated a movement of resistance against the usurper Huerta. In Jalisco, the armed uprisings against the general multiplied.[44]

Like Constitucionalista, Villista, and Zapatista men and women, Apodaca, at the age of twenty-nine, launched an intense campaign against General Huerta and the Catholic Church from August 1913 to June 1914, before the Constitucionalistas took Guadalajara on July 8, 1914.[45] Apodaca's action provoked feelings of scandal, fear, and rejection among some members of the Jalisco rural Catholic Church. On October 13, 1913, three priests of Mascota informed the archbishop of Guadalajara, Francisco Orozco y Jiménez,

FIG. 11. Atala Apodaca Anaya, ca. 1914. Courtesy of Colección Independencia y Revolución en la Memoria Ciudadana, file 49 (Atala Apodaca Anaya), BCCG-CO-CIRMC.

FIG. 12. Andrés and Atala Apodaca Anaya, ca. 1914. Courtesy of Colección Independencia y Revolución en la Memoria Ciudadana, file 49 (Atala Apodaca Anaya), BCCG-CO-CIRMC.

"that Saint Atala Apodaca is undermining the social edifice of Catholicism, unabashedly denigrating the teachings of Christ, son of God; therefore, it is necessary that Your Excellence draw the line for this woman, corrupted in soul, and perhaps in body—whose corruption is always lesser."[46] The priests requested that the archbishop of Guadalajara dictate a pastoral to indicate that "they do wrong in going to listen to anti-Catholic conferences . . . and that they incur in heresies condemned a thousand times over by the Sovereign Pontiffs."[47] Said pastoral should also combat pornographic establishments and the impious press. They considered this an opportune time to defend the rights of the Catholic Church and rescue those who were on the verge of falling into the "eternal abyss."[48] Furthermore, various Catholic schoolteachers subjected her to constant hostility and humiliation. Catholic imagery embarked on a social construction with regard to Apodaca that sought to cultivate "a mortal hatred for her among the girls." According to the *Boletín militar*, "She was called offensive epithets, slandered, and in the final days of the Mier administration, she found herself entangled in the gossip of a fanatical teacher who, motivated by some patriotic verses recited by a boy, accused her of impiety and of countermanding the provisions of the C.N."[49]

In contrast with the Catholic perspective that reproved the actions of Apodaca, General Agustín Olachea of the Fifteenth Battalion of Sonora ensured that daily newspapers of Guadalajara such as *La gaceta*, *El gato*, and *El demócrata* among others publish the activities of Apodaca.[50] According to Olachea, she "distributed and posted in public places copies delivered to her by the Junta Revolucionaria Constitucionalista of a proclamation of the Army, the speech of [senator] Belisario Domínguez [against the abuses of the Huerta regime that he gave in the Senate on September 17, 1913] and a memorandum of the Junta itself, dated December 12, 1913, declaring illegal and fraudulent the sale of goods of the Nation approved by the so-called Huertista chamber; all this, while outwitting Huertista espionage and persecution."[51]

Apodaca's anticlerical and Antihuertista efforts bore fruit in early 1914. Anticlericals, liberals, Constitucionalista military officers, and Masons considered her an extraordinary and influential woman capable of achieving social change by modernizing and secularizing Mexican society. Anticlericals and Constitucionalistas applauded her leadership, while the Catholic Church lashed out at her work.[52] On January 18, 1914, the magazine *Alianza* reviewed the recognition in honor of Atala Apodaca held at the Teatro Degollado. In attendance at the artistic matinée were around three thousand people.[53] At this ceremony the LAP renewed its board of directors, reporting its achievements over the course of the year 1913. The schoolteacher Blanca de Baducci sang Giuseppe Verdi's romance *Un Ballo in Maschera*. Apodaca gave a speech on virtue. Railroad machinist Francisco García Sánchez gave an address, and the railroad guild bestowed him with a gold medal as a show of admiration and gratitude for his meritorious labor and talent. The event ended with the singing of an aria, popular poet Enrique C. Villaseñor recited a composition dedicated to Apodaca, and the Gendarmerie Band played the "Hymn to Juárez."[54] The correspondent of the *Alianza* article stated that Apodaca was no common woman because she had caused both amazement and enjoyment. He wrote that "her presence indicates a new stage of activity and struggle, ideals and efforts, aspirations and hopes; because she is a star of the greatest magnitude."[55] He described her with shades of a revolutionary nationalism as follows: "Extremely modest and humble; in her Indian countenance sparkle a pair of pure Mexican eyes, revealing all the grandeur of her soul and the kindness and stoic nature of her heart. Her speech is simple, smart, eloquent, and convincing. Her voice is of powerful timber, her gestures possess the authority, nerve, and grace of the Aztec blood, and her ideal, her ambition, her supreme aspiration, her golden dream are THE REDEMPTION OF HER PEOPLE."[56]

From the perspective of liberal male citizenship, Apodaca Anaya evinced individual, domestic, and social virtues while showing wisdom, temperance, valor, and industriousness. According to her, these were elements fundamental to any liberal, free, and responsible citizen. The correspondent of *Alianza* was unable to transcribe her speech of over one hour, but he was able to capture some of her thoughts, such as the following: "WISDOM: 'Only he who is wise can be good, only he who is good can be wise'; TEMPERANCE: 'Only the man who dominates his passions is free'; VALOR: 'The valiant man forges his future as running water carves out its channel'; INDUSTRIOUSNESS: 'There is no man more miserable than he who has no need for fatigue.'"[57] Like Sárraga Hernández and other anticlerical revolutionary leaders, Apodaca Anaya argued that theological virtues were only "used to fanaticize and cover up their evils and immoralities."[58] The publication *Alianza* did not highlight that during this ceremony, Apodaca had "the temerity to rebuke the usurper and assassin Victoriano Huerta," perhaps due to the harsh repression that said administration had wielded.[59] According to Irene Robledo (1890–1988), while those in attendance did listen to Apodaca's points of view, they did not debate with her because they were afraid due to the tense political situation Guadalajara was experiencing. Robledo mentioned that it was surprising that the Catholic government did not repress her political activities, although it clearly did not approve of her ideas.

Apodaca's Carrancista Role

After the arrival of the Constitucionalistas in Guadalajara on July 8, 1914, the activism and visibility of Apodaca, Centro Bohemio, and the LAP increased. On July 18, Apodaca organized an anniversary celebration to commemorate the death of Benito Juárez and gave a speech at the Teatro Degollado.[60] The event was followed by a military parade from the Palacio de Gobierno to the Jardín de Escobedo, led by generals Manuel M. Diéguez, Lucio Blanco, and Benjamín Hill with troops from Sonora. In this civic act, Miguel Medina Hermosilla and Apodaca gave speeches. Apodaca was baptized the "Zárraga of Jalisco."[61] As with the funerals of French politicians in the nineteenth century studied by Ben-Amos Avner,[62] the distribution of hierarchies of power became evident during the ceremony at the Teatro Degollado: the governor and General Diéguez entered at the same time; the secretary general of government, Aguirre Berlanga; the private secretary Lieutenant Colonel Fernando Valenzuela; the assistant chief of staff Fausto Topete; General Brigadier Benjamín Hill, and Miss Apodaca, "who was given the place of honor and received thunderous applause from the select yet sizable audience that filled the seats."[63] Despite being a woman and despite her work against the Catholic Church and the Huerta regime, her dynamism, intelligence, and brilliant oratory placed her on equal footing with the Constitucionalista military officers. Moreover, Diéguez had employed Apodaca as a cultural lieutenant of Carrancismo.

As an ardent Maderista, Apodaca began her speech with addresses that praised the virtues "of the great democrat and liberator" Madero. She compared him to Hidalgo and Juárez. Apodaca referred to the Tragic Ten Days, to clericalism, and to the Constitucionalista movement and its generals.[64] From a perspective imbued with the strong liberal heritage of the nineteenth century, she stated that future generations "would see in Hidalgo the liberator, in Juárez the reformer, and in Madero the democrat and martyr."[65] She recognized the struggle of liberal men against the clergy in the nineteenth century and that the libertarian cry lived on in men who followed in the footsteps of the defense of the constitution and the rule of law. She exalted the masculinity of various men who, despite their differences in ethnicity, social class, and generation, were joined by their contributions to the emancipation of Mexico. She asked "that no one rest until all that which is contrary to the good functioning and order of our republic has been slain."[66] She ended by reading a poem that she wrote for Madero before he became president of the republic: "There was a priest; he rose up in arms / and liberated us from Spain, / and there was an Indian whose feat / freed us from Rome. / And tomorrow, be not amazed / upon taking Chapultepec, / when History says: A man / freed us from Tuxtepec." At that moment, the liberal vision of Apodaca made no reference to the sexual difference between men and women; she merely attributed the leadership of these changes to men. The audience gave her a heartfelt round of applause. The event ended with the "Hymn to Juárez."

In July 1914, General Diéguez named Apodaca school inspector, referring to her as a "distinguished teacher and orator."[67] On August 2, Apodaca gave another speech in honor of General Diéguez at the Teatro Degollado in which the same protocol was followed as before, with Diéguez and other generals entering the hall together with Apodaca.[68] Her speech addressed clericalism and revolution, the moralization of the people, and virtue and labor. The *Boletín militar* indicated that numerous ladies attended this event and that the LAP would renew its activities. And so it did—starting on August 8, every Sunday, the organization offered conferences at the Teatro Degollado.[69]

In addition to the ongoing military campaign of the Constitucionalistas in western Mexico under the command of General Diéguez, an intense civic and propaganda campaign was also launched in favor of their cause and against clericalism in Guadalajara. The LAP, the Centro Bohemio, anticlerical teachers like the Apodaca sisters, and fledgling labor organizations attempted to transform the consciences of citizens through different civic ceremonies and conferences. Not unlike the talks given by the LAP and Apodaca, the Centro Bohemio publicized its conferences. Members of the Centro Bohemio collaborated on artistic tasks with teachers Atala and Laura Apodaca and

Dolores Nieves Viuda de Lavat in civic, educational, and sports events at the Normal School, the Teatro Degollado, and the Hospicio.[70]

Despite crop shortages and outbreaks of epidemics, the political participation of peasant men and women, educators, and the incipient organized labor movement was increasingly visible. These social groups would become key political forces in the day-to-day formation of the new revolutionary state and social figures who sought to implement social policies. The case of Apodaca is an excellent example of how women joined the Constitucionalista cause and struggled for the transformation of gender relations by means of female autonomy.

Like Belén de Sárraga Hernández, Apodaca Anaya stood out for being an anticlerical woman with Jacobin tendencies and as an intelligent and superb orator who captivated her audience. As early as October 1913, Catholic priests had identified her as dangerous. As for the anticlericals and Constitucionalistas, Apodaca suited them perfectly by attacking their main enemy, the Catholic Church, and removing its most faithful allies: women.

In August 1914, Apodaca Anaya founded and presided over the Círculo Liberal Josefa Ortiz de Domínguez (CLJOD), which had strong ties to the Constitucionalista government.[71] Meetings were held at the Jalisco Normal School for women. The first meeting was presided over by the director of public instruction, Doctor Felipe Valencia, and the founding president of the LAP, and nearly five hundred people were in attendance.[72] Apodaca and the liberal women won a cultural and political space with the establishment of the CLJOD, but they maintained the vertical structure of male patriarchal power in their inaugural ceremony. Male presence not only gave legitimacy to their organization, but it also demonstrated their strong ties to Constitutionalism. During this solemn session, new members were registered, and a board of directors was named: Atala Apodaca as president and Miss Valencia, sister of the doctor of the same last name, as vice president. Doctor Valencia announced that the Teatro Principal would be available for future conferences of the CLJOD. The first proposal in this session was Apodaca's, in which she suggested that the CLJOD recognize the valor and selflessness of the Fifth and Fourteenth Battalions of Sonora, currently in Manzanillo, with banners embroidered by the members of the CLJOD. Apodaca stated that the banners would be delivered during the patriotic festivities on September 16.[73]

In an open letter to Atala Apodaca published in the *Boletín militar* on August 15, 1914,[74] Nicolás Sivón congratulated Apodaca for her labor as an inspector of public instruction, for her speeches, and "for her meritorious labor in favor of the emancipation of the woman already initiated in the female Círculo Liberal Josefa Ortiz de Domínguez, of which you are the worthy founder."[75] Like Sárraga, Sivón, and other anticlericals, Apodaca sought to liberate women from religious fanaticism by means of a civic education. They believed that this way, they would build a "fatherland, great and happy." Sivón believed that the Constitucionalista government (young, energetic, and progressive) and Apodaca would give "the *coup de grâce* to all the abuse, deceit, and crimes of those people who only aspire to live at the expense of the ignorant and the fanatical."[76]

After this session of the CLJOD and editorials and texts in favor of the Diéguez administration and his anticlerical policies, there was a strong response from the Catholic hierarchy and from Catholic men and women of various social classes and organizations. As a Constitucionalista governor, Diéguez confiscated church property, closed churches and parishes, expelled clergy, forced Archbishop Orozco y Jiménez into exile, and later had him arrested.[77]

The Diéguez administration was painted as "an enemy of the faith and of beliefs as cruel and barbarous, rousing the spirits of the credulous and foolish, against the Revolution."[78] With regard to Apodaca, according to the *Boletín militar*, "the holier-than-thous who will not rest today spread the rumor that the teacher . . . has been commissioned to break into homes—like the agents of Father Correa—to become informed of the religious education of children. That the government pays spies to learn whether religion is being taught in private schools and to prohibit worship, and other such foolishness."[79] Another action of the Catholic resistance against Apodaca was the posting of leaflets, anonymous and typewritten. Through these, the ladies of Jalisco asked Governor Diéguez to prohibit Apodaca's speeches. According to the *Boletín militar*, her conferences were "drawing many former believers away from the Church and as a consequence, Sunday alms have declined."[80]

Apodaca responded that this propaganda "affects them in no way and on the contrary, their labor from now on will be more active, to drench the people in knowledge making known the truth come what may, in favor of liberal institutions."[81] This strong, tenacious Catholic resistance caused the anticlerical momentum of the recently created CLJOD and of Apodaca to veer toward a Jacobin anticlericalism. The CLJOD met regularly. The Diéguez administration requested that they embroider six more flags to be distributed among the ranks of the Constitucionalista army.[82] In counterbalance to the campaign against Apodaca, liberal employees of commerce presented her with a gold medal on October 18 in recognition of her propaganda efforts.[83] In the midst of all this, Atala Apodaca taught a class in logic, psychology, and morality at the Normal School starting in September 1914.[84]

Like the LAP and the Centro Bohemio, the CLJOD held conferences at the Teatro Principal.[85] Atala's sister Laura Apodaca, also a teacher, also collaborated with these organizations, discussing the role of education in the transformation of the country and the "labor of the authorities to ennoble Mexican women."[86] By means of her participation in these organizations, Atala Apodaca promoted the organization of workers and the dissemination of revolutionary ideas. To achieve the politicization of the masses, every Sunday starting on September 13, 1914, she offered "revolutionary" chats at the Teatro Principal that were attended by male and female teachers, students from the Normal School, working-class men and women, and Apodaca's acquaintances.

In October 1914, Apodaca requested a leave of absence from her teaching position to travel to Mexico City and, from there, to the Aguascalientes Convention.[87] However, the files and letters she sent to the Ministry of National Defense fail to confirm her attendance. That month, she supported the electrical workers' strike and organized parties to raise funds for them.[88] On October 30, 1914, Apodaca, as an inspector of public schools, informed the municipal president of Guadalajara, Luis Castellanos Tapia, that the greater part of the children who attended public schools were extremely poor. This condition deprived them of the joys that children were entitled to. She requested one hundred pesos to buy toys and sweets for underprivileged children to be delivered on December 25. Her petition was approved. In November, Apodaca gave another speech in collaboration with the LAP in the township of San Agustín, in the Guadalajara municipal area. In San Agustín, Laura and Atala Apodaca established the Club Liberal Benito Juárez, composed mainly of men and of a few women.[89] For the Catholics, her appointment symbolized the disintegration of the education system.[90] Starting in December, she carried out an intense campaign in rural and urban areas in favor of the revolutionary cause, in order to "preach the true gospel of constitutionalism [to] open the eyes of so many ignorant and fanatical people under the influence of the clergy, the direct cause of the disgraces of our hapless country."[91]

Following the fierce attack by Julián Medina and the Villistas on Guadalajara, on December 11, 1914, the Diéguez administration relocated to Ciudad Guzmán (December 12, 1914). Apodaca accompanied Diéguez and his army. On February 18, 1915, the Apodaca sisters collaborated in the battle of Sayula Hill between Constitucionalistas and Villistas. Atala carried out tasks of propaganda and persuasion; Laura and the students from the Normal School tended to the wounded.[92] Following this military campaign, Diéguez retreated to Colima. There, Apodaca, her group, Samuel Ruiz Cabañas, and Zuno expanded their propaganda efforts.[93] The Constitucionalista administration of Colima awarded a gold medal to Atala.[94] Her speeches from this period feature the phrase "We must annihilate Villa," which caused the Villista governor Julián Medina to strip her of her appointments as inspector and teacher.[95]

After the defeat of the Villistas at Las Juntas, Toluquilla and El Castillo, south of Guadalajara, on April 16, 1915, Apodaca renewed CLJOD gatherings, congratulated the *Boletín militar* on its anniversary for its editorial work in defense of liberty and justice, and organized a grand festival on the forty-second anniversary of the death of Juárez.[96] The press reported, "There can be no doubt. There is talent there, there is energy, there is a revolutionary woman."[97] Despite the fact that the Constitucionalista administration of Jalisco restored her appointments as a school inspector and professor of physics and chemistry at the Normal School, she participated in the Division of the West in the battles of Trinidad, Guanajuato, in April 1915.[98] There, General Diéguez dedicated a photograph to her that reads, "To the eminent liberal lady Atala Apodaca as a souvenir of her stay at Camp Trinidad during the battle."[99]

Likewise, Apodaca and the CLJOD collaborated in other civic acts to honor Diéguez and Álvaro Obregón during their visit to Guadalajara and during the September 15 festivities dedicated to Hidalgo.[100] In August, Apodaca and the CLJOD called on the general citizenry to join and donate funds to finance the production of two gold medals to honor the "hapless widows" of Madero and Pino Suárez during the celebrations of the anniversary of the revolution on November 20. Apodaca and the CLJOD invoked the most noble feminine sentiments to award two gold medals, recruiting "patriotic women to this task that is an act of justice that honors us, and that the jackal named Victoriano Huerta may tremble upon finding himself singled out by the indignation of Mexican women."[101] Another act of recognition of the CLJOD was the gift of a pencil portrait of General Diéguez to his mother, composed by the Centro Bohemio artist Amado de la Cueva.[102]

In November 1915, Apodaca clarified that several people proposed the project to form societies for the protection of underprivileged children and had provided snacks, toys, clothing, and school supplies at public schools and sought to build a workshop-school for children between the ages of ten and fourteen.[103]

By March 1916, destitution, typhus, and smallpox in Guadalajara and statewide had expanded in alarming numbers.[104] The groups of female beggars asking for alms in the commercial houses in downtown Guadalajara drew attention; there was a shortage of basic items, and hunger became evident among the people.[105] Moreover, from 1910 to 1917, several women from different social classes participated in and became more visible in the military confrontations as colonels, propaganda officers, and female soldiers, or *soldaderas*.[106] By March 19, 1916, the military command of Guadalajara announced an agreement with the federal government to form "a general status report of widows, orphans, and parents who have lost their husbands, fathers, and sons serving in the army. Similarly, those same members of the army who during a campaign, were rendered unfit for service."[107] Apodaca believed that to ensure triumph over the Villistas, her presence was required in Mazatlán, Guaymas, and Hermosillo. The local press in these cities and in Guadalajara reviewed the resounding success of her conferences and her excellent speaking skills.[108] Upon her return to Guadalajara, a private party was organized to honor her and General Ramón F. Iturbe.[109] In May 1916, the campaign of the Catholic Church against Apodaca had surpassed the borders of Guadalajara and Jalisco.[110]

In June 1916, Apodaca Anaya was interviewed together with Carranza in the port of Veracruz as a "commissioner of the government of Jalisco to manage the shipment of war materiel destined for the so-called Division of the West."[111] According to Apodaca, upon her return she "renewed labors with greater enthusiasm, because the words of [Carranza] were a powerful stimulus, fortifying her faith and instilling new energies. I distributed at the camp 500 buttons with photograph and with warm words, I urged the soldiers to triumph alongside the predestined redeemer of the Mexican people: Venustiano Carranza."[112] In July 1916 Carranza, as the head of the Constitucionalista Army, named her president of the Comisión Nacional de Estudios y Propaganda Nacionalista, a position she held from 1916–17.[113] Carranza commissioned her to organize a tour across the republic together with eight artists, writers, teachers, painters, and poets in order to "spread cultural and patriotic propaganda throughout the republic, giving conferences and publishing an illustrated newspaper [*Argos*] in order to carry into practice all of the ideals that the Revolution."[114] The tour lasted eleven months, during which different states and cities were visited (from Ciudad Guzmán, Colima, Culiacán, and Hermosillo to Los Angeles, California, in the United States).[115] This group was formed by the editor of *Argos* magazine, Samuel Ruiz Cabañas, who would become Apodaca's husband in November 1917.[116] Apodaca constituted the Comisión with gender equity, ensuring that it included an equal number of four men and four women. The women were schoolteachers; the men were illustrators, cartoonists, printers, musicians, authors, and journalists. Their working agenda was to hold conferences to unify the revolutionary creed; to offer patriotic, socioliterary, pedagogical conferences; and to support public education and lift morale.[117]

After several years of holding conferences, participating in military battles, and responding to the attacks of the Catholic Church, on August 13, 1916, Apodaca Anaya assessed the revolution and the scenario the war had left behind. From a freethinking perspective, she analyzed gender relations, practices, and representations of female and male. She honed her ideas on the social role of women and men and meditated on the future role of educated, emancipated women.[118] On August 13, 1916, in the first issue of *Argos*, Apodaca published an article entitled "El papel social de la mujer mexicana." She argued, in this magazine, that women had a special place. She claimed that the revolution would empower women and enhance their important role in educating children. Even though the matter of war was almost resolved, there remained social issues that could not always be addressed with gunfire. For Apodaca, "man has spoken of his rights; woman has spoken only of her duty. Woman fights with more faith than man because she always contemplates sacrifice. . . . Someday, woman will be appropriately educated in liberty; in female gardens will be cultivated that rare flower, willpower; women will possess individual worth and initiative; and man will be compelled to always be respectful to beings who are his equal, who can compete with him."[119]

Apodaca Anaya shows here her political transformation from a "neutral" liberal stance (between the ascent of Maderismo, the struggle against Huerta, and the arrival of the Constitucionalistas to Guadalajara) to a position critical of the actions of men and women during the armed struggle, especially during the U.S. invasion of April 1914 and the fight against clericalism. She distinguishes between the rights assigned to men and the duties ascribed to women. With a utopian vision, Apodaca sustains that the most significant transformations will take place in the role of women, thus leading to their liberation.

Urban Spaces Disputed by "Red" and "White," 1917–19

After the passage of the Constitution of 1917, with radical proposals in some of its articles—especially the 3rd, 5th, 13th, 27th and 130th—the participation of Catholic men and women and those who favored the revolutionary cause intensified.[120] Their politicization and radicalization triggered transgressions in the social order and changes in the culture of gender and politics. Some Catholic and liberal women who were already politicized became organized, mobilizing to defend and preserve their respective identities, practices, and representations. However, their actions, discourses, and representations did not align with the constructions of culture and gender that were held by revolutionary leaders and different members of the Catholic Church with regard to women. The revolutionary leaders were disquieted by the fact that women were so conservative and controlled by the Catholic Church. They perceived them as a social force that complicated the processes of modernizing and secularizing society. On the other hand, the Catholic Church was scandalized by the anticlerical speeches of liberal women, given that they symbolized the diabolical influences (of Masonry and socialists) that caused chaos in the family and society. Both revolutionary leaders and the Catholic Church summoned men and women to defend their ideals and programs. Revolutionary leaders and the Catholic Church required the active participation of men and women; therefore, both saw themselves forced to change their notions of how they imagined men and women: the former, exclusively in the public sphere, and the latter, mainly in the domestic sphere, in "their role as discreet, kindly and Christian women."[121] When the new revolutionary state tried to control education, religious practices, and public life, the Catholic Church turned to the support and mobilization of its own organizations of young people, women, and workers.

Catholic organizations had constructed a sense of solidarity and a strong Catholic identity between men and women that helped them challenge the power and legitimacy of the revolutionary government. The successful mobilization of Catholics (of different social classes, generations, regions, and genders) between 1918 and 1919 became an example of what they could achieve in other parts of Mexico. Catholic men and women, whether or not they were members of an organization, played an important role in the resistance to anticlerical laws. According to Robert Curley, in Guadalajara, nine thousand women endorsed different protests, while nineteen thousand men signed petitions.[122] Men and women found themselves compelled to defend their Catholic identity; upon doing so, they became political figures, reacting against the attacks on the Catholic Church.

Even though the Catholic discourse indicated that women were "the angel of the home," they left that house to defend their Catholic identity. During this process, Catholics were empowered and became political figures and public mothers. This is illustrated by the following case in point: after the Constitucionalistas converted the Cathedral of Guadalajara and some churches into military headquarters, the ADCG protested at the Government Palace in order to demonstrate to Governor Manuel Aguirre Berlanga that they did not approve of "the blasphemies published and approved by the government, that profaned churches, persecuted and executed priests, and prohibited Catholic schools."[123] In 1916, Catholic women continued to protest and broke the seals on the doors of churches that had been closed by the government. They were threatened by the municipal president of Guadalajara, who communicated to them that if they continued with such actions, they would be arrested. Yet they continued to protest and lobby to change Diéguez's anticlerical policies.[124]

By May 1918, Governor Manuel Bouquet's anticlerical policies, the arrest of Archbishop Orozco y Jiménez, and the restrictions on the number of priests and churches generated more tensions among the Constitucionalistas and the Catholic hierarchy, triggered more Catholic protests, and the organization of a massive resistance movement. On July 6, 1918, the ADCG, the recently founded Asociación Católica de la Juventud Mexicana (ACJM), the Academia Miguel Cervantes, and other Catholic organizations planned and led a campaign to defend Archbishop Orozco y Jiménez.[125] On July 8, 1917, all these organizations distributed fliers in every home of Guadalajara to protest the arrest and the regulations of Decree 1913. Between July and August, the distribution of flyers and the call to post them in the windows of each home continued.[126] Men, women, children within Catholic organizations participated in this mass mobilization.[127] All of them demanded that the governor and the state Congress revoke the decree. Catholic women participated in the protests: the Catholic ladies of cities and towns, schoolteachers, workers, servants, and employees. More than two hundred women from the ADCG sent letters protesting these unjust policies.

According to Ignacio Dávila Garibi and Salvador Chávez Hayhoe, young men were energetically opposed, in a virile fashion, while Catholic ladies manifested their suffering and disinterest in the following terms: "There are moments when womankind, in her resignation and suffering, cannot help but make herself heard when she is wounded in that which she loves most and is most worthy of love. She may fall silent before any offense against her; but before the outrage of her Faith, which is the strength and vigor of her life, womankind will always raise a sublime cry of protest."[128]

Not all Catholic women manifested their frustration in terms of feminine suffering or disinterest. Eighty-five Catholic schoolteachers demanded the repeal of the decree based on their individual rights as granted by the Constitution of 1917. These teachers couched their petition in the following terms: "Among us, as all Catholics, there is a sentiment of respect for the established authority, that is deeply rooted and forms part of our being as an exclusively Catholic teaching; and therefore, we condemn the Revolution for having risen up in arms, but we also condemn, with the same energy and conviction, arbitrariness, and the abuse of authority."[129]

The schoolteachers built their civic citizenship based on individual rights that allowed them to consider themselves Mexican social subjects. As citizens, the Catholic teachers manifested their right to protest and demanded that the state change its anticlerical policies on the grounds that they were being deprived of their liberty.

Female employees and workers were also in disagreement. The Unión Profesional de Empleadas de Comercio (Professional union of Catholic female employees) adhered to this public complaint over unjust legislation.

Simultaneously, 120 female catechists, servants, and workers of the Santa Zita Conference built their protest around their duty "not only to love, venerate and respect our sacrosanct Catholic Church, and express reverential gratitude towards our most Illustrious Prelate, but also as a matter of conscience."[130] Some Catholic working women perceived their role in society to be one of respect and obedience to their superiors. Like the Catholic schoolteachers, ninety-four female catechists, domestic workers, servants, and workers at the centers of the Sacred Heart of Jesus and Our Lady of Guadalupe argued that Decree 1913 had turned them into slaves of despotism. These women sustained that "in the Republic, all are born free, not as slaves"; therefore, their right to practice their religion ought to be protected, not attacked.[131]

On July 7, 1917, over one hundred women from the ADCG interviewed the interim government, Manuel Bouquet, and asked him to rescind the decree. The governor declared that this demand ought to be posed to General Diéguez. After this meeting, 150 people, mostly married women, walked from the Government Palace to the train station and proposed to Diéguez that he reconsider the case of Archbishop Orozco y Jiménez.[132] Despite this protest, Diéguez could not believe that most Catholics in the state of Jalisco would reject Decree 1913. To convince Diéguez of the magnitude of their discontent, the Catholics protested before the train station on July 22, 1918. The reported figures of how many people attended the gathering vary from ten thousand to sixty thousand.[133] Diéguez refused to receive the Catholic commission and preferred to give a speech to the Catholics from the balcony. At the end, Diéguez and the Catholics could not negotiate to reach an agreement. Catholics from different social classes showed their strong solidarity. The police dissolved the protest, jailing several, and one woman was killed.[134] After this mass mobilization, the state Congress restricted even more the number of priests in the state. On July 25, 1918, the legislature published Decree 1927, allowing only 243 priests; there were around one thousand.[135]

Catholics continued to struggle by means of an extensive program of lobbying and several tactics of resistance. In early August 1918, Guadalajara awoke as a city in mourning. Every home had a black ribbon tied in a bow outside; the Catholic women chose to dress in black as a symbol of resistance and participated in marches. Their bodies became powerful symbols of active resistance and protest. The Catholics called for a boycott of all unnecessary activities or entertainment: no parties, no music or carriages or streetcars, and purchases were reduced to a minimum.[136]

Catholics abstained from attending churches designated by the government for the celebration of Mass as a form of protest against this policy. They attended mass at the churches of Zapopan and San Pedro Tlaquepaque. Thus, they showed that they would decide which congregations to attend and that they would not tolerate state intervention in the regulation of religious practice. This was their way of demonstrating that they did not recognize Decrees 1913 and 1927. Moreover, Catholics carried out campaigns against government newspapers such as *El occidental* and *Diario de Jalisco*.[137] In Catholic newspapers such as *La palabra* and *La lucha*, Catholics published a list of the members of the Masonic lodges in Guadalajara and asked the Catholic community to make their purchases only in those shops and read only those newspapers that did not belong to Masons. This general boycott against the Constitucionalista government and its followers spread from Guadalajara to the entire state.

A delegation of women from the ADCG lobbied President Carranza regarding the religious question in Jalisco. In Mexico City, the ladies obtained the support of other Catholic organizations. The Catholics of Guadalajara received notes and letters of support and solidarity from Catholics in Aguascalientes and Toluca and Mexicans who lived in Chicago.[138] The Catholics continued lobbying for reform of Decree 1913. President Carranza offered to intervene in this conflict and discuss it with Diéguez.[139] Finally, on February 4, 1919, Diéguez repealed Decrees 1913 and 1927.

Catholics were successful in their challenge to the power and legitimacy of the state Congress and the Constitucionalista government. Their mobilization strengthened the Catholic identity of their organizations. New Catholic newspapers, like *El obrero* and *La época*, appeared to orient and evangelize the working class. In April 1919, the first Catholic Workers' Congress was held in Guadalajara; this event provided impetus for the growing Catholic organizations. Also, as part of these protests, Catholic women gained awareness of their role in safeguarding and regenerating society.[140] Catholics believed that they had reconquered their political and social arenas. Those Catholics who were former members of the PCN organized the Partido Democrático (Democratic party) in the state of Jalisco and, federally, the Partido Nacional Revolucionario (National revolutionary party). These parties included moderate Maderistas who opposed the candidacy of General Álvaro Obregón.[141]

The Centro Radical Femenino (Women's Radical Center)

When Catholic mobilization reached its peak on July 18, 1918, radicalized women from the COM reacted by organizing themselves as the Centro Radical Femenino (CRF) and gave their "sympathy vote to the authorities for their conduct against the clerical masses; for Decree 1913 and its regulation, for the expulsion of Archbishop Orozco y Jiménez."[142] On August 16, 1918, after several meetings, 140 women founded the CRF in order to work toward the de-fanaticizing of women, under the slogan "labor and emancipation."[143] The executive committee of the CRF was composed of María Trinidad Hernández Cambre, as general secretary; María Guadalupe Padilla, as secretary; Rosalina Gutiérrez, as secretary of the exterior; María Panduro, as secretary of the interior; and Carmen Hernández Cambre, as treasurer.[144] These schoolteachers and workers of the CRF promoted their Jacobian anticlericalism and helped the government follow through on the tenets of the Constitution of 1917. The CRF created its own newspaper with sections dedicated to education, finance, and social issues. It also announced that various local and national organizations would be established. In September 1918, the CRF published its first issue of the newspaper *Iconoclasta*.[145] Of the CRF schoolteachers, ten had studied at the Normal School of Jalisco, but there are no clear indications of the others' occupations or marital status. The CRF called on nonorganized women to join their struggle and form an alliance with the CLJOD, led by Atala Apodaca. The women of the CRF and the CLJOD made efforts to counteract the Catholic mobilization. By mid-1918, the anticlericalism of Apodaca took on radical hues, with antireligious tendencies.

These women drew on the anarcho-syndicalist ideas of the COM and their close relationship with the socialist feminist Evelyn Roy—wife of Manabendra Nath Roy—who linked them and Apodaca to other Mexican feminists and anticlericalists of the Consejo Feminista Mexicano (CFM) who also sought the economic, social, and political emancipation of women.[146] Probably, the First Feminist Congress of 1916 also contributed to the profession of atheism by Apodaca and the women of the CRF. This participation of anticlerical women initiated a practice that would question the traditional, apolitical, domestic feminine ideal by promoting the image of the secular "modern woman."[147]

The women of the CRF were opposed to the commonly accepted representation that visualized all women as fanatical Catholics. Generally, women were considered to be the "angel of the home," the moral guardians of family, men, and society. This representation of women linked them strongly to Catholic morality. Like the Constitucionalistas and editorialists of the *Boletín militar* and *Acción*, the women of the CRF recognized that many women were sanctimonious Catholics and therefore tried to demonstrate to Guadalajara society that they were anticlerical Jacobins. Their actions, speeches, and representations demonstrated that the radical liberal tradition was not only masculine; women could also possess a strong anticlerical identity.

Tensions grew because the Constitution of 1917 recognized individual rights for all citizens. Catholics and non-Catholics employed them differently. Liberal and atheist women like the Apodaca's sisters recurred to their individual rights to denounce the violation the Catholics were committing of religious restrictions and their continued propaganda in favor of female fanaticism. The Catholics, meanwhile, brandished their individual rights to defend their religious freedom. Therefore, both groups used the constitution in different ways for different ends, showing their internal contradictions. To illustrate this, Laura Apodaca defended her anticlerical identity by demanding that the judge jail the Catholic women. In consequence, she provided a list of female Catholic catechists and schoolteachers, to speed up the process.[148]

Gender, Religious, and Political Identities in Dispute

The Jacobin anticlericalism of the women of the CRF placed them on equal footing with the revolutionary leaders. This alleged equality and likeness erased the differences between men and women; new gender identities destabilized the heterosexual hegemony of the gender order. This caused a lot of fear, noise, and discomfort to society at large. Despite this fear and rejection, the women of the CRF, such as Apodaca, were perceived as exceptional fighters and won the right to participate in the male political world because they were not "traditional" women. The CRF challenged the Catholic representation of the feminine ideal that revolved around the Virgin Mary—a woman who was both mother and virgin. The anthropologist Ana María Alonso indicates that "*the Mother* represents the natural and divine feminine virtues of purity, chasteness, and modesty. The virgin is devout, self-sacrificing, sweet, timid, submissive, humble, and affectionate."[149]

From July to November 1918, the anticlericalism of the CRF went from a radical stance to an antireligious one. The Catholic press reacted immediately. *La lucha*, a Catholic newspaper, attacked the women of the CRF and described them as "*icono-plastas*"—a play on *iconoclasts* using the term for "nuisance"—radical old maids, ridiculous clowns who did not belong to the middle classes, pure lowlifes who were dark-skinned and homely.[150] The Catholic press caricatured them and doubted that they would achieve their goal because they "were not worthy of even the left pinky fingernail of the latest demon."[151] Despite this sharp attack, the Catholic press showed the fear they caused among Catholics that feminism, Jacobin anticlericalism, and the antireligious would gain traction and strength among the populace. That is why they attempted to stress that they were a small, hopeless minority. The Catholics wanted them to be perceived thus because they violated the norms of behavior for women.

Despite this sharp mockery and critique, the women of the CRF continued their iconoclast campaign. Jacinta Curiel (1906–2002), a student from the Normal School and the second female physician to graduate from the Universidad de Guadalajara, recalled that Apodaca gave speeches about atheism at the Teatro Degollado. There, Apodaca used to say, "If God exists, then this theater ought to collapse. [After waiting for a moment] See, God does not exist, because the theater is still standing."[152] In the newspaper *Iconoclasta*, anticlerical women proclaimed that they were completely against the ignorance that propped up the Catholic Church because it impeded the progress of the masses. The CRF and Apodaca, both in their newspaper and in their school, favored liberty in learning to promote social justice and destroy the capitalist system. In this way, children would learn how to profess solidarity with the workers of the world. The children of workers affiliated to the COM attended iconoclast Sunday school.

The schoolteacher Carmen Hernández Cambre, one of the founders of the CRF, stated that the CRF was proud of its iconoclast school for boys and girls given that there, a class consciousness was developed and the values of unity and solidarity were promoted. The teachers from this school thought that children should not receive punishment but, on the contrary, ought to receive incentives for their intellectual development. The children collected money and donations to help offset the needs of the school.¹⁵³ Some girls who were pioneers of this school were later leaders in the feminist and labor movement of Guadalajara, as illustrated by the case of María Guadalupe Martínez Villanueva, who, together with María A. Díaz, founded the Círculo Feminista de Occidente (CFO; 1927–2002) and was a leader of the women's section of the Federación de Trabajadores de Jalisco (FTJ).

In January 1919, Elisa Estrada García, secretary of the interior of the CRF, requested from the Guadalajara city government license to use the Teatro Degollado every fifteen days in the afternoons. The CRF sought to put into practice its action program by means of "a series of educational conferences touching on different points about art, industry, philosophical or of any order they present themselves, because it has been noted that liberalism has been heading into decadence due to a lack of cultural meetings."¹⁵⁴ The Guadalajara city council approved her request, but only "on the condition that your conferences not touch on political or religious issues."¹⁵⁵ Moreover, they would have to deposit Mex$200 in order to guarantee "any imperfections you may cause to said arena, given that we have observed that with this sort of meetings, it always ends up damaged."¹⁵⁶ This conditioned consent restricted the actions of the CFR, which was already a political and anticlerical organization. The Guadalajara city government attempted to stop the violence triggered by religious matters, given that there had already been considerable wear and tear between the Constitucionalista government (state and municipal) and the Catholics, polarizing the residents of Guadalajara. The CRF did not have the approval or the backing of the state or the federal government, unlike Belén de Sárraga in 1912 or Atala Apodaca from 1914 to 1916. As the CRF was affiliated with the COM, it presented itself as an autonomous, combative organization. Carranza, in August 1916, had shut down and repressed the workers' strikes of the COM for upsetting the social order. The Guadalajara city council perceived the CRF as a pressure group and a political minority; therefore, implicitly, it did not consent to its radicalization. The Mex$200 they requested was a significant sum, especially if one considered that most industries and businesses did not pay the daily minimum wage required by regulation. For example, in April 1919, workers from the La Experiencia textile factory complained before the governor because they were compensated with insignificant wages of Mex$4.05 per week. With this, they were able to buy only beans and corn, and it was not enough to cover the remaining expenses of their families, which caused them to feel humiliated and incapable of confronting "the frightful crisis."[157] If women earned lower wages than men, they would hardly be able to come up with the Mex$200 required by the Guadalajara Ayuntamiento.

On March 9, 1919, the CRF, the iconoclast school, the COM, and the Masonic Lodge of the Universal Rite of Gonzalo Lecuona organized a conference at the Teatro Principal. Governor Luis Castellanos did not authorize this, but the organizers changed the venue to Salón Tívoli. On May 1, the CRF, the iconoclast school, and the COM served food to 250 workers. At both meetings, the organizers disseminated ideas of solidarity among the working class.[158] At this meal, the family of Guadalupe Martínez confirmed its commitment to liberal values, the Mexican revolution, social justice, and the "Red" organized labor movement.

Revolutionary and labor leaders like Rosendo Salazar and Zuno Hernández perceived the women of the CRF as "exceptional fighters" in Jalisco. In the national arena, the revolutionaries recognized the political labor of feminists like Hermila Galindo, Elvia Carrillo Puerto, and Elena Torres, who were also seen as exceptional political fighters.[159] By the end of 1919, anticlerical conferences had not contributed to diminishing Catholic religious practices in Guadalajara society but, on the contrary, had politicized and radicalized society. Despite how little information there is about why the CRF and the CLJOD were shut down, the interviews I conducted allowed me to establish connections and influences of Apodaca and the CRF with several of their students at the Normal School; they instilled them with the ideal of promoting a secular civic culture.

Teaching Practice and Politics, 1920–77

At the age of thirty-six, on January 28, 1920, Apodaca wrote to President Carranza to request work for her husband, Samuel Ruiz Cabañas (who had been the director of the Talleres Gráficos [Printers' workshops]), his brother Rafael Apodaca (who had been a machinist for the Division of the West), and for herself. Each one had to settle urgent economic commitments. It was suggested that her husband be ratified as director of the Talleres Gráficos and that her brother be reinstated as a machinist, and she wanted to be appointed professor of national language and grammar at the Normal School in Mexico City.[160] In 1920, Apodaca returned to the capital in order

FIG. 13. Atala Apodaca Anaya with two Constitutionalists, ca. 1914. Courtesy of Colección Independencia y Revolución en la Memoria Ciudadana, file 49 (Atala Apodaca Anaya), BCCG-CO-CIRMC.

to be appointed regional federal inspector; she was also principal of the Quetzalcóaltl School, where she established school breakfasts.[161] Apodaca likely did not continue with the CLJOD during her stay in Mexico City in early 1920 because it was an organization that had been founded in Guadalajara during the ascent of Constitutionalism, strongly linked to Carranza and Diéguez. Carranza's decision in 1920 that his presidential successor be Ignacio Bonilla—not a military man but a diplomat—irritated the general from Sonora, Álvaro Obregón. He launched the Agua Prieta Plan to repudiate the Carranza administration and restart his own revolution. Following Carranza's assassination in May 1920, it was not convenient for Apodaca to openly declare her Carrancista affiliations.

Even though Obregonismo broke away from Carrancismo, Apodaca and Zuno (an Obregonista) always maintained their anticlerical position and strong ties of friendship and politics, created together with the Centro

Bohemio in 1912. Both had been state inspectors during the Diéguez administration. Apodaca invariably congratulated Zuno for his political achievements as president of the Partido Liberal Jalisciense (Jaliscan liberal party), as a state deputy, municipal president of Guadalajara, and governor of Jalisco. Apodaca returned to Guadalajara in 1924 during Zuno's administration as governor (1922–25), during which anticlerical and populist policies were promoted. She was reinstated in her position as school inspector in September 1924. As a state inspector, she verified that state educational programs were respected in private schools. She always supported the protestant school, the Instituto Colón, in its recognitions at the end of the school year because it provided a non-Catholic education.[162] One month later, in October, she resigned to take her position as honorary representative of Jalisco in Mexico City. The Dirección General de Educación of Jalisco (General department of education) designated her to inform the Jalisco state government of educational and cultural issues and plans from the nation's capital that might contribute to the improvement of statewide education.[163]

Given the imminent breakout of the Cristero War and the resignation of Zuno as governor due to strong pressure for him to be impeached because of his resistance to the centralist politics of President Plutarco Elías Calles, in April 1926, the Dirección General de Educación Primaria y Especial of Jalisco (General department of primary and special education) once again named Apodaca technical inspector of the first school zone of the state.[164] Despite the differences between the state and federal government with regard to regional autonomy, both wanted the implementation of anticlerical policies. The anticlerical stance of Apodaca contributed to the guidelines of secular education being carried out. She visited municipal areas and established contacts with the municipal boards of education. However, she performed this commission only up until 1927 because her health deteriorated, compelling her to retire from her post.[165] From 1928 to 1934, she was director of the Departamento de Enseñanza Primaria y Normal (Department of primary and normal education) for the state of Jalisco.

Like other women who participated in the Mexican Revolution, on August 31, 1946, the Secretaría de la Defensa Nacional (National defense ministry) officially recognized Atala Apodaca as a veteran of the revolution; she was sixty-two years old.[166] This was a significant recognition, as there were thousands of women who applied for this but only 432 were recognized as

FIG. 14. President Venustiano Carranza, 1917. Courtesy of Colección Independencia y Revolución en la Memoria Ciudadana, file 49 (Atala Apodaca Anaya), BCCG-CO-CIRMC.

veterans.[167] Generals Amado Aguirre, Ramón Iturbe, and Agustín Olachea certified and provided detailed information about her actions as a Maderista, Antihuertista, and Constitucionalista. Apodaca in her request attached newspaper clippings from Guadalajara, Mazatlán, and Culiacán to reconstruct and provide testimonials of her significant revolutionary contributions.

Not long after her recognition as a veteran, in March 1948 she joined the progressive forces of Jalisco and formed part of the state's organizing committee of the Partido Popular (PP). At the start of the administration of President Miguel Alemán Valdés (1946–52), there was a conflict between the Partido Revolucionario Institucional (PRI) and Vicente Lombardo Toledano, as representative of the Central de Trabajadores de México (CTM). From this fallout, Lombardo founded the PP in 1947 to recover the Mexican Revolution; he fell back on socialism to provide his ideological leftist foundation and maintained tense relations with the Partido Comunista Mexicano (PCM) and the autonomous, combative labor unions. According to Elisa Servín, "The formation of the Partido Popular [took place] in the context of a reconfiguration of the left that was express[ed] at the Round Table of Mexican Marxists to which Lombardo was summon[ed] in January 1947."[168] The PP might object to the "revolutionary regime," but it would not confront it. Although the PP did not dispute the political arenas of the PCM and the PRI, it did seek recognition in the public sphere. For Servín, "at the start of the Cold War, Miguel Alemán was not interested in sustaining an alliance with someone who, in the eyes of the belligerent anti-Communism of that era, hysterically expressed in the press that he was the direct representative of Moscow."[169] The organizing committee of the PP was formed by men and women who were peasants, employees, professionals, and workers. Apodaca was part of the state women's commission of the PP, in which one student, two textile workers, one schoolteacher, one nurse, and one housewife were participants. The manifesto of the PP specified that they would struggle for independence and national sovereignty; they would maintain, purge, expand, and deepen the democratic system of the country; they would respect the freedom of political assembly; they would encourage the country's economic development; they would back scientific knowledge; they would procure the improvement of living standards; and they would defend national and international peace.[170] At the age of seventy-two, in 1958, Atala

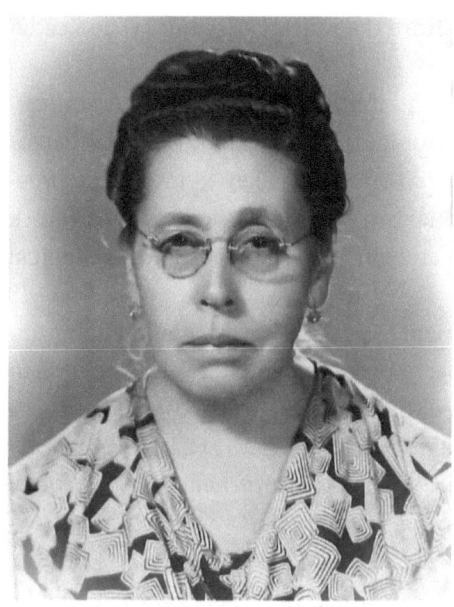

FIG. 15. Atala Apodaca Anaya, ca. 1946. Courtesy of Colección Independencia y Revolución en la Memoria Ciudadana, file 49 (Atala Apodaca Anaya), BCCG-CO-CIRMC.

Apodaca was a candidate for senator for the PP, but she did not obtain the votes necessary to win.[171]

At the age of sixty-three, in April 1947 Apodaca was named a classroom teacher at Escuela Urbana 64 and commissioned to the psycho-pedagogical office of the Cultural Department; she performed both jobs from 1947 to 1953.[172] As a principal and teacher at Escuela Urbana 64, she participated in school expositions and pedagogical conferences. In March 1947, Apodaca requested from Heliodoro Hernández Loza, municipal president of Guadalajara, that the Ayuntamiento transfer the school from the Colonia Villaseñor to a home on Belén Street because said academic center did not meet suitable conditions. Apodaca stated that in the Belén Street location, there were significant educational staff working under the teachers Aurelia Guevara and Aurelio Ortega. At the age of sixty-nine, in 1953, she became principal of the Escuela Federal José Clemente Orozco; she completed tasks related to the festivities of the Year of Hidalgo and represented Jalisco in the acts commemorating the battle of the Alhóndiga de Granaditas. In 1954, she was designated honorary principal of the Escuela Rural Severo Díaz in Sayula, Jalisco.[173] In 1955, even before she retired in 1956, she showed interest in the patriotic festivities of the schools.[174] She continued to be active in civic ceremonies to honor Jalisco liberals from the nineteenth century, dedicated to Ramón Corona or Benito Juárez.

Rodolfo González Guevara, president of the PRI regional executive committee in Mexico City, recognized Apodaca's intense labor to José Parres Arias, head of the State Cultural Department, as a key figure to the preservation of the liberal and revolutionary history of Jalisco. Apodaca's work had contributed to defending Mexican principles of liberty and ideological independence.[175]

Notably at the time of her retirement, Apodaca Anaya would attempt to publish her essay. I have been unable to discover whether it was printed in the end. From 1956 to 1967, she edited the following works: *Globalización de la enseñanza* (1953), *Homenaje al generalísimo dn. José María Morelos y Pavón* (1965), and *Homenaje al primer jefe del ejército constitucionalista Venustiano Carranza y a los diputados constituyentes por el estado de Jalisco en el cincuentenario de la constitución reformada, de los Estados Unidos Mexicanos, 1917* (1967). On March 27, 1957, the government of Jalisco awarded her the Manuel López Cotilla Medal for her contributions to statewide education.[176] In 1957, at the age of seventy-three, she retired as a teacher and as an inspector.

At the age of seventy-nine, in 1963, the Secretaría de la Defensa Nacional accepted the entrance of Atala Apodaca into the Mexican Legion of Honor because she met the requirements of Articles 3 and 25 of the foundational decree of this body, meaning she became a member of the Division of Legionnaires of the state of Jalisco.[177] On February 1, 1949, President Alemán established the Mexican Legion of Honor, to be directed by the Secretaría de la Defensa Nacional. The mission of the Mexican Legion of Honor, as an apolitical group, was to heighten and preserve the outstanding events of history, to maintain an understanding and tradition of the various groups that had carried out some military tasks. To enter this legion, it had to be proven that one was a defender of the country, that one was a precursor or veteran of the Mexican Revolution, and that the quality of one's conduct and military and civic performance were worthy and honorable.[178] Apodaca met every one of these requirements, and she could prove it.

Toward the end of her life, Apodaca suffered from economic want and health issues. Apodaca and Zuno maintained a friendly epistolary exchange for many years in which they discussed liberal, artistic, and Masonic themes, and also, she asked him for economic and moral support during her old age.[179]

In 1969, Apodaca traveled to Mexico City, accompanied by her daughter Carmen, to sell the library of her late husband, Samuel Ruiz Cabañas, and to prepare herself "to die well," but she did not achieve her objective, given that her economic and health problems were relentless. When she was eighty-seven years old, in 1971, Apodaca went to Zuno in search of help for "disability and worse yet, the ingratitude, indifference, and dangerous complications on the part of Carmen, my adopted daughter."[180] When she passed away on August 30, 1977, at the age of ninety-three, Professor Ramón García Ruiz, head of the Department of Education, stated in the obituary published in *El informador*, "A distinguished teacher had died / Who through her brilliant labor in classrooms and social struggle always stood out for her clear conduct / Let us spread the best of her teachings among the children of Jalisco."[181]

The history of the life of Atala Apodaca Anaya shows that she passed through different processes and stages. Her practices and speeches from the end of the decade of 1910 have remained in a negative light in the memory of local history in Guadalajara, significantly undermining her actions throughout her career in education and politics. Upon reconstructing her life and providing context as part of the fierce disputes between the Constitucionalista and Catholic agendas, one can gain an understanding of why her liberal nineteenth-century culture became radicalized when she declared herself to be not only anticlerical but moreover an atheist. This caused revolutionaries and Catholics alike to see her as an "exceptional woman" who did not fit into the traditional role model for women. This male perspective pushed aside her struggle for the promotion of secular, modern civic culture based on education as well as her project to train a "new, modern woman." However, gender analysis has permitted the realization of a more balanced analysis of the figures involved in the revolutionary process, thus rejecting the vision that proposes that only revolutionary military leaders were the creators of social and educational policies.

4

María Arcelia Díaz

Labor and Women's Politics within the Context of the Construction of the Postrevolutionary State of Guadalajara

In late 1922, the leaders of the Catholic Union of La Experiencia agreed during an assembly to assassinate "the Bolshevik" María Arcelia Díaz (1896–1939), a *trocilera*, or textile worker, who acted as secretary general of the Unión Obrera de La Experiencia (UOLE), a labor organization that supported the revolutionary government. This agreement "was warmly applauded" by a priest and a political commissary, "who were present and form[ed] part of the board of directors of that union."[1] At the meeting, one of those present indicated that they had already attempted to assassinate her but had been unable to find her at home alone. Once they caught wind of this resolution, a group of streetcar operators and textile workers affiliated with the Federación de Agrupaciones Obreras de Jalisco (FAOJ) and a member of the Confederación Regional Obrera Mexicana (CROM) called a meeting in the area surrounding the factory to defend Díaz, asking the governor of Jalisco, Antonio Valadez Ramírez, to put an end to the hostilities and threats that were being aimed at the members of the UOLE.[2] To the leaders of the Catholic Union, the priest and the political commissary, this protest confirmed that Díaz would not desist from demanding the fulfillment of workers' rights. A significant labor contingency backed her. It is noteworthy not only that this Catholic organization tried to end her life but that labor organizations mobilized to avoid her assassination, which begs the question, Who was María Arcelia Díaz?

Díaz did not fit the image of an unqualified, apolitical, submissive woman. Nor did she resemble the woman who, because she had left home to work in a factory, had lost her moral values and chosen the path of prostitution. Nevertheless, the state (both Porfirista and revolutionary), the Catholic Church, labor leaders, journalists, politicians, legislators, educators, industrialists, and certain middle-to-upper-class feminists debated these perceptions and fears, given the growing visibility and presence of the working woman in urban centers.[3] The strongest polemic arose when women began to actively participate in politics. Díaz formed part of a generation of women who joined the revolutionary process, the conflict between church and state, the organized labor movement, and the incipient feminist movement to demand women's rights—civil, social, economic, and political. Like Belén de Sárraga and Atala Apodaca, Díaz forged political bonds and friendships in regional, national, and international arenas with other women who challenged traditional gender values and, in so doing, generated anxiety, fear, and upon occasion, threats of violence, as illustrated by the assassination attempt against her, the "Bolshevik."[4]

Through analysis of Díaz's different jobs, her political career, and her life, this chapter shows how she gradually built her leadership and coalitions with other working-class unions during the 1910s and 1930s. These labor and political experiences allowed Díaz to move beyond a stance that fought for social justice to favor a feminist consciousness and women's rights. Díaz's feminist consciousness crystallized in the establishment of one of the most enduring working-class feminist organizations: the Círculo Feminista de Occidente (CFO), focused on addressing the demands and needs of working women in general. Therefore, I argue that the reconstruction of Díaz's life and labor career contributes to the ongoing debate about representation and revisits the question posed by Gayatri Chakravorty Spivak: Can the subaltern speak?[5]

Family, Labor, and Union Background

María Arcelia Díaz was born in La Escoba, in the municipal area of Zapopan, Jalisco, in 1896. She was the daughter of J. Merced Díaz, a farmer, and Francisca Rendón, a homemaker.[6] Her history comes in fragments, as would be expected given her gender and working-class background. Most of the biographies dedicated to her adopt an apologetic and heroic viewpoint to underline her suffering and vicissitudes. Díaz was transformed from an exploited *trocilera* (a female worker who operated a machine for spinning, weaving, or finishing textiles) to a union leader who fought for men and women in the textile industry of the Guadalajara region. Following the death of her father, at eight years old Díaz began working for the Compañía Industrial de Guadalajara to support her mother and her brothers.[7] Like many wage earners of that era, she worked sixteen-hour days with no contract, under unsanitary conditions, and with no labor rights whatsoever. Because she was a child, she would fall asleep during her workday among the empty bobbin boxes.[8] Several Díaz biographies claim that her elder companions taught her to read and write "on the looms, with the chalk used to mark blankets."[9] This anecdote speaks to an informal written culture and literacy shared among members of the Mexican working class. Her written culture was interwoven with reading culture. Díaz read the manifestos of the Flores Magón brothers that called for political change as well as the newspapers *La luz* and *La antorcha* and the publications of the Casa del Obrero Mundial (COM).[10] It is not known how Díaz obtained or interpreted these readings, if it was customary to practice reading out loud, or who bought these bulletins and circulated them. Despite these information gaps, I find that what Jesús A. Martínez stated in his study regarding reading and readers of Madrid in the nineteenth century applies in the case of Díaz, in the sense that "one only reads if three elements come together: knowledge (literacy), power (economic position and access to distribution), and interest (personal stimuli and motivations)."[11] Like German, English, and French working men and women who wrote their autobiographies in the late nineteenth and early twentieth centuries, Díaz provided clues regarding how her literacy contributed to her politicization and unionization.[12]

In 1908, when she was twelve years old, Díaz worked at Río Blanco, the textile factory that replaced La Escoba and witnessed the first textile strikes in the Guadalajara region.[13] In 1910, at the age of fourteen, her participation in organizing a labor union led to her being fired.[14] Díaz and her family migrated from Guadalajara to Amatlán, Puebla, where she worked for seven years in a textile factory. There, she married Pablo Aranda, with whom she had two sons who passed away as children.[15] With regards to her companion, we are unaware whether he was also a textile worker, how long their relationship as a couple lasted, at what age their sons passed away or the cause of their death, or how these events may have affected Díaz's personal life and political career. Despite these silences, we do know that Díaz's textile labor evolved within a context where strikers and textile leaders commonly migrated to different regions in search of work.[16] Díaz and her family, like most textile workers, participated in a vibrant political culture that fed the protests and organizing that made the Mexican Revolution (1910–17).[17]

In 1917, the Díaz family returned to Guadalajara with a political culture based on combativeness and the struggle for workers' rights. During that period many of the workers, including textile workers, appropriated revolutionary discourse to obtain what they called "social justice." Thus, the alliance of the labor movement with Constitucionalistas recognized workers as an important political force that would aid the construction of the new revolutionary state and the establishment of new political institutions.[18] Upon her arrival in Guadalajara, Díaz observed that the minimum wage was not paid for workers, nor was the eight-hour workday respected, and many workers were obliged to complement their salary with overtime to cover basic needs. Likewise, due to widespread unemployment, there were desperate people in search of any job to be able to survive. These conditions favored the statewide violation of all that was stipulated in Article 123 of the constitution.[19]

Labor was not the only sector of society concerned with working and living conditions. Industrialists, business interests, and intellectuals all sought solutions to the labor problem. In June 1911, for example, Carlos Robles Gil, Joaquín Aceves, and other citizens of Guadalajara proposed that the governor establish a labor department, as President Francisco León de la Barra (1911) had done, because they thought that this new agency would aid in the country's pacification.[20] In November 1913, José Arreola Adame, José G. Montes de Oca, and Miguel Mendoza López Schwerdtfeger suggested to the governor that he create a labor department in Jalisco. From the perspective of the social sciences, these men argued that such a department would help design social reforms, establish an employment agency, mediate between capitalists and laborers, and keep statistical records. These liberal intellectuals felt the labor problem required, invariably, fair solutions that would address agrarian and educational issues.[21]

While these proposals were being developed to solve the labor problem, men and women in the textile industry had already carried out a general strike to demand the payment of minimum wage. After the arrival of the Constitucionalistas in Jalisco in July 1914, the implementation of the minimum wage was a highly contentious affair. The owners of textile factories in the region were opposed to paying an equal minimum wage to men and women. Men were seen as heads of household and more skilled, while women were perceived as dependents.[22] In late 1914, the workers at the factories of Río Grande and Atemajac experienced major confrontations with their respective administrators because they refused to comply with the minimum wage. The workers complained to Governor Manuel M. Diéguez, specifying that they often worked only twenty hours a week or not at all. Some workers were fired without reason. Even though they always behaved "honorably and with dedication to their jobs," their families went hungry. They only went on a "peaceful strike" because management would not negotiate. They requested that the governor balance the scales of justice and asked him, "How is it that [the owners] still even consider bringing into practice the privileges granted by Porfirian tyranny?"[23] Between October 1916 and July 1917, men and women from the Río Grande factory complained of the terribly unsanitary conditions inside the factory and again threatened a strike. Workers Benito Gómez and Florencio Herrera petitioned the governor to pay workers in gold coins, given that the factory owners refused to do so. The workers invoked their constitutional rights to demand the establishment of an arbitration board.[24] In late 1917, the workers of Río Grande protested further cuts in the work week, which would mean lower take-home pay and threaten their capacity to meet their most basic needs. According to these workers, a family of four needed on average Mex$8.65 to buy four liters of corn, one kilogram of beans, a small package of coal, a liter of limestone, half a kilogram of salt, chili peppers, tomatoes, onions, two bars of soap, a half kilogram of lard, matches, and kindling and pay rent for their home and electricity.[25] The conflicts grew more acute when the liberal union and Catholic group in Río Grande clashed over collections for the religious festivities held on December 12. Liberal workers wished to channel that money into a school for adults and claimed that the Catholics were a minority, predominantly composed of women and led by a "friar."[26]

The social Catholic movement in Jalisco had evolved as an alternative to the improvement of social and material conditions of the masses, to control the excesses of capitalism and avoid the spread of socialist thinking. When the PCN dominated the governorship and the legislature from 1912 to 1914, laws were decreed that were in keeping with Catholic social action. Therefore, the competition between the Catholic project and the Constitucionalista agenda triggered major clashes during the decades of 1910 and 1920.

Textile factories served as the location of many of these conflicts between Catholics and libertarian organizations, which were referred to at the time as "Red." In 1918, there were conflicts between Catholic workers—affiliated with Catholic female circles for working women and the Liga Protectora de la Obrera (LPO), which sought to "regenerate women and young people by means of moral and material assistance" and was led by the ADCG—and the Reds at La Experiencia and Río Grande. At La Experiencia, Díaz confronted the LPO. This Catholic organization tried to recruit young people to instill moral values in them, but they took no interest in improving and regulating female labor and thus failed to attract most of the women workers. Díaz, together with the Centro Radical Femenino (CRF)—an anticlerical and iconoclast organization affiliated with the COM led by teacher María Trinidad Hernández Cambre and linked to the Consejo Feminista Mexicano (CFM, or Mexican feminist council)—vigorously protested the use of religion to indoctrinate and control women workers.[27] Díaz, Apodaca, and the CRF favored organizing women in ways that countered a Catholic vision of womanhood: a "new woman" with radical ideas, a blend of anarcho-syndicalism, socialism, and communism.

In the early 1920s, Díaz collaborated in some elementary schools of Guadalajara to teach the girls handcrafts and instruct them in the importance of their families' struggle to improve their living conditions.[28] It was through this work that she met Guadalupe Martínez and her sisters, young women who would go on to study at the Jalisco Normal School and attend CRF Sunday school at the COM. Later, Guadalupe would become a key political leader in the organized labor movement in Jalisco.[29] This was the beginning of Díaz's relationship with progressive middle-class schoolteachers. Together, they participated in the creation of unions and women's organizations to combat Catholic associations and expand women's sphere of action in 1920s Guadalajara.

From Invisible Working Woman to Visible Textile Leader

The petitions of textile workers during the decade of 1910 that are preserved at the Archivo Histórico de Jalisco (AHJ) are basically demands and complaints presented by certain leaders (Benito Gómez and Ángel Cervantes) in representation of the men and women of the textile industry of Guadalajara. What few traces there are of Díaz refer to her brush with the LPO. She became increasingly visible as a textile worker and leader in the 1920s. As the gender historian Joan Scott has pointed out, the relationship between invisibility and visibility has long been interwoven with unequal power relations.[30] This author draws from the concept of invisibility proposed by Michel Foucault, who contends that a person or a group were invisible if they possessed three characteristics: perceived as "Other," subordinated, and considered a passive entity. Díaz fulfilled these conditions.

Díaz transformed these elements in a radical manner (subordination, perception as "Other," and passivity) by means of a politicization that she experienced individually because of the alliance established between revolutionary governors and workers. The 1920s in Jalisco was a period of intense social and political mobilization promoted by the governors Basilio Badillo (1921–22) and José Guadalupe Zuno Hernández (1923–26), who implemented anticlerical, populist, and radical measures to strengthen their political position, which favored the organization of men and women in the labor market and educational system. These governors struggled against the proposal of Catholic social action and created their social base by means of political exchanges with the masses. Zuno promoted the creation of organizations of peasants, workers, and teachers in which he incorporated women so that they could demand the distribution of lands and the establishment of schools for the children of peasants and workers. Although they associated him with President Álvaro Obregón, Zuno was opposed to the centralist policy of the CROM to organize and dominate the local labor movement.[31] To provide greater autonomy to workers and counteract the influence of the CROM, on September 17, 1924, Zuno created the Confederación de Agrupaciones Obreras Libertarias de Jalisco (CAOLJ) with members from Grupo Acción.[32] In 1925, he invited David Alfaro Siqueiros, Amado de la Cueva, Hilario Arredondo, and Roberto Reyes Pérez—prominent communists who lived in Mexico City—to participate in the organized labor movement. These individuals would go on to collaborate closely with the CAOLJ to expand their base beyond the mostly artisans and service workers to include industrial workers (miners, textile workers, and electricians).[33] Through the Liga de Comunidades Agrarias de Jalisco and the CAOLJ, the two most important Zunista organizations, their affiliates engaged on several fronts. To counteract the Catholic social action movement, Zuno decreed Catholic associations to be illegal and that his government would recognize only non-Catholic organizations. As a counterweight to the policies of the federal government, which sought to repress Zuno's regional policies, he passed legislation on the autonomy of municipalities, as well as the legislative and judicial branches. The CAOLJ backed independent unions and strikes and struggled against the scabs of the CROM and the authoritarian policies of the Secretaría de Industria (Ministry of industry), which prevented the autonomy of the organized labor movement. The Zunistas and their communist allies combated the exploitation of workers by local and foreign industrial companies (in mining, the electric industry, and textiles). In 1927, the Zunistas and communists were radicalized, forming the Confederación Obrera de Jalisco (COJ).

The alliance between Zuno and the masses generated social programs and projects, such as the Colonia Obrera (Workers' neighborhood) and the Casa Amiga de la Obrera (Friendly house for women workers), a school and daycare for the children of single mothers. Various worker and labor organizations found the political space to make demands, as was the case when María A. Díaz requested that Governor Zuno decree a state law against extreme exploitation.[34] In addition to being a leader, Díaz was a political operator and negotiator. Along with other organized workers, she influenced Zuno to pass the State Labor Law in 1923, which, echoing constitutional article 123, recognized the right of female workers to maternity leave, daycares, the minimum wage, and equal pay for equal work. The 1923 law empowered working women and men as they fought for the enforcement of the minimum wage, the right to organization, contracts, and rest on Sundays.

The Profile of the Employment Structure of Men and Women in 1920

To understand the political participation of women and Díaz's leadership in the region of Guadalajara, it is necessary to examine the gendered organization of the labor force in the decade of 1920. The 1921 census included information for the entire region, without distinguishing between towns and cities.[35] It sheds light on trends in the distribution of the workforce and cultural and gender constructs of the occupations of men and women that resembled the discourses of the state and the Catholic Church, which distinguished between the public and private spheres.

According to the 1921 census, the people of Jalisco were concentrated in domestic labor (50 percent), followed by agriculture (36 percent), industry (6 percent) and commerce (3 percent); construction, bureaucracy, office workers and mining all registered very small percentages (See table 1). These numbers showed the tendency in Jalisco toward agricultural labor. The high

Table 1. Labor force distribution in Jalisco by sector and by sex, 1921

	Men	Percentage	Women	Percentage	Total	Percentage
Agriculture	291,589	76.28	1,060	0.25	292,649	36.0
Mining	1,706	0.45	—	—	1,706	0.20
Industry	35,387	9.26	13,246	3.07	48,633	6.0
Construction	6,082	1.59	36	—	6,118	0.75
Commerce	19,309	5.05	4,987	1.6	24,296	3.0
Public administration	2,139	0.56	24	—	2,163	0.26
Professions	2,964	0.78	2514	0.58	5,478	0.67
Domestic labor	2,219	0.58	404,492	93.87	406,711	50.0

Source: Dirección de Estadística Nacional, *Censo general de habitantes, 1921* (Mexico: Talleres Gráficos de la Nación, 1928).

percentage of domestic labor can be explained not only because there were more women than men but also because the constructions that dominated what was considered male and female in these areas strongly influenced the categories used in this census, although the definitions used in each category are not specified. The occupational segregation meant that men were concentrated in agriculture (76 percent) and had less representation in industry (9 percent) and commerce (5 percent), while women dominated domestic labor (93 percent), with some presence in industry (3 percent) and commerce (1 percent). Contrasting the sex composition in each sector provides further insight into the differing constructions of male and female labor. For example, men were predominant in agriculture (99 percent), mining (100 percent), construction (99 percent), and public administration (98 percent); therefore, they were concentrated in "male" occupations related to the public sphere and those with "menial labor" that "highlighted male physical strength." In contrast, women were predominantly employed in domestic labor (99 percent), an occupational field that references the private sphere. However, these broad categories and their high indices masked different activities of women in the home (embroidery, sewing, cooking, caring for others, washing, and knitting) that generated products and offered services for other people. These activities have not been recognized as work; women

Table 2. Textile industry workers in the Guadalajara region, 1906–35

	1906		1911		1920		1935	
	MEN	WOMEN	MEN	WOMEN	MEN	WOMEN	MEN	WOMEN
Río Blanco	33	77	23	77	—	—	—	—
La Experiencia	37	63	28	72	39	61	—	—
Atemajac	17	83	—	—	55	45	—	—
Río Grande	—	—	91	9	62	38	80	20

Source: Dawn Keremitsis, "La doble jornada de la mujer en Guadalajara, 1910–1940," *Encuentro* 1 (1984): 42–44, 48.

have carried them out under different conditions within the domestic sphere as part of the labors of the home, in artisanal industry, in home delivery workshops, or as activities complementary to the raising of children.[36]

There were also significant percentages of women in professions (45 percent), industry (25 percent), and commerce (20 percent). The professional percentage indicates the importance of the role of women in private and public schools as schoolteachers and office workers. In fact, these sectors represented not only the female labor force, given that from them, women's political organizations emerged. In this context, organizations of Catholic, "Red" (a broad term referring to progressive social forces), anarchist, socialist, and communist workers sought to gain control over female workers during the 1920s. It stands out that during this period, the number of textile workers was diminishing (due to mechanization, the economic crisis, and the organized labor movement led by men who sought only to preserve male jobs), while the numbers of office workers (mainly schoolteachers) and women's political organizations (especially in the service sector) increased. In the oldest textile factories of the Guadalajara region (Río Blanco and La Experiencia), more women were hired between 1906 and 1920, while the new and modern companies (Atemajac and Río Grande) employed mostly men. Díaz worked at La Experiencia, a factory that was unable to compete with the economic expansion of more modern industries. This is one of the processes that marked her significantly.

The Asociación de Damas Católicas de Guadalajara (ADCG), together with the Catholic organizations (Confederación Católica del Trabajo [CCT] in

1920—which later became the Confederación Nacional Católica del Trabajo [CNCT] in 1922), organized female textile workers, schoolteachers, commercial and domestic employees, and women in general into labor unions for both sexes or solely for women.[37] They also established parochial schools and women's centers where women learned to sew, knit, and embroider and received religious education that emphasized the different roles of men and women in keeping with their social class. The Catholic ladies represented themselves as "the feminine ideal" who promoted love and Christian charity and who would seek the instruction of women workers on morality and honorability; that is to say, the efforts of the Catholic ladies stressed the moralization of women above all else. During the 1910s and 1920s, they created two labor unions: one for female schoolteachers (Unión Profesional de Maestras del Sagrado Corazón de Jesús y de la Asunción) and one for female employees (Unión Profesional de Empleadas de Comercio).

From Working Woman to Modern Woman

At the age of twenty-six, Díaz was a charismatic young woman who had been politicized by major events that influenced her way of wielding her leadership—the death of her father during her childhood, unfavorable working conditions, the death of her children, violent conflict in the textile industry in Amatlán, and the clash between Catholics and "Reds" in Jalisco. Like Eufrosina Moya, the *Negra Moya* (1907–69), leader of the coffee workers in Veracruz, these events probably marked her desire to enter politics. Her perseverance in the labor and union struggle and her dedication, discipline, and shows of support for others allowed her to form a political clientele. Her struggle for justice established her legitimacy among "Red" political leaders.

During the 1920s, archival data illustrate the transformations of Díaz's political work, from the defense of the labor rights of working-class men and women to a struggle centered on the needs and problems of women. In early 1922, María A. Díaz, representing a group of female coworkers, filed a complaint with the Labor Department against the assistant director of La Experiencia factory for not taking actions against a female worker for her insulting and arbitrary treatment of other female workers. Díaz asked for her removal.[38] Although she did not provide details, it is most likely that this female worker belonged to and supported the Catholic labor union;

FIG. 16. Unión Obrera de La Experiencia board of directors in 1922, including María A. Díaz (*seated at center*). From Fábrica La Experiencia, *Cien años de actividad social en la fábrica "La Experiencia 1851–1951"* (1951).

it is likely that this request was not attended to or resolved as requested by Díaz and her coworkers. On May 1, 1922, Díaz and workers from the three textile factories in the region of Guadalajara declared their support for Luis C. Medina, founder of the COM in that city, in his electoral campaign for the municipal presidency.[39] On May 22, 1922, workers at La Experiencia formed a union. María Arcelia Díaz, Ignacio E. Rodríguez, Pedro M. Chávez, Timoteo Durón, Juventino Servín, and others created the Unión Obrera de La Experiencia (UOLE), with the motto "For the collective good," affiliated with the FAOJ-CROM. The issues of the UOLE overlapped with those of the FAOJ-CROM, which sought to eliminate the obstacles that prevented the common good. The leaders of the FAOJ-CROM believed that "in order to free the proletariat, it is necessary to transform protest and indignation into dignity, organization, and action."[40] Díaz was elected general secretary, and the committee included J. Refugio González, J. Francisco González, Heraclio Navarro, and María Juárez.[41] With the emergence of the UOLE, Díaz and the members of the board of directors of that union were very active: they defended workers who had been unjustly fired; they complained of the abuses of doormen who allowed Catholic workers to arrive late, but not Reds; and they demanded the investigation of poor working conditions, the lack of medical services, and low salaries.[42]

Following the attempt on her life in 1922, Díaz decided to carry a pistol to protect herself and to assert greater authority in her political practices. She was a brown-skinned woman of medium height and slim build. The people who knew her remember that she always wore her hair in a bun, smooth skirts, long-sleeved blouses, cufflinks, and low-heeled shoes. She spoke in a low voice and had a way with words. People describe her as intelligent, a true fighter, and a leader who knew how to listen.[43] Her dress and demeanor spoke of an austere woman who did not seek to emphasize her femininity or her sexuality. She presented herself with a masculine bearing in public as a way of countering stereotypes of women as apolitical, motherly, and dependent.

On August 1, 1923, Díaz approached the Labor Department to file a complaint against the director of the La Experiencia factory for having unjustly suspended her. At the time, Díaz was employed as a *trocilera* and earned a weekly salary of nine pesos. The company justified the dismissal with the argument that Díaz had been granted permission to be absent from work for one day and had taken two. In her defense, Díaz pointed out that the travel time required to consult with an attorney in Ocotlán obliged her to take an extra day off work. She emphasized that she "did not [believe it to be] fair solely because of one day of justifiable delay, given that during the entire time [that] she worked at the aforementioned factory, she never failed to fulfill her obligations."[44] She received Mex$120, the equivalent of three months' salary and considered her lawsuit to be over.[45]

After her dismissal, she extended her union labor to other textile (Atemajac, Río Blanco) and paper (El Batán) factories. Díaz participated in forming the Unión Libertaria de Obreros de Río Blanco (1924), the Unión de Obreros Libertarios de Atemajac (1924), and the Sindicato Progresista Libertario Obreros del Batán (1925).[46] She filed demands against the factory of Atemajac, the Compañía Industrial de Guadalajara, the Compañía Hidroeléctrica de Chapala, and other employers.[47] She carried out meticulous labor inspections of the different departments of textile factories, reporting if there were broken machinery or tool shortages, and she insisted on the payment of the minimum wage. Díaz was successful in her fight against factory directors who were abusive to textile workers. On April 7, 1925, Díaz, as general secretary of the Sindicato Libertario de Obreros de Río Blanco, requested that the Labor Department immediately remove the director of the Río Blanco Factory, Mr. Enrique Ladewig, from his position "due to the fact that he is quite a bad element for the workers, and also an impossible person to deal with."[48] They argued that countless complaints had been registered against this director because he had reduced their salaries, insulted them, mistreated them, and occasionally threatened them. By 1925, Díaz showed an increasingly determined attitude. Her union practices shifted from negotiation to the assertion of power. This transformation is evident in the shift of the union's motto; while the Unión Obrera de La Experiencia's motto in 1922 was "For the collective good, health and social revolution," the Sindicato Libertario Obreros Río Blanco (Libertarian workers' union of Río Blanco) adopted the motto "By the might of reason or by the might of might" in 1925.[49] Díaz's empowerment echoes that of Eufrosina Moya and Sofía Castro, leaders of the coffee industry in Veracruz, studied by historian Heather Fowler-Salamini.[50] Like other labor leaders, Díaz made public her disapproval of antiunion workers. Unlike some labor leaders, Díaz did not spend her union quotas in the cantinas, nor did she use the funds for personal and family expenses or on potential lovers, as womanizers did.

In 1925, Díaz was the first labor representative of the local textile industry at the Municipal Board of Conciliation and Arbitration. She asked that the Río Blanco factory respect the minimum wage for an eight-hour workday and that overtime be duly compensated.[51] On March 3, 1925, the state Congress asked the head of the Labor Department for information regarding Díaz's services as honorary inspector of the textile factories in Atemajac, Río Grande, and Río Blanco because she requested compensation for her services.[52] The Labor Department clarified that she had been provided with identification as an honorary inspector but that she had not been named to that position, clarifying that those services had been carried out of her own volition. In other words, the Labor Department merely conceded her space in the margins. Nevertheless, Díaz had forged ahead in her efforts for enforcement of the law.[53] Eventually, Zuno granted her a salary and named her inspector of the Higher Council of Health, a position considered to be more proper for female public service in that it dovetailed with maternalist policy.[54]

Although Díaz did not draft the proposal for a social policy program for the working class in the Guadalajara region, in different petitions made before the Labor Department, it is possible to note that she suggested labor, health, and housing reforms that would benefit textile workers. She continued to recommend that the minimum wage be paid, that overtime be compensated, and that factories possess good electrical service in order to avoid abrupt machinery stoppages, given that such interruptions ruined the fabric and the workers were then obliged to pay for the damage out of their own wages. She demanded that the factories offer good health services. To compensate for low salaries, she suggested that textile factories charge lower rent on the houses they provided for workers, that the cost of electricity be lowered, and that workers be allowed to grow vegetable gardens so that their families could consume what they planted.[55] Only the demand for the minimum wage was met.

The Founding of the Círculo Feminista de Occidente

By 1926, Díaz directed the Centro Evolucionista de Mujeres (CEM) in Guadalajara, whose motto was "For the improvement of women," and formed part of the Bloque Independiente de Agrupaciones Obreras (Independent bloc of worker's associations).[56] In this organization, she continued her policy of unionization and loyalty to labor associations that also backed labor leaders. In 1927, Díaz and seven women established the Círculo Feminista de Occidente (CFO) and affiliated it with the Confederación de Obreros de Jalisco (COJ).[57] The CFO brought together female textile workers, tortilla makers, millers, schoolteachers, students of the Normal School, theater employees, ticket takers, domestic workers, and housewives. Among the activists, there were schoolteachers who had come from working-class families with anticlerical and liberal educations. Laura Rosales, who at the time was a student at the Normal School, shared those origins. Her father was a weaver at the Río Grande factory and had fought against Catholic organizations in the decade of 1910. Guadalupe Martínez also came from a liberal, anticlerical, working-class family and became a schoolteacher. Her father was an electrician who had participated in the foundation of the COM in Guadalajara in 1914. Her mother worked in the textile factories and was a distant relative of Díaz.

The articles of incorporation of the CFO stipulated that the organization had been functional for some time and that its main goal was to struggle for the moral and material progress of female workers through its commissions of labor, justice, and welfare. Like Catholic organizations at the time, the CFO implemented a campaign for the moralization of society; however, it offered a morality based on women's rights. The CFO promoted the image of a new woman, one who was politically informed regarding her civil, political, and social rights. They chose combative, radical, and extraordinary figures as their icons: French anarchist Louise Michel (1830–1905), one of the main figures of the Paris Commune (1871); the Marxist and Social Democratic German Jew Rosa Luxemburg (1871–1919); the Russian socialist feminist Alexandra Kollontai (1872–1952); the six hundred women of Haymarket Square, where American anarchists were martyred in their struggle for the eight-hour workday; and Carmen Morales, a labor leader who wore red and black in the Labor Day parades of Mexico City. With these female representations, the CFO sought to create a new morality that would destroy the passive, apolitical image of women and old prejudices that cataloged women as not apt to receive an education beyond what was necessary to be able to fulfill their domestic activities.

In line with the approach taken by Sárraga and the Apodaca sisters, Díaz and the members of the CFO focused part of their work on education, and the Círculo was converted into a center of literacy and political orientation. By 1933, in an article in the press titled "Reflections Regarding Womankind," Díaz set forth her vision on the working woman and the modern woman.[58] She felt that it was up to women to work with honor and that they were agents of social change because they ought not to be slaves in chains, that they could be good, useful, honorable, and help others but that they had to modernize and leave their Catholic values and practices behind. She argued that "woman, properly prepared for the myriad fields of action that life today presents, will and always should be, a mother, as a wife, as a sister," and that she would attain "a greatness in the home, at the office, and on the factory floor."[59] She set forth a maternalistic perspective that aligned with that of the new revolutionary state but also with that of the Catholic Church, in the sense that women ought to serve others. The novelty lay in that this conception expanded the functions of women because it invited them to work, to obtain an education, and to modernize. Díaz believed that these new roles would form a new generation of strong women who would defend their political, social, and civil rights. She stated that only through education could women struggle for their ideals and, at the same time, occupy positions and practice professions considered more appropriate for men. She concluded that womankind would move to the foreground and tell life, "Look at me, nothing can keep me down! I am strong in my femininity! I will form a strong generation! I have conquered you!!"[60]

By 1934, Díaz and the CFO had published their own newspaper titled *Fémina roja*, in which they demanded equal pay for equal work, that women be accepted in any kind of employment, and that more female workplace and health inspectors be hired. They invited female workers to join unions to defend their rights.[61] They encouraged women to urge their husbands to also join unions because this was a path to improve the welfare of their families. Only a few issues of *Fémina roja* were published, probably during a year.

Díaz and the CFO worked closely with the leaders of the COJ because they shared the notion that women could change from god-fearing to revolutionary. The members of the CFO, workers, and schoolteachers like Irene Robledo, Concha Robledo, and Guadalupe Martínez helped women workers—seamstresses, servants, trimmers, tortilla makers, oil makers, and bakers—organize their unions.[62] They were taught how to read and write, tools that were fundamental to their union struggle. They acquired a culture of civic duty by attending and organizing festivals, patriotic parades, reading circles, lectures, and sports activities. Díaz advocated that the quotas paid to the CFO be used to fund medicine, to cover the basic needs of female workers who were without income, and to assist various students of the Normal School in completing their studies. The case of Consuelo Ruiz illustrates these practices. In her oral exam to obtain her teaching certificate, she presented the topic of "the fighting instincts of women" to explain the search for social justice and the emancipation of women. Ruiz stated that Díaz had taught her "to never look back, to always look forward, because in that way, women would win."[63] They also participated in electoral campaigns.

Díaz, the CFO, and her followers were even more radicalized following the implementation of the socialist educational project (1934–40). They were in favor of the project and participated in the establishment of night schools. They demanded that vacancies for female teachers at public schools be granted only to those who were revolutionaries and that the female section of

FIG. 17. María A. Díaz and other members of the CFO during their visit to Salto Jalisco, 1936. Courtesy of Belén Martínez Villanueva.

the Partido Nacional Revolucionario (PNR) in Jalisco be directed by women with experience in organizing working women. The CFO also launched a campaign in favor of female suffrage and organized the third National Congress of Women Workers and Peasants, held in Guadalajara in 1934.[64] Díaz, Guadalupe Martínez, and the members of the CFO formed an integral part of public opinion, frequently appearing in *El jalisciense* (local newspaper and organ of the PNR). They published articles regarding the role of women in the public sphere as mothers, workers, and women with political, social, and civil rights. They participated in the local and national debate regarding the expansion of women's public engagement. Both the official party and female labor organizations—at the regional and national level—created women's sections. María Díaz, representing Jalisco, was the only authentic labor organizer to attend the national convention that transformed the PNR into the Partido de la Revolución Mexicana (PRM). By the end of the 1930s, Díaz already enjoyed legitimacy and prestige among political circles and hence was included in the Jalisco delegation to the PRM convention. Moreover, Díaz and the CFO formed part of a political faction led by Heliodoro

FIG. 18. Letterhead of María A. Díaz for Círculo Feminista de Occidente. Courtesy of Guadalupe Martínez.

Hernández Loza (1898–1990) of the Federación de Trabajadores de Jalisco (FTJ), which participated in the Arbitration Board.

In 1939, Governor Silvano Barba González named Díaz welfare inspector.[65] Her political career, administrative record, and activism had permitted Díaz to go from being an exploited textile worker to a textile leader, a representative of women workers at the Arbitration Board, a labor inspector, feminist leader, representative of the labor sector in the PRM, and welfare inspector. Her intense political work allowed her mobility in the union, state, and party bureaucracy. Although Díaz had dedicated her efforts to protecting women's political rights, her latest appointment led her to concentrate on social policy, an area allegedly more well suited to women. However, by the end of that same year, Díaz had died, and the CFO lost its most radical leader.

That same year, Guadalupe Martínez assumed the presidency of the CFO, and its name changed to the Círculo Feminista de Occidente María A. Díaz (CFOMAD). The CFOMAD was active from 1939 until 2002, when Martínez passed away. It is worth clarifying that its members always referred to that organization as the CFO and believed that it had been founded in 1927. They became part of the organized labor movement and were recognized as a legitimate organization. Díaz formed a group of women who worked for more than five decades in the women's sections of the FTJ and the PRI. Some of them were female union leaders, others were city council members or congressional deputies, and only Guadalupe Martínez came to occupy offices of popular election on several occasions, such as federal and state deputy or senate seats.

In 1941 Ana María Hernández, federal labor inspector and president of the Instituto Nacional de Ayuda a la Madre Soltera (National welfare institute for single mothers), along with the CFO and the Liga de Mujeres 10 de Mayo de la Colonia Francisco Villa (Mexico City), founded the Centro de Capacitación Femenina María A. Díaz to honor her memory.⁶⁶ In a similar vein, every year, the members of the CFOMAD commemorate her death.

From Leader to Myth and Symbol

On November 29, 1939, an independent newspaper from Guadalajara reported on the front page that the textile leader María Arcelia Díaz (1898–1939) had died. This event was "cause for mourning at the revolutionary centers of Guadalajara . . . due to the loss of one of the oldest standard bearers of the people."⁶⁷ This newspaper emphasized that Díaz was widely known for her union struggle in Jalisco and predicted that her funeral would be "a true show of sorrow" due to the affection and recognition she had gained by being identified as a tireless "socialist fighter."⁶⁸ The following day, that same daily related on the front page how and who had paid for her posthumous homage and made a detailed description of the different stages of her funeral arrangements. Díaz's body was reverently transferred from her home to the FTJ to be watched over by labor groups and members of the CFO—the literacy and political training center that Díaz had founded in 1927 and that had since become affiliated with the organized labor movement.⁶⁹ Her coffin was taken to the FTJ so that final tribute could be paid to her on the part of labor organizations and women. To honor her work, her coffin was wrapped in two flags: one national (of Mexico) and the other proletariat (red, to represent the workers' struggle).⁷⁰ More than thirty-three political, labor union, teacher, and student organizations stood guard and sent floral arrangements. Both the Federal Education Division and the State Department of Education ordered that each one of the local federal and state schools, the so-called Article 123 centers, and night schools appoint a commission to attend the burial at the Municipal Pantheon. The funeral procession was attended by numerous figures and union representatives who marched down the streets of the city.⁷¹ Before lowering the coffin into the tomb, various ladies of the CFO praised Díaz's life and emphasized that she was "the founder of women's labor unions in Jalisco and the figurehead of feminine vindication,"⁷² a sincere fighter who did not seek riches and who never remained "silent before the sorrows of her poor brethren."⁷³ Like in the French Republican funerals of the state analyzed by Avner Ben-Amos, at Díaz's the values of the political group of the CFO and the FTJ (discipline, loyalty, and so on) interacted. The center of that coalition was the TFJ building and her mobile coffin (carried from Díaz's home to the RTJ and the Mezquitán Cemetery) to draw attention to her status as a fighter for labor unions.[74]

Since the death of María A. Díaz from a heart attack in 1939 to 2002, the CFO, the Sindicato de Trabajadores Automovilistas de Jalisco (SUTAJ), and the FTJ held acts of transference of cultural memory to honor and remember her life and political career.[75] It is vital to point out the importance of these acts and their continuity over the course of sixty-two years. Year after year, this political group composed of teachers, nurses, men, and women workers of the tortilla industry, as well as urban bus drivers and workers in general, celebrated with tributes and funereal ceremonies that included songs, marches played by the CFO band, poems, speeches, and a play regarding her labor and union careers. These rituals had a twofold purpose. On one hand, they reinforced values and bonds not only within the founding group of the CFO but also with the political labor union family that created the CFO, with the drivers of the SUTAJ, and with the labor leaders of the FTJ. On the other hand, a political border was created that prevented building bridges with the new generations of the working class. The preoccupation of this political group formed between the 1920s and 1930s and consolidated in the 1940s with preserving Díaz's figure is striking. The women of the CFO promoted discursive and theatrical representation of Díaz to highlight and preserve the way in which she taught loyalty and discipline to the labor movement—characteristics highly valued in the maintenance of political cohesion and power—and to counteract growing union dissidence once the clientelist and authoritarian practices of the organized labor movement and the party began to be severely questioned in the late 1950s.

In order to understand how the figure of María A. Díaz was constructed and reconstructed, I believe it is pertinent to establish a timeline of this cultural memory that allows us to distinguish how it evolved through time. I have already mentioned the chronicles of the newspaper *Las noticias* that stressed the sorrow and pain shown by feminist, labor, and socialist groups upon the loss of a recognized and respected leader at her death. How was her figure created and re-created after her death? These are questions that will guide me through this section.

Ten days after Díaz's death, a woman named María de Jesús S. de Preciado, probably affiliated with the CFO, dedicated a poem titled "To the Tireless

Heroism of our Sister and Teacher" to Díaz, in which she highlighted her sufferings and struggles. In this poem, the author did not specify concrete dates of the battles Díaz took part in, nor did she list which battles they were. She also did not indicate what her profession was or her political affiliation, nor do we know if it was read during another tribute.[76]

This brief poem contrasts starkly with *La mujer mexicana en la industria textil*, written by Ana María Hernández (schoolteacher of Querétaro and federal inspector of the Labor Department in Mexico City), given that therein, the author incorporated a small biography of Díaz and a chronicle of her funeral, which stated, "From this day forward, María A. Díaz is a symbol to women and the Mexican proletariat, to whom she bequeathed, by her example of struggle and sacrifice, great teachings."[77] *La mujer mexicana* was a book dedicated to female textile workers, whose history, Hernández believed, had been "written in blood [... and it would produce...] a responsible generation, with class consciousness, that would overcome inter-union conflict and unify workers."[78] It is not known how many working men and women of Mexico read this book, but Hernández's intention was that Díaz be evoked as a fighter who formed part of Mexican labor history and who ought to be remembered.

In July 1940, the CFO paid the first tribute to Díaz at the SUTAJ headquarters. The program included musical pieces such as the "Marcha María Arcelia Díaz," "Mujer de Occidente," "Alma Tapatía," and the "Himno Obrero"; a profile was presented, an acrostic was read, the declamation "To María" was recited, the representative of the SUTAJ spoke, and an elegy was presented.[79] The structure of this act of mourning showed that the recognition paid by the CFO and the SUTAJ to Díaz, due to its seriousness, was very much similar to the civic celebrations that ritualized the collective memory of the Mexican nation.[80] The CFO and the SUTAJ recalled their bonds with Díaz and the experiences they shared in the labor struggles spanning the 1920s and 30s. Through Díaz's figure, they initiated their own historical narrative of the collective memory centered on Díaz, her union, and political family. The "Marcha María Arcelia Díaz" was written by Guadalupe Martínez, one of the founders of the CFO. In the "Marcha," Martínez refers to the fact that Díaz was always a leader who guided the workers and protected them, uniting them so that they would fight for their rights, which was the reason why they remembered her.[81] On the other hand, the "Himno Obrero," written by Víctores Prieto on May 1, 1940, invited workers to remain united and be guided by honor, work, and science, values that ought to form part of their duty and social action.[82]

I do not have in my possession the program of the second memorial ceremony, but I do have fragmented information. A letter sent by Magdalena Velasco de la Mora from Córdoba, Veracruz, to the executive committee of the CFOMAD in November 1941 recalled some of Díaz's practices and speeches. The letter said she had taught them to "not back down, [to move] always forward and so, triumph" and that "Jalisco never loses and when it loses, it takes away"—a saying that Díaz proffered at the 1934 Congreso Nacional de Mujeres Obreras y Campesinas in Guadalajara when she beat the communists. Velasco believed that these practices and heroic speeches should not be forgotten and declared, "Jalisco never loses due to the emancipation of its women, and it takes away because of [its] justice."[83] That same year, Joaquín Cano wrote a few lines for the second tribute and maintained that Díaz deserved a statue in Guadalajara "because her role was great and sublime: the emancipation of womankind, especially the working woman."[84]

The programs of tributes four through six were very similar to the first, with a formal and ritualized structure in which members of both the CFO and SUTAJ participated, as well as the FTJ, in the SUTAJ building. In some invitations, it was specified that there would be two memorial ceremonies: one at the municipal cemetery in the morning and the other at the SUTAJ at night. Starting with the eighth tribute in 1947, two transformations took place: one was spatial, given that the memorial act was transferred from the facilities of the automotive union to the Workers' Federation building. That year, Hernández Loza had already retaken leadership of the latter, and added to the program was a speech by a representative of the Partido Revolucionario Institucional (PRI). Her historical narrative had begun to be associated with that of the dominant political party.

In 1949, on the tenth anniversary of Díaz's death, the teacher Josefina C. de Gorjón presented a biographical profile in which she referred to María A. Díaz as a multidimensional figure, given that she was a worker of humble means as well as a forerunner and a pioneer of labor unions. She recalled that together with other female textile workers from Jalisco (like Guadalupe Rendón and María Juárez), María Arcelia challenged the bosses to create the labor union affiliated to the CROM in 1922 and succeeded in

FIG. 19. Pamphlet of María A. Díaz's death anniversary. Courtesy of Guadalupe Martínez.

composing a strong faction. She indicated that the Mexican Revolution was Díaz's school, recognizing her as one of the members of the feminist movement in Guadalajara and the founder of the CFO. She mentioned that during her lifetime, she confronted envy, intrigue, and ingratitude, but "she did not wish to overshadow the triumphs of others, nor sell out her principles."[85]

On the eleventh anniversary (1950), the memorial program was governed by the same structure. The speech read by one of the members of the SUTAJ, like that of the teacher Gorjón from the previous year, emphasized Díaz's humble origins, her commitment to the workers, the persecution she had suffered, and her death—all the while immersed in the greatest poverty "because she never accepted kickbacks."[86] This year, the importance of one of Díaz's mottos, the emancipation of women, was not mentioned. These contrasting visions of Díaz by women and men were more evident in the monthly FTJ newspaper during the mid-1950s until 1960. On the one hand, the newspaper promoted scientific motherhood for working-class women, while on the other, it emphasized the constant struggle women faced for acceptance in the realms of unions and party politics.[87] Representations of Díaz were reaccommodated to the political motives of the FTJ. This occurred for both political and personal reasons. Guadalupe Martínez and Heliodoro Hernández Loza were married in 1949. Following that year, Guadalupe moderated her political discourse of female liberation to emphasize the role of women in benefiting others.

Guadalupe Martínez de Hernández Loza published a small pamphlet dedicated to Díaz on the thirty-fifth anniversary of her death, in 1974. In contrast with earlier biographies, in this one, Martínez expressed her position regarding the figure of Díaz after more than three decades—and the effect of time on her memory. Therefore, she specified, "we don't know how many years it takes for truth to become fiction, facts to become legend, and the legend starts to form history in our acts, that become doctrine, that become banners in our vocation."[88] She succinctly presented the origins of Díaz, extracts from her childhood and the harsh workdays she experienced in the textile factories, and the ways in which she challenged patronizing patterns and contributed to the improvement of women's education. She highlighted María Arcelia's role in founding beloved and trusted labor organizations. She mentioned that the textile town La Experiencia had a street with her name. She concluded that Díaz was found among the ranks of other women who

FIG. 20. Mural at the Federación de Trabajadores de Jalisco. Author photograph.

had struggled, such as Elvia Carrillo Puerto and Rosa Torres of Yucatán, Hermila Galindo of Veracruz, and Florinda Lazos León of Chiapas. And yet with all this, the struggle must continue.

The image of María A. Díaz in this pamphlet is like the representation of a schoolteacher. It is not an original photograph of her but a heavily retouched portrait. If compared to photographs from the time of the creation of the UOLE in 1922 and that of the CFO in 1937, in this one from 1974, as well as those included in the first memorial tribute under the official role of the CFO, the use of spectacles, a suit jacket, and serious countenance are noteworthy. In the photographs dated 1922 and 1937, Díaz looks more serene. Perhaps Guadalupe Martínez chose that profile because she was a schoolteacher and, in doing so, revisited her own ideals of womanhood. During the 1920s, teachers upheld the archetypes promoted by the Secretaría de Educación Pública (SEP) and by Gabriela Mistral—archetypes of teachers as disciplined and strong. In an increasingly feminized profession, they invoked masculine qualities.[89] However, Martínez's perspective differed from that of the SEP and Mistral; she believed that mothers and schoolteachers should not be apolitical. Instead, she held a politicized vision of the schoolteacher as someone who should actively work to improve the living and working conditions of both the masses and women. Díaz represented all of this.

That same year the new FTJ building was inaugurated (1974), and the following year, a mural was painted in its auditorium; however, it does not

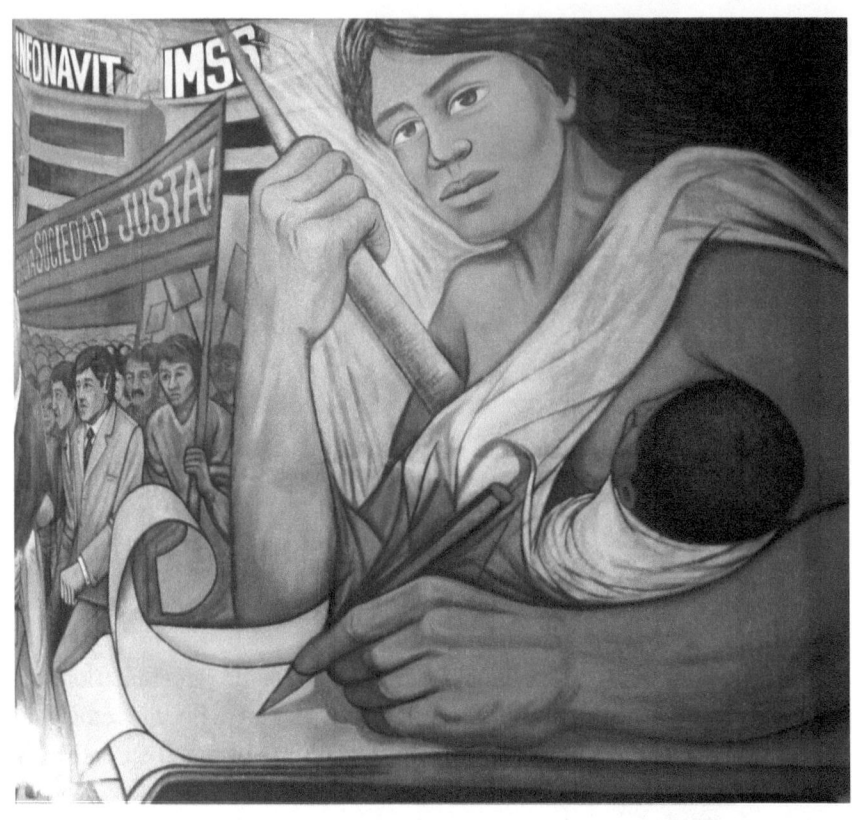

FIG. 21. "The Motherland" depicted in the mural of the Federación de Trabajadores de Jalisco. Author photograph.

bear a date for composition, nor is it known who designed and painted it. This image gives us an idea of how the leaders of that organization perceived the role of men and women in the organized labor movement and how Díaz was remembered. At the center of the mural, the figures of male labor leaders stand out (Fidel Velásquez of the CTM, Heliodoro Hernández of the FTJ, and Blas Chumacero of the FTP), accompanied by only two female leaders (Díaz and Martínez), and in the background are the workers exploited by industries, who struggle and march to demand their labor rights. Women workers were not painted, but they did include the Motherland as a marginal female figure. In this mural, the countenance of Díaz is very similar to that of the image seen in the pamphlet from 1974, in which she

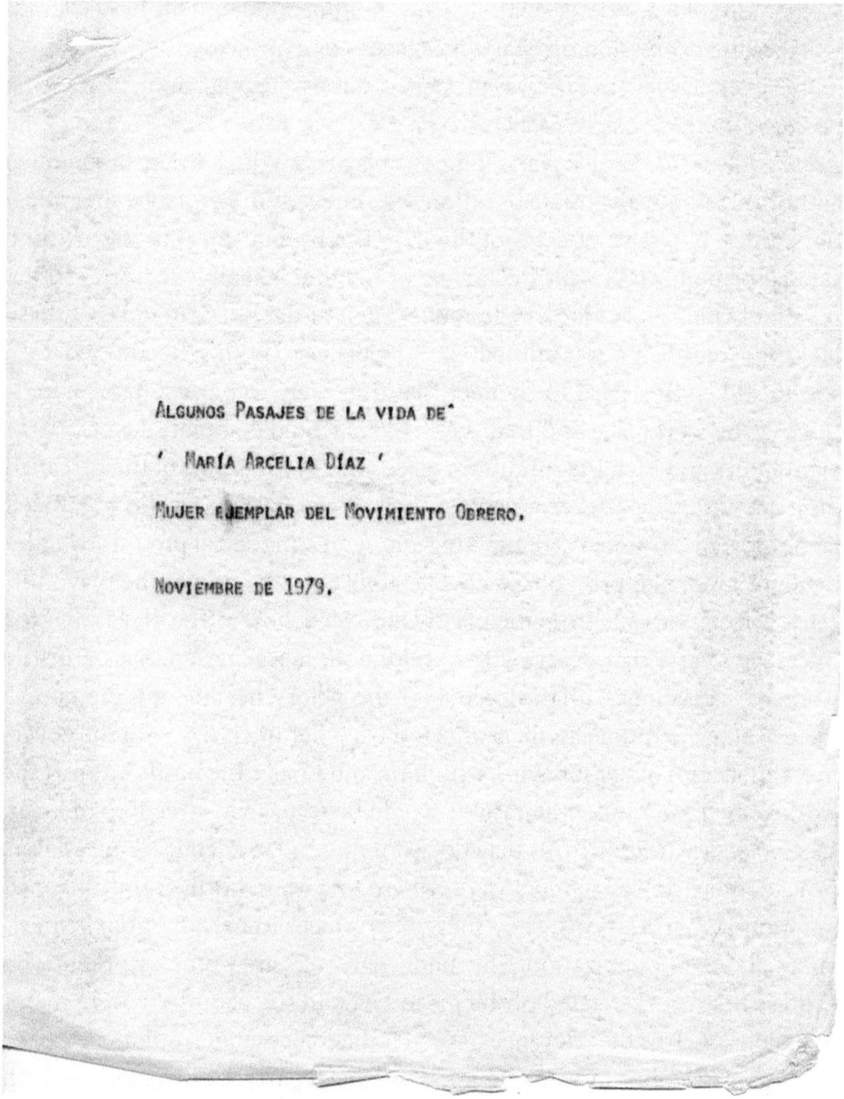

ALGUNOS PASAJES DE LA VIDA DE

' MARÍA ARCELIA DÍAZ '

MUJER EJEMPLAR DEL MOVIMIENTO OBRERO.

NOVIEMBRE DE 1979.

FIG. 22. Title page of the play *Some Passages from the Life of María Arcelia Díaz*. Courtesy of Guadalupe Martínez.

looks more like a serious schoolteacher holding a document in her hand, whereas the expression on Martínez's face is one of sorrow.

In November 1979, a play was presented at the FTJ auditorium, titled *Some Passages from the Life of María Arcelia Díaz: An Exemplary Woman of the Labor Movement*. Twelve pages long, the play was written by an anonymous author in a political climate of union discontent and dissidence that questioned the repressive policies of the FTJ. The Federación was maintaining said labor policy still with the arrival of the first assembly factories to the region of Guadalajara in the late 1960s. The FTJ did not demand that these factories fulfill what was stipulated in labor laws (both state and federal), specifically with regard to the fact that they were to have suitable conditions at the workplace and that the workers would complete a workday of eight hours and earn the minimum wage. The FTJ was part of the so-called political alliance between the state, the official party, and the organized labor movement, aimed at containing and repressing social protests by independent unions to promote political stability. As the title of the play indicates, select moments from the life of Díaz were chosen. The play is divided into seven parts that describe her childhood, her experiences as a textile worker, her relations with the foreman of the factory, her attempts to improve the working conditions in the textile industry, her interview with the governor, the success of her lobbying with him, and finally, the notification of the workers that their individual rights would be respected—freedom of labor, speech, and education. This play does not present any details about María's private life (who her parents were, where they were born, and if they had any political affiliation); they merely emphasized certain labor experiences and her politicization. The main characters are women workers who express their work-related problems to Díaz. In the play, there were major omissions, such as the relevance of gender difference among union members, the organized labor movement, and the official party. Confrontations with bosses and foremen were selectively highlighted. A positive and courageous image was provided of those men who supported her in her union struggle, such as other textile workers and the governor. The authoritarian policies that Díaz implemented to instill discipline and loyalty were not mentioned, nor were the political differences she may have had with other women allied with the labor movement. The FTJ and CFOMAD arduously sought discipline and loyalty, practices that were highly valued and rewarded. For that reason, it was fundamental to them to selectively reproduce Díaz's labor participation. She was the model to be followed by the new generations of the FTJ and PRI because they presented her as someone who had a strong bond with the needy but who would neither endorse dissidence nor question the authoritarianism of these corporate institutions. I have no information regarding whether it was ever staged, who performed the play, who produced it, or who and how many were in the audience. But it does illustrate how the group of the CFO gradually transformed technologies of cultural memory. This short, schematic play is an example of this.

By 1983, the CFO was celebrating the fiftieth anniversary of its foundation. At the ceremony, they underlined the fact that since 1933, weekly sessions had been held. However, the first tributes in the 1940s and the certificate of foundation of the CFO indicate that its establishment was before 1933. What stood out in the memorial celebration of 1983 was its more institutionalized discourse, linked to the historical narrative of the dominant party. Díaz was identified as a member of the working class who had been struggling and inspired since 1929 by the postulates of the Partido Revolucionario Institucional (PRI). That year, the party was still the PNR, not the PRI. To the leader of the CFO, Guadalupe Martínez, the PNR and the PRI were the same institution, given that they shared a common past. By 1983, it was evident there had been a major change to the memorial ceremony, which had been transformed from a tribute and ritual that praised the figure of Díaz into a celebration that spoke to the career and participation of the Jaliscan woman in the political and social circles of Mexico. In other words, it should be considered that women were still re-creating and rethinking how to commemorate Díaz and the past of the CFO. In addition to the evening memorial service, there were also other cultural events, and the anniversary of Adolfo Ruiz Cortines was celebrated.

After the death of Hernández Loza on May 30, 1990, the new leaders of the FTJ expelled the women of the CFO from the building they had shared. The CFO could no longer rely on administrative personnel to assist them in the logistics of anniversary events. The last visit of the Martínez sisters, Guadalupe and Dolores, to the tomb of María A. Díaz at the Mezquitán Cemetery was on November 28, 2001. Early the following year, in January 2002, both passed away. As the FTJ-CFO political faction fell apart, along came the transition from a corporate state to a neoliberal one, where

FIG. 23. Mural at the Labor Department of the State of Jalisco. Author photograph.

workers' demands were no longer a priority. Simultaneously, citizens more forcefully demanded the crystallization of democratic change in electoral processes and the Mexican political system. This had repercussions on the PRI, which was weakened, and the historic alliance between that party and the organized labor movement. As a result, the unions and their worn-out federations confronted the violation of their labor rights daily.

Of all the women in the early twentieth century, Díaz stands out as a feminist worker who struggled for women's rights. Research regarding feminism in Mexico has concentrated on studying middle-class feminists who were often schoolteachers or held some profession, such as doctors or lawyers. Feminists Hermila Galindo and Elvia Carrillo Puerto are frequently associated with the revolutionary strongmen who served as their patrons.[90] Few cases of working women who held political office and were feminists have been salvaged through serious study.[91]

The case of María A. Díaz helps us understand the interconnections between feminism—regional, national, and international—revolutionary strongmen, the organized labor movement, and the conflict between church and state, but above all, it helps us understand the political and gender negotiations that took place in daily life during the formation of the new state and new political relations of power. Diaz's case also highlights the shifting dynamics of power in her subaltern status as "the Other," transforming her marginalization and invisibility into empowerment and visibility. The family life and the labor, union, and political career of Díaz is fragmented because, as Jean Franco has rightly pointed out, the positions of discourse have been characterized by a series of clashes, discontinuities, and violence.[92] Her life story illustrates how her family and labor background were a strong influence that would later turn her into a union leader and defender of the rights of women. Also, her case helps us understand how women workers participated in and influenced the revolutionary process by means of an alliance with the new state and with other women. Díaz played a crucial role in the dispute between Catholic and Red unions; in strikes; as a union leader; as president of two women's organizations (CEM and CFO); as a labor, health, and welfare inspector; as a representative of workers before the Board of Conciliation and Arbitration; and as a delegate from Jalisco to the convention for the creation of the PRM. These roles present her as an exceptional woman due to her intense political and union work. Paradoxically, the new revolutionary state, on a local level, did not grant her the legitimacy that would have placed her at the center of the debate on labor policy. On the contrary, it allowed her to wield pressure from the margins as an "honorary" labor inspector, or by appointing her as social welfare inspector and working exclusively maternalistic policies. Her legacy was the creation of a political agenda for working women in the workplace, in her union, in the organized labor movement, and in the official party.

For sixty-two years, the CFOMAD celebrated different memorial events with different characteristics, in which they created and constructed their own historical narrative depending on the period and their audience. Those of the 1940s and 50s were quite formal, very similar to civic ceremonies. Over the decades they lost that formality, in part because this political group failed at integrating many young people. Their elderly or founding members died off, grew sick, or retired. In some cases, their daughters or nieces continued to attend. However, over all this time, the Martínez sisters, Guadalupe and Dolores, were the promoters and organizers of tributes to Díaz; they sought to selectively re-create her actions and interweave them with those of the CFO, the SUTAJ, and the FTJ. They were perceived as outstanding historical figures in the union struggle; they always wanted to keep this record alive because it dignified them, allowing them to lay claim to recognition for their work and their political project of instilling discipline and loyalty in the working class. They considered it to be more important to promote the unity of workers with certain benefits than an autonomous, combative labor movement. Through these rituals, the women of the CFO identified themselves as heirs to a revolutionary class culture yet would not publicly admit that they had adapted to authoritarian, corporate, and patriarchal political and labor structures. All this, they silenced and denied.

5

María Guadalupe Martínez Villanueva
The Mobilization of Women and Corporatist Politics

In early 2002, María Guadalupe Martínez Villanueva, the widow of Heliodoro Hernández Loza (1906–2002), left this life. Her political career is representative of a generation that participated not only in the revolutionary process (1918–40), the construction of the new state, and the formation of modern corporate institutions but also in cacique union practices. Due to the authority and control she came to possess, the press in Guadalajara presented Martínez Villanueva as a female icon of the PRI regime in Jalisco.[1] Her name was almost always associated with that of Heliodoro Hernández Loza (1898–1990), who was the leader of the Federación de Trabajadores de Jalisco (FTJ) for forty-three years and general secretary of the Sindicato Único de Trabajadores Automovilistas de Jalisco (SUTAJ). However, Martínez did not participate actively in politics because she was Hernández's wife and hence charged with functions of social volunteerism, as is the case of all those who are married to municipal presidents, governors, and presidents of the republic. However, upon examining her life story and political career, it becomes evident that she entered politics long before she even met him.

In this chapter, I will describe how Martínez not only created a political space to discuss matters related to working women and women in general but also contributed to and collaborated in the training of a political faction of men and women who would aid in the consolidation of the *cacicazgo* and union bureaucracy of Hernández Loza. Both were political and cultural go-betweens with different needs and demands who moved among male and female workers of the official party, the government, and other labor leaders. As leaders of the organized labor movement, they backed conservative policies that controlled and subjugated workers with the objective of achieving economic development and political stability in the region.

In general, studies about the organized labor movement and rural, urban, and labor *cacicazgos* have focused solely on male figures.[2] If women are mentioned in *cacicazgos*, they are not analyzed from a gender perspective.[3] However, the historians Francie Chassen-López and Heather Fowler-Salamani have delved into female *cacicazgo* from a gender perspective. Chassen-López analyzes the case of Juana Catarina Romero on the Isthmus of Tehuantepec and her use of informal politics during the Porfiriato to become a cacique.[4] She suggests that access to economic power by means of the accumulation of wealth allowed Juana Catarina Romero to wield economic and political authority over her clientele on the Isthmus of Tehuantepec to such a degree that she came to be more important than the political boss of that region. Fowler-Salamini, on the other hand, identifies a flexible, collective postrevolutionary female *cacicazgo* within the Sindicato de Obreras Escogedoras de Café de Córdoba, affiliated with the CROM, from 1930 to 1960.[5] The case of Guadalupe Martínez is also a collective female *cacicazgo* but one within a hierarchical union structure characterized by male domination. This chapter examines how Heliodoro Hernández and Guadalupe Martínez's *cacicazgo* was constructed and consolidated, how it was reproduced, and how it declined. As in any other union *cacicazgo*, these "*cacias*, strongwomen, encouraged solidarity and union discipline through obligatory participation in union activities and the stigmatization of undesirable behavior. They exploited the closed shop stipulation promised in the constitution (1917) to shut out newcomers. They compelled female workers to attend weekly meetings on Tuesday evenings and when they were absent, publicly scolded them or even threatened to dock their wages for the day."[6] Fowler-Salamini concludes that men and women alike practiced strong-arm tactics. In counterbalance to the male union strongmen, the strongwomen of Orizaba did not resort to physical violence to discipline their affiliates. Rather, they relied on "the threat of job loss to negotiate commitments and maintain discipline inside or outside the factory."[7] The power of these caciques was more subtle and flexible.

By exploring the lives of Heliodoro Hernández and Guadalupe Martínez as part of the same union and *cacicazgo*, we see that their political alliances were significant not only as a couple but as one that mediated between their superiors and their base. From this gender perspective, the following questions emerge: Who was Guadalupe Martínez? Who was Heliodoro

Hernández Loza? When and how did each of them enter the organized labor movement and politics? What was the gender order each of them promoted? What bonds were there between Hernández and his working-class male base? What kinds of contacts were there between Hernández and the female sections of the FTJ and PRM/PRI? What were the interactions like between Martínez and her working-class female base? What bonds were there between Martínez and the male sections of the FTJ and PRM/PRI? How were the notions of traditional patriarchy, the modernization of patriarchy, and traditional and revolutionary motherhood adjusted and negotiated within a male-dominated hierarchically structured labor union in the FTJ?

To answer these questions, first I must examine why the studies regarding caciquismo, or bosses, have not included women as an integral part of cacique power and why studies of women and gender use other categories to analyze women in politics rather than resorting to the cacique concept. Both perspectives analyze issues of power and politics, but they begin from different theoretical questions and therefore arrive at different answers. I argue that the combination of both makes the term *politics* less rigid, allowing us to explore the activities and cultural politics of men and women as coparticipants in *cacicazgos*, in the construction of the new state, and in corporate institutions. This kind of analysis contributes to distinguishing and comparing different discourses and practices in terms of what a man or a woman ought to be in politics. However, these discourses and practices were by no means static. They changed depending on the conflicts they faced to adapt and survive new political conditions. Secondly, to analyze these ambivalences, I present the story of the lives and political careers of Martínez and Hernández, how each of them changed over time, and how they consolidated their *cacicazgo* in the late 1940s. Their *cacicazgo* was achieved by means of political exchanges between their base and their superiors that translated into wage increases, benefits, union and bureaucratic positions, and political loyalties.

Finally, I conclude that three factors were crucial to ensure that the *cacicazgo* of Heliodoro Hernández and Guadalupe Martínez would last well into the 1990s: (1) Strong loyalty to Fidel Velásquez and the CTM and the PRI, manifested in a following very close to the so-called historic alliance—a coalition between workers, the party, and the state that was assembled to control the labor movement and benefit industrial development. Likewise, their political support was shown through the mobilization of major blocs during the electoral campaigns and political meetings. (2) They did not break away from their base political group formed during the 1930s, 40s, and 50s because they established a system of brokering political allegiances. The members of their political group were also required to show them loyalty and fidelity. (3) Finally, in the late 1950s and early 60s, two new groups—women and youth—played a central role in counteracting criticism of the authoritarian Mexican political system. The long-in-coming recognition of the right to women's suffrage (in 1947 and 1953) allowed Martínez, together with other women from the labor sector of the FTJ and the PRI, to win electoral office and provide state and federal representation as deputies, senators, and city council members starting in the late 1950s. Through these posts, they not only contributed to extending the control over electoral districts wielded under the *cacicazgo* of Hernández Loza, but they also created a forum for women's issues within the FTJ and PRI, albeit through a vertical, authoritarian power structure. They did not allow new generations to seek more democratic, less authoritarian practices upon entering this group. There was room made only for those youths trained within their own rank and file. However, following the death of Hernández in 1990, the fragmentation of this political family began. The divisions were accentuated because Hernández and Martínez had no descendants. They did, however, create very strong bonds with fictive kin—"sons" and "daughters" who were loyal followers during their lifetimes.

Shaping Jalisco's Political Landscape through Women's Activism and Union Power

The life and political career of Martínez Villanueva show some elements similar to the characteristics of traditional caciques. She fulfilled the role of a political and cultural go-between for the female workers and male leaders of the organized labor movement and the official party.[8] Her role as a mediator was determined by the influences of different processes—the revolutionary process, the conflict between church and state, the emergence of the labor movement, the incipient feminist movement, the Normal School, and changes in the labor force. Likewise, various people or different groups wielded a great influence on her to fulfill the role of political and cultural intermediary. Government functionaries would contribute significantly to her becoming a legitimate leader with a certain degree of authority.

FIG. 24. *Effective Suffrage, No Reelection*, tableaux vivant, 1912. Biographical album "Una mujer y su destino," 1. Courtesy of Guadalupe Martínez.

First and foremost, Martínez Villanueva was a product of the proletarian origins of her family and the nineteenth-century liberal ideas of her father, David Martínez. Her parents came from textile towns—Juanacatlán and La Escoba. Her father was a house painter and electrician; her mother, María Villanueva, was a textile worker. Her case is outstanding because her father introduced her to the labor movement and politics as early as the mid-1910s. As a liberal, David Martínez participated in the antireelectionist clubs to defeat the Porfirio Díaz dictatorship and to support the candidacy of Francisco I. Madero. He favored the Constitucionalista government of Manuel M. Diéguez (1914–19), which promoted anticlericalism. He collaborated in the founding of the Casa del Obrero Mundial (COM) in Guadalajara. Influenced by anarcho-syndicalist ideas, the COM sought to do away with the capitalist system and the power of the Catholic Church, encouraging workers to go on strike and organize through labor unions. David Martínez brought Guadalupe along to COM meetings and registered her in their iconoclast school, directed by anticlerical schoolteachers who were pioneers in the feminist movement in Guadalajara, such as Atala Apodaca.[9] In this school, Guadalupe fraternized with the children of workers, who learned that they ought to free themselves from the Catholic religion, favor the unionization of workers, and support the ideals of the Mexican Revolution of 1910.

David Martínez instilled nineteenth-century liberal values in his children so that they would feel "love for their fatherland." Martínez taught his children great respect for the 1857 constitution and for Benito Juárez, who had freed Mexico from French intervention. He taught them to value democracy, justice, and the dignity of working people. These values were transmitted through tableaux vivant at workers' meetings that they acted themselves and that were later consigned to paintings.[10] Likewise, David Martínez brought not only liberal ideals into his home but also those of the COM. He asked his children and wife to stop attending church, given its participation in the exploitation of workers.[11] He believed that this practice would free his children from exploitation and religious ideals, allowing them to become teachers and intellectuals with active roles in society and the public sphere.

Emergence of Female Political and Cultural Intermediation: The Founding of the Círculo Feminista de Occidente (CFO)

These nineteenth-century liberal and working-class values intertwined with Martínez's Normal School formation and with the development of the labor movement in Guadalajara. Upon completing her studies at the Normal School in 1927, Martínez became one of the founders of the CFO.[12] Like María A. Díaz in her initial stage, from 1927 to 1930, the CFO worked with female cracker makers, women in the tortilla-making industry, female shoemakers, domestic workers, and seamstresses so that they could form their own unions. Likewise, it promoted secular morality as an alternative to Catholicism. This new morality sought to grant women civil and labor rights—that is to say, the right to have a job, a minimum wage, to form a union, and to demand equality in the workplace as indicated in the 1917 constitution. Within the CFO, women were encouraged to reproduce the combative approach of the German Rosa Luxemburg, the Paris Commune radical Louise Michel, the Russian Alexandra Kollontai, and the six hundred women of Haymarket Square, where anarchists were martyred in their struggle for an eight-hour workday.[13]

During this period, men and women in the organized labor movement learned through coercive practices (physical and verbal violence) the practices of discipline, honor, and responsibility within the male-dominated union hierarchical structure. In the CFO, Martínez observed how María A. Díaz carried out her political work with other working women in the Labor Department and with Governor Ramírez. Díaz taught CFO members the meaning of "Jalisco never loses, and when it loses, it takes away," especially when it came to politics.[14] For Díaz and the women of the CFO, this slogan meant possessing sufficient strength and control to gain the upper hand—by nondemocratic, violent means if necessary. Violent tactics were not exclusive to men. Like male labor leaders, Díaz and the women of the CFO learned that in politics, it was important to partake of both coercion and negotiation to consolidate a political force. They knew they could not remain on the margins of the political and labor organizations directed by men. They had to form alliances with them to exert pressure and achieve their own goals.

This was evident in the Second National Feminist Congress of Women Workers and Peasants that was held in Mexico City in 1933, where there was a strong, violent confrontation between the communists and members of the PNR over women's emancipation.[15] Whereas the communists argued for separate organizations for women and workers, the PNR favored integrating women into the organizations under its tutelage.[16] As a result of these intense debates and disagreements during the Congress, two permanent commissions were formed: one of communists and the other of PNR members. The CFO participated in the latter. As a representative of the CFO, Díaz suggested that the Third Congress be held in Guadalajara in 1934. Because the CFO decided to take the Congress out of Mexico City, the communists refused to

FIG. 25. The board of directors of the Círculo Feminista de Occidente. Biographical album "Una mujer y su destino," 1. Courtesy of Guadalupe Martínez.

recognize the PNR commission and did not attend the following Congress in Guadalajara. Despite the absence of the communists, during the following Congress, some of the CFO workers and teachers carried firearms and sharp weapons to ensure their dominion.[17]

The information I gathered from various archives did not allow me to learn with precision exactly how long Martínez was secretary general of the CFO, but I was able to identify the following years: 1932, 1934, 1939–40. In 1934, she was also director of *Fémina roja*, a newspaper dedicated to the social doctrines of women's groups in the COJ. In 1940, she became secretary general of the state committee of the Frente Único Pro Derechos de la Mujer. As was the case with the flexible female *cacicazgo* of the coffee pickers of

Orizaba, this fragmented data regarding the CFO indicates that the board of directors rotated between the schoolteachers Martínez, Concha Robledo, Ramona Aguilar, and Amalia Mendoza throughout the 1930s and into the 1950s. These last two women ran for posts of popular election and represented the women's labor sector in the administration of the Ayuntamiento of Guadalajara and as state deputies. Meanwhile, Martínez Villanueva traded the office of secretary general of the CFO for more important political positions: secretary of feminine action on the regional committee of the PRI and FTJ. Throughout her life, Martínez directed and supervised the activities of the CFO, and toward the end, she became president of this organization.

Formation of a Women's Political Group within the Labor Movement

The analysis of the formation of the CFO women's political group and its collaboration with the conservative faction of Hernández Loza in the late 1920s and early 1930s helps us understand how the *cacicazgo* of the labor union that would form years later came into being. Specifically, the case study of the politicization and unionization of women in the corn-grinding industry illustrates how CFO workers allied with teachers; established a coalition with Heliodoro Hernández Loza, leader of the COJ; and negotiated within sometimes violent situations.

The labor of discipline and integration of the political faction of the CFO can clearly be appreciated in the case of Ana María Hernández Lucas, a former leader of six hundred tortilla makers and member of the CFO who was politically trained by Martínez. The women of the CFO and those of the corn-grinding industry allied to denounce the abuses of the owners of the corn mills and the macho, corrupt practices of their coworkers and union leaders who, in addition to failing to defend them, collaborated with the mill owners to dismiss them from qualified positions. And yet they still charged them union quotas to be spent in the cantinas.[18]

Hernández Lucas mentions that Díaz and Martínez Villanueva were always present when they were needed for the union struggle.[19] They were counseled on how to organize a union, how to carry out a strike, how to draft their demands, and how to agree to negotiate only after their demands had been met. Likewise, Ana María Hernández thought of Díaz and Martínez Villanueva as sisters, as part of her family, because they always took an interest in working women, asking whether they had eaten, whether they had paid their rent or needed any money. If they had problems, Díaz and Martínez would assist them. But in turn, Ana María Hernández recalls that she and other female leaders like Refugio Santa María (leader of dough dispensaries) and Jovita Robles (leader of corn grinders), among others, had to learn certain rules to become female leaders and direct women in the corn-grinding industry: they had to convey to their base the importance of loyalty to their union and their political base, as well as avoid being seen as mere "political agitators." They were loyal to the group of Heliodoro Hernández and Catarino Isaac (1910–94), leader of the corn grinders. During a process that brought with it great violence, they followed instructions, even though the events resulted in the murder of a shoe shiner. They refused to acknowledge the group opposing Hernández and applied the closed-shop rule at work and in their labor unions.[20]

These female leaders and their subordinates learned the golden rules of political barter: discipline, responsibility, and solidarity in May Day parades, political protests,[21] and electoral campaigns. In exchange, the COJ and, later on, the FTJ would back them in their demands for salary increases, annual vacations, rest on Sundays and holidays, insurance in the event of sickness and maternity leave, support for their basketball teams, and finally, opportunities for promotion inside and outside their labor unions. They followed Heliodoro Hernández's strategies by using extortion and going on strikes to exert pressure so that a set number of workers would be employed.[22]

Hence the 1930s were one of the most crucial, yet ambivalent stages in the career of Martínez and the CFO. On the one hand, they advocated in favor of women and working women, with literacy campaigns, unionization, and politicization. They became part of the female section of the PNR and joined the Frente Único Pro Derechos de la Mujer (FUPDM). Martínez in particular fought for the rights of working women, helping them organize (above all those in the corn-grinding industry); she taught them to read and write, given that these were key tools in the labor union struggle; she participated in the establishment of night schools for workers; she favored the introduction of a socialist education; she participated in two (out of three) feminist congresses for working women and peasants (1933–34); and she demanded before the state committee of the PNR that the feminine section be represented by a woman from the working class, given that she would

FIG. 26. Heliodoro Hernández Loza and María Guadalupe Martínez, labor leaders of the Federación de Trabajadores de Jalisco. Biographical album "Una mujer y su destino," 1. Courtesy of Guadalupe Martínez.

already have had experience in the formation of political organizations. She strongly opposed this section being directed by a woman from the middle class, exerting pressure for her to be replaced by a CFO representative. Finally, she joined the massive campaign of the FUPDM, together with the CFO, in its struggle for women's suffrage in the mid-1930s.

On the other hand, Martínez Villanueva and the women of the CFO joined the conservative wing of the COJ represented by Heliodoro Hernández Loza, who, in turn, had formed a coalition with the Callista governor Sebastián Allende (1932–35). Together, they promoted a campaign against communist leaders who had worked in textiles, mining, and the electrical power industry, implementing a labor policy against strikes, stoppages, and sabotage.[23] Those workers who followed Heliodoro Hernández would have secure employment in any public works—highway and street construction, urbanization—overseen by Governor Allende.[24]

Despite this environment of political agitation, due to the effects of the 1929 economic crisis that generated the displacement of major traditional business by small, more dynamic and numerous industries;[25] widespread unemployment; a change in the configuration of the labor force from industrial, qualified workers to farm workers, artisans, and workers in the service industry; and the resurgence of progressive forces in the 1920s, allied with Cardenismo, Governor Allende sought social stability in order to encourage industrial development. Meanwhile, Heliodoro Hernández took advantage of this opportunity to try to consolidate his leadership of the COJ but with more conservative, less combative or autonomous politics than the communists—politics that tended to favor workers in the service area.[26]

Which begs the question, Why did this alliance take place between the women of the COJ and its conservative wing? Despite his conservative and pro-working-man politics, Hernández permitted access to women to consolidate his leadership position. It is likely that he imagined that once the cause was won, women would return to their "traditional and natural" role as wives and mothers of the working class, thus abandoning politics and the workplace. However, this was not the case. The women of the CFO felt entitled to work side by side with men, but they were not willing to push aside their own agenda regarding women's issues. They exerted pressure to conserve that space within the COJ and PRN.

Creation of a Political Family

Most of the studies about the organized labor movement and the *cacicazgo* of Hernández Loza have pointed out his corrupt and nepotistic politics, but they have not described in detail how he created his base or the relationship it had with women.[27] Once Hernández had become the leader of service sector workers, he then forged different kinds of bonds with different men and women; he imposed himself as the patriarch and cacique in order to fulfill the functions of a moral guide and protector while, at the same time, recurring to coercion. He protected male and female workers through the creation and consolidation of his labor unions so that they would become a loyal, faithful base. Although he unequally distributed the benefits of the consolidation of his *cacicazgo*, working-class men and women and their respective families benefited not only through the assurance of jobs and labor contracts that guaranteed a minimum wage, annual vacations, and medical insurance but also through the promotion of education, housing, and sports. His innermost circle succeeded in forming part of the union bureaucracy by occupying elected office as *regidores*, members of city council, and local and federal deputies.

As a public figure, he practiced paternalistic relations with men, not unlike those of a father with his sons. The case of Catarino Isaac (1910–94), a leader of the corn grinders, illustrates this kind of relationship. Isaac was orphaned at the age of eight. His father had been a sweeper in the San Juan de Dios market. Hernández exerted pressure for Isaac to inherit the position of his father because he had no other kind of professional training. Afterward, he brought Isaac, his mother, and his sisters to work in the corn-grinding mills. There, Isaac got his start as a loader and distributor of dough. He would later form part of the board of directors of the Sindicato de Trabajadores en Molinos para Nixtamal y Similares (STMNS) and eventually held the post of general secretary. In the fierce struggle for the unionization of workers in the corn-grinding industry, Catarino Isaac formed an alliance with Heliodoro Hernández and the women of the CFO. Isaac's career was also similar to that of Hernández because after being secretary general of the STMNS, he was also secretary general of the FTJ from 1938 to 1939 and 1990 to 1993. Likewise, he was elected a deputy of congress twice: once federal (1942–45) and once state (1971–73).[28] Not unlike Hernández, he transformed the motto of the CTM—"For the emancipation of Mexico"—to support "the emancipation of the worker." Moreover, the closest followers and relatives of Isaac became owners of corn-grinding mills themselves. Initially, Isaac was Hernández's "fictive kin" son, but later they became compadres to strengthen and confirm not only their family ties but their political ties as well. In addition to the male line, the bonds of *compadrazgo* (co-parenting) were extended among women as well. The group of Hernández and Martínez became an extended family that spent birthdays, baptisms, and saint's days together.[29]

Meanwhile, Hernández also established paternalistic relations with the women of the FTJ. Anita Hernández, a tortilla-making leader, opined that Heliodoro was an exemplary and inspirational leader. He taught them the values of honesty, education, respect, and discipline.[30] He instructed them not to be agitators, underscoring that "one must always work face forward, chin high, hat tilted and scarf on; never with heads bowed, and always looking out for the betterment of the workers."[31] For Anita Hernández and other men and women of the corn-grinding industry, changing their submissive attitude toward owners and foremen and feeling proud of their labor identity made them feel that they could exercise their rights.

The relationship Hernández formed with María Guadalupe Martínez Villanueva was different from those he sustained with Catarino Isaac and Anita Hernández. The latter two were his loyal followers, as if they were his own children. But Martínez, unlike most men and women in the service area who did not know how to read and write, was trained as a schoolteacher and saw herself as an intellectual representative of workers, whose mission it was to mediate between them and governmental institutions in order to improve their labor and living conditions. Whereas Catarino Issac and Anita Hernández came from recently organized sectors of the workforce, Martínez already had some political experience because her father had introduced her to the progressive wing of the organized labor movement and the feminist movement. Even though she was a woman—and it was frowned upon for women to participate in politics—Martínez was not at as much of a disadvantage as the men and women who worked in the service industry. Her education, political experience, and political base composed of women in the CFO placed her on a relatively equal footing regarding Hernández.

They had both participated in politics to consolidate a political group; they both had ambitions of power. Once they formed an alliance in the early 1930s, both Hernández and Martínez knew that they were a perfect match. Thanks to Martínez, Hernández could provide a certain degree of literacy to working men and women; she politicized them and instructed them in the importance of the history of Mexico and of the working class so that they could acquire civic values of discipline and social mobility. Likewise, Martínez promoted not only the formation of unions by women but also their support of their husbands by organizing and attending union meetings. Martínez, in turn, constructed a forum through Hernández where women's issues could be discussed.

In the 1940s, the CFO continued its literacy work, providing moral education by instilling values aligned with the political and social goals of the organization—such as loyalty to the labor movement, support for social justice, the improvement of workers' lives, civic responsibility, and discipline—to the working class affiliated to the COJ-FTJ and advancing the struggle for female suffrage. The CFO expanded to include issues of social welfare, education, hygiene, nutrition, and urbanization. Moreover, the CFO pointed out corrupt practices in the police force, the Department of Transit, and state medical services.[32] These wide-ranging actions of the CFO fit into a turn of events that took place during the presidency of Manuel Ávila Camacho (1910–46), when labor took a more conciliatory position in exchange for agrarian reform and socialist education. Ávila Camacho backed a maternalistic policy that conceived of women in terms of their reproductive capacity rather than their political capacity. Women were responsible for the upbringing and caretaking of children, as well as the well-being of the community. Aside from the implementation of these welfare-based and maternalistic policies, in that same decade other major transformations took place: the reformation of the Electoral Code, the institutionalization of the PRI in 1946, and the recognition of female suffrage in the municipal political arena approved by the Congress on December 23, 1946, and published on February 12, 1947.

Like in the 1930s, Martínez and the CFO campaigned again in favor of women's suffrage in the 1940s. Instead of using a confrontational stance toward the state and its representatives, they preferred to present themselves as a group that had been fighting at the local level for women's social, labor, and political rights, that had political experience and could elaborate solid social policies to the municipal government. They were aware that President Miguel Alemán, congressmen, senators, and PRI's political leaders agreed with the idea that the participation of women in the municipality was very similar to the care required by the family, the home, and the care work. Male political leaders believed that the active participation of women in public life in the municipality would not pervert them because the municipality was like home. They also thought that this way would prepare women in politics and public life. On December 12, 1946, Congress approved with seventy-seven votes and one against the presidential initiative to reform Article 115. In Jalisco, the legislative reform process was carried out in August 1948 and was incorporated into the state constitution in September of that year. It was agreed to release women to exercise their civil rights instead of making it mandatory.

It was in this context that Martínez and the CFO supported Heliodoro Hernández Loza during his campaign to run as *presidente municipal* (major) of Guadalajara for the biennial period of 1947–48. After Hernández Loza's electoral triumph, toward the end of 1946, some schoolteachers from the CFO delivered to some of the newly elected *regidores* (male members of city council) some proposals of social policies that they could implement in the following years. The CFO schoolteachers addressed various problems and issues in relation to the lack of welfare to improve the standard of living. Through these proposals they sought the creation of social programs devoted to literacy, civics, hygiene, and small cottage industries. They considered the problem of children on the streets, specifically their vagrancy and criminality; child labor in the factories and workshops; and widespread infant mortality due to malnutrition. They suggested that childhood and juvenile delinquency be attended to beyond the Escuela Correccional (juvenile institute) by means of a court formed by a doctor, a schoolteacher, and a lawyer, stressing that these positions ought to be filled by women due to their "honorable spirit . . . and maternal instinct."[33] They also urged that a zone of tolerance be established to control prostitution. These proposals of the CFO were in keeping with the public welfare and maternalist policies of the state of Jalisco and the PRI. Detailed research remains to be carried out regarding which of these initiatives were enacted and the results they obtained. Some of these, such as municipal academies, were launched by Dolores Martínez, Guadalupe's sister.

On many occasions, a series of negotiations and accommodations took place, as is illustrated by the marriage of Hernández and Martínez in 1949. Once they were married, Hernández allowed Martínez to continue giving classes in mathematics and calligraphy in the Normal School.[34] However, Martínez was not willing to sacrifice the political work that had situated her as a leader with a defined female political group in both the FTJ and the PRM/PRI. She did agree to stop working so that Hernández could act as the "provider of the household."

In the FTJ and in the PRI, Martínez controlled and handled the female sections. She succeeded in mobilizing over two hundred women who participated in electoral campaigns and political meetings. In keeping with the times, they received scientific instruction on how to be good mothers and wives, although there was also a very clear distinction between them and those who were leaders.³⁵ Leaders required workshops not on motherhood but rather on labor politics.³⁶ However, by the time Martínez ran for federal deputy in the second district in 1958, the discourse about women had changed completely. The leaders of working women, schoolteachers, and housewives were all summoned to join the campaign of the first woman from the labor sector to seek elected office. Their participation in her campaign was not only justified, but their presence was also required to support Martínez's work as deputy in the inauguration of schools and regional CFO centers.

Consolidation of the Hernández-Martínez *Cacicazgo*

In the 1950s, after she was married and the right to women's suffrage in federal elections was passed in 1953, Martínez Villanueva consolidated her function as a cacique and political broker. Her strength and power are represented in a mural painted in the Department of Labor in the early 1990s. Martínez Villanueva is at the center, mediating between two other caciques: Heliodoro Hernández Loza of the FTJ and Francisco Silva Romero of the CROC. It is a representation of the authority she wielded as a mediator. She compelled them to negotiate to determine which electoral districts, municipalities, and unions they would control, thus bringing violent confrontations to an end.³⁷ In the end, they agreed that Hernández would control the municipal area of Guadalajara and Silva Romero would control Tlaquepaque.

As Anita Hernández recalls, Martínez not only established order between the top union bosses; she was also opposed to leaders being irresponsible, womanizers, or alcoholics. She recriminated them when they failed to fulfill their responsibility to protect their workers. Martínez always expressed her opinion, either to Hernández himself or to politicians, governors, or presidents of the republic. According to Anita Hernández, she did not like to be contradicted. In a similar vein, within the PRI she indicated who ought to become an elected *regidora* or *regidor*, female or male member of city council, or local or federal deputies, reviewing with extreme care the proposals that were made to her.

Despite being very authoritarian, Martínez had a loyal following that included female attorneys, ticket takers, cashiers, seamstresses, nurses, office workers, judges, schoolteachers, waitresses, and workers in the footwear, corn-grinding, or textile industries, as well as vendors of flowers and nopal cactus leaves. Vendors, the so-called Marías, followed her faithfully because she always defended them whenever the authorities tried to remove them from the markets.[38] She maintained the practice of a politics of reciprocity with her base, whom she helped in their daily struggles, in turn demanding that they respond when their presence was required at political meetings. Anita Hernández explains what kind of assistance Martínez provided her in the 1950s when her mother died and she lost the baby she was expecting. The owner of a corn-grinding mill gave her only ten pesos for the burial. Given the lack of economic support from her boss, Heliodoro Hernández, Martínez, and Isaac covered all the expenses for both burials. This kind of moral and economic sustenance were fundamental to these bases and reinforced their feeling of belonging to a political family.

In his study of political families in Jalisco, Javier Hurtado found that fifty-eight political figures formed part of the Hernández bloc, one of the most numerous political families in Jalisco—which included those of Zuno, Ramírez, García Barragán, González Gallo, and Silva Romero. Hurtado found that it was one of the families with the greatest number of elected offices: 112, not counting those occupied by the patriarchy and within the labor unions. Hernández Loza occupied the largest number of offices and the one with the longest political career.[39] In the long run, they did not obtain posts in federal ministries or governorships, but they did succeed in maintaining their local power in Electoral Districts 2 and 15. However, compared to other organizations within the PRI, they apparently failed to become dominant because the CNOP controlled more electoral districts than the FTJ. All in all, they did stand out because Hernández and Martínez were those who came to have the most elected offices, while at the CNOP, representatives always changed.[40]

Within their bases, those who succeeded in occupying elected office also had ascending careers within the unions, until they reached the position of secretary general. As secretary generals, they not only had to be faithful and loyal to Hernández and Martínez, but they also had to improve working and living conditions for the base. For example, Juan Ramírez, leader of the Textile Union of the Atemajac Factory, created the first playground for the workers' children. He also built houses, introduced electric wiring, and collaborated in the construction of the Juan Palomar School. This labor allowed him to become state deputy (1953–57).[41] Similarly, Genaro Vega, driver and member of the SUTAJ, performed different tasks within the union but was also charged with the creation of other unions. He collaborated in the establishment of the Benito Juárez School in Mezquitán. Later, he was elected to city council three times and local deputy once.

As for the women inside the FTJ, they also had rising careers in their unions. However, it is worthy of note that there was not only a distinction of social class between schoolteachers and women workers but also a marked difference in their level of education. The schoolteachers came to be state deputies and *regidoras* (female members of the city council), such as, for example, Amalia Mendoza (1965–67), Ramona Aguilar, and Laura Rosales, whereas the workers were more limited because they only knew how to read and write. Only Anita Hernández, a tortilla maker, became an alternate *regidora*, for the municipal area of Guadalajara.

Upon examining the head of the Hernández-Martínez *cacicazgo*, we may observe that Heliodoro Hernández was a local deputy five times (1933–35, 1941–43, 1949–53, 1968–71, 1974–77), a federal deputy twice (1943–46, 1964–67), a senator of the republic twice (1982–85, 1985–88), and mayor of Guadalajara (1947–48). As for Martínez, she was federal deputy twice (1958–61, 1970–73), local deputy twice (1977–80, 1989–92), and alternate senator once (1964–70). Hernández and Martínez occupied the same electoral offices on a state and federal level. Although there is a numerical difference, this is because women obtained the vote very late—not to mention the right to run for office. As for their bases, there were significant differences between men and women and among women themselves. Men were obliged to complete elementary school to gain access to electoral office as city council members and deputies, while women needed more schooling. Only schoolteachers came to be female members of city council and deputies. Their level of education set them apart and excluded other loyal leaders who mobilized a lot of women workers, as I have already indicated in the case of Anita Hernández, who led six hundred tortilla makers.

Social Policies under the Hernández-Martínez *Cacicazgo*

The social policies of both Hernández and Martínez were focused on three main areas: housing, education, and recreational activities, such as sports and theater. From a gender perspective, Hernández reproduced a male vision that favored men as heads of the household entitled to become homeowners or small business owners of, for example, corn-grinding mills, cornmeal

FIG. 27. The CIRFO female basketball team in 1937.
Courtesy of Belén Martínez Villanueva.

dispensaries, tortilla-making shops, or taxi and truck companies. Meanwhile, Martínez focused on the functions of education and literacy. Like Hernández, through these activities, she contributed to the reproduction of a traditional family model where the man was the head of household and women played the role of mothers, first and foremost.

Hernández and Martínez recurred to education to indoctrinate their base and to be more disciplined, civilized, and productive. It was a means of combating ignorance and vice.[42] Hernández and Martínez hoped that the children in their base would finish school and choose professional careers; these soon-to-be professionals would be able to solve the problems of the working class and soon form part of their political family and union bureaucracy. To complement their educational program, Hernández and Martínez edited their newspaper entitled *Jalisco ceteme* at the end of the 1950s and during the 1960s.[43] This newspaper presented Hernández and Martínez as major intellectuals and labor leaders who were making history as responsible, revolutionary citizens linked to the Mexican Revolution and to labor leaders

FIG. 28. The CIRFO basketball team with Guadalupe Martínez, 1943. Courtesy of Belén Martínez Villanueva.

of the nineteenth and twentieth centuries who were able to understand the sufferings of the working class. However, *Jalisco ceteme* silenced their repressive labor practices. Finally, Hernández and Martínez encouraged dedication to sports and the theater. They formed teams for women and men in soccer and basketball and groups for music and choir. This was a means not only of control but of recreation for workers.[44]

Criticism of the Opposition and Use of Male Language

Starting in the mid-1940s, the CTM-FTJ implemented policies of coercion to discourage or eliminate any actions or movements within unions that sought to challenge the established authority or push for more radical changes and dissidence. Essentially, they sought to maintain control and prevent any opposition from within the labor movement. Despite these repressive politics, some autonomous movements emerged among the miners, oil workers, and railroad workers in the late 1950s. During that decade, fears of division within the CTM-FTJ increased yearly because they could not put an end to criticism from the communists and PAN supporters. The leaders of the CTM-FTJ used virile language to reaffirm their masculine identity. If they were men, then they ought to fight for their organizations. The following fact illustrates this: in a birthday party for Hernández Loza in 1959, Fidel Velázquez confirmed that the FTJ was one of the best federations in the country due to its large number of members, characterized by their loyalty and discipline. Moreover, they had struggled against the "corrupt communists," especially the textile factory Celanese Mexicana.[45] Therefore, in the FTJ there were no cowards, weaklings, or fearful men because no internal divisions were allowed.[46] In fact, Hernández Loza rejected the idea of opposition to Velázquez by those who sustained that he was a "rotten leader." On the contrary, according to Hernández, Velásquez was a guiding light who had dedicated his life to solving workers' problems.[47]

In contrast, two newspapers in Guadalajara—*El informador* and *El occidental*—did not agree with the CTM-FTJ view of male identity. These newspapers confirmed that men who did not respect democracy in electoral contests and in unions because they resorted to shock groups and were involved in co-opting votes for the PRI were not responsible. These men were womanizers, alcoholics, "sheep, opportunistic cowards and brown-nosers."[48] Responsible men would respect and fight for a democratic nation while remaining sober and faithful to their families. Efraín González Luna (1898–1964), one of the founders of the PAN and a fighter for democracy, became a role model because he represented these characteristics. Hence men like Velásquez and Hernández Loza did not represent manly features, according to the gaze of these periodicals.[49]

Despite these differences in opinion regarding male identity in Guadalajara in the public eye, the defense of labor leaders did not put an end to the criticism and attacks against the CTM. In fact, this kind of questioning only increased in the 1960s. The Cuban Revolution (1959) and the student movement of 1968 fueled a reinforcement of the criticism of authoritarian practices. The discourse of the CTM, focused on strengthening unity, continuing with a revolutionary and patriotic participation, and identifying its enemies—the Catholic Church, big business, and communist leaders—and accepting self-criticism, was lacking.[50] The dissidence continued during the 1960s and 1980s among electrical workers and teachers.

The Role of Women in Confronting Attacks against the CTM

It is important to point out that Fidel Velázquez was publicly opposed to the campaign for the women's vote in 1952 and 1953. He held that it was more important to improve living conditions than grant the right to vote in federal elections to women. In this campaign, the PRI, PAN, and Partido Popular Socialista (Socialist popular party) took an interest in the female electorate because women would significantly increase their base of possible voters. Women had struggled since the decade of 1910 to obtain greater recognition in politics, and finally, in 1953, the right to women's suffrage was granted.[51] After that, women were presented as a strong political contingent, mobilized by the CTM to counteract the emergence of criticism from union dissidence.

In 1957, the CTM brought together more than seven hundred women for the First National Congress of the Federación Mexicana de Organizaciones Femeninas (Mexican federation of women's organizations). The goal of this meeting was to promote labor unity in unions, the workplace, and among working families. According to the CTM, the significant participation of women showed the practice of liberty and democracy within unions.[52] However, women were unable to advance their own autonomy within the CTM. They had to be loyal and disciplined. Even though women of the CTM learned from combative role models, they had learned through experience that to have mobility within their organizations, it was very important to follow the golden rules of fidelity and obedience. Women had to actively counteract the criticism of dissidents but at the same time fulfill the traditional roles that were assigned to them: maintaining and reproducing moral families and CTM organizations—schools, civic tours, press, sports, theater, and musical groups.[53]

During decades of the 1960s and 70s, Martínez's discourses blended several themes: her cultural memory of her political group, the struggle for women's suffrage, her legitimacy as a union and political leader, and the discrimination of women within the PRI. In 1967, at the age of sixty-two, during a commemoration of the death of María A. Díaz at the FTJ, Martínez narrated how the CFO was formed, who it comprised, how they began to work, and where they had met. She indicated that the women affiliated with the CFO learned the values of friendship, fraternity, and protection as well as how to give advice. This speech contrasted with the ones she had pronounced in 1934 regarding the new and revolutionary woman and with those of 1957 ("How We Women Think"), given that now she emphasized the suffering that they experienced because they were "persecuted and even punished for defending [their] integrity, dignity, and independence."[54] She pointed out that as young people, by "playing, playing, we did our part in social and union work."[55] She proudly emphasized that the CFO was the oldest women's organization in Mexico to hold weekly sessions, that it had always been part of the FTJ, and that its origins traced back to the COM. In this group, various people came to be official representatives before the Junta Central de Conciliación y Arbitraje, the first *regidoras*, female members of the city council of Guadalajara, and federal and state deputies. She sustained that her group knew how to conquer these places with responsibility and serve her state, fatherland, and citizenship. In this discourse, Guadalupe gave subtle indications that those who formed part of the CFO ought to be disciplined and "socially, politically, and morally prepared" because if they failed to show loyalty, discipline, and submission, they could not form part of this faction. They were repressed or pushed aside, as María A. Díaz taught her during the 1920s and 30s, or as she learned alongside Heliodoro Hernández during the 1930s and 50s. She provided nuance for these authoritarian practices by affirming that the participation of the CFO was based on work with "dignity and honesty." Before a growing criticism among dissident groups and the opposition, Guadalupe concentrated on emphasizing these final two values to legitimize her leadership in the FTJ-CFO and the PRI.

At the age of sixty-four, in a speech she argued that women were closer to the problems of the community because these conflicts were like those that began at home. The women of the PRI had to collaborate to resolve such issues. She saw a significant improvement in women's employment opportunities, particularly in traditionally male-dominated industrial sectors—over thirty thousand women were working in the electronics industry, in spare parts, and in painting and others were working with modern machinery like textiles, in hat making, in biscuit making, in mills, and in packing factories, among others. She indicated that in the electronics industry, women were preferred "due to their cleanliness, labor responsibility and performance."[56] This idea contrasts radically with her position of defense of the working woman and her rights in the 1930s. In the late 1960s, Guadalupe considered it important for women to have jobs, while failing to consider how female workers were treated in the *maquiladora* industry: as cheap labor that represented a risk if they unionized because the FTJ-CFO promoted cordial relations between capital and labor while repressing autonomous, combative unions.

In the year 1974, fissures became visible between the political faction of the FTJ-CFO and the PRI. In a tribute to Adolfo Ruiz Cortines a year after his death, Guadalupe told how the struggle for women's suffrage had taken place: there was a bill proposed during the presidency of Lázaro Cárdenas, but it was not ratified. She indicated that in 1947, women's suffrage was recognized in the municipal arena. She referred to the fact that since 1928, women struggling in the CFO fought for political and social citizenship. She indicated that from 1928 to 1953, "the interventions of women in various cases, despite the effective action of women within the Partido Revolucionario Institucional, were never taken into account."[57] On this occasion, she fused the name of the PNR with its foundation. Guadalupe rendered this tribute to Ruiz Cortines because he had taken women into account and kept his promises, as shown by the appointment of the first federal deputy for Baja California, Aurora Jiménez. She recalled her participation in the first electoral contest in which women exercised the right to vote. The forerunners of women's suffrage were militant in the PNR, PRM, and PRI. She surprisingly stated, "We women, as citizens of Mexico, are not interested in being *regidoras*, we are not interested in being deputies, we are not interested in being governors or presidents of the Republic, *we are interested in using our vote to choose the best men, so that Mexico may be happier*," and hence, she shows how throughout her political career, she had not only moderated and accommodated her combative, radical language from the 1930s but also assimilated this political culture, albeit with ambivalences and paradoxes.[58]

Regarding the debate around women's suffrage, Guadalupe mentioned that certain feminists considered that failing to grant the vote would be a discriminatory act. She declared herself in favor of generating legislative reforms to diminish the segregation of women, which, she argued, continued to persist. She compared the presence of women and men in teaching to illustrate her point. She pointed out that many times, schoolteachers at most took charge of a classroom, while men quickly ascended to administrative posts. She also indicated that something similar took place in the unions formed mostly by women, given that their general secretaries were almost always men. She asked herself if once her husband died, the peasant's wife might in fact inherit his land. She also questioned what went on with divorce and why *patria potestad* was a privilege enjoyed by fathers, without taking mothers into account. She pointed out that there were very few women in labor courts. She indicated that women had been "given what we deserve, bit by bit, while gentlemen are showered by the bucketful."[59] Guadalupe held women responsible for this contrasting situation of barriers that did not allow for the expansion of the presence of women in electoral office:

> Because we are pusillanimous; because we dare not have an opinion, because we dare not talk about the *leeches that exist in our Party*; because we dare not say that we are treated with injustice; because we have ourselves to fall from the grace of our leader or our Secretary General; companions, I believe that Don Adolfo Ruiz Cortines did not give us the vote to become ornamental; he gave us the vote so that a handful would become Deputies and strut about with the pride of their jurisdiction; he told us we were Citizens of Mexico because he wanted men and women to share this responsibility.[60]

She invited members of the PRI to leave apathy and fear behind and rise. This is an indication that the political group of Guadalupe did not reproduce itself; some had died, while others retired from the ranks due to her strong-arm authoritarianism. Perhaps Guadalupe had lost her negotiating side, which she had proudly displayed in the 1920s and 30s, since she was already sixty-nine years old. She always tended to manifest a strong personality as a leader. Her long career and her struggles to impose her ideas and projects had allowed her to exercise her authority and her power. In the late 1960s, her authoritarian political culture and her age made it difficult for her to build bridges with younger generations. These are examples of splits and fissures that had begun to form not only within the PRI but within her own group as well.

In her speech regarding judicial equality read in 1975 at the National Female Assembly of the Extraordinary Congress of the Federación Obrera Femenil of the CTM, within the context of the International Women's Year, she spoke of promoting economic rights, the development of women, and reforms to civil procedure codes to eradicate discriminatory articles. Like in other dissident Mexican movements—railroad workers, electricians, and doctors—that questioned the authoritarianism and the antidemocratic and authoritarian practices of the Mexican State, feminists of the 1970s questioned the patriarchal state and authoritarianism of families. Many of them had participated in the student movement of 1968 that questioned the failures of the economic model known as "The Mexican Miracle" (1940–70): the corrupt, authoritarian, and antidemocratic practices of the PRI. The women who participated in the student mobilization became radicalized, developing a gender-based struggle that was more subversive and transgressive than that of their male peers. They challenged and redefined traditional notions of womanhood, expanded spaces for female participation, and confronted the political practices of the male-dominated Mexican left, which had largely ignored the issue of women's subordination.[61] These feminists did not participate in the international conference dedicated to the International Women's Year in 1975, but they did organize a congress.[62]

By interweaving the categories of cacique, social class, corporatism, and gender, we not only problematize and enrich both perspectives; by examining them together, it is possible to clarify how over time, the relations of power and the conceptualization of politics in the organized labor movement changed in the official party, in women's organization, and between men and women. The life stories, political careers, and cultural politics of Hernández and Martínez show how these were transformed throughout their lives. In the case of Hernández, he maintained a strong influence in the traditional culture of Los Altos of Jalisco, one that was suited to a state and labor politics that favored working men. His interventions as a union leader, politician, and businessman made him see the importance of negotiating with different groups. Despite his traditional way of doing politics, he accepted the inclusion of women in his political family to consolidate his leadership. This was highly significant. In counterbalance, Martínez changed her combative labor politics and her struggle for the emancipation of women for a more moderate position to consolidate her political group and her presence in politics. However, this subordination allowed her to form part of the power structures of the FTJ, the official party, and union bureaucracy. Both figures appropriated the nineteenth-century saying "Jalisco never loses, and when it loses, it takes away" to indicate that despite a series of changes brought on by the Mexican Revolution of 1910, in politics there were still antidemocratic, strong-arm, and violent practices that were very useful to them in ensuring that their *cacicazgo* would last until the 1990s.

During the Cardenista politics of the masses in the 1930s, the themes of equality, the new woman, the revolutionary woman, and social justice may be identified. During the boom of the Mexican Miracle and the political modernization of the country in the 1950s, the concepts of mutilated democracy, modern democracy, and social democracy stand out. Once the crisis of the Mexican Miracle drew near and strong criticism of the authoritarian political system began to gestate, notions of honor, honesty, and dignity stood out. The latter were used by Guadalupe and other union leaders like Heliodoro Hernández and Fidel Velázquez to justify their prolonged leadership, gained by means of violent struggle in the period from 1920 to 1940. Overall, all the categories that Martínez used and re-created in her speeches reflect and contextualize the changes and the social, cultural, political, and economic processes that she experienced, from active social participation in civic society during the revolutionary period (1910–29), passing through the incorporation into corporatist and authoritarian state structures (1930–50), to the beginning of fragmentation of this political system (1960–70). The texts about citizenship also show and give indications of how she constructed, modified, adjusted, and assimilated different stages of the Mexican political system and labor and gender politics in the organized labor movement affiliated with the state. Martínez transitioned from advocating for women's fervent autonomy and independence to adopting a more maternalistic approach to gain access to political citizenship. Motherhood legitimized women's participation in politics, positioning them as entering public life to serve others: the fatherland and their husbands, brothers, and sons. Ironically, she had strongly opposed this idea in 1933 when the female section of the PNR was created in Jalisco. Despite these maternalistic concessions, she was ambivalent about the broader participation of women in elected positions. Her proposals can be seen as early initiatives akin to today's quota laws. However, she struggled to grasp why women continued to face "invisible" barriers, or the so-called glass ceiling, that hindered their advancement within political structures. Her argument only partially explained the exclusion of women from elected positions. Martínez's approach to political culture illustrates the evolving process of constructing citizenship in its various forms—social, economic, and political—yet always within a male-dominated political framework.

6

María Guadalupe Urzúa Flores
Advocate and Modernizer of Jalisco Rural Politics

On December 7, 2004, a Jaliscan congressman announced to the state legislature that María Guadalupe Urzúa Flores (1912–2004) had passed away. According to this state representative, Urzúa Flores was an outstanding and well-known member of the Jalisco branch of the PRI at the national, regional, and local levels. He stated that Urzúa Flores "was a brilliant advocate for the dispossessed, who always shared her knowledge and fought for educational issues."[1] He finished by recognizing that she promoted many public works and asked his fellow Congress members to observe a minute of silence. Her long and successful political career and her actions in the public sphere (female member of the city council of San Martín Hidalgo, federal congresswoman on four occasions, and mayor twice) show that she was more of an advocate, or *gestora*, than a broker, or *cacica*. She wielded power to modernize rural areas in coastal and central Jalisco. Starting in the 1940s, she promoted health and educational programs, pushed for land reform, and promoted public works, including the construction of nursing homes, dams, an electrical power grid and highways, potable water, postal services, telephones, wells, and watering holes for livestock.

The story of Urzúa Flores helps us explore how individual experiences in rural Mexico during the postrevolutionary period of state formation (1917–40) and the emergence of the "Mexican Miracle" (1940–70) intertwined with broader changes and processes such as the sanitation of Mexican society, the modernization of patriarchy, the rationalization of domesticity, rural migration to the United States, demographic changes, the execution of land reform, the building of modern political corporatist institutions, and the incorporation of women in public posts after women's municipal suffrage was granted in 1947.[2]

The concept of advocate versus *cacica* implies different conceptualizations of power. By my understanding, an advocate refers to someone who promotes and struggles to find solutions for specific local issues to benefit communities but does not necessarily belong to said communities.[3] The advocate is committed to social services and problem-solving and influences public policy. She may or may not have an institutional affiliation to a labor union, political party, or social or political organization. Her role is to identify local needs and become a cultural or political intermediary among different institutions and cultural, political, and social forces. She is highly familiar with the structure of state bureaucracy and identifies influential political figures and decision-makers, which becomes a key factor in persuading or dissuading them. Through speech and writing, an advocate makes her demands, needs, and local issues heard and, moreover, visible, channeling them through different government agencies.[4] In order to solve these particular local issues, she lobbies and negotiates with various figures through formal and informal resources, using social and political networks at different moments of public policy, especially in the public sphere.[5] A favorable result contributes to creating an image of legitimacy and prestige among those who receive the benefits of her public works.

My idea of the cacique is based on extensive historiographical literature, which has defined him as a political boss or strongman whose authority stems from informal sources and who arbitrarily wields personal political power over a region or a locale, one where he is capable of mediating between his local base and the political, economic, social, and cultural powers that be. The cacique acts through clientelist and paternalist channels and, upon occasion, uses violence. The cacique wields control over wealth, honor, public office, and political power. He receives support from family networks, godfathers, friends, fellow activists, and clients, and he is seen as a cultural and political intermediary among his subordinates and his own superiors—that is to say, one who is capable of articulating different political cultures and creating bonds between them. To his superiors, the cacique must show obedience, handle information, and rely on political support while, at the same time, his subordinates must be loyal and faithful and fulfill the obligations and positions that are assigned to them.

Despite the fact that there are differences between the advocate and the cacique, they have both been important figures and cultural and political intermediaries in the clientelist, paternalist Mexican political system.[6] The postrevisionist analysis of caciquismo, the Mexican Revolution, and the revolutionary process of state formation have examined the role of cultural and political intermediaries and have emphasized negotiation, resistance, and reaccommodation among subalterns, state agencies, political leaders, communities, and political parties, among others.[7] Despite the fact that this is a very important contribution, I argue that we have neglected the role of advocates in political negotiations. Some caciques were also advocates, as was the case of General Marcelino García Barragán.[8] However, not all advocates were caciques, like Urzúa Flores. Caciques and advocates were key figures in the social contract of the PRI given that they placed emphasis on the growing infrastructure incentives to compensate for the unequal distribution of wealth nationwide. Like the recent historical studies about *cacicas* of the nineteenth century and postrevolution that have critically examined the concept of caciquismo and gender, I believe that this analysis may also be applied to that of advocates and advocacy. These exercises in advocacy are not exclusively male or female.[9] The category of gender helps us explain why individuals focus solely on attending to certain issues, whom they recur to, and how they attempt to solve them to benefit a specific group in keeping with their social class, ethnicity, gender, and generation.

In this chapter, I explore how Urzúa Flores emerged as a rural leader, enjoyed a long political career in public office, and became a political and cultural intermediary between local, state, and federal groups to represent peasants and women. I argue that Urzúa constantly confronted the shifting power dynamics among caciques, peasants, politicians, government agency representatives, state political parties, opposition political parties, and women. On one hand, in the local and regional arenas, it would seem that during the 1940s and 1950s, she stayed at the margin of the politics of authoritarian rural caciques like Marcelino García Barragán (1895–1979) in Autlán, Alfonso G. Ceballos in San Martín Hidalgo, or Basurto Limón in Zacoalco, in the southern region of Jalisco. On the other hand, in the federal arena, both agrarian reform and full female suffrage in 1953 empowered Guadalupe Urzúa Flores, peasants, and women. Urzúa Flores became familiar with legal codes and knew how to use them on different levels to advocate for peasants and women. First, I discuss her family background, delineating the local context of San Martín Hidalgo and the shifting political forces among caciques. Second, I go into detail regarding Guadalupe's campaign to build a local hospital to show how she became a local leader and advocate. Third, I analyze her ideas regarding the role of women, women's needs, and her proposal for a land reform specifically aimed at peasant women before women's suffrage was granted in 1953, coinciding thus with the rationalization of domesticity and the modernization of the patriarchy. Finally, I briefly trace her role as federal deputy and as *presidenta municipal* (major). I argue that the case of Guadalupe Urzúa helps us rethink what it meant to be a charismatic and influential woman in rural Mexico in the post-1940s period while creating an in-depth analysis of a person who devoted her life to public service in favor of forgotten peasants. I contend that current feminist scholars need to study and think more about these kinds of women and how to name them: *cacicas* or advocates.

Family Background

María Guadalupe Urzúa Flores was born on the Chapala Riviera in Jocotepec, Jalisco, on December 12, 1912.[10] At this moment, what little information I have about Guadalupe's family background is fragmented. However, a few scattered clues suggest that she grew up in the bosom of a liberal family of professionals—teachers and pharmacists—probably from the incipient rural middle class of the late nineteenth century. The family was originally from Jocotepec. Her father was José Urzúa Gutiérrez, who came from a family of musicians and was himself a musician. According to an interview with Manuel Urzúa (Guadalupe's nephew), her grandfather was Gerardo Flores, a physician who had belonged to Benito Juárez's personal guard.[11] Between the War of Reform (1857–60) and the French Intervention (1862–67), Juárez had asked Flores to stay in San Martín Hidalgo because there was no general practitioner in the region. Doctor Flores settled in the town, married, and had five children: Rosario, Francisco, Julia, Amelia, and María Guadalupe.

José Urzúa Gutiérrez married Rosario Flores Monroy, a schoolteacher who graduated with a degree from the Normal School of Jalisco in 1896.[12] The Urzúa family had two children: Manuel and Guadalupe. The death of her mother shaped Guadalupe's life.

Her father decided to keep and raise the boy in Jocotepec, while the little girl was sent to live with her maternal aunts in San Martín Hidalgo, a village eighty kilometers southwest of Guadalajara.

Growing Up in a Rural Community

Urzúa Flores's childhood and adolescence were immersed in a local context with agrarian disputes, the emergence of new political actors such as ejidatarios, and politics controlled by caciques. After General Manuel M. Diéguez and the Constitucionalista army controlled Jalisco in mid-1914, some local leaders in San Martín Hidalgo became Agraristas: Valentín García, Elías Cedano, Silvestre Coracero, Isaac Pérez, and Manuel Hoyos Garza. The latter used Carranza's Agrarian Law of 1915 to back his request that his lands be restituted. In 1916, Venustiano Carranza visited San Martín Hidalgo and publicly recognized the agrarian leaders. In 1919, a presidential resolution granted lands to peasants in San Martín. As a result, the Comité Local Agrario was formed.[13] During the 1920s, this committee requested the extension of lands for ejidos and requested the creation of new ejidos for other landless peasants. San Martín became a community divided among peasant leaders, peasant organizations, and political leaders. There were violent clashes that intensified during the Cristiada (1926–29), especially between Agraristas and Cristeros. During the 1930s, Alfonso G. Ceballos, a Cardenista Agrarista, ruled the village, using force and electoral imposition to maintain control. Ceballos created his own political bloc and threatened those factions opposed to his cacique politics or resisting agrarian reform. In the mid-1930s, the followers of Callista governors of Jalisco—Sebastián Allende (1932–35) and Everardo Topete (1935–39)—and those who supported the Cardenista governor, Silvano Barba González (1939–43), and Ceballos's political bloc had a contentious political relationship. The incorporation of Ceballos into municipal politics and his careful regulation of the municipal government in the 1930s allowed him to develop his political career in the following stages: alternate senator (1936), federal congressman (1940–43), member of city council in Guadalajara, and head of the Departamento de Agricultura y Ganadería (Department of agriculture and livestock) of Jalisco (1950).[14] In the mid-1930s, the alliance between Ceballos's group and the cacique Basurto Limón of Zacoalco became visible. They were both key rural anticlerical caciques and agrarian leaders who fought against the Cristeros and benefited from agrarian reform. They both wielded influence in their places of origin and won municipal presidencies by controlling local electoral processes, fraudulent elections characterized by violence and the duplication of ballots, causing mistrust and discontent. Their political power and influence allowed Ceballos and Limón to become owners of large ranches after having been revolutionary leaders. Political power also brought economic returns, and by the 1940s, Ceballos had become the owner of one of the largest ranches in the region.[15]

From Childhood to Youth

As a child, Guadalupe was sensitized to the suffering and poverty of these ill people. Guadalupe's uncles and aunts—Julia, Amelia, María Guadalupe, and Francisco—heralded from the rural middle class. Most worked as teachers, but Julia, a pharmacist, also owned a drugstore in San Martín Hidalgo.[16] Urzúa learned from observing the role of the pharmacist how to serve the rural poor, including those who visited the drugstore to receive treatment for their leprosy. Historically, leprosy had been seen as a consequence of poverty, marginalization, and exclusion; in terms of the makers of public policy in Mexico, poor peasants represented the diseased social body. This "race" was preventing the modernization of the country.[17] Peasants were supposed to enjoy sanitary conditions. Their "drinking, gambling, praying, womanizing, and violence [had to] be curtailed."[18]

Guadalupe developed a very close relationship to her aunt Julia. From her she learned five moral and civic values, as well as significant practices: (1) everyday living is earned through hard work; (2) it is important to serve others, especially the dispossessed; (3) if one gets involved in public service, one should always be honest and never make use of public money for personal needs; (4) avoid participating in politicking; and (5) distrust men intensely. The last rule was probably the result of Julia's rape by J. Trinidad López, the municipal president of San Martín Hidalgo, in 1927.[19] Guadalupe did not take all this advice to heart. Instead, she began her own process of individualization, giving these values and practices another meaning and reconfiguring them to contribute to the sanitary conditions of rural Mexico, the modernization of the patriarchy, and the rationalization of domesticity.[20] Perhaps her aunt's distrust of men affected Guadalupe in another way. She certainly used her beauty to attract, manipulate, and work with men in the political sphere, but always with the objective of serving others, the underdogs, more honestly. Her strategy was one of control of what might

FIG. 29. Flores Monroy family. Guadalupe is next to the bride. Courtesy of Colección María Guadalupe Urzúa Flores at the Biblioteca Carmen Castañeda García, CIESAS Occidente.

form part of her private life, keeping her romantic and intimate relations with men entirely separate.

Like the seven agrarian leaders of *The Princes of Naranja* studied by Paul Friedrich, Guadalupe also lost a relative in early infancy and was in contact with local politics, sparking her desire to change policy, struggle for agrarian reform, and gain access to power. In her childhood, she met a few political leaders, and in 1922, at the age of ten, Guadalupe skipped school and went to the town square to hear José Guadalupe Zuno (1923–26).[21] Zuno's speeches during his gubernatorial campaign were populist and anticlerical, his stance regarding agrarian reform was progressive, and he spoke of the rights of peasants and workers.[22] Guadalupe Urzúa took notes during the speech and was particularly impressed by Zuno's use of the term *camaradas*, or comrades. Zuno realized that she was writing down what he and his followers were saying and decided to introduce himself to Guadalupe. From that moment forward, they would become firm friends. Guadalupe also enjoyed hearing Silvestre Coracero's stories about the agrarian movement in San Martín Hidalgo. In accordance with a romanticized biography by one of her loyal followers, as a child, Guadalupe asked Coracero if he could show her his plot of land. He replied with tears in his eyes that it had been taken away. Guadalupe promised him she would return it when she grew up.[23]

According to Roderic Ai Camp's brief political biography, Guadalupe started her studies at the Josefa Ortiz de Domínguez school in San Martín Hidalgo. She then finished her primary education at the school next to the Normal School in Zacoalco de Torres.[24] In Guadalajara, she attended a middle school and studied at a secretarial school for three years.[25] At the Academia Comercial "Vizcarra" in Guadalajara, she received training in commercial law and shorthand with the aim of becoming a secretary. Here she acquired the rudiments of written culture needed to send letters and petitions on behalf of the community, peasants, and women. All this proves that her education was more liberal than religious.

By the end of the 1920s, Guadalupe had become a happy, dynamic, and attractive young woman who enjoyed mariachis and carnivals—so much so, in fact, that she organized the "Flechero district mariachi." Her taste for this kind of music may be explained in part because her town was located close to two communities that claim to be the birthplace of mariachi: Cocula and Tecolotlán. This attraction to social activities is reflected in the fact that in 1931 she was elected the princess of the carnival of San Martín Hidalgo.[26] The carnival permitted the development of joyfully profane speech in order to overturn social hierarchies. Those with sufficient economic means went to Ameca to enjoy the costume balls, parades with allegorical floats, the flowery ritual combat, and the prank of smashing eggshells filled with confetti on those who were taken unawares. Her participation in the public sphere (the carnival and beauty contests) helped reinforce in her a secular culture that coincided with the political practices of the corporatist state. The carnival interacted with traditional Catholic customs, folk culture, and the public sphere of the PNR to appeal to broader, more fragmented audiences of rural policies in modern Mexico.[27]

Due to her beauty and cheerful character, Guadalupe had several suitors—young men vying for her attention who fell in love with her. Likely, she enjoyed putting her sexuality and body on display as a young white

FIG. 30. María Guadalupe Urzúa Flores in her youth. Courtesy of Colección María Guadalupe Urzúa Flores at the Biblioteca Carmen Castañeda García, CIESAS Occidente.

woman who provided contrast with the peasant women and ranch wives of San Martín Hidalgo. Despite these suitors, however, she decided to take on a public role in her community. In Urzúa Flores's experience, married women always suffered a lot.[28] Therefore, she resolved to take charge of her sexuality and became another type of woman: one who promoted the modernization of patriarchy and sought the transformation of traditional gender roles through civic, labor, and agrarian reforms. She fought for the rights of women and children in the family and workplace, access to birth control, and rural health care, all without radically changing the patriarchy.[29] These social programs and practices coincided with the rationalization of domesticity promoted by the Secretaría de Educación Pública and other government agencies, which supported "'modern' notions of health, hygiene, medicine, household organization, and child development."[30]

In the 1930s, Guadalupe began to engage in politics. At the age of twenty-one, in 1933, she met Lázaro Cárdenas during his presidential campaign tour. As a schoolteacher, she also worked at the Centro Cultural Deportivo "Hidalgo" and organized the Academia de Capacitación Femenil Municipal, a workshop that gave instruction on cooking, embroidery, shorthand writing, and English. Guadalupe also created a theater group called Hidalgo through which she raised funds for building a basketball court. She participated in a program for planting trees and building a road to the town's cemetery and Alameda. In 1935, at the age of twenty-three, Urzúa lobbied for the construction of the highway from Guadalajara to Barra de Navidad along the southern coast of Jalisco.[31] At the same time, Colonel Marcelino García Barragán, military chief of Sayula and of the Fourth Cavalry Regiment, tried to exert influence over regional businessmen, governors, and federal bureaucrats for the construction of the highway to Autlán and Barra de Navidad.[32] Urzúa's and García Barragán's lobbying confirms Benjamin Fulwider's point that "the state success [in constructing roads] was the result of collaboration between local and national powerholders, rather than the top-down imposition of an expanding 'leviathan' state. This process necessarily involved compromise as well as collaboration and was often piecemeal and ad hoc as state leaders tried various policy approaches and changed their position based on the results."[33]

By the mid-1930s, Urzúa had established clear agrarian and political affiliations. In 1936, at age twenty-four, she joined the Female Section of the Comité Agrario Regional (Regional agrarian committee). Two years later, in 1938, she became the secretary of feminine action of the Comité Campesino (Peasant committee) of Jalisco of the Partido de la Revolución Mexicana (PRM) and a founding member of the Confederación Nacional Campesina (CNC).[34]

By her midtwenties, Guadalupe had also made it clear that she identified with the social issues of the dispossessed: the poor, leprous peasants. Soon, she became known as *voluntariosa*, or headstrong, as someone who lobbied, raised money, negotiated, and succeeded in public works being made in favor of the community and agrarian reform. Her interest and commitment to eliminate leprosy and to improve the living conditions, health, educational, and communication services of her people distinguished her as a social fighter. For Guadalupe, the quest for social justice was of the utmost importance. At the entrance of her house, there was a mural that read "If you love liberty and fight against injustice, come inside, and welcome home."

Although Guadalupe had close ties to local ejidatarios, she was not an extreme agrarian rebel who sought a radical redistribution of wealth. Rather, she sought to improve peasant living standards. These actions dovetailed with PRM-PRI politics and helped explain her visibility and extraordinary political career. Paradoxically, due to her active participation in politics, her sexuality was questioned. According to some, there was a rumor that claimed that Guadalupe captivated important politicians who enabled her to carry out important public works projects. Her political work and beauty set off two reactions: the first linked her beauty to the nineteenth- and twentieth-century image of the "femme fatale" or "erotic siren" who attracted, manipulated, and destroyed men.[35] The second alluded to the idea and cultural fear dominant in the twentieth century that a woman lost her femininity and honor once she entered politics.[36] From the perspective of those looking up from below, this gossip was rooted in discrimination; from the opposite view, it highlights the interplay of agency, power, and sexuality through a gendered lens. Parallels may be drawn between these intertwined ideas, illustrated in the case of Urzúa Flores and María Dolores Estévez Zuleta (alias Lola "La Chata"), a female drug dealer who amassed considerable wealth and power during the 1930s.[37] Although Urzúa Flores and La Chata had different physical appearances—one was young and conventionally pretty, the other short, stocky, with "negroid" features and gold-capped teeth according to Harry J. Anslinger, director of the Federal Bureau of Narcotics in the United States—both ruptured the normative expectations of what it meant to be a woman and to have access to and take advantage of complex webs of power.[38] Both drew significant attention from men with influence because they defied the image of female morality. These women used their capacity for agency, power, and sexuality to influence politics and drug trafficking.

During the following decades, as an incipient and visible advocate, Guadalupe continued to be involved in various public works: the Fourth Centennial Celebration of San Martín Hidalgo (1940), the construction of a local hospital and a popular library (1941), the establishment of the first literacy center for peasant women (1942), and the creation of a local board of trustees to fight leprosy (1947), together with Doctor José Barba Rubio. She was the secretary of the Comité Local de Mejoras Materiales (Local committee for material improvements, 1949–52), lobbied for the establishment of a telephone line (1952), and was also president of the hospital board of trustees and vice president of the local government council (1953). Beginning in the 1940s, Urzúa promoted the construction of schools and roads, was the state representative of feminine action for the Liga de Comunidades Agrarias y

FIG. 31. Construction of the hospital at San Martín Hidalgo, Jalisco. Courtesy of Colección María Guadalupe Urzúa Flores at the Biblioteca Carmen Castañeda García, CIESAS Occidente.

Sindicatos Campesinos de Jalisco (Jaliscan league of agrarian communities and peasant unions), and on a federal level, she was in charge of the women's section of the Confederación Nacional Campesina (CNC) and vice president of the national women's section of the PRI.

A Fundraising Campaign for a Hospital

The Constitution of 1917 made public health the responsibility of the federal state.[39] During the 1920s and 1930s, a radical community of doctors from the Colegio de San Nicolás in Morelia, Michoacán, strove to spread scientific health services throughout the country's ejidos. For them, "poor health and deficient sanitary conditions were examples of social injustice."[40] According to Ana María Kapelusz-Poppi, this program "saw bringing modern health care to the countryside as one step toward the construction of a classless society in post-revolutionary Mexico."[41] The administrative structures and central offices of the Secretaría de Salud (Health ministry) in Mexico City toned down this radical perspective and promoted social modernization and economic progress.[42] Ejido medical services lasted from 1936 to 1940 and "contributed to making the right to modern health care part of the notion of citizenship in postrevolutionary Mexico."[43] The law was designed primarily to serve skilled rural and urban workers and address the high rate of infant mortality and infectious diseases such as dysentery, malaria, leprosy, and tuberculosis. Paradoxically, during this decade many medical and technological paradigms changed drastically. Increasingly, experts held that medicine ought to examine not only illnesses but their causes and the proper therapy to address them. That is to say, the medical field should attend to the health of individuals and their community, design preventive measures, and procure a suitable working environment while at the same time promoting the training of professionals and technicians in health services and, finally, building clinics and hospitals.[44]

By using her experience as secretary of social affairs and health for the Comisariado Ejidal, in 1941 Guadalupe decided to launch a public fundraising campaign for a hospital in San Martín Hidalgo.[45] She sent several letters to the officials of Hacienda y Crédito Público (Ministry of finance and public credit) and to the Dirección de Bienes Nacionales (National assets department), the governor of Jalisco, and natives of San Martín who lived in Chicago to request a plot for the building of a hospital because there was no health facility in town. She suggested a piece of land next to El Calvario Church as being best suited for the construction and clarified that in the event her request was approved, there would be no religious influence, nor would it be for her personal gain. She lacked the resources for construction and believed that this project and fundraising campaign were "in fulfillment of a humanitarian and patriotic responsibility, given that the task I propose surpasses by far my means to bring it to fruition."[46] By 1944, as president of the Pro-Hospital Committee of San Martín Hidalgo, Guadalupe had itemized the cost of the hospital. The total budget was Mex$20,151.01. In the same year, the Dirección de Bienes Nacionales granted the requested plot of land for building the hospital, and the committee got to work.

In mid-1945, without her aunt's consent, Guadalupe went to Mexico City to talk with Doctor Baz, who was head of the Secretaría de Salud at the time, about the public health problem in San Martín Hidalgo: the ostracized leprous peasants. A picture in her personal archive indicates that she had an interview with Doctor Baz and representatives from the Federación Nacional de Escuelas Técnicas (National federation of technical schools).[47] Because Guadalupe studied in a rural peasant school in Zacoalco that was linked to rural normal schools in 1931, she identified with the grievances and demands of students from rural normal schools during their mobilizations in the 1940s. Students demanded beds, sheets, an increase in the daily food ration, and scholarship stipends.[48] In that interview, she asked Doctor Baz if he could grant her some funds to complete the construction of the hospital and to hire the necessary staff to run it. Baz promised to assess her request and make a proposal. Local legend has it in San Martín that her beauty impressed the minister so much that she was granted her request. The information I obtained from her personal archive indicates that following this approval, she took on the work herself.

Meanwhile, the committee and Guadalupe worked very hard in their fundraising campaign by sending letters to federal, state, and local representatives of state agencies and to braceros in the United States. They also sponsored bullfights, sold drinks at local cantinas, sold bread and flowers, and organized fundraising parties (*kermesses*). By 1946, the committee obtained a letter notifying them that they would receive Mex$10,000 from the Secretaría de Salud. However, they only received Mex$5,000. Guadalupe wrote again to Doctor Baz to inform him of their progress, describing in detail the precarious economic condition of her hometown and requesting an extra Mex$60,000 in funds. Two years later, in 1948, the committee agreed to use the Mex$5,000 in the building of "a septic tank, plaster, floors, two bathrooms, and a main entryway." In 1949, the committee received another Mex$2,500. By then, Urzúa approached Beatriz Velasco de Alemán, President Miguel Alemán's wife, to ask for her financial support. Mrs. Velasco not only represented an alternative route to the president; Guadalupe approached her as a political strategy. These actions formed part of a political agenda of municipal presidents, governors, and wives of federal presidents to monitor, promote, and resolve issues related to public health and welfare. In 1951, Guadalupe wrote to President Alemán requesting his assistance. She explained to him that "through many sacrifices, construction of the hospital in San Martín Hidalgo has been partially completed, however, much still remains to be done."[49] By 1952, the hospital received Mex$250 monthly to cover expenses. By 1953, the project had evolved significantly. At that point, Guadalupe itemized all the personnel, carpentry, painting, plumbing, electricity, furniture, and equipment still needed. The budget had increased to Mex$87,896. In order to run the hospital, the committee proposed that young local women be trained by the town's doctors. Women could receive a three-month training session in vaccination, the use of some medical instruments, medical prevention, and hygiene. With that knowledge, these women could work in the hospital, receive a modest salary, and serve their family and society. The committee asserted, "To serve others is a duty imposed by the supreme cause, GOD. Prepare yourself to supply relief to the humble homes of their sufferings, with your knowledge and experience. Don't throw away this opportunity that has presented itself. If you are not a mother, remember that every woman is potentially a mother and that you should prepare yourself for maternal love while harvesting more sublime experiences."[50] They appealed to young women by using a maternalistic discourse with the predominant idea that women had to serve others.

While Urzúa Flores raised funds for this project, she also helped her aunt Julia at the dispensary to assist lepers. At the beginning of 1945, Guadalupe became a sixth officer of the Dirección de Epidemiología (Epidemiology department) as part of the campaign to fight leprosy. Her strong will and intense fundraising and lobbying in San Martín Hidalgo and Mexico City contributed to the construction of a hospital and the founding of a dermatology clinic. Both the hospital and the clinic were key in the successful elimination of leprosy over the course of the next thirty years. Guadalupe obtained training as a nurse at the Cruz Verde to cure people with leprosy, and because she did not show signs of rejection toward the sick, many were very grateful for her work. In this manner, Guadalupe began to broaden her political base. She completed the hospital in the mid-1950s, and many people were able to receive health services. At the unveiling ceremony of the statue of Guadalupe Urzúa in San Martín Hidalgo in June 2009, a leprosy survivor expressed his gratitude for Urzúa's insistence that he receive cures and treatment. He stated that he owed her his life and added that Guadalupe and a physician had visited every home in the region to ensure lepers would receive medical attention. Many survivors were able to continue to lead productive lives.

During the 1940s, Urzúa also founded a library and organized the centennial celebrations of her town. From 1949 to 1952, she was secretary of the Junta de Mejores Cívicas y Materiales (Board of civic and material improvements) of San Martín Hidalgo, and from 1953 to 1955, she was a member of town council in charge of the Comisión de Tesorería, Salud y Educación (Treasury, health, and education commission).

From Health and Public Works to Women's Issues in the 1950s

Mexican women had campaigned for women's suffrage since the 1910s. In 1930, the Frente Único Pro Derechos de la Mujer led a strong movement for this cause but was unsuccessful. In 1950, the issue gained force once again as different women's associations mobilized and pushed for female suffrage. The debate focused on issues of social equality and difference. According to Gabriela Cano, "In the mindset of the Ruiz Cortines administration women had no social relevance in and of themselves, as individuals with their own rights. They were important in as much as they supported their man in his daily struggle and as long as they carried out their role as mother. Only then were they recognized as possessing specific moral virtues."[51]

During Adolfo Ruiz Cortines's presidential campaign in 1952, Guadalupe organized a group of women that waited for him at the highway and forced the presidential bus to stop. Ruiz Cortines asked who Guadalupe was. Some local people pointed out that she was "a willful woman" who worked very hard for her community and was an elected councilwoman from San Martín Hidalgo. Ruiz Cortines allowed her to board the bus. In doing so, Guadalupe was able to establish political connections that allowed her to transcend the sphere of local politics. After Ruiz Cortines was elected president and granted women the right to vote in 1953, Guadalupe launched a very successful political career in elected office. She was the first federal congresswoman from Jalisco and one of the first five federal congresswomen in Mexico.[52] She benefited from Ruiz Cortines's policy of sharing power with local leaders, often by appointing his friends and close followers to public office.[53]

In April 1953, the PRI held the Primer Congreso Nacional de Mujeres (First national women's congress). As a councilwoman, Guadalupe Urzúa presented a paper entitled "Women's Issues." This was a turning point in Guadalupe's agenda as she expanded from public health and public works to women's issues. Her actions were similar to the findings of other studies regarding female consciousness, gender interests, and collective action among women.[54] The shift illustrates the conceptualization of female consciousness that Temma Kaplan used in her study on the women of Barcelona.

She focuses on gender rights, social concerns, and survival. According to Kaplan, "Those with female consciousness accept the gender system of their society; indeed, such consciousness emerges from the division of labor by sex, which assigns women the responsibility of preserving life."[55] These actions by women, focusing on the defense of their community, had revolutionary consequences because they politicized social community networks.

In her presentation to the Congress, Guadalupe asserted that a woman was the foundation of the household. Therefore, the state had a duty to respect her, protect her, and maintain her dignity. She claimed the Mexican legislature had paid little attention to women and that there was no law to prevent abuse by men. Guadalupe requested that the legislative body create regulations to guarantee respect for women in all walks of life. She argued that

> working women must receive a fair wage that meets their needs and should not be forced to work more than 9 hours as stated by the Labor Code. It is also necessary to establish training centers where women can be properly instructed and to stop the influence of fanaticism that atrophies their mind. In a poor home, women lack everything, because of the meager wage of their husbands or their own salaries, and are unable to produce strong and well-nourished children; hence, there is a high rate of infant mortality, due to the anemic state of many families, which is prejudicial to childhood, because without abundant and nutritious diet, the child is incapacitated to assimilate scientific knowledge and thus, the child, society and the Fatherland lose.[56]

Guadalupe requested effective laws for women to punish medical doctors who gave health certificates to people with venereal diseases; to extend health services, especially to prostitutes; to provide vaccinations to prevent diphtheria, smallpox, and typhus; to buy corn mills and sewing machines; and to give women an idea of civic culture and grant them dignity as women, wives, and mothers. She thought of Mexican women as aware of their own rights, with a high sense of responsibility, with model households, as real partners of their husbands, and with good children "to forge a great and respected fatherland."[57]

Guadalupe not only lobbied for social programs for San Martín Hidalgo, but she also started working with councilwomen from other towns. In May 1953, a group of councilwomen of the municipalities of Guadalajara, Tamazula de Gordiano, Puerto Vallarta, Ahualulco de Mercado, and San Martín Hidalgo participated in the Primer Congreso Municipal (First municipal congress) organized by the governor Agustín Yáñez (1953–59) to be held in Guadalajara to delve into the same issues stated in her presentation mentioned above. I have identified only four councilwomen for Jalisco in this point in time. Their participation must have increased over the following years. With the reform to the Electoral Code in 1946, the institutionalization of the PRI that same year, and women's suffrage on a municipal level in 1947, the president of Mexico had the power to control electoral processes and incorporate new political forces—such as that of women, for example.[58] Their role was to recruit new members to the PRI to expand the base and thus counteract dissident movements. Recent studies regarding women leaders argue that the trend of women's participation in Jalisco politics evolved. In the 1950s women had the opportunity to be elected as councilwomen, federal deputies, and state deputies. By the 1960s, they were already municipal presidents and, in the 1970s, alternate senators.[59] More research remains to be done to learn how many more councilwomen there were in Mexico and to demonstrate whether the Jalisco trend is representative of the nation as a whole.

In July 1953 Guadalupe gave a paper at the Primer Congreso Nacional de Mujeres about the reforms needed in the agrarian code to grant women the same rights as men. Like Concha Michel, a schoolteacher and communist in the 1930s, Guadalupe demanded the right of peasant women to receive land and to reform Article 54, fraction 1.[60] She argued that Mexican peasant women had worked in the fields, participated actively in peasant's movements, and been involved in community efforts to demand equal rights for men and women. For Guadalupe, though, the principal role of peasant women was that of moderator, not agitator. Instead, she believed that "peasant womanhood" would become "an example of courage, patience, and perseverance." She concluded that the revolution was indebted to the Mexican peasant woman for her active participation in the movement.

After the closing of the Primer Congreso Nacional de Mujeres, Guadalupe became the national representative of peasant women at the CNC. She expanded her role from advocate and councilwoman to that of policymaker. On August 9, 1953, Guadalupe proposed to the president's secretary the design of a policy directed toward peasant women. She proposed to organize women into Ligas Femeniles and to inform them of the president's proposals

FIG. 32. María Guadalupe Urzúa as a deputy outside the Congreso de la Unión, surrounded by peasant women. Courtesy of Colección María Guadalupe Urzúa Flores at the Biblioteca Carmen Castañeda García, CIESAS Occidente.

for solving their economic, agrarian, and everyday problems. She also proposed to promote the formation of boards for moral, civic, and material improvement and to participate in the president's revolutionary program.

As part of her agenda as secretary of feminine action for the CNC from 1953 to 1956, she designed the policy that sought to organize peasant women for the implementation of agrarian, civic, social, and political activities in agreement with state agrarian and educational policies. For example, she privileged maternalist policies that promoted schools, childcare centers, school breakfasts, and childcare centers to support mothers with young children. She programmed a three-week educational and technical training for peasant women about Mexican history, politics, and the economy as well as civic education, pediatrics, hygiene, crops, agrarian and industrial law, literacy, rural tourism, sports, and physical education. Through these workshops, women received "scientific" instruction on how to be good mothers and wives and how to engage in civic and political life through the CNC and the PRI.[61]

How did Urzúa Flores regard peasant women? Like many urban teachers and policymakers, she took for granted that these women ought to reproduce traditional female gender roles. In her personal archive, there is a text that describes in detail her ideas in this regard. She envisioned the peasant woman as loving her country, her land, and her school. Her land, because she had cultivated it with her own hands and because it provided the means for subsistence for her children. Guadalupe desired economic prosperity, political equality, and social unity for rural homes. She longed to establish justice to do away with social differences. This was a democratic principle. She concluded, "In this way, I will fight against all opposition to the ideal that lives and grows more fertile each day in my female awareness."[62]

Urzúa Flores's ideas of peasant women were not only gender constructs, but they were also intertwined with class and race formations. As a deputy, she wore suits that contrasted with peasants' garb. This, her behavior, and her body language give us an idea of the persistence of racial and class hierarchy in a paternalist and clientelist system. Urzúa Flores's views on peasant women mirrored her broader perceptions of women, as reflected in a decalogue she created for the Volunteer Female Army, Protector of Childhood and Public Health, which emphasized the vital role of mothers in ensuring the well-being and upbringing of children.

Throughout 1953, Guadalupe lobbied for the construction and connection of roads between several communities and San Martín Hidalgo with the main highway (the crossroads of Santa María and Ipazoltic) and their connection to the Guadalajara-Barra de Navidad highway. She helped various ejido owners in Tepehuaje and San Martín Hidalgo who demanded the right to receive lands.[63]

The 1955 Federal Elections for Congress

The 1955 elections, and the campaign leading up to it, provoked heated debate. Various editorials in the newspaper *El informador* questioned electoral transparency, criticized the fraudulent practices of the PRI that made it very difficult for the PAN to change the balance of power in politics, disapproved of the president's absolute control of the selection of who could run for federal deputy, satirized the meaning and function of these federal/state representatives, denounced the role of violent and repressive caciques in local politics, and cast doubt upon the real emergence of women as voters and as elected officials.[64] In Jalisco the most contentious electoral district was Autlán. The town became a kind of electoral laboratory and tested the strength of local PRI-backed caciques while highlighting the PAN struggle for electoral transparency. The elections also raised the profile of women in politics. Urzúa Flores was one of the first women to run for office as a federal deputy and to confront the political strength of Efraín González Luna and General Marcelino García Barragán. González Luna, one of the founders of the PAN and a presidential candidate, was born in this town and possessed a strong and important network of relatives and friends. General García Barragán, also from the region, had shown a special interest in modernization during his administration of a military officer and as a governor.[65] During the electoral campaign, six hundred conservative women of Autlán denounced to *El informador* that it was no accident the voting booths had been installed so far out of town.[66] They claimed that it was only possible to get there by horse. In this election, many people voted for Guadalupe because of her legitimacy in the region, earned through her successful public works in San Martín de Hidalgo. After her victory, Carlos Pineda Flores, a PAN state deputy denounced the victory of Urzúa Flores, arguing that the PRI had made use of prohibited practices. He requested that Congress deny her appointment as a federal deputy. She refuted the accusation, arguing that she had campaigned in nineteen towns (Atengo, Autlán, Ayutla, Casimiro Castillo, Cihuatlán, Cuautitlán, Cocula, El Limón, El Grullo, Ejutla, La Huerta, Juchitlán, Villa Purificación, San Martín Hidalgo, Tenamaxtlán, Tecolotlán, Tonaya, Unión de Tula, and Venustiano Carranza) and that she had won with a clear majority of 22,476 votes to 5,471 for the PAN.[67] She criticized the PANista federal congressman because he did not follow the civic and moral principles that González Luna had practiced. The latter's son, Javier González Luna, had already recognized Guadalupe's landslide. The PAN and women had triggered strong fears that they could destabilize the hegemony of the PRI through another Cristiada. However, women voted mostly for the PRI, and five women from that party were elected.[68]

As a federal deputy, Urzúa visited her rural electoral district frequently and sponsored a wide range of public works and services: a hospital in Autlán, mobile health brigades, schools in various towns, an increase in the number of federal teachers, the introduction of drinking water in Tecolotlán, paved streets in San Martín Hidalgo, and the construction of water wells. She sought to demonstrate that when Jaliscan women were elected to public posts, they could bring social programs to completion. During this period, the Departamento Agrario (Agrarian department) recognized that Guadalupe was a deputy who represented the peasants and began to grant deeds for redistributed land. *El informador* described every one of her achievements, thus countering negative views of women in politics.[69] Before she was elected deputy, Urzúa was a correspondent at *El informador*, which may explain why her achievements were reported. However, this positive view of her work contrasted with a caricature published in the same newspaper representing the image of a man on his knees, praying that his wife would never become a congresswoman.[70] The woman depicted displays an authoritarian attitude. Another cartoon, drawn by Freyre, presents the first congresswomen as mermaids on the shore, alongside congressmen armed and ready to hunt them.[71]

Despite these representations that ridiculed them, women continued to enter politics, as is illustrated by the case of Guadalupe and many others. She served as a federal deputy four times (1955–58, 1964–67, 1970–73, and 1976–79) and always represented the central and coastal regions of Jalisco at the CNC, which encompassed nineteen municipalities.[72]

FIG. 33. Freyer's cartoon depicting the election of the first federal congresswomen in 1955. Courtesy of Colección María Guadalupe Urzúa Flores at the Biblioteca Carmen Castañeda García, CIESAS Occidente.

Besides being a federal congresswoman, at the federal level, Urzúa also served as general secretary of the feminine section of the CNC several times (1953–56, 1958, and 1964–67).[73] At the state level, she was in charge of the feminine section of the Liga de Comunidades Agrarias y Campesinas of Jalisco (Jaliscan league of agrarian and peasant communities, 1951–53 and 1966–70). For Guadalupe, being a federal deputy meant being in an ideal position to modernize rural Mexico through public works. Federal deputies had the space needed to maneuver and a certain degree of autonomy to challenge local authoritarian caciques, as the following example illustrates. In 1957, as a federal congresswoman representing the electoral district of Autlán, she co-opted the presidential candidate Adolfo López Mateos's campaign slogan "Caciques last as long as people want them to" as a diagnosis of the region's problems.[74]

This slogan became a warning to local strongmen: the federal government would no longer tolerate arbitrariness.[75] She identified nine problems and proposed various pathways to find solutions and to ensure that they would form part of the public agenda. These were as follows: a lack of economic autonomy among peasant women, a need for irrigation water for agriculture, soil erosion, a lack of guarantees in the price of agricultural products, inequitable exploitation of forests, a need for the creation of new population centers for ejidatarios without land, a lack of agricultural credits, the politics of caciquismo, and a shortage of schools and rural schoolteachers. She expressed that these problems were not only local but national as well. With regards to local caciquismo, Guadalupe demanded guarantees from the presidential candidate for peasants given the abuse, deaths, and privations of liberty that had been suffered by some people.

Her complaint coincided with the public accusation published by Mrs. Mariana Moreno de Pelayo in *El informador* regarding the murder of her son Ruperto and her husband, Feliciano Pelayo, perpetrated by Dionisio Flores González in Autlán.[76] In a full-page announcement, Mrs. Moreno stated that in 1955, rural inhabitants of Autlán lived in constant fear of violence and lacked the rule of law. Both Urzúa's denunciations and those of Mrs. Moreno shed light on the degree of violence of local caciques. Their voices also showed that there was not just one cacique in the Autlán region. These caciques subsisted in tandem with presidential power, strengthened by the legislative and political reforms of 1946. According to Rogelio Hernández Rodríguez, "It was recognition that the federal government could not multiply itself in order to guarantee on its own the stability of the states. Coexistence was a result of a tacit distribution of responsibilities in which it was accepted that local powers could not be overlooked and that, moreover, they could be functional in terms of the political system."[77] Of caciques in the region, General García Barragán was the most well known. As a military officer and as a governor, he sought the modernization of the coastal region through public works (schools, roads, garbage dumps, irrigation systems, and farm machinery). García Barragán and Urzúa Flores probably met in the 1930s when they were both negotiating the construction of the highway to Barra de Navidad, but they definitely overlapped when the general visited San Martín Hidalgo during his campaign for governor in 1942.[78] Guadalupe did not form part of his political base, and García Barragán had to respect the decision of President Ruiz Cortines, who had chosen her as a candidate for federal deputy.[79] Guadalupe proved capable of challenging the caciquismo of the general in Autlán. He was excluded from political participation in the PRI and was forced into a political vacuum. As governor of Jalisco (1943–47), he was accused in 1947 of refusing to approve a law that increased the years of the position of governor (from four to six). In 1950, he went into self-exile from the military and politics. Around 1952, he headed the presidential campaign of General Miguel Henríquez Guzmán for the Federación de Partidos del Pueblo (Federation of people's parties), who ran against the candidate for the PRI, Adolfo Ruiz Cortines.[80] By virtue of the fact that García Barragán did not maintain his loyalty and preferred to support Henríquez, this action was seen as an attempted coup. Gabriel Torres states that this situation created a power vacuum that allowed for political negotiation and the reconfiguration of local networks of power.[81] According to José Eduardo Zárate, "García Barragán oversaw modernizing the coast and part of southern Jalisco. . . . His most important project, and the one that allowed him to become the region's 'strongman' of the region, was the settlement of the coast; . . . the so-called 'march to the sea' that began in 1944 and continued for several decades. . . . García Barragán inherited a wide network of *cacicazgos* based on the control of municipal governments, *ejidos*, and producer organizations, that became stronger and more consolidated in the succeeding decades through the integration of interest groups linked by bonds of family and business ties."[82]

Between 1959 and 1964, the central power of some *cacicazgos* was undone and local powers useful to the federal authorities were incorporated.[83] López Mateos invited García Barragán to lead the military zone in Guadalajara, thus reintegrating him into the military.[84] In 1964 he became minister of the Secretaría de la Defensa Nacional.

Los Lupistas

Guadalupe Urzúa created a political bloc popularly known as the *lupistas*. Her most loyal and faithful followers were Tomás García Tadeo, who became a mailman thanks to Guadalupe; Jesús Camacho Barreto, a teacher who later became mayor of San Martín Hidalgo; and Juan Díaz, who was from the same town. She also formed an alliance with local agrarian leaders in the neighboring villages of Cihuatlán and Casimiro Castillo.

Urzúa Flores's supporters were predominantly peasants and ejidatarios. Her female base was organized around the female section of the ejido. These peasant women, however, were not as visible as her male supporters, perhaps because of the violence, both symbolic and physical, that she faced throughout her political career. She was threatened many times for favoring and promoting land reform, but her male supporters protected her when opposing political forces threatened her. According to Urzúa Flores, even though their opponents wanted to assassinate her, they told her that they did not kill her because she was a woman. In time, she would recall that many men disapproved of a woman participating in politics, but she never confronted or challenged them. On the contrary, Urzúa always acted in a very careful manner. Nevertheless, she gained numerous enemies due to her support of Agraristas and agrarian reform.[85] Guadalupe established good political relations with the presidents Lázaro Cárdenas, Adolfo Ruiz Cortines, Adolfo López Mateos, and Luis Echeverría Álvarez as well as with the governors Juan Gil Preciado and Enrique Álvarez del Castillo.

The changing balance of power between the three sectors of the PRI—CNC, CTM, CNOP—can be demonstrated by the predominance of Guadalupe in the selection of candidates for municipal president following the death of one of the most powerful local caciques from the 1930s to the 1950s. During the 1950s and 1960s, she established strong ties with federal and state political networks, influenced local politics, and named some candidates as municipal presidents.[86] However, during the 1970s, the weakening of the peasant section within the PRI in Jalisco became evident, unlike the growing power and importance accrued by the CNOP. According to Jaime Sánchez Susarrey, the CNC was Jalisco's third political force and hence the weakest sector of the official party. It only controlled one electoral district.[87] The strongest sector was the CNOP, followed by the working-class sector. In the 1970s, a PRI faction of the CNOP attempted to do away with her. This movement was composed of local corn producers and allied with Guillermo Cosío Vidaurri (who formed part of the CNOP and later became municipal president of Guadalajara and governor of Jalisco). They displaced the *lupistas* from the municipal government from the 1970s to the 1990s (despite a brief resurgence between 1977 and 1979, when Jesús Camacho was municipal president).

Over the following two decades, Urzúa Flores was municipal president twice: the first time in her native town of Jocotepec, from 1983 to 1986, and the second time, from 1997 to 2001 in San Martín Hidalgo. By the late 1990s, Guadalupe had diabetes. She was old and got disoriented easily due to the onset of senility. After the PRI had suffered two defeats in San Martín Hidalgo in the '90s, a faction of PRI operators noticed that when she attended the inauguration of a library in the community of Tepehuaje, she was recognized by many people who greeted her with affection, gratitude, and respect. This faction believed that by harnessing Guadalupe's popularity and taking advantage of her legitimacy, the PRI could recover that political arena. Many people knew that Guadalupe was being used, but nobody did anything about it. What's more, Guadalupe felt she had the right to run for the municipal presidency due to her lengthy social and political career. Perhaps due to the onset of Alzheimer's disease, she was unable to realize that her time had passed. Meeting minutes of the municipal council in San Martín recorded that, several times, she proposed acquiring a plot of land to build a hospital. She had lost her sense of space, time, and memory. During this period, mismanagement was registered in the township. In 2004, Guadalupe Urzúa Flores died alone and with no possessions in an asylum in Jocotepec, Jalisco, at the age of ninety-one.

Using a long-term perspective along with the analytical categories of cacique, advocate, and gender, the case of Urzúa Flores helps us identify and distinguish different phases and processes in Mexican twentieth-century politics—ranging from the construction of the new revolutionary state to the development of modern corporatist institutions and, eventually, to their decline. Likewise, this political career and life story contribute to an understanding of not only the various practices and representations of women and politics but, above all, the historic periodization of women in politics: their organization, how they joined state agencies and politics, and how they shared and participated in electoral processes by running for electoral office.

Guadalupe initially entered politics because of her great sensitivity and solidarity with the dispossessed. She did not belong to a local political family or regional *cacicazgo*. She worked very actively for her community, lobbying and negotiating for the construction of libraries, highways, social welfare centers, schools, hospitals, and dams. She entered politics at a very young age. She became an advocate who earned her legitimacy and prestige thanks to the public works she backed and brought to completion. This allowed her to create a political bloc, the *lupistas*, while wielding influence over local electoral processes and creating political networks at the local, regional, and federal levels. She became politicized during the revolutionary process by the marginalization she encountered among poor peasants with leprosy, and she promoted the modernization of the patriarchy and the rationalization of domesticity. Perhaps because she never married, Urzúa had no limits and was able to develop her political career as she wished. She used her power to improve her community and the living conditions of poor peasants. The length of her political career contrasted markedly with the short political trajectory of most women of her generation, like Hermila Galindo (who asked the Constitucionalista deputies to include women's suffrage in the 1917 constitution), Elvia Carrillo Puerto, or Amalia Castillo Ledón. These women played important roles at certain times in certain spaces and often relied on the patronage of their brothers or husbands. Guadalupe was not a radical peasant leader, but she contributed significantly to expanding the role of women within the PRI after the municipal vote was granted in 1947, the electoral reform of 1946, and the institutionalization of the PRI. In this party, women became reformers within their communities and within the PRI itself. Women and young people were crucial to renovating the PRI in the 1950s and 60s, as a counterbalance to the dissident movements that appeared over those same two decades. Urzúa Flores was an unusual case within the PRI. According to Roderic Ai Camp, she was the most successful woman on a federal level in the late 1970s. Her political career compares to that of any man, at a time when such a career was uncommon. However, the liberal perspective of Camp made invisible the inequalities between men and women in politics and society in general and what it meant to be a strong woman in rural Mexico after the 1940s. As feminist academics, we need to think more closely about this kind of woman and how to name her: cacique or advocate. Further discussion of each category is required.

Epilogue

The five women of this book—Belén de Sárraga, Atala Apodaca, María Arcelia Díaz, Guadalupe Martínez Villanueva, and Guadalupe Urzúa Flores—enrich the transnational discussion on the impact of organized women in social movements and social policy during the emergence of welfare states (1880–1940) as well as the fight for broader women's rights—civic, economic, labor, political, and social. Historian Katherine M. Marino characterizes this broad perspective as *feminismo americano*, which encompasses the diverse contributions of these women to social movements and the advancement of women's rights. They were long-lived, except for the textile worker Díaz. They formed part of two cultural and political generations that interacted. Four of them were born and studied during the Porfirio Díaz regime. The activism of Sárraga, Apodaca, and Díaz, viewed through a transnational lens, reveals new forms of activism, new modes of identity, and ideas about citizenship. From a very young age, Martínez accompanied her father to the cultural events of antireelectionist clubs, while Sárraga, Apodaca, and Díaz played important roles in the Maderista movement, the Madero presidency, the anti-Huerta movement, Constitutionalism, the emergence of the organized labor movement, and the revolutionary period. Sárraga, Apodaca, and Díaz experienced the changes in the Porfirio Díaz regime triggered by the Mexican Revolution of 1910. The cases of Martínez and Urzúa provide excellent illustrations of the practices and representations of an authoritarian and corporatist postrevolutionary policy. Sárraga's, Apodaca's, Díaz's, Martínez's, and Urzúa's arguments were based on changes proposed to political movements and theories of the nineteenth and twentieth centuries (anarcho-syndicalism, anticlericalism, Spiritism, liberalism, freethinking, and Masonry). These transformations resulted in cultural constructs of femininity, masculinity, politics, and education.

Through a range of complex political and cultural discourses, Sárraga, Apodaca, Díaz, Martínez, and Urzúa gained recognition as subjects of social change. By resisting male patriarchal power and the influence of the Catholic Church, they significantly enhanced women's presence in society. Figures such as Laura and Atala Apodaca, along with Hermila Galindo, participated in processes that feminist historians have deemed a rationalization of domesticity and modernization of the patriarchy. They transformed traditional gender roles by means of agrarian, civil, labor, and political reforms that granted greater rights to women and children inside the home and at the workplace while also promoting hygiene campaigns to support national development. Hence a new concept of political and social reform was born: "the new woman," "the civic woman," and "the modern, politicized woman."

The analysis of the political careers and lives of these five women shows that they did not possess a unitary identity or fixed consciousness. On the contrary, they formed part of an ongoing ideological change that led them to become women with varying positions on gender and politics over the course of their lifetimes. Their story was captured by various sources: albums, biographies, songs, letters, interviews, labor demands and complaints, memoirs, articles in magazines and newspapers, poems, and the daily registries of debates in the Congreso de la Unión and the city council. The study of their history—the deconstruction of their actions, speeches, subjective experiences, cultural memories, and representations—refutes their invisibility and marginalization in education, the public sphere, and politics during the twentieth century in Mexico. Even though they were born and raised in different places (rural and urban, in Spain and Mexico) they all received a strong liberal education, which allowed them to complete studies at the Normal School, in commerce, and at universities. Only Díaz, the textile *trocilera*, had no elementary school education, yet her literacy aided her access to and mobility within the bureaucracy of the new Mexican State. The literacy, education, and professional training of these five women were accompanied always by cultural practices of reading essential to their politicization in labor-related experiences and their presence in the public sphere. They grew, studied, and were politicized in rural and urban environments, where they experienced and observed stark social inequalities. Their ability to write was useful to them, enabling them to not only draft letters and compose petitions but also edit magazines and newspapers that voiced the opinions of women, workers, farm women, and freethinkers. They were all nourished by different trends of thought and contributed to their dissemination.

In the case of Sárraga, it has been documented how Masonry and Spiritism greatly influenced her thinking. As for Apodaca and Martínez, the mark left by the presence of Masonic lodges at labor events or their strong bonds with "grand masters" are referenced, but I was unable to corroborate their initiation or development within Masonry. A liberal education with pronounced anticlerical heritage from the nineteenth century, Masonry, and freethinking influenced the ideas of Apodaca, Díaz, Martínez, and Urzúa, all of whom valued the social constructs of law, justice, the people, and Benito Juárez.

These women contributed to the modernization of Mexico's lower strata. Each one of them organized associations that, at first, included men and women and, afterward, only women and that fought for secular education and agrarian, civil, labor, and political rights. Their struggles focused on the defense of subaltern groups (men and women who were peasants, the working class, and women in general) to provide them with an education, labor rights, land plots, highways, hospitals, and housing.

Apodaca, Díaz, and Martínez were strongly linked to the organized labor movement, which led in turn to the organization of unions to defend both men and women. Moreover, each of them established women's associations, some of them with a maternalist agenda, as was the case of the female leagues of the CNC backed by Urzúa during the 1950s and 60s.

Following the displacement of women in the textile and tortilla industries during the 1920s and 30s and given the fact that the demands of women workers were not attended to by union leaders, Díaz radicalized her political stance. With the establishment of the Círculo Feminista de Occidente, Díaz and Martínez struggled for the basic demands of women: equal salary, collective contracts, minimum wage, and the right to unionize, direct labor organizations for women and, of course, support for the literacy of working women. They traded their struggle for a program that addressed the demands and needs of women, excluding male workers.

The five women of *Freethinkers and Labor Leaders* joined political parties, formed part of the board of directors of said parties, and directed the women's sections of peasants and workers in them. Sárraga, Apodaca, Martínez, and Urzúa ran for offices of popular election, after women's suffrage was recognized in Spain (1931) and in the municipal (1947) and federal arenas (1953) in Mexico. However, only Martínez and Urzúa became federal deputies, municipal presidents, or alternate senators. The other two lost their political races. Their presence in offices of popular election and mobility among these allowed them to wield power in different manners: as *cacicas* or as advocates. Their political performance and achievements were diverse. All of them show the long, difficult road women have faced. As the U.S. American political analyst Jo Freeman has stated, they took one step at a time.[1] However, this did not necessarily imply linear progress.

These five cases of women shed light on the arguments of Elizabeth Dore and Maxine Molyneux, who state that the liberal policies of the state affected gender relations, that secularization had effects (both positive and negative) on the configuration of the classification of gender, and "that female activism ensured that some account was taken of women's interest. Yet concessions from governments were piecemeal, usually minimal, and the arenas of decision-making power remained largely impermeable to female accession until the century's close."[2] Their lengthy life stories and political careers illustrate the participation of women and their collaboration in diverse movements and processes, such as European freethinking. The expansion of the freethinking across the American continent was made possible by its adaptation to different national, regional, and local circumstances as well as their adhesion to the Maderista movement, their active participation in the resistance against Victoriano Huerta, and their role in the emergence of labor, feminist, and peasant movements. Their actions highlight the political phases that women experienced throughout the twentieth century. Their practices and representations broke away from the tropes of "the angel of the home," "the victimized and exploited female worker," and "the lost woman."

The women featured here were affected by the social inequalities, exploitation, and poverty experienced by the dispossessed and oppressed, including women. Their personal and professional lives involved labor struggles and advocacy for policies like equal pay for equal work and the expansion of labor laws to include rural and domestic workers. This advocacy not only occurred locally but also intersected with transnational women's movements. Personal tragedies, such as the violent deaths of relatives, further motivated figures like Díaz and Urzúa to pursue political change and social justice. These women did not act in a vacuum. They were allied with major revolutionary figures (Madero, Diéguez, Carranza, Zuno, and Calles), labor leaders (Hernández Loza), politicians, and presidents of the republic (Madero, Carranza, Calles, and Ruiz Cortines) who favored the construction of a new Mexican State.

The coalition formed by these influential politicians and the five women of *Freethinkers and Labor Leaders* modified the culture of gender and politics. They negotiated feminine and masculine spaces, discourses, practices, and representations in education, politics, agrarian reform, and labor. They contributed to the modernization of a patriarchy, which was based on unequal power structures differentiated both horizontally and vertically. They proceeded quickly from household to factory or classroom and, finally, entered politics. Different moments in their political careers exemplify cultural change in their various spheres—economic, political, and social—and how spaces and discourses expanded in favor of women, albeit still under male domination. They destabilized traditional social constructs of male citizenship—such as military service, wage earning, and civic commitment—transforming them to obtain assistance and support. The political bloc of Martínez, a fundamental part of the union *cacicazgo* of the FTJ, aimed to preserve the revolutionary class culture they had built through civic, funereal, and labor rituals. They denied and silenced corporatist and patriarchal authoritarian political and labor structures. Additionally, the case of Martínez illustrates how a political power couple (she and Hernández) negotiated between themselves, their supporters, and their political faction, as well as governors and presidents of the republic, within the union bureaucracy during their four-decade *cacicazgo*.

What unites these women are not only the two cultural generations to which they belonged and interacted but also the "threads of the story" that encompass anticlericalism, women's emancipation, their political participation, and "the trail they left behind" of their contacts, encounters, and networks.[3] To disseminate their ideals, they recurred to magazines and newspapers: *Argos* (1916–17), *Rumbos nuevos* (1925–27), *Fémina roja* (1934), and *Jalisco ceteme* (1950–60).

Each of these women made major contributions. They not only fought for a secular education to emancipate women from the influence of the Catholic Church and its robust Catholic social action movement but also developed proposals for civic education. Through this instruction, they sought to legitimize the modern woman, endowed with social and political rights and responsible for educating loyal citizens to the nation. Sárraga and Apodaca focused on advocating for women's right to education, a strategy they viewed as more transcendental than the struggle for women's suffrage. Education granted freedom of thought, enabling individuals to make independent decisions—an idea that was revolutionary and remains valid today.

Despite all this, the contributions of these five women were forgotten because they transgressed the established gender order in politics. The actions of revolutionary leaders were seen as natural due to their anticlerical, combative, Masonic, and military revolutionary stances. Sárraga, Apodaca, Díaz, Martínez, and Urzúa challenged and destabilized the male-dominated constructs of what was considered political or revolutionary. Their literacy and education were crucial in advocating for the right to work, to equal wages, to create unions for workers and peasant organizations. Their women's associations played a significant role in shaping the corporatist politics of the PRM-PRI, except for Apodaca, who was affiliated with the Partido Popular of Vicente Lombardo Toledano.

Paradoxically, they reproduced gender inequalities in political parties and their women's organizations. They advocated for a greater presence of women in formal politics. They lobbied for more roles for women in unions, the women's sections of the PRI, and in the labor and peasant sectors and electoral races—not only as voters but also as candidates in electoral races. Although their actions and politics did not dismantle patriarchal power, they contributed to the modernization of the corporatist politics of the PRI throughout the twentieth century.

APPENDIX

Table 3. Mexico's population ages ten years and older according to literacy, illiteracy, and sex in Mexico, 1895–2000

	1895		1900		1910		1921		1930		1940	
	NUMBER	PER-CENT	NUMBER	PER-CENT	NUMBER	PER-CENT	NUMBER	PER-CENT	NUMBER	PER-CENT	NUMBER	PER-CENT
Total	10,301,030	100.0	9,822,220	100.0	10,809,090	100.0	10,528,622	100.0	11,748,936	100.0	12,960,140	100.0
Men	5,089,465	49.4	4,819,686	49.1	5,286,213	48.9	5,074,276	48.2	5,681,300	48.4	6,806,218	52.5
Women	5,211,565	50.6	5,002,534	50.9	5,522,877	51.1	5,454,346	51.8	6,067,636	51.6	6,153,922	47.5
Literate	1,843,292	17.9	2,185,761	22.3	2,992,076	27.7	3,564,767	33.8	4,525,035	38.5	5,416,188	41.8
Men	1,090,214	59.1	1,277,203	58.4	1,680,918	56.2	1,878,434	52.7	2,460,614	54.4	3,401,089	62.8
Women	753,078	40.9	908,558	41.6	1,311,108	43.8	1,686,333	47.3	2,064,421	45.6	2,015,099	37.2
Illiterate	8,457,738	82.1	7,636,459	77.7	7,817,064	72.3	6,973,855	66.2	7,223,901	61.5	7,543,952	58.2
Men	3,999,251	47.3	3,542,483	46.4	3,605,295	46.1	3,195,842	45.8	3,220,686	44.6	3,405,129	45.1
Women	4,458,487	52.7	4,093,976	53.6	4,211,769	53.9	3,778,013	54.2	4,003,215	55.4	4,138,823	54.9
Does not specify	—	—	—	—	—	—	—	—	—	—	—	—
Men	—	—	—	—	—	—	—	—	—	—	—	—
Women	—	—	—	—	—	—	—	—	—	—	—	—

	1950		1960		1970		1980		1990		2000	
	NUMBER	PER-CENT	NUMBER	PER-CENT	NUMBER	PER-CENT	NUMBER	PER-CENT	NUMBER	PER-CENT	NUMBER	PER-CENT
Total	20,708,657	100.0	23,829,338	100.0	32,334,732	100.0	37,927,410	100.0	49,610,876	100.0	62,842,638	100.0
Men	10,142,621	49.0	11,773,023	49.4	15,979,368	49.4	18,500,443,	48.8	23,924,966	48.2	30,043,824	47.8
Women	10,566,036	51.0	12,056,315,	50.6	16,355,364	50.6	19,426,967	51.2	25,685,910	51.8	32,798,814	52.2
Literate	11,766,258	56.8	15,848,653,	66.5	24,657,659	76.3	31,475,670	83.0	43,354,067	87.4	56,841,673	90.5
Men	6,123,450	52.0	8,294,844	52.3	12,701,534	51.5	15,955,272	50.7	21,575,645	49.8	27,780,949	48.9
Women	5,642,808	48.0	7,553,809	47.7	11,956,125	48.5	15,520,398	49.3	21,778,422	50.2	29,060,724	51.1
Illiterate	8,942,399	43.2	7,980,685	33.5	7,677,073	23.7	6,451,740	17.0	6,161,662	12.4	5,942,091	9.5
Men	4,019,171	44.9	3,478,179	43.6	3,277,834	42.7	2,545,171	39.4	2,305,113	37.4	2,233,244	37.6
Women	4,923,228	55.1	4,502,506	56.4	4,399,239	57.3	3,906,569	60.6	3,856,549	62.6	3,708,847	62.4
Does not specify	—	—	—	—	—	—	—	—	95,147	0.2	58,874	0.1
Men	—	—	—	—	—	—	—	—	44,208	46.5	29,631	50.3
Women	—	—	—	—	—	—	—	—	50,939	53.5	29,243	49.7

Source: Instituto Nacional de Estadística Geografía e Informática, *Estadísticas históricas de México* (Mexico: INEGI, 2000).

NOTES

Introduction

1. Hernández, *La mujer mexicana*, 41; "Llegó a Guadalajara D. Belem de Zárraga," *El informador*, Guadalajara, January 11, 1923, 8, HDEI; "Belén de Sárraga," *El informador*, Guadalajara, January 12, 1923, 8, HDEI.
2. Marino, *Feminism for the Americas*, 4-6.
3. By cultural generation, I mean a group of individuals who share common experiences that took place in the historic past—experiences that marked them culturally as a group, given that they share similar objectives and recognize themselves as a community.
4. Elias, *El proceso de la civilización*; Scott, *Gender and the Politics*.
5. Elias, *El proceso de la civilización*, 12.
6. Elias, *Conocimiento y poder*, 125-26.
7. Cejudo Ramos, *El gobierno no pueda más que dios*; Porter, *Working Women in Mexico City*; Porter, *From Angel to Office Worker*; Vaughan, *Cultural Politics in Revolution*; Vaughan, "Modernizing Patriarchy"; Vaughan, Cano, and Olcott, *Sex in Revolution*.
8. Ginzburg, *Threads and Traces*, 1; Bayly et al., "*AHR* Conversation," 1441-64.
9. Pratt, "Repensar la modernidad," 55.
10. Pratt, "Repensar la modernidad," 70.
11. Pratt, "Repensar la modernidad," 70.
12. Maza, "Stories in History," 1493-1515.
13. Vaughan, *Portrait of a Young Painter*, 4. For a comparative vision of new biography, see Banner, "Biography as History"; Bazant, *Laura Méndez de Cuenca*; Bazant, *Biografía*; Cano, *Se llamaba Elena Arizmendi*; Chassen-López, *Mujer y poder*; Fowler-Salamini, "Algunas reflexiones sobre las feministas"; Nasaw, "Introduction"; Oikión Solano, *Cuca García*; Spiegel, "Comment on a Crooked Line"; Vasquez Montaño, *Ethel Duffy Turner*; Lau Jaiven and McPhail Fanger, *Rupturas y continuidades*; Arrom, *La Güera Rodríguez*; and Vaughan, "Pensar la biografía."

14. Vaughan, *Portrait of a Young Painter*.
15. Bazant, *Caminos docentes*, 17.
16. Chassen-López, *Mujer y poder*, 4.
17. Chassen-López, *Mujer y poder*, 10.
18. Scott, *Only Paradoxes to Offer*, 16.
19. Personal Narratives Group, *Interpreting Women's Lives*, 5; Smith Crocco, Munro, and Weiler, "In Search of Subjectivity," 7, 12.
20. Franco, *Las conspiradoras*, 11.
21. Deans-Smith and Joseph, *Special Issue*; Knight, "Mexican Revolution"; Knight, *Mexican Revolution*; Rubin, "Decentering the Regime"; Spenser and Levison, "Linking State and Society"; Vaughan, *Cultural Politics in Revolution*.
22. Vaughan, *Cultural Politics in Revolution*, 8.
23. Joseph and Nugent, *Everyday Forms of State Formation*; Knight, *Mexican Revolution*; Vaughan, *Cultural Politics in Revolution*; Curley, *Citizens and Believers*.
24. For an excellent and exhaustive review of teachers in the revolutionary process, see Vaughan, "Women School Teachers," 106–24; and Vaughan, *Cultural Politics in Revolution*. For a discussion of the soldaderas, see Salas, *Soldaderas en los ejércitos mexicanos*; Salas, "Soldadera in the Mexican Revolution"; and Rocha Islas, *Los rostros de la rebeldía*.
25. Fowler-Salamini, "Género y la Revolución Mexicana," 391.
26. Fowler-Salamini, "Género y la Revolución Mexicana."
27. Ramos Escandón, "Gender, Work, and Class Consciousness," 87–88. Also see Lau Jaiven and Ramos Escandón, *Mujeres y revolución*. The Grupo Ácrata was an association of nurses who worked together with the Batallones Rojos, a military group of workers created in 1915 to support the Constitutionalist cause of Venustiano Carranza. They both formed part of the Casa del Obrero Mundial. See Rivera Carbó, "Esther Torres," 50.
28. Rocha Islas, "Las mujeres en la Revolución mexicana"; Rocha Islas, *El álbum de la mujer*.
29. I draw from the conceptualization of Carole Pateman to better understand the modern concept of "patriarchy" as a systematic exercise by men over women in social and sexual relations that, in fact, are relations of domination and subordination. See Pateman, "Patriarchal Welfare," 231.
30. O'Malley, *Myth of the Revolution*; Fowler-Salamini and Vaughan, *Women of the Mexican Countryside*.
31. Ramos Escandón, *Presencia y transparencia*; Ramos Escandón, "Mujeres mexicanas"; McGee Deutsch, "Gender and Sociopolitical Change."
32. McGee Deutsch, "Gender and Sociopolitical Change," 271.
33. Fowler-Salamini and Vaughan, *Women of the Mexican Countryside*.

34. Lau Jaiven, "Una vida singular"; S. J. Smith, *Gender and the Mexican Revolution*; Cano, "Adelina Zendejas"; Cano, "Las feministas en campaña"; Cano, "Revolución, feminismo y ciudadanía"; Ramos Escandón, "Mujeres mexicanas"; Ramos Escandón, "Metiéndose en la *bola*"; Ramos Escandón, "Mujer y poder en el cardenismo"; Vaughan, Cano, and Olcott, *Sex in Revolution*; Schell, *Church and State Education*; Olcott, *Revolutionary Women in Postrevolutionary Mexico*; Cano, *Se llamaba Elena Arizmendi*.
35. Ruiz, *Challenge of Poverty and Illiteracy*; Britton, *Educación y radicalismo en México*; Britton, "Teacher Unionization"; Vaughan, *Cultural Politics in Revolution*; Civera Cerecedo, "La historiografía del magisterio en México"; Civera Cerecedo, *La escuela*; Galván and López, *Entre imaginarios y utopías*.
36. Britton, "Teacher Unionization"; Raby, *Educación y revolución social en México*; Martínez Moya and Moreno Castañeda, *La escuela de la revolución*; Chavoya Peña, *Poder sindical en Jalisco*.
37. Olcott, *Revolutionary Women*, 20.
38. Barlow et al., "Modern Girl around the World," 245–94.
39. Dore and Molyneux, *Hidden Histories of Gender*; Duby and Perrot, *Historia de las mujeres*; Fauré, *Enciclopedia histórica*; Gómez-Ferrer et al., *Historia de las mujeres*; Johnson-Odim and Strobel, *Expanding the Boundaries*.
40. Some historians such as Victoria de Grazia, Mary Kay Vaughan, and Susan Besse have called this new relationship between women and the state the "modernization of the patriarchy," due to the incorporation of more egalitarian ideas in gender roles in social policies in the early twentieth century and due to a more active participation of women in the public sphere regarding vaccination, literacy, hygiene, and antialcoholic campaigns, though as second-class citizens. This modernization did not seek to fracture male power or erase traditional gender roles; rather, it sought only to modernize them. See Vaughan, *Cultural Politics in Revolution*; de Grazia, *How Fascism Ruled Women*; Besse, *Restructuring Patriarchy*.
41. See especially the analysis in Fauré, *Enciclopedia histórica*.
42. Molyneux, "Twentieth-Century State Formations," 68.
43. Fowler-Salamini, "Género y la Revolución Mexicana."
44. The origin of the term is "*kassequa*," hispanicized as "cacique" to refer to the autochthonous legal representatives of the Indian republics. See de la Peña Topete, "Poder local, poder regional." The bibliography is vast, so I will mention only a few: Friedrich, *Rebelión agraria*; Joseph, *Revolution from Without*; Falcón, *Política y caciquismo*; Bartra, *Caciquismo y poder político*; Brading, *Caudillos y campesinos*; Knight and Pansters, *Caciquismo in Twentieth-Century Mexico*; de la Peña Topete, "Populism, Regional Power"; Guerra, *México*; Knight, "Cultura

política y caciquismo"; Martínez Assad, *Estadistas, caciques y caudillos*; Salmerón Castro, "Caciques"; Lomnitz-Adler, *Las salidas del laberinto*; Salmerón Castro, *Los límites del agrarismo*; Pansters, *Citizens of the Pyramid*; Pansters, *Política y poder en Puebla*; Purnell, *Agraristas and Cristeros of Michoacán*; Fallaw, *Cárdenas Compromised*.

45. Salmerón Castro, "Caciques," 109.
46. De la Peña Topete, "Poder local"; Salmerón Castro, "Caciques"; Joseph, "El caciquismo y la revolución."
47. Knight, "Cárdenas, Caciquismo."
48. Kellogg, *Weaving the Past*; Chassen-López, "Patron of Progress"; Fowler-Salamini, "'La Negra Moya'"; Fowler-Salamini, "Caciquismo, sindicalismo."
49. Buve, "Caciquismo." For a very interesting analysis of Indigenous widowed female caciques in the colonial era, see Muriel, "Las viudas"; and Ochoa and Vicuña Guengerich, *Cacicas*.
50. Cárdenas García and Guerra Manzo, *Integrados y marginados*, 29.
51. Pansters, *Goodbye to the Caciques?*, 349–76.
52. Scott, *Only Paradoxes to Offer*, 14.
53. Molyneux, "Twentieth-Century State Formations."
54. Olcott, *Revolutionary Women*, 11, 17, 19–20.
55. Batliwala, "Meaning of Women's Empowerment"; Kabeer, *Realidades trastocadas*.
56. Kaplan, "Female Consciousness and Collective Action," 545.
57. Alvarez, *Engendering Democracy in Brazil*, 24; Molyneux, "Mobilization without Emancipation?," 232–34.
58. Koven and Michel, *Mothers of a New World*.
59. Brush, "Love, Toil, and Trouble"; Ladd-Taylor, *Mother-Work*.
60. Threlkeld, *Pan American Women*; Olcott, *International Women's Year*; Marino, *Feminism for the Americas*; Hernández, *For a Just and Better World*.
61. Pratt, "Repensar la modernidad," 56.
62. I especially refer to the struggle and dispute among those who supported the influence of religion in society and those who sought to privilege the points of view of the state to replace the strong dominion of the church over society, an unequal process of long duration known as secularization. For a discussion of this concept, see McLeod, *Secularisation in Western Europe*.

1. The "Modern Woman"

1. Apodaca, *Educación de las jóvenes*.
2. Pratt, "Repensar la modernidad," 55.
3. O'Dogherty Madrazo, *De urnas y sotanas*, 237.
4. Cárdenas Ayala, *El derrumbe*.

5. Márquez Carpet, *Las grandes encíclicas sociales*, 236.
6. O'Dogherty Madrazo, *De urnas y sotanas*.
7. Cárdenas Ayala, *El derrumbe*, 235.
8. It encompassed more than seven thousand male and nine thousand female workers. See Ceballos Ramírez, *El catolicismo social*, 30.
9. National Catholic congresses were held in the cities of Oaxaca (1903), Morelia (1904), Guadalajara (1906), and again in Oaxaca (1909). Catholics also held regional agricultural congresses (1904–6) and two Social Weeks (1908–9). At these congresses, it became evident that there were two main trends in Mexican Catholicism: the conciliatory and the intransigent. See Barbosa Guzmán, *La iglesia y el gobierno civil*.
10. Partido Católico Nacional, *Acción política de los católicos*; Partido Católico Nacional, *Programa y estatutos*.
11. Cárdenas Ayala, *El derrumbe*, 436.
12. Cárdenas Ayala, *El derrumbe*, 238.
13. Cárdenas Ayala, *El derrumbe*, 421.
14. Ceballos Ramírez, *El catolicismo social*, 399.
15. Barbosa Guzmán, *La iglesia y el gobierno civil*, 86–87.
16. Miguel Palomar y Vizcarra, a lay Catholic, proposed the founding of Cajas Raiffeisen, which was based on the concepts of charity and labor. This was an attempt to substitute the banking system and create co-ops run by workers. The model for these funds was taken from German rural credit funds. See Curley, *Citizens and Believers*, 39, 64, 68, 90, 285, 81, 363, 79.
17. Curley, *Citizens and Believers*, 177–78; Méndez Medina, *La cuestión social en México*; Barbosa Guzmán, *La iglesia y el gobierno civil*, 117.
18. In a consular report, they described him as "wealthy, handsome, and proud." The Orozco y Jiménez family was from Zamora, Michoacán. He studied at the Collegio Pio-Latino of Rome, known for its focus on social action. Orozco y Jiménez was archbishop of Guadalajara from 1913 to 1936. His arrival in Guadalajara was on the same day as the fall of President Francisco I. Madero to the military coup of General Victoriano Huerta in February 1912. See Burton, "Resistance and Accommodations," 84; Camberos Vizcaíno, *Francisco el grande*.
19. *La gaceta de Guadalajara*, March 3, 1913, quoted in Barbosa Guzmán, *La iglesia y el gobierno civil*, 123.
20. Barbosa Guzmán, *La iglesia y el gobierno civil*, 126–33.
21. Tamayo Rodríguez, *Los movimientos sociales*, 67.
22. On April 26, 1913, the ADCG was founded. Dávila Garibi, *Memoria histórica*, 2. The Círculo de Estudios Sociales León XIII was established in June of 1913. Barbosa Guzmán, *La iglesia y el gobierno civil*, 127–28.

23. Archbishop Orozco y Jiménez was director; Catalina Palomar de Verea was President; Emilia Hayhoe de Chávez was Secretary; and Teresa Zavala de Fernández del Valle was Treasurer. See Dávila Garibi, *Memoria histórica*, 3.
24. Vaca, "Devociones y trabajos," 90–121; Arrom, "Mexican Laywomen"; Arrom, "Mobilization"; Arrom, "Las Señoras de la Caridad"; Boylan, "Mexican Catholic Women's Activism"; Boylan, "Género, fe y nación."
25. Vaca, "Devociones y trabajos," 9, 84–91.
26. O'Dogherty Madrazo, "Restaurarlo todo en Cristo," 130.
27. Schell, "Honorable Avocation for Ladies," 79, 81, 84–85; Schell, "Las mujeres del catolicismo social."
28. Dávila Garibi, *Memoria histórica*, 6.
29. Dávila Garibi, *Memoria histórica*, 102.
30. Dávila Garibi, *Memoria histórica*, 14.
31. O'Dogerthy Madrazo, "Restaurarlo todo en Cristo," 145–46.
32. Barbosa Guzmán, *La iglesia y el gobierno civil*, 136.
33. Barbosa Guzmán, *La iglesia y el gobierno civil*, 137.
34. According to Laura O'Dogherty Madrazo, by 1914, the PCN had almost disappeared, maintaining only a presence in the legislature of Jalisco. See Cárdenas Ayala, *El horizonte democrático*, 42–50; Cárdenas Ayala, *El derrumbe*, 412–21; O'Dogerthy Madrazo, *De urnas y sotanas*.
35. Aldana Rendón, *Manuel M. Diéguez*, 13.
36. Aldana Rendón, *Manuel M. Diéguez*, 12.
37. Dávila Garibi, *Memoria histórica*, 10.
38. Katz, *Life and Times*, 481.
39. The Villistas occupied Guadalajara from December 16, 1914, to January 18, 1915. From February to April of 1915, the Villistas controlled certain parts of Jalisco. See Murià, *Historia de Jalisco*, 486; Vargas Reynoso, "Siete meses."
40. Michel Pimienta, *Episodios históricos*, 25–36; Katz, *Life and Times*, 482–83.
41. See chapter 3 for a more detailed analysis of the participation of women Constitucionalistas.
42. Urzúa Orozco and Hernández, *Jalisco, testimonio de sus gobernantes*, 257–74.
43. Curley, "'Avanza el desierto'"; González Flores, *La cuestión religiosa en Jalisco*, 390.
44. González Flores, *La cuestión religiosa en Jalisco*, 382–83; Barbosa Guzmán, *La iglesia y el gobierno civil*, 164–68.
45. Michel Pimienta, *Episodios históricos*, 9–10.
46. Dorantes, Castillo Ramírez, and Tuñón Pablos, *Irene Robledo García*, 46–48.
47. Dorantes, Castillo Ramírez, and Tuñón Pablos, *Irene Robledo García*, 48.
48. Pedersen, *Family, Dependence*, 54.

49. The newspapers I use in this chapter tend to be anarcho-syndicalist (*Acción*) and Constitucionalista (*Boletín militar*). *Acción* was the organ of the Confederación Revolucionaria, Delegación de Occidente (Western delegation of the revolutionary confederation). It was within the framework of Constitutionalism. An afternoon daily newspaper, it defended the fulfillment of individual autonomy and the right to collective bargaining. It informed the public of the activities of the Casa del Obrero Mundial in Jalisco and nationwide, as well as labor associations. The *Boletín militar* was the organ of propaganda of the Constitucionalistas, especially Venustiano Carranza and Manuel M. Diéguez in Jalisco, to announce their military feats and legislative works. It was published from July 1914 to June 1916, and its director was N. Valenzuela. "El deber de la mujer," *Acción*, Guadalajara, August 5, 1915, FE/BPEJ; "Lo que el pueblo mexicano ha sido y lo que puede llegar a ser," *Acción*, Guadalajara, July 7, 1915, FE/BPEJ; "Programa de educación y enseñanza," *Acción*, Guadalajara, August 3, 1915, FE/BPEJ; "Sección editorial: La Ley contra la embriaguez," *Boletín militar*, Guadalajara, August 20, 1915, FE/BPEJ.

50. T-1-914, box T-bis "C," 1914, file no. 5906, AHJ, FT; T-1-914, file 578, AHJ, FT; T-1-914, box T-bis "C," 1914, file no. 5912, AHJ, FT; T-1-917, box T-bis "D," 1916–18, file no. 5929, AHJ, FT; T-8-917, box T-38 bis "O," file no. 8588, AHJ, FT; T-1-917, box T-bis "D," 1916–28, file no. 5930, AHJ, FT; T-2-917, box T-10 bis "D," file no. 7071, AHJ, FT; T-2-917, T-10 bis "B," 1917, file no. 7068, AHJ, FT; T-2-917, box T-10 bis "D," file no. 7069, AHJ, FT; T-1-917, box T-bis "D," 1916–18, file no. 5940, AHJ, FT; T-1-916, box T-bis "D," 1916–18, file no. 5925, AHJ, FT; T-3-917, box T-19 bis "J," file no. 7846, AHJ, FT.

51. Porter, *Working Women in Mexico City*; "Campaña anti-alcohólica," *Boletín militar*, Guadalajara, March 7, 1916, 3, FE/BPEJ; "El servicio militar obligatorio, es el mejor método para convertir en hombres aptos y útiles a nuestros ineptos desocupados," *Boletín militar*, Guadalajara, May 24, 1916, 2, FE/BPEJ; Leonidas, "La cuestión obrera," *Boletín militar*, Guadalajara, March 4, 1916, 2, FE/BPEJ; Soledad Muñoz, "Petición para que no se cierre el Mercado Libertad los domingos en la tarde," in T-1-914, box T-bis "C," 1914, file no. 5907, AHJ, FT.

52. Keremitsis, "La doble jornada," 42–44, 48.

53. T-1-914, box T-bis "C," 1914, file no. 5911, AHJ, FT.

54. T-1-914, box T-bis "C," 1914, file no. 5906, AHJ, RT; T-1-914, file no. 578, AHJ, RT; T-1-914, box T-bis "C," 1914, file no. 5912, AHJ, RT; T-1-917, box T-bis "D," 1916–18, file no. 5929, AHJ, RT; T-8-917, box T-38 bis "O," file 8588, AHJ, RT; T-1-917, box T-bis "D," 1916–28, file no. 5930, AHJ, RT; T-2-917, box T-10 bis "D," file no. 7071, AHJ, RT; T-2-917, box T-10 bis "B," 1917, file no. 7068, AHJ, RT; T-2-917, box T-10 bis "D," file no. 7069, AHJ, RT; T-1-917, box T-bis "D," 1916–18,

file no. 5940, AHJ, RT; T-1-916, box T-bis "D," 1916-18, file no. 5925, AHJ, RT; T-3-917, box T-19 bis "J," file no. 7846, AHJ, RT.
55. Vaughan, *Cultural Politics in Revolution*, 197.
56. Reséndez Fuentes, "Battleground Women"; Cano, *Se llamaba Elena Arizmendi*; Poniatowska, *Las soldaderas*; Salas, "Soldadera in the Mexican Revolution"; Salas, *Soldaderas en los ejércitos mexicanos*; Villegas de Magnón, *La rebelde*; Islas, "Las mujeres en la Revolución Mexicana." See the discussions of Friedrich Katz regarding the role of women in the Mexican Revolution and the diverse presence of women in the Maderista, Villista, and Constitucionalista forces. Katz, *Life and Times*, 290-92.
57. The COM was created on July 15, 1912, in Mexico City. Ácrata was founded in 1915. Paula Osorio, Jovita Estrada, Carmen Velásquez, and Maclovia Pachecho formed part of Ácrata. See Rivera Carbó, "La Casa del obrero Mundial," 249, 340.
58. S. J. Smith, *Gender and the Mexican Revolution*; Porter, *Working Women in Mexico City*; Vaughan, *Cultural Politics in Revolution*; Knight, "Revolutionary Project, Recalcitrant People"; Knight, "Popular Culture."
59. Vaughan, *Cultural Politics in Revolution*.
60. See the editorials and biographies of *Boletín militar* published from September 1914 to May 1916. "8 de julio de 1914," *Boletín militar*, Guadalajara, July 8, 1914, 1, FE/BPEJ; "Coronel Juan José Ríos, Jefe del 14 Batallón," *Boletín militar*, Guadalajara, October 18, 1914, 1, FE/BPEJ; "¿Cuál es la teoría del poder público revolucionario?," *Boletín militar*, Guadalajara, November 1, 1914, 2, FE/BPEJ; "Datos biográficos del Sr. Gral. Manuel M. Diéguez," *Boletín militar*, Guadalajara, September 6, 1914, 5, FE/BPEJ; "Elementos civiles en la revolución: Lic. Manuel Aguirre Berlanga," *Boletín militar*, Guadalajara, September 13, 1914, 4, FE/BPEJ; "La honorabilidad privada y la pública," *Boletín militar*, Guadalajara, November 5, 1914, 2, FE/BPEJ; "La peregrinación del caudillo constitucionalista," *Boletín militar*, September 5, 1914, 2, FE/BPEJ; "La Revolución sobre los personalismos," *Boletín militar*, Guadalajara, September 3, 1914, 2, FE/BPEJ; "Labor de cobardes," *Boletín militar*, Guadalajara, October 18, 1914, 2, FE/BPEJ; "Los hombres nuevos como funcionarios y soldados," *Boletín militar*, Guadalajara, September 6, 1914, 2, FE/BPEJ; "Manifiesto: Gral. Don Manuel M. Diéguez, Gobernador y Comandante del Estado, dirige a la Convención de Aguascalientes," *Boletín militar*, Guadalajara, November 10, 1914, 1, FE/BPEJ; "Pueblo de Jalisco," *Boletín militar*, Guadalajara, November 14, 1914, 1, FE/BPEJ; "Señor Coronel Ernesto Damy, Jr.," *Boletín militar*, Guadalajara, December 6, 1914, 2, FE/BPEJ; "Sr. Gral. Alvaro Obregón," *Boletín militar*, Guadalajara, August 30, 1914, 1, FE/BPEJ; "Sr. Gral. Dn. Francisco Murguía," *Boletín militar*, Guadalajara,

November 8, 1914, 1, FE/BPEJ; "Teniente Coronel Esteban B. Calderón," *Boletín militar*, Guadalajara, November 1, 1914, 1, FE/BPEJ; "Biografía y características de Carranza," *Boletín militar*, Guadalajara, July 8, 1915, 9, FE/BPEJ; "Documentos para la historia: La contestación del general González a los convencionistas," *Boletín militar*, Guadalajara, July 8, 1915, 3, FE/BPEJ; "Honradez del constitucionalismo," *Boletín militar*, Guadalajara, August 1, 1915, 6, FE/BPEJ; "Carranza, el gran reformador," *Boletín militar*, Guadalajara, March 4, 1916, 3, FE/BPEJ; "Hombres de la revolución," *Boletín militar*, Guadalajara, March 4, 1916, 1, FE/BPEJ; Salvador Martínez Alomía, "Venustiano Carranza y el Constitucionalismo," *Boletín militar*, Guadalajara, September 3, 1914, 3, FE/BPEJ; Martínez Alomía, "Venustiano Carranza y el Constitucionalismo," *Boletín militar*, Guadalajara, September 4, 1914, 4, FE/BPEJ.

61. "Ideas y Hombres," *Boletín militar*, Guadalajara, July 3, 1915, 1, FE/BPEJ.
62. "El clericalismo y el nuevo régimen," *Boletín militar*, Guadalajara, July 25, 1914, 1, FE/BPEJ.
63. "El clericalismo y el nuevo régimen," *Boletín militar*, Guadalajara, July 25, 1914, 1, FE/BPEJ.
64. Apodaca, *Educación de las jóvenes*, 9.
65. Apodaca, *Educación de las jóvenes*.
66. "Discurso pronunciado por el joven Daniel Galindo en la matinée de los estudiantes preparatorianos con motivo de la apertura del año escolar de 1914 a 1915," *Boletín militar*, Guadalajara, October 9, 1914, 4, FE/BPEJ.
67. "Discurso pronunciado por el joven Daniel Galindo en la matinée de los estudiantes preparatorianos con motivo de la apertura del año escolar de 1914 a 1915," *Boletín militar*, Guadalajara, October 9, 1914, FE/BPEJ.
68. "Discurso pronunciado por el joven Daniel Galindo en la matinée de los estudiantes preparatorianos con motivo de la apertura del año escolar de 1914 a 1915," *Boletín militar*, Guadalajara, October 9, 1914, FE/BPEJ.
69. For a broader discussion of the introduction of Auguste Comte to Mexico, see Zea, *El positivismo en México*; and Córdova, *La ideología*, 53–78.
70. Constitucionalista propaganda in favor of their own cause significantly contrasts with the robbery and pillaging that Venustiano Carranza allowed among his followers. These actions gave rise to the verb *carrancear*.
71. Antonia Ortiz, "Constitucionalistas, la Patria os espera ¡Corred a salvarla!," *Boletín militar*, Guadalajara, July 10, 1915, 2, FE/BPEJ.
72. Alter Ego, "¿Qué Pretendía el Villismo?," *Boletín militar*, Guadalajara, July 3, 1915, 7, FE/BPEJ.
73. "Nuestro Primer Aniversario," *Boletín militar*, Guadalajara, July 15, 1915, 1, 12, FE/BPEJ.

74. Arrom, "Mexican Laywomen"; Arrom, "Las Señoras de la Caridad."
75. Reyismo refers to a popular urban movement that supported General Bernardo Reyes as a candidate to the vice presidency of 1910. José López Portillo y Rojas and Rodolfo Reyes, the son of General Reyes, led this movement. Their slogan was "The people want Reyes!" See Guerra, *México*, 144–230; Knight, *Mexican Revolution*, vol. 1, 47–55. The Flores Magón brothers were middle-class intellectuals who created the Partido Liberal Mexicano in 1907 to topple the Porfirio Díaz dictatorship. They published *Regeneración* to disseminate ideas against the Díaz regime and to favor social justice and political reform. See Cockcroft, *Precursores intelectuales*; Dorantes, Castillo Ramírez, and Tuñón Pablos, *Irene Robledo García*, 35–36.
76. Dorantes, Castillo Ramírez, and Tuñón Pablos, *Irene Robledo García*, 39.
77. For a more in-depth discussion of these organizations and other women teachers of Jalisco, see chapter 3.
78. Dorantes, Castillo Ramírez, and Tuñón Pablos, *Irene Robledo García*, 39.
79. Scott, *Gender and the Politics*, 44–50.
80. Orellana Trinidad, "'La mujer del porvenir,'" 136.
81. Rössler and Fanning, "Mujer"; Pavissich, *Mujer antigua y mujer moderna*; Delgado Capeans, *La mujer*.
82. Rössler and Fanning, "Mujer."
83. For a historical and theoretical discussion of the debates revolving around difference and equality, see Scott, *Only Paradoxes to Offer*.
84. Vaughan, "Cultural Approaches," 300–301; Vaughan, "Modernizing Patriarchy," 194, 197, 200.

2. Belén de Sárraga Hernández

1. Throughout the life of Belén de Sárraga, primary sources refer to her as Belén Sárraga, Belén de Sárraga, or Belén de Zárraga. According to María Dolores Ramos, after her divorce from Emilio Ferrero in 1911, Belén adopted "de Sárraga" to display her new, liberated identity.
2. Belén de Sárraga's arrival in Mexico was news in various daily newspapers of the capital and the cities she visited. "Sección Ecos de la Semana," *El abogado cristiano*, Mexico, August 15, 1912, 4, HNDM/UNAM.
3. "Test of Intellect Recognizes No Sex," *Mexican Herald*, September 6, 1912, 2, HNDM/UNAM.
4. "Test of Intellect Recognizes No Sex," *Mexican Herald*, 2, HNDM/UNAM.
5. "Test of Intellect Recognizes No Sex," *Mexican Herald*, 2, HNDM/UNAM.
6. Pérez Ledesma, "Por tierras," 387.
7. There are discrepancias regarding the birthdate of Sárraga. Various sources claim she was born in 1872, 1873, or 1874. See Ramos Palomo, "Un compás"; Ramos

Palomo, "Federalismo, laicismo, obrerismo, feminismo"; Ramos Palomo, "Belén de Sárraga"; Ramos Palomo, "Radicalismo político, feminismo y modernización"; Ramos Palomo, "Mujer, asociacionismo"; Vitale and Antivilo, *Belén de Sárraga*.
8. Herrera, Guzmán, and Navarro Angulo, *Belén de Sárraga*, 10.
9. Ramos Palomo, "Belén de Sárraga," 693; Herrera, Guzmán, and Navarro Angulo, *Belén de Sárraga*, 10.
10. Sanabria A., *Republicanism and Anticlerical Nationalism*, 141.
11. Ortiz Albear, "Masonería y feminismo," 424.
12. Sanabria A., *Republicanism and Anticlerical Nationalism*, 141.
13. Delgado Criado, *Historia de la educación*, 468; Álvarez Lázaro, *Cien años de educación en España*, 265.
14. Herrera, Guzmán, and Navarro Angulo, *Belén de Sárraga*, 10.
15. Ramos Palomo, "Un compás," 81; Ramos Palomo, "Radicalismo político, feminismo y modernización," 35.
16. Ramos Palomo, "Un compás," 80.
17. Vitale and Antivilo, *Belén de Sárraga*, 146.
18. Anderson, *European Universities*, 221–23.
19. Ortiz Albear, *Mujeres masonas en España*, 346.
20. According to Ramos Palomo, her daughter Libertad died at the age of nine due to sunstroke in Málaga, and her son, Víctor Volney, committed suicide. In her Mexican naturalization file dated 1940, Sárraga recorded that she had one son: Demófilo Danton Ferrero, of U.S. nationality and born in Valencia. Ramos Palomo, "Belén de Sárraga," 706.
21. Monroe, "Cartes de visite," 119–53; Pérez Ledesma, "Por tierras," 389; Ramos Palomo, "Belén de Sárraga," 700; Tortolero Cervantes, *El espiritismo*, 41–47; Walkowitz, *La ciudad*, 333–70.
22. Monroe, "Cartes de visite," 122.
23. Monroe, "Cartes de visite," 124.
24. Monroe, "Cartes de visite," 128.
25. Walkowitz, *La ciudad*, 344.
26. Walkowitz, *La ciudad*.
27. Walkowitz, *La ciudad*, 346.
28. Ramos Palomo, "Belén de Sárraga," 698; Cumberland, *Mexican Revolution*, 33–34.
29. Walkowitz, *La ciudad*, 344.
30. Its mottos were "Liberty, justice, and fraternity" (the Masonic symbols of the triangle, the draftsman's square, and the compass) and "Fight against hypocrisy and ignorance! Stand up for science and truth!" Ramos Palomo, "Radicalismo político, feminismo y modernización," 47; Ramos Palomo, "Un compás" 87.

31. Pérez Ledesma, "Por tierras."
32. Ramos Palomo, "Federalismo, laicismo, obrerismo," 136.
33. Ramos Palomo, "Federalismo, laicismo, obrerismo," 389.
34. Pérez Ledesma, "Por tierras," 390.
35. Ortiz Albear, *Las mujeres en la masonería*, 52–54, 60, 64, 70, 75.
36. Ramos Palomo, "Belén de Sárraga," 697.
37. Ramos Palomo, "Belén de Sárraga," 697.
38. Ramos Palomo, "Belén de Sárraga," 697–98.
39. Herrera, Guzmán, and Navarro Angulo, *Belén de Sárraga*, 10.
40. Sanfeliú Giménez, *Republicanas*, 98.
41. Ramos Palomo, "Federalismo, laicismo, obrerismo, feminismo," 139.
42. Ramos Palomo, "Belén de Sárraga," 38, 41.
43. Ramos Palomo, "Radicalismo político, feminismo y modernización," 37.
44. Ramos Palomo, "Radicalismo político, feminismo y modernización," 38.
45. Ramos Palomo, "Radicalismo político, feminismo y modernización," 38.
46. Pérez Ledesma, "Por tierras," 392–94.
47. Ramos Palomo, "Federalismo, laicismo, obrerismo, feminismo," 132–33.
48. Ramos Palomo, "Un compás," 82–93.
49. Asociación de Mujeres Librepensadoras in Barcelona (1896), Asociación General Femenina in Valencia (1897), Asociación de Mujeres Librepensadoras in Mahón (1899), Sociedad Progresiva Femenina of Málaga (1900), Asociación de Damas Liberales in Uruguay, Asociación de Mujeres Universitarias in Buenos Aires (1906), and the Federación Anticlerical Femenina in Ecuador (1930). Herrera, Guzmán, and Navarro, *Belén de Sárraga*, 10; Ramos Palomo, "Belén de Sárraga," 695.
50. Expediente naturalización, 1926, 43-29-62 III/21.2 (46) / 1780; 34-13-32 VII/21.3/931; 34-13-32 VII/521.3/931, AHGE-SER, FMH; Ramos Palomo, "Belén de Sárraga," 695.
51. Sárraga, *El clericalismo*, 8.
52. Ramos Palomo, "Federalismo, laicismo, obrerismo, feminismo," 158.
53. According to Ramos Palomo, Belén and Emilio were married (1894–1911) for seventeen years and then separated in 1911. Afterward, she initiated a relationship with her personal secretary, the anticlerical writer Luis Porta Bernabé. Ramos Palomo, "Belén de Sárraga," 694, 706.
54. Sárraga, *El clericalismo*.
55. Sárraga, *El clericalismo*, 8.
56. Sárraga, *El clericalismo*, 15.
57. Sárraga, *El clericalismo*, 95–96, 99–100.
58. Sárraga, *El clericalismo*, 72, 75, 227–28, 288–89.
59. Sárraga, *El clericalismo*, 305.
60. Sárraga, *El clericalismo*, 192.

61. Sárraga, *El clericalismo*, 200.
62. Sárraga, *El clericalismo*, 200.
63. Sárraga, *El clericalismo*, 198–202.
64. Tortolero Cervantes, *El espiritismo*, 214.
65. Tortolero Cervantes, *El espiritismo*, 224.
66. Tortolero Cervantes, *El espiritismo*, 18.
67. Tortolero Cervantes, *El espiritismo*, 15, 18.
68. Tortolero Cervantes, *El espiritismo*, 20.
69. Vaughan and Lewis, *Eagle and the Virgin*, 9.
70. Duffy, *Saints & Sinners*, 248.
71. "Notes of the Passing Day," *Mexican Herald*, Mexico City, August 28, 1912, 8, HNDM/UNAM; "Interesante velada en el teatro Xicotencatl," *El diario*, Mexico City, August 28, 1912, 5, HNDM/UNAM; "Una notable conferencista," *El abogado cristiano ilustrado*, Mexico City, August 29, 1912, 546, HNDM/UNAM. According to Pérez Ledesma, "in later years, the program was modified to make room for current issues—such as 'the American question,' or the European War and the response of the Catholic Church—and, above all, the plight of the working class, some of whose organizations were now sponsors of her public speaking events. Finally in 1930, it seems that the main theme, at least in the texts that have been published, were criticisms of the papacy and its actions throughout history." Pérez Ledesma, "Por tierras," 399; "Hoy será la conferencia de la Sra. B. de Sárraga," *El diario*, August 15, 1912, 6, HNDM/UNAM; "La conferencia de la Sra. Belén de Sárraga," *El imparcial*, August 16, 1912, 1, HNDM/UNAM; "La conferencia de hoy," *El correo español*, August 17, 1912, 4, HNDM/UNAM; *La esperanza*, August 17, 1912, 7, HNDM/UNAM; "¿Hasta cuándo *El país* dejará de ser jesuita?" *La patria: Diario de México*, August 31, 1912, 1, HNDM/UNAM; Paper of Record (PR), "Una distinguida conferencista y oradora española en México," *El diario*, Mexico City, August 12, 1912, 1, HNDM/UNAM; "Está en México una conferencista española," *El diario*, Mexico City, August 12, 1912, 4, HNDM/UNAM; "Hoy será la conferencia de la Sra. B. de Sárraga," *El diario*, Mexico City, August 15, 1912, 6, HNDM/UNAM; "Segunda conferencia de Da. Belem de Sárraga," *El diario*, Mexico City, August 18, 1912, 2, HNDM/UNAM; "Conferencia de la Sra. Doña Belén de Sárraga," *El diario*, Mexico City, August 18, 1912, 13, HNDM/UNAM; "Cuarta conferencia de la Sra. Belén de Sárraga," *El diario*, Mexico City, August 23, 1912, 8, HNDM/UNAM; "Quinta conferencia de Dña. Belén de Sárraga," *El diario*, Mexico City, August 12, 1912, 1, HNDM/UNAM; "La sexta conferencia de la Sra. Belén de Sárraga," *El diario*, Mexico City, August 24, 1912, 3, HNDM/UNAM; "Fiesta estudiantil a la Sra. de Sárraga," *El diario*, Mexico City, August 25, 1912, HNDM/UNAM; "La conferencia de la Sra. Belén de Sárraga," *El diario*, Mexico City,

August 25, 1912, 9, HNDM/UNAM; "Interesante velada en el Teatro Xicotencatl," *El diario*, Mexico City, August 28, 1912, 5, HNDM/UNAM; "Se dice que hablará en la Alameda Da. Belén de Sárraga," *El diario*, Mexico City, August 30, 1912, 3, HNDM/UNAM; Sárraga, *La evolución del pensamiento*.

72. For a feminist, historical, and sociological discussion, see Ryan, "Gender and Public Access," 260–85; Fraser, "Repensar el ámbito público," 23–58; and Calhoun, introduction to *Habermas*, 1–50.

73. "Test of Intellect Recognizes No Sex Madam De Sarraga Says," *Mexican Herald*, Mexico City, September 6, 1912, 2, HNDM/UNAM.

74. Tortolero Cervantes, *El espiritismo*, 216.

75. "La conferencia de ayer," *El correo español*, Mexico City, August 16, 1912, 1; "La conferencia de ayer," *El correo español*, Mexico City, August 28, 1912, 4; "La Sra. Belém de Sárraga, 'El País' y el Centro Asturiano," *El correo español*, Mexico City, August 31, 1912, 4; "Centro Asturianos," *El correo español*, Mexico City, September 4, 1912, 1; "El asunto del Centro Asturiano y la Sra. Belén de Sárraga," *El correo español*, Mexico City, August 16, 1912, 1.

76. "Homenaje a la Sra. Sárraga," *La patria*, Mexico City, September 8, 1912, 12.

77. "Sección editorial," *El faro*, Mexico City, August 30, 1912, 8, HNDM/UNAM.

78. "Libertad y eso," *El mañana*, Mexico City, September 3, 1912, 4, HNDM/UNAM; Tortolero Cervantes, *El espiritismo*, 217.

79. "La semana en revista," *El faro*, Mexico City, September 6, 1912, 4, HNDM/UNAM.

80. "Aquí se respetan las manifestaciones de pensamiento," *El mañana*, Mexico City, September 9, 1912, 3, HNDM/UNAM.

81. Yankelevich, "El Artículo 33 constitucional," 358.

82. "Ecos de la semana," *El abogado cristiano*, Mexico City, September 12, 1912, 4, HNDM/UNAM.

83. "Más adhesiones a la protesta contra Doña Belén de Sárraga," *El país*, September 2, 1912, 4, HNDM/UNAM; Pérez Ledesma, "Por tierras," 405.

84. "La primera conferencia de doña Belén de Sárraga," *Nueva era*, August 16, 1912, 8, FRHN/UNAM, quoted in Tortolero Cervantes, *El espiritismo*, 217.

85. "Actualidades: Doña Belem de Sárraga," *La patria*, Mexico City, September 14, 1912, 2, HNDM/UNAM.

86. "Desde Jauja," *Revista mexicana*, 1915–20, Texas, April 8, 1917, 34, HNDM/UNAM.

87. "La Señora Jacobina," *La mañana*, Mexico City, September 3, 1912, 1, HNDM/UNAM.

88. "¿Puede la mujer mezclarse en la política?," *El regional*, Guadalajara, September 27, 1912, 2, FE/BPEJ.

89. "Notes of the Passing Day," *Mexican Herald*, Mexico City, October 23, 1912, 8, HNDM/UNAM; "De actualidad: La señora Belén de Sárraga en San Luis Potosí,

Éxito sorprendente," *El faro*, October 25, 1912, Mexico City, 678, HNDM/UNAM; "Notes of the Passing Day," *Mexican Herald*, Mexico City, November 2, 1912, 8, HNDM/UNAM; "Notes of the Passing Day," *Mexican Herald*, Mexico City, November 6, 1912, 8, HNDM/UNAM; "Notes of the Passing Day," *Mexican Herald*, Mexico City, November 15, 1912, 8, HNDM/UNAM; "Notes of the Passing Day," *Mexican Herald*, Mexico City, November 19, 1912, 8, HNDM/UNAM; "Gratas impresiones de un viaje evangelista," *El faro*, Mexico City, November 22, 1912, 11, HNDM/UNAM.

90. "De actualidad: La señora Belén de Sárraga en San Luis Potosí; Éxito sorprendente," *El faro*, Mexico City, October 25, 1912, 12, HNDM/UNAM.
91. "De actualidad," *El faro*, Mexico City, October 25, 1912, 12, HNDM/UNAM.
92. "De actualidad," *El faro*, Mexico City, October 25, 1912, 12, HNDM/UNAM.
93. "La bomba de El Regional," *El correo de Jalisco*, Guadalajara, October 15, 1912, 1, FE/BPEJ; González Navarro, *Cristeros y agraristas*, vol. 1, 263; González Navarro, *Masones y cristeros en Jalisco*, 26.
94. Aldana Rendón, *Del reyismo al nuevo orden*, 151–82; Cárdenas Ayala, *El derrumbe*, 390–99.
95. Aldana Rendón, *Del reyismo al nuevo orden*, 1, 177.
96. Decrees were made regarding the good of the family, rural credit banks, taxes favoring the state and municipal area, the exercise of academic freedom, the independence of municipal areas, and proportional representation. Barbosa Guzmán, *La iglesia y el gobierno civil*, 106.
97. "Espiritismo," *El regional*, Guadalajara, June 11, 1912, 2, FE/BPEJ; "La doctrina espiritista es herética," *El regional*, Guadalajara, June 13, 1912, 2, FE/BPEJ; "El liberalismo en bancarrota," *El regional*, Guadalajara, June 14, 1912, 2, FE/BPEJ; "El espiritismo y la salvación final del género humano," *El regional*, Guadalajara, June 14, 1912, 2, FE/BPEJ; "El espiritismo en sus prácticas," *El regional*, Guadalajara, June 15, 1912, 2, FE/BPEJ; "Consecuencias de las prácticas espiritistas," *El regional*, Guadalajara, June 18, 1912, 2, FE/BPEJ; "La francmasonería niega la espiritualidad e inmortalidad del alma humana," *El regional*, Guadalajara, July 10, 1912, 2, FE/BPEJ; "Libertad, igualdad, fraternidad: El gran embuste de la masonería," *El regional*, Guadalajara, July 12, 1912, 2, FE/BPEJ; "Igualdad y fraternidad masónicas," *El regional*, Guadalajara, July 16, 1912, 2, FE/BPEJ; "La masonería es enemiga de la familia," *El regional*, Guadalajara, July 25, 1912, 2, FE/BPEJ; "La masonería es enemiga de la propiedad," *El regional*, Guadalajara, August 8, 1912, 2, FE/BPEJ; "En qué ha de terminar la señora Sárraga," *El regional*, Guadalajara, October 2, 1912, 2, FE/BPEJ.
98. "La biblia y la antigüedad," *El regional*, Guadalajara, October 20, 1912, 2, FE/BPEJ.

99. "La conferencia de hoy," *El regional*, Guadalajara, October 20, 1912, 1, FE/BPEJ.
100. "La bomba de El Regional," *El correo de Jalisco*, Guadalajara, October 15, 1912, 1, FE/BPEJ.
101. "La llegada de la Sra. Sárraga fue un triunfo," *El correo de Jalisco*, Guadalajara, October 11, 1912, 1, FE/BPEJ.
102. "Fue brillante la conferencia, dada antenoche, por la Sra. Belén de Sárraga: La multitud la acompañó a su alojamiento en medio de aclamaciones," *La gaceta de Guadalajara*, Guadalajara, October 15, 1912, 1, FE/BPEJ.
103. "La primera conferencia de la señora Sárraga," *La libertad*, Guadalajara, October 14, 1912, 3, FE/BPEJ; "Sección editorial: Un pagano entre cristianos; Trayectorias humanas," *La gaceta de Guadalajara*, Guadalajara, October 15, 1912, 2, FE/BPEJ.
104. "La conferencia de anoche," *La libertad*, Guadalajara, October 16, 1912, 2, FE/BPEJ; "La mujer: Segunda conferencia de la Sra. Belén de Sárraga," *El correo de Jalisco*, Guadalajara, October 16, 1912, 1, FE/BPEJ.
105. Belén de Sárraga, *La conciencia libre*, 1, 1906, quoted in Sanabria A., *Republicanism and Anticlerical Nationalism in Spain*, 146, 212.
106. Sanabria A., *Republicanism*, 146.
107. Enríquez Vargas, "La cultura política."
108. "La última conferencia de la Sra. Sárraga," *La libertad*, Guadalajara, October 21, 1912, 2, FE/BPEJ.
109. Ramírez Hurtado, "Una feminista," 276.
110. Ramírez Hurtado, "Una feminista," 276.
111. "Actuaciones de Doña Belem de Sárraga," *La patria*, Mexico City, September 14, 1912, 2, HNDM/UNAM; "De actualidad: La Sra. Belén de Sárraga en San Luis Potosí; Éxito sorprendente," *El faro*, Mexico City, October 25, 1912, 678, HNDM/UNAM.
112. Herrera, Guzmán, and Navarro Angulo, *Belén de Sárraga*, 48.
113. Ramos Palomo, "Federalismo, laicismo, obrerismo, feminismo," 126.
114. *Lectura dominical: Órgano del apostolado de la prensa*, Madrid, November 12, 1899, V, no. 306, 7, HDBNE; *Lectura dominical: Órgano del apostolado de la prensa*, Madrid, March 2, 1902, IX, no. 426, 8, HDBNE.
115. "Bodas de plata de una profesionista mexicana," *El diario*, Mexico City, August 21, 1912, 7, HNDM/UNAM; "La glorificación de la primera doctora mexicana," *El diario*, Mexico City, August 23, 1928, 8, HNDM/UNAM.
116. Navarrete, *La masonería en la historia*, 129–31.
117. "¡Adelante!," *El correo de Jalisco*, Guadalajara, October 17, 1912, 1, FE/BPEJ.
118. Herrera, Guzmán, and Navarro Angulo, *Belén de Sárraga*, 58.

119. *Periódico oficial del estado de Yucatán: Diario oficial*, Yucatán, November 8, 1916, HNDM/UNAM.
120. *Periódico oficial del estado de Yucatán: Diario oficial*, Yucatán, January 22, 1916, 379, HNDM/UNAM; *Periódico oficial del estado de Yucatán: Diario oficial*, Yucatán, November 11, 1916, 3787, HNDM/UNAM; *Periódico oficial del estado de Yucatán: Diario oficial*, Yucatán, December 23, 1918, 797, HNDM/UNAM.
121. Cano, "México 1923"; Cano, "Las feministas en campaña"; Olcott, *Revolutionary Women*, 203–26; Macias, "Felipe Carrillo Puerto," 333–34; Ramos Escandón, "Desafiando el orden legal"; S. J. Smith, *Gender and the Mexican Revolution*; Peniche Rivero, "El movimiento feminista," 32–34.
122. "Después de la propaganda de la señora Sárraga," *El abogado cristiano*, Mexico City, November 28, 1912, 755, HNDM/UNAM.
123. "El Evangelista Mexicano y la Sra. Sárraga," *El abogado cristiano*, Mexico City, February 6, 1913, 82, HNDM/UNAM.
124. Pérez Ledesma, "Por tierras," 405; Tortolero Cervantes, *El espiritismo*, 225.
125. Article 3 promoted an obligatory secular education in elementary schools and prohibited religious schools; Article 5 did not recognize religious vows; Article 13 denied the legal status of religious organizations; Article 27 enforced agrarian reform and the nationalization of national resources, stipulating that religious associations did not have the right to possess properties, and finally, these properties were to form part of national property; Article 130 specified that the state would control religious practice. See Bantjes, "Saints, Sinners, and State Formation," 137; Comisión Nacional para la Celebración del Sesquicentenario de la Proclamación de la Independencia Nacional y del Cincuentenario de la Revolución Mexicana, *Diario de los debates*, 1181–229.
126. In 1920, the Episcopado Mexicano established the Secretariado Social Mexicano (SSM) not only to reconcile different ideas and coordinate all the lay Catholic organizations on a national level but also to counteract the consolidation of non-Catholic labor organizations belonging to the CROM. The SSM transformed the activities of lay Catholics from an electoral policy (1912–14) to a Catholic social action that promoted associations of Catholic men and women. The goal was to strengthen the Catholic organizations with a certain national orchestration based on the principles of Catholic social action in which different social classes, generations, and sexes would play different roles within a corporatist society. The SSM coordinated the following institutions: the Unión de Damas Católicas Mexicanas, composed of women of the elites; the Asociación Católica de la Juventud Mexicana (ACJM) for young Catholics; the Juventud Femenina Católica Mexicana (JFCM) for young women; the Orden Caballeros de Colón for men; and the Confederación Nacional Católica del Trabajo (CNCT). These

organizations worked on different and diversified cultural, economic, political, and social fronts: savings funds, catechisms, study circles, Catholic schools (elementary, parochial, and vocational), mutual aid societies, national meetings, labor unions, the publication of various materials, and morality plays. With this impetus, they launched a campaign against the international advance of Bolshevism, socialism, and the presidential candidacy of Álvaro Obregón, whose discourse in favor of the masses was considered radical. O'Dogerthy Madrazo, "Restaurarlo todo en Cristo," 133; Hanson, "Day of Ideals," 17–18.

127. "Dio su primera conferencia la Sra. De Sárraga," *El informador*, Guadalajara, August 26, 1922, 6, HNDM/UNAM; "Se solicitó el Teatro Degollado para traer a Belén de Sárraga," *El informador*, Guadalajara, December 12, 1922, 6, HNDM/UNAM; Gallegos, *Apuntes para la historia*.

128. Herrera, Guzmán, and Navarro Angulo, *Belén de Sárraga*, 40.

129. Herrera, Guzmán, and Navarro Angulo, *Belén de Sárraga*, 42.

130. Herrera, Guzmán, and Navarro Angulo, *Belén de Sárraga*, 17, 19.

131. Herrera, Guzmán, and Navarro Angulo, *Belén de Sárraga*, 30.

132. De los Reyes, *Cine y sociedad en México*, 107, 10.

133. "Dio su primera conferencia la Sra. De Sárraga," *El informador*, Guadalajara, August 26, 1922, 6, HNDM/UNAM; "Tuvo un colosal éxito en su conferencia Doña Belem de Sarraga," August 28, 1922, 6, HNDM/UNAM; "Se solicitó el Teatro Degollado para traer a Belén de Sárraga," *El informador*, December 12, 1922, 5, HNDM/UNAM; "Hoy arribó a," *El informador*, Guadalajara, March 7, 1923, 4, HNDM/UNAM.

134. Dorantes, Castillo Ramírez, and Tuñón Pablos, *Irene Robledo*, 56–57; Gruening, *Mexico and Its Heritage*, 440–41; Tamayo Rodríguez, *La conformación del Estado moderno*, 103–66; Fernández Aceves, "José Guadalupe Zuno Hernández."

135. "Belenes y espárragos," *El cruzado*, Guadalajara, August 13, 1922, 3, FE/BPEJ.

136. "La Zarraga viene . . . ," *El cruzado*, Guadalajara, December 24, 1922, 2, FE/BPEJ.

137. "A las escotadas," *El cruzado*, Guadalajara, July 30, 1922, 1, 4, FE/BPEJ; "Caricia a las semidesnudas," *El cruzado*, Guadalajara, August 13, 1922, 1, 4, FE/BPEJ; "La mujer moderna," *El cruzado*, Guadalajara, September 10, 1922, 3, FE/BPEJ; "Las dos modas," *El cruzado*, Guadalajara, November 26, 1922, 1, 2, FE/BPEJ; "Cosas de la moda," *El cruzado*, Guadalajara, April 8, 1922, 1–2, FE/BPEJ; "Oigan de la moda," *El cruzado*, Guadalajara, March 25, 1923, 2, FE/BPEJ.

138. "Lo que la mujer puede hacer," *El cruzado*, Guadalajara, August 6, 1922, 4, FE/BPEJ; "Lo que la mujer puede hacer II: Sección femenina," *El cruzado*, Guadalajara, August 6, 1922, 4, FE/BPEJ; "La mujer virtuosa," *El cruzado*, Guadalajara, September 10, 1922, 3, FE/BPEJ; "Misión de madre," *El cruzado*, Guadalajara, October 15,

1922, 1, FE/BPEJ; "La mujer católica jalisciense," *El cruzado*, Guadalajara, September 23, 1923, 3, FE/BPEJ.
139. "Genealogía maldita: Lo que son los bolcheviques," *El cruzado*, Guadalajara, August 27, 1922, 3, FE/BPEJ; "Genealogía maldita I: La masonería y el liberalismo," *El cruzado*, Guadalajara, July 9, 1922, 4, FE/BPEJ; "Genealogía maldita II: La masonería y el liberalismo," *El cruzado*, Guadalajara, July 16, 1922, 3, FE/BPEJ; "Genealogía maldita III: Hazañas del socialismo," *El cruzado*, Guadalajara, July 30, 1922, 3, FE/BPEJ; "Genealogía maldita IV: El bolcheviquismo en México," *El cruzado*, Guadalajara, July 20, 1922, 3, FE/BPEJ; "Catolicismo, socialismo, liberalismo," *El cruzado*, Guadalajara, July 30, 1922, 1, 4, FE/BPEJ; "Los impíos," *El cruzado*, Guadalajara, November 12, 1922, 1, 2, 4, FE/BPEJ; "Feminismo," *El cruzado*, Guadalajara, June 17, 1923, 1, 3, 7, FE/BPEJ; "La desvergüenza del feminismo," *El cruzado*, Guadalajara, June 24, 1923, 4, FE/BPEJ; "Los enemigos," *El cruzado*, Guadalajara, June 17, 1923, 1, 3, FE/BPEJ.
140. Gallegos, *Apuntes para la historia*.
141. "La Iglesia en la política," *El cruzado*, Guadalajara, January 21, 1923, 2, quoted in Preciado Zamora, *Por las faldas del Volcán*, 108.
142. Curley, "'Avanza el desierto,'" 54.
143. Meyer, *La cristiada*, 124.
144. Pérez-Rayón, "El anticlericalismo en México," 125.
145. Article 33 stipulated that foreigners could not participate in Mexican politics. Comisión Nacional, *Diario de los debates*, 1192.
146. Junco, *La sra. Belén de Sárraga desfanatizando*.
147. Junco, *La sra. Belén de Sárraga desfanatizando*, 5.
148. "Hoy arribó a ésta la Conferencista Belén de Sárraga," *El informador*, Guadalajara, March 7, 1923, 4, HNDM/UNAM; "El diputado Aguilera y Miranda pide," *Periódico oficial del estado de Zacatecas*, May 26, 1923, 587, HNDM/UNAM.
149. File 35, inventory 5765, FAPECFT.
150. File 45, inventory 5332, FAPECFT-AEC.
151. Fernández Aceves, "Las mujeres graduadas."
152. File 6, inventory 3580, FAPECFT-AEC; file 99, inventory 5681, FAPECFT-AEC; file 8, inventory 1474, FAPECFT-AEC.
153. File 789, inventory 706, FAPECFT-FSG.
154. Ramos Palomo, "Federalismo, laicismo, obrerismo, feminismo," 161.
155. File 789, inventory 706, FAPECFT-FSG; Sárraga, *Conferencia sustentada*; González Navarro, *Cristeros y agraristas*, vol. 2, 43.
156. Sárraga, *Conferencia sustentada*, 14–15.
157. *Boletín de la Universidad del Sureste*, Yucatán, June 1, 1924, 61, HNDM/UNAM; Obaya, Barredo, and Ricardo, *Valoraciones*, 105.

158. "Llegó anoche a la capital la conferencista Doña Belén de Sárraga," *El demócrata*, Mexico City, July 2, 1924, 9, HNDM/UNAM.
159. Luis Porta Bernabé was an anticlerical writer, seven years younger than Belén de Sárraga, who accompanied her on her travels as her personal secretary. Ramos Palomo, "Belén de Sárraga," 706.
160. File 45, inventory 5332, FAPECFT-AEC.
161. Casasola, *Historia gráfica*, 1730–31; Herrera, Guzmán, and Navarro Angulo, *Belén de Sárraga*, 6.
162. Camberos Vizcaíno, *Francisco el grande*; Rius Facius, *De Don Porfirio a Plutarco*; Meyer, *La cristiada*, vol. 2.
163. Meyer, *La cristiada*, vol. 2, 110–11, 14–21.
164. Bantjes, "Saints, Sinners, and State Formation," 138.
165. More than one hundred people led by the Presbyterian José Joaquín Pérez y Budar took possession of the church La Soledad to end diplomatic relations with the Vatican and demand greater equality in the distribution of power and wealth among Mexican priests. Vaca, "Devociones y trabajos," 107; Olivera Sedano, *Aspectos del conflicto religioso*, 99–106; Reich, *Hidden Revolution*, 12; Meyer, *La cristiada*, vol. 2, 148–56; Barbosa Guzmán, *La iglesia y el gobierno civil*, 297–99; Buchenau, *Plutarco Elías Calles*.
166. Expediente naturalización, 1926, 43-29-62 III/21.2 (46) / 1780; 34-13-32 VII/21.3/931; 34-13-32 VII/521.3/931, AHGE-SER, FMH.
167. Belén Sárraga, "Propósitos: La redacción," *Rumbos nuevos*, April 1925, 1, FAPECFT.
168. Manuel Navarro Ángulo and Belén Sárraga, "Nuestro saludo: La redacción," *Rumbos nuevos*, April 1925, 2, FAPECFT.
169. Sárraga, "Propósitos: La redacción," FAPECFT.
170. Navarro Ángulo and Sárraga, "Nuestro saludo: La redacción," FAPECFT.
171. "A recoger el guante," *El cruzado*, Guadalajara, February 25, 1923, 2, 4, FE/BPEJ.
172. "A recoger el guante," *El cruzado*, Guadalajara, February 25, 1923, 2, 4, FE/BPEJ.
173. The conservative military leaders of the LNDLR honored Agustín de Iturbide (the leader of Spanish descent who negotiated Mexico's independence from Spain in 1812 and affirmed the supremacy of the Catholic Church); Lucás Alamán, one of the first conservative leaders following independence; and Miguel Miramón and Tomás Mejía, two generals who supported the French intervention (1862–67) and the empire of Maximilian of Austria (1864–67). Martial Court found Maximiliano, Miramón, and Mejía guilty and condemned them to death. The LNDLR rejected liberals, freemasons, and Yankees. It was nationalist and modern; it favored Italian fascism, with the clear dream of creating an elite society. They envisioned a cooperative, just, and Catholic society. Meyer, *La cristiada*, vol. 1, 65–68.

174. Belén Sárraga, "Conferencia: Velada en el Arbeu," *Rumbos nuevos*, Mexico City, year 1, no. 1, April 1925, 11–12, FAPECFT.
175. "Banquete de promiscuación," *Rumbos nuevos*, Mexico City, year 1, no. 2, May 1925, 6–7, FAPECFT.
176. "Sra. Belén de Sárraga está en Michoacán organizando una serie de conferencias," Archivo Municipal de Zamora, Gobernación, 1925, file 5; "Correspondencia de Colima," *El informador*, July 13, 1925, 6, HNDM/UNAM; "Correspondencia de Colima," *El informador*, July 17, 1925, 4, HNDM/UNAM; "Visita Toluca," *El demócrata*, December 9, 1925, 12, HNDM/UNAM.
177. "Una salida de tono de *El universal*," *Rumbos nuevos*, Mexico City, year 1, nos. 4 and 5, July and August 1925, 53–54, FAPECFT.
178. "Una salida de tono de *El universal*," *Rumbos nuevos*, 53, 54, FAPECFT.
179. "Enseñanza laica, no religiosa," *Rumbos nuevos*, Mexico City, year 1, no. 1, April 1925, 23, FAPECFT; José Vasconcelos, "Enseñanza laica pero no sectaria," *El universal*, year 9, vol. 35, no. 3038, section 1, 3, FAPECFT; "¡¡Oiga Excélsior!!," *Rumbos nuevos*, Mexico City, year 1, nos. 4 and 5, July and August 1925, 56, FAPECFT.
180. "Maniobras clericales en el Congreso Internacional de Mujeres de la Raza," *Rumbos nuevos*, Mexico City, year 1, nos. 4 and 5, July and August 1925, 41, FAPECFT.
181. Peniche Rivero, "El movimiento feminista," 54.
182. Preciado Zamora, *Por las faldas*.
183. "Troops Save Quito Orador: Special Cable," *New York Times*, January 9, 1930, 5.
184. "Belén Sárraga en Málaga," *El heraldo de Madrid*, Madrid, December 23, 1931, 11, HDBNE.
185. Margarita Andiano, "Mujeres de ayer y hoy: Belén de Sárraga," *Crónica*, April 3, 1932, 15, HDBNE.
186. Ortiz Albear, *Mujeres masonas en España*; Ramos Palomo, "Mujer, asociacionismo."
187. Domínguez Prats, "Intelectuales españolas en el exilio de México," 1245.
188. "Falleció ayer Doña Belén de Zárraga," *El nacional*, Mexico City, September 10, 1950, section 1, 1, HDBNE; "La muerte de la Sra. Belén de Zárraga," *El nacional*, Mexico City, September 11, 1950, 24, HDBNE; "Falleció ayer en esta capital Doña Belén de Zárraga," *El universal*, Mexico City, September 10, 1950, section 1, 24, HDBNE.
189. "Guadalajara en 1914," *Jueves de excélsior*, Mexico City, November 13, 1958, 24, HDBNE; "Provocó malestares," *El porvernir*, Monterrey, February 12, 1973, 12, HDBNE; "Zárraga, invitada para catequizar revolucionarios," *Impacto*, Mexico City, November 24, 1971, 31, HDBNE; "Charlas sobremesa," *El informador*, Guadalajara, December 14, 1977, 5, HDBNE; "Charlas sobremesa," *El informador*, Guadalajara, May 17, 1980, 5, HDBNE.

3. Atala Apodaca Anaya

1. Orozco Cano, *La educación en Ciudad Guzmán*, 85.
2. Dore, "One Step Forward," 3–32.
3. Dore, "One Step Forward," 3, 15.
4. Molyneux, "Twentieth-Century State Formations," 68.
5. Ramos Escandón, *Ciudadanía carente*, 17.
6. S. J. Smith, *Gender and the Mexican Revolution*, 29.
7. Molyneux, "Twentieth-Century State Formations," 52–53.
8. Macias, *Contra viento y marea*, 52–59, 87–94.
9. McGee Deutsch, "Gender and Sociopolitical Change"; S. J. Smith, *Gender and the Mexican Revolution*.
10. For a comparative analysis, see table 3, "Population Ages Ten Years and over According to Literacy, Illiteracy, and Sex in Mexico, 1895–2000"; Civera Cerecedo, "Mujeres, cultura escrita"; and Instituto Nacional de Estadística Geografía e Informática, *Estados Unidos Mexicanos*.
11. Aldana Rendón, *Manuel M. Diéguez*; Dávila Garibi, *Memoria histórica*; Dorantes, Castillo Ramírez, and Tuñón Pablos, *Irene Robledo García*; García Alcaraz, "Poder, educación y religión"; Ibarra Ibarra, "Atala Apodaca"; Instituto Nacional de Estudios Históricos de la Revolución Mexicana, Instituto de Investigaciones Legislativas de la H. Cámara de Diputados, *Las mujeres*; Martínez Moya and Moreno Castañeda, *La escuela de la revolución*, 7; Mendieta Alatorre, *La mujer*; Mendoza Lozano, "Atala Apodaca"; Moreno Ochoa, *Semblanzas revolucionarias*; Salazar, *Las pugnas de la gleba*; Vaca, *Los silencios de la historia*; Zuno Hernández, *Anecdotario del Centro Bohemio*; Zuno Hernández, *Reminiscencias de una vida*.
12. Other studies indicate that Atala Apodaca was born in Techaluta, Jalisco. See Instituto Nacional de Estudios Históricos de la Revolución Mexicana, *Las mujeres*, 43.
13. When I interviewed various relatives of Apodaca's who still reside in Guadalajara, they mentioned that they are unaware of the details of her life because she broke off relations with her relatives after she declared herself to be an atheist. The family conserved its Catholic identity and did not want to be associated with her political and educational activities. Her relatives are unaware if anyone kept her personal archive. Laura Apodaca Casillas, unrecorded interviews by the author, Guadalajara, Jalisco, November 21, 2000, and January 16, 2003; Rosa del Carmen Apodaca López, unrecorded interview by the author, Guadalajara, Jalisco, November 21, 2000; Atala Apodaca, file 1397, AHJ, DEP, REB.
14. Vaca, *Los silencios de la historia*.

15. Myrna Cortés argues that the liberals of the late nineteenth century in Guadalajara sought urban renewal, including the introduction of paved streets with cobblestones; the construction of public markets; the renovation and construction of squares; the creation of gardens; the introduction of stagecoaches (1864), the telegraph (1868), the streetcar (1880), the railroad (1888), and electrical streetlights (1884); control over cemeteries; and the installation of factories. For a more detailed analysis of liberal urbanization, see Cortés Cuesta, "Modernidad y representaciones sociales," 47–91.
16. Aldana Rendón, "Masonería y revolución en Jalisco"; de los Reyes, "El impacto de la masonería"; González Navarro, *Masones y cristeros en Jalisco*; Martínez Moreno, "Masones en defensa"; Navarrete, *La masonería*, 46; Téllez-Cuevas, *El papel de la masonería*; Trueba Lara, *Masones en México*.
17. Barrancos, "Maestras, librepensadoras y feministas"; Gran Logia Femenina de Chile, *Mujeres con mandil*; Ortiz Albear, *Las mujeres en la masonería*.
18. Two known cases of female Masons in Jalisco are those of Rosa Navarro (1850–92) and Catalina Álvarez Rivera (1862–?). Navarro was a schoolteacher in Nayarit who had completed her professional studies in Guadalajara; she wrote pedagogical articles for the Guadalajara newspaper *Las clases productoras* and in *Violetas del Anáhuac*, and she founded the Xóchilt Masonic lodge, probably in 1882. Álvarez Rivera was also a schoolteacher and formed part of the Xóchilt lodge. She drafted articles for the newspaper *El libre y aceptado Masón* and established the female Masonic lodge Aurora in Ahualulco de Mercado. Vázquez Leos, *La masonería femenina*; Velasco López, "La mujer y la masonería"; Wright de Kleinhans, *Mujeres notables mexicanas*.
19. See chapter 1. Apodaca, *Educación de las jóvenes*, 22–23.
20. The French Republican author Victor Hugo contributed to the first French newspaper of socialist women, *La voix des femmes*. He was one of the few Republican writers who recognized the rights of women. Like other French Republicans of the nineteenth century, Victor Hugo believed in a viable Republican democracy that could encompass the sovereign aspirations of the people. The main demand of radical Republicans was universal suffrage. Likewise, they were concerned over social issues—the burden of the poor in general and the urban masses in particular. Their rhetoric was laden with the language of justice, liberty, and equality. See Accampo, "Gender, Social Policy"; McMillan, *France and Women, 1789–1914*.
21. No. 112, AHJ, AE, LEPN.
22. Ibarra Ibarra, *Educadores jaliscienses*, 48–50; Instituto Nacional de Estudios Históricos de la Revolución Mexicana, *Las mujeres*, 43–44; Vaca, *Los silencios*

de la historia, 197. However, her retirement file documents her employment in Guadalajara from 1905 to 1913. Atala Apodaca, file 1397, AHJ, DEP, REB.
23. Martínez Moya and Moreno Castañeda, *La escuela de la revolución*, 7.
24. Aldana Rendón, "Masonería y revolución en Jalisco," 24.
25. Ramírez Flores, *La revolución maderista en Jalisco*, 37–39, 54, 56.
26. Zuno Hernández, *Historia de la revolución*, 48–49. Hermila Galindo was in a similar situation, having also given "a welcome speech to Carranza upon his triumphant march into the capital after the fall of the counterrevolutionary regime of General Victoriano Huerta." See Macias, *Contra viento y marea*, 53.
27. Cárdenas Ayala, *El derrumbe*, 6, 282.
28. Cárdenas Ayala, *El derrumbe*, 6, 410.
29. Ramírez Flores, *La revolución maderista en Jalisco*, 136.
30. Ramírez Flores, *La revolución maderista en Jalisco*, 154.
31. Ramírez Flores, *La revolución maderista en Jalisco*, 159.
32. The ordinary session of the Valentín Gómez Farías Club on April 17, 1910, was attended by "the distinguished misses Carlota Tejeda, María Guadalupe Sotomayor, and Elvira Cárdenas and the no less esteemed ladies Carlota Cueva Vda. de Tejeda, Josefa de la Peña, and Julia Fernández de Olea." Ramírez Flores, *La revolución maderista en Jalisco*, 149–50.
33. Cano, *Se llamaba Elena Arizmendi*, 70–71.
34. Lau Jaiven and Ramos Escandón, *Mujeres y revolución*, 136.
35. Aldana Rendón, *Del reyismo al nuevo orden*, 1, 172–73; Cárdenas Ayala, *El derrumbe*, 6, 386.
36. Aguirre, *Mis memorias de campaña*, 95; Aldana Rendón, *Manuel M. Diéguez*, 161.
37. "Nuestras ilustraciones: Atala Apodaca," *Alianza*, February 2, 1914, 30–32, HNDM/UNAM.
38. The founders of the Centro Bohemio were Zuno, Carlos Stahl, Xavier Guerrero, and Ramón Córdova. Other members were Ixca Farías, Enrique Díaz de León, Amado de la Cueva, Alfredo Romo, Joaquín Vidrio, Carlos Orozco Romero, José Luis Figueroa, Samuel Ruiz Cabañas, and David Alfaro Siqueiros. Camacho Becerra, "Síntomas de la vanguardia," 10.
39. Camacho Becerra, "Síntomas de la vanguardia," 48.
40. Camacho Becerra, "Síntomas de la vanguardia," 51.
41. Camacho Becerra, "Síntomas de la vanguardia," 50.
42. Aldana Rendón, *Manuel M. Diéguez*, 161.
43. Vaca, *Los silencios de la historia*, 197; Aldana Rendón, *Manuel M. Diéguez*, 161.
44. Aldana Rendón, *Del reyismo al nuevo orden*, 1, 189–93; Ramírez Flores, *La revolución maderista en Jalisco*, 60.

45. File no. XI/481.5/103, box 61, year 1956, ASDN, OP, DACH.
46. Sr. Francisco Orozco y Jiménez, years 1912–18, file 20, box 2, AHAG, GS, OS.
47. Sr. Francisco Orozco y Jiménez, years 1912–18, file 20, box 2, AHAG, GS, OS.
48. Sr. Francisco Orozco y Jiménez, years 1912–18, file 20, box 2, AHAG, GS, OS.
49. "Sección editorial: Las maestras convenencieras y fanáticas," *Boletín militar*, Guadalajara, August 18, 1914, 2, FE/BPEJ.
50. File Atala Apodaca de Ruiz Cabañas, D/112/M-85, ASDN, DACH.
51. File Atala Apodaca de Ruiz Cabañas, D/112/M-85, ASDN, DACH.
52. "El zapatismo de la prensa," *El diario de occidente*, Guadalajara, February 16, 1914, 2, FE/BPEJ.
53. "Nuestras ilustraciones: Atala Apodaca," *Alianza*, February 2, 1914, 30, HNDM/UNAM.
54. "Nuestras ilustraciones: Atala Apodaca," *Alianza*, February 2, 1914, 30–32, HNDM/UNAM.
55. "Nuestras ilustraciones: Atala Apodaca," *Alianza*, February 2, 1914, 30, HNDM/UNAM.
56. "Nuestras ilustraciones: Atala Apodaca," *Alianza*, February 2, 1914, 30, HNDM/UNAM.
57. "Nuestras ilustraciones: Atala Apodaca," *Alianza*, February 2, 1914, 30, HNDM/UNAM.
58. "Nuestras ilustraciones: Atala Apodaca," *Alianza*, February 2, 1914, 30, HNDM/UNAM.
59. File no. XI/481.5/103, box 61, year 1956, ASDN, OP, DACH.
60. "18 de Julio," *Boletín militar*, Guadalajara, July 17, 1914, 1, FE/BPEJ.
61. "18 de Julio: El festival de ayer," *Boletín militar*, Guadalajara, July 19, 1914, 3, FE/BPEJ.
62. Ben-Amos, "El centro sagrado del poder: París y los funerales de Estado republicanos," 27–48.
63. "La velada en el Degollado," *Boletín militar*, Guadalajara, July 21, 1914, 4, FE/BPEJ.
64. "Discurso: Pronunciado por su autor el 28 del actual," *Boletín militar*, Guadalajara, July 25, 1914, 4, FE/BPEJ; "Discurso: Pronunciado por su autor el 28 del actual," *Boletín militar*, Guadalajara, July 26, 1914, 4, FE/BPEJ; "Discurso: Pronunciado por su autor el 28 del actual," *Boletín militar*, Guadalajara, July 28, 1914, 4, FE/BPEJ.
65. "Discurso: Pronunciado por su autor el 28 del actual," *Boletín militar*, Guadalajara, July 28, 1914, 4, FE/BPEJ.
66. "La velada en el Degollado," *Boletín militar*, Guadalajara, July 21, 1914, 4, FE/BPEJ.

67. "Instrucción Pública: Nombramientos," *Boletín militar*, Guadalajara, July 29, 1914, 1, FE/BPEJ; Departamento de Educación Pública, Relación de Expedientes dados de baja por renuncias, jubilaciones, abandono de empleo y fallecimiento, Atala Apodaca, file 1397, AHJ.
68. "Gran Teatro Degollado," *Boletín militar*, Guadalajara, August 2, 1914, 1, FE/BPEJ.
69. Atala Apodaca also participated in many of the LAP conferences. "Festival en el Degollado: La Liga Amigos del Pueblo," *Boletín militar*, Guadalajara, August 8, 1914, 1, FE/BPEJ; "Gran conferencia en el Teatro Degollado," *Boletín militar*, Guadalajara, August 9, 1914, 1, FE/BPEJ; "La matinée en el Degollado," *Boletín militar*, Guadalajara, August 25, 1914, 1, FE/BPEJ; "Conferencia en el Degollado," *Boletín militar*, Guadalajara, August 30, 1914, 8, FE/BPEJ; "La pasada conferencia," *Boletín militar*, Guadalajara, September 1, 1914, 2, FE/BPEJ; "La conferencia en el Degollado," *Boletín militar*, Guadalajara, September 5, 1914, 1, FE/BPEJ; "La conferencia en el Degollado," *Boletín militar*, Guadalajara, September 8, 1914, 1, FE/BPEJ; "Opulencia y Miseria," *Boletín militar*, Guadalajara, September 10, 1914, 4, FE/BPEJ; "La conferencia de hoy," *Boletín militar*, Guadalajara, September 13, 1914, 5, FE/BPEJ; "Por el Degollado," *Boletín militar*, Guadalajara, September 20, 1914, 1, FE/BPEJ; "La conferencia de hoy," *Boletín militar*, Guadalajara, December 6, 1914, 4, FE/BPEJ; "Las conferencias de la Liga Amigos del Pueblo," *Boletín militar*, Guadalajara, August 10, 1915, 7, FE/BPEJ.
70. "Las conferencias del Centro Bohemio," *Boletín militar*, Guadalajara, August 8, 1914, 1, 2, FE/BPEJ; Zuno Hernández, *Anecdotario del Centro Bohemio*, 33.
71. The *Boletín militar* in different articles named the CLJOD in various ways. It was called the Círculo Feminista Josefa Ortiz de Domínguez and the Sociedad Femenina Josefa Ortiz de Domínguez.
72. "Por el Círculo Liberal Feminista Josefa Ortiz de Domínguez: Sesión solemne," *Boletín militar*, Guadalajara, August 27, 1914, 6, FE/BPEJ.
73. "La pasada conferencia," *Boletín militar*, Guadalajara, September 1, 1914, 1, 2, FE/BPEJ.
74. "Carta abierta a la Srita. Profesora Atala Apodaca," *Boletín militar*, Guadalajara, August 15, 1914, 3, FE/BPEJ.
75. "Carta abierta a la Srita. Profesora Atala Apodaca," *Boletín militar*, Guadalajara, August 15, 1914, 3, FE/BPEJ.
76. "Carta abierta a la Srita. Profesora Atala Apodaca," *Boletín militar*, Guadalajara, August 15, 1914, 3, FE/BPEJ.
77. On May 31, 1918, proxy governor Manuel Bouquet by means of degree 1913 permitted only one priest per parish to attend to five thousand churchgoers. On July 13, 1918, the legislature published the regulations of decree 1913 ordering that each priest register before the Ministry of the Interior, and that to officiate

mass, he must obtain the permission of the same agency. See Fernández Aceves, "Political Mobilization of Women in Revolutionary Guadalajara," 81; Barbosa Guzmán, *La iglesia y el gobierno civil*, 6; Boylan, "Mexican Catholic Women's Activism, 1929–1940"; Curley, *Citizens and Believers*; Dávila Garibi, *Memoria histórica*; González Flores, *La cuestión religiosa en Jalisco*.

78. "Sección Editorial: El cuarto poder," *Boletín militar*, Guadalajara, August 28, 1914, 2, FE/BPEJ.
79. "Sección Editorial: El cuarto poder," *Boletín militar*, Guadalajara, August 28, 1914, 2, FE/BPEJ.
80. "¿Pasquines tenemos? ¡Por ahí les duele!," *Boletín militar*, Guadalajara, September 3, 1914, 1, FE/BPEJ.
81. "Por el Círculo Liberal Feminista Josefa Ortiz de Domínguez," *Boletín militar*, Guadalajara, September 4, 1914, 1, FE/BPEJ.
82. "Ocho hermosísimas banderas," *Boletín militar*, Guadalajara, September 13, 1914, 5, FE/BPEJ; "Citatorio," *Boletín militar*, Guadalajara, October 17, 1914, 5, FE/BPEJ; "La conferencia de hoy," *Boletín militar*, Guadalajara, October 18, 1914, 4, FE/BPEJ.
83. "Obsequio a la Srita. Prof. Atala Apodaca," *Boletín militar*, Guadalajara, September 22, 1914, 5, FE/BPEJ.
84. Atala Apodaca, file 1397, AHJ, DEP, REB.
85. "La matinée en el Degollado," *Boletín militar*, Guadalajara, August 25, 1914, 1, FE/BPEJ.
86. For an analysis of Laura Apodaca's speech, see chapter 1. "Teatro Degollado," *Boletín militar*, Guadalajara, September 27, 1914, 8, FE/BPEJ; "La conferencia del domingo," *Boletín militar*, Guadalajara, September 29, 1914, 1, FE/BPEJ.
87. "Viajera," *Boletín militar*, Guadalajara, October 25, 1914, 4, FE/BPEJ.
88. "Continua la huelga," *Boletín militar*, Guadalajara, October 20, 1914, 4, FE/BPEJ.
89. "Una pequeña población da ejemplo de alto espíritu liberal," Guadalajara, November 24, 1914, 3, FE/BPEJ; "La conferencia de hoy," *Boletín militar*, Guadalajara, November 29, 1914, 1; "La conferencia de ayer," Guadalajara, December 1, 1914, 1, FE/BPEJ.
90. Vaca, *Los silencios de la historia*.
91. "La señorita Atala Apodaca en viaje de propaganda: Va a predicar el evangelio del constitucionalismo," *Boletín militar*, Guadalajara, December 8, 1914, 1, FE/BPEJ; File no. XI/481.5/103, box 61, year 1956, ASDN, OP, DACH; *Diccionario histórico*, 54, INERHM.
92. González Navarro, *Cristeros y agraristas en Jalisco*, 194.
93. Zuno Hernández, *Anecdotario del Centro Bohemio*, 26.
94. File no. XI/481.5/103, box 61, year 1956, ASDN, OP, DACH.

95. Atala Apodaca, file 1397, AHJ, DEP, REB.
96. Atala Apodaca, file 1397, AHJ, DEP, REB.
97. File no. XI/481.5/103, box 61, year 1956, ASDN, OP, DACH.
98. These appointments lasted from April 16, 1915, to October 31, 1924. Departamento de Educación Pública, Relación de Expedientes dados de baja por renuncias, jubilaciones, Atala Apodaca, file 1397, AHJ, DEP, REB.
99. File no. XI/481.5/103, box 61, year 1956, ASDN, OP, DACH.
100. "El ornato," *Boletín militar*, Guadalajara, August 5, 1915, 1, FE/BPEJ; "Excitativa," *Boletín militar*, Guadalajara, September 14, 1915, 2, FE/BPEJ.
101. "Mujeres del pueblo de México," *Boletín militar*, Guadalajara, August 31, 1915, 1, 5, FE/BPEJ.
102. "Retrato del general Diéguez," *Boletín militar*, Guadalajara, November 25, 1915, 4, FE/BPEJ.
103. "Invitación," *Boletín militar*, Guadalajara, August 5, 1915, 1, FE/BPEJ; "Hijos del pueblo," *Boletín militar*, Guadalajara, November 7, 1915, 5, FE/BPEJ; "La Srita. Atala Apodaca hace unas aclaraciones," *Boletín militar*, Guadalajara, November 9, 1915, 8, FE/BPEJ.
104. "La mendicidad en Guadalajara crece," *Boletín militar*, Guadalajara, March 1, 1916, 1, FE/BPEJ; "La peste de la viruela se desarrolla," *Boletín militar*, Guadalajara, March 2, 1916, 1, FE/BPEJ; "Algunos casos de tifo," *Boletín militar*, Guadalajara, March 4, 1916, 4, FE/BPEJ.
105. "Las mujeres pordioseras," *Boletín militar*, Guadalajara, March 26, 1916, 12, FE/BPEJ; "Carestía de los artículos," *Boletín militar*, Guadalajara, March 28, 1916, 8, FE/BPEJ.
106. The *Boletín militar* reviewed the endeavors of the colonel Mrs. Ramona Reyes Vda. de Flores of Sinaloa and the female soldiers in Guadalajara. "Heroína de la revolución y coronela del ejército constitucionalista, la Sra. Ramona Reyes Vda. de Flores," *Boletín militar*, Guadalajara, October 13, 1914, 6, FE/BPEJ; "La Sra. Ramona Reyes Vda de Flores," *Boletín militar*, Guadalajara, October 27, 1914, 1, FE/BPEJ; "Regresan a Mazatlán, Sinaloa," *Boletín militar*, Guadalajara, November 7, 1914, 1, FE/BPEJ; "Las mujeres . . . las he visto," *Boletín militar*, Guadalajara, July 24, 1915, 7. For a broader discussion of women in the armed struggle of 1910, see Cano, "Inocultables realidades del deseo," 35–56; *Las mujeres en la revolución*, INEHRM; and Lau Jaiven and Ramos Escandón, *Mujeres y revolución*.
107. "Se hará un Estado de viudas y huérfanos," *Boletín militar*, Guadalajara, March 29, 1916, 7, FE/BPEJ; "Muy importante al público," *Boletín militar*, Guadalajara, April 19, 1916, 6, FE/BPEJ.
108. "La conferencista Srita. Atala Apodaca en Mazatlán," *Boletín militar*, Guadalajara, March 3, 1916, 4, FE/BPEJ; "La conferencia de la Señorita Atala Apodaca,"

    Boletín militar, Guadalajara, March 3, 1916, 4, FE/BPEJ; file no. XI/481.5/103, box 61, year 1956, ASDN, OP, DACH.
109. "Una fiesta de carácter íntimo," *Boletín militar*, Guadalajara, March 5, 1916, 1, FE/BPEJ.
110. "La señorita Atala Apodaca, confundida con una dama extranjera, iba a ser lapidada en Tepic," *Boletín militar*, Guadalajara, May 9, 1916, 4, FE/BPEJ.
111. Certificate awarded to Atala Apodaca on July 1, 1916, file 9711, 1889–1920, CEHM-CARSO, APJEC; Zuno Hernández, *Anecdotario del Centro Bohemio*, 73–75.
112. File no. XI/481.5/103, box 61, year 1956, ASDN, OP, DACH.
113. Vaca, *Los silencios de la historia*, 198; file 49, Atala Apodaca, box 40, Informe de la Comisión de Estudios y Propaganda Nacionalista, July 8, 1917, CIRMC, BCC-CO.
114. File 49, Atala Apodaca, box 40, Informe de la Comisión de Estudios y Propaganda Nacionalista, July 8, 1917, CIRMC, BCC-CO.
115. File no. XI/481.5/103, box 61, year 1956, ASDN, OM, DACH; letter from the governor of Sinaloa, General Angel Flores, to Venustiano Carranza about the patriotic and cultural endeavors of Atala Apodaca, November 15, 1916, file 11792, 1889–1920, CEHM-CARSO, APJEC.
116. File no. XI/481.5/103, box 61, year 1956, ASDN, OM, DACH.
117. File 49, Atala Apodaca, box 40, Informe de la Comisión de Estudio y Propaganda Nacionalista, July 8, 1917, CIRMC, BCC-CO.
118. *Argos*, first period, no. 1, August 13, 1916, quoted in Mendoza Lozano, "Atala Apodaca."
119. *Argos*, first period, no. 1, August 13, 1916, quoted in Mendoza Lozano, "Atala Apodaca."
120. Comisión Nacional para la Celebración del Sesquicentenario de la Proclamación de la Independencia Nacional y del Cincuentenario de la Revolución Mexicana, *Diario de los debates*. The Constitucionalista press published some of these Constitucionalista reforms and the decrees that they passed. See "Cual debe ser la obra del gobierno," *Boletín militar*, Guadalajara, August 29, 1914, 2, FE/BPEJ; "Documentos del gobierno constitucionalista: Decreto no. 21," *Boletín militar*, Guadalajara, August 28, 1914, 6. FE/BPEJ; "Documentos del gobierno constitucionalista: Ley del Descanso Obligatorio," *Boletín militar*, Guadalajara, September 11, 1914, 2, FE/BPEJ; "El cambio de la Escuela de Artes y Oficios del Estado," *Boletín militar*, Guadalajara, August 29, 1914, 1, FE/BPEJ; "El gobierno se interesa por mejorar la situación del pueblo," *Boletín militar*, Guadalajara, August 26, 1914, 6, FE/BPEJ; "El porvenir de la instrucción en Jalisco," *Boletín militar*, Guadalajara, July 28, 1914, 2, FE/BPEJ; "Hoy se colocará la primera piedra de la Escuela Normal Juárez," *Boletín militar*, Guadalajara, September 20, 1914,

1, FE/BPEJ; "La escuela laica oficial y la escuela parroquial," *Boletín militar*, Guadalajara, September 9, 1914, 2, FE/BPEJ; "La instrucción de hoy un gran paso," *Boletín militar*, Guadalajara, August 30, 1914, 4, FE/BPEJ; "La Ley de Instrucción Laica a la luz del derecho constitucional," *Boletín militar*, Guadalajara, September 23, 1914, 4, FE/BPEJ; "Queda abolida en el Estado la enseñanza religiosa," *Boletín militar*, September 5, 1914, 1, FE/BPEJ; "Se impulsará a la niñez estudiosa," *Boletín militar*, Guadalajara, August 28, 1914, 1, FE/BPEJ; "Se les hará justicia los labradores pagándoles debidamente su trabajo," *Boletín militar*, Guadalajara, October 9, 1914, 1, FE/BPEJ; "Sección editorial: Mas sobre el descanso dominical y las horas de trabajo," *Boletín militar*, Guadalajara, September 19, 1914, 2, FE/BPEJ; "Sección editorial: Sobre el descanso dominical y las horas de trabajo," *Boletín militar*, Guadalajara, September 16, 1914, 2, FE/BPEJ; "Sección editorial: Sobre el descanso dominical; Decreto 31," *Boletín militar*, Guadalajara, September 20, 1914, 3, FE/BPEJ; Marcelino Cedano, "El problema de Instrucción Pública," *Boletín militar*, Guadalajara, September 12, 1915, 7, FE/BPEJ; Manuel M. Diéguez, "Decreto no. 29: Reformas en la Instrucción Pública," *Boletín militar*, Guadalajara, September 15, 1914, 1, 4, FE/BPEJ; "Decreto no. 47: Reformas sobre Instrucción Pública," *Boletín militar*, Guadalajara, November 13, 1914, 1, 2, FE/BPEJ.

121. "Los consejos de un canónigo y la labor de las mujeres," *Boletín militar*, August 4, 1914, 2, FE/BPEJ; "Siempre 'ellas' instrumentos de los curas: Una anécdota del Gral. Hill," *Boletín militar*, Guadalajara, July 23, 1914, 1, FE/BPEJ; Sección Editorial, "El pueblo mexicano sosteniendo colegios en Europa," *Boletín militar*, Guadalajara, August 27, 1914, 2, FE/BPEJ.
122. Curley, *Citizens and Believers*.
123. Ulloa, *La Constitución de 1917*, 431.
124. González Flores, *La cuestión religiosa en Jalisco*, 383–83; Barbosa Guzmán, *La iglesia y el gobierno civil*, 6, 171.
125. The organizations that joined this mobilization were Unión Profesional de Empleadas, Liga de la Preservación de la Juventud, Escuela Normal Libre para Señoritas, Asociación Hijas de María, Círculos de Estudios "Juventud Femenina," and Unión Profesional de Maestras, as well as Sunday schools, Catechism associations, and Círculos de Estudio. See Dávila Garibi, *Memoria histórica*, 23–24; González Flores, *La cuestión religiosa en Jalisco*, 423–28.
126. Dávila Garibi and Chávez Hayhoe, *Colección de documentos*, 9–15.
127. According to Dávila Garibi and Chávez Hayhoe, the Catholic organizations that protested in Guadalajara were as follows: Agrupaciones Catequísticas de Señoritas, Unión Profesional de Empleadas, Círculo de Estudios Santo Tomás de Aquino, Congregación de la Buena Muerte, Asociaciones Eucarísticas de Señoras,

ADCG, Catequistas del Sagrado Corazón de Jesús, Círculo Central de Estudios, las Asociaciones de Hijas de María Inmaculada, Asociaciones Piadosas, Asociación de Santa Zita, Asociación de los Santos Ángeles, la ACJM, Unión Profesional de Profesoras, Centro de Estudios Juventud Femenina, Congregación de Nuestra Señora de Guadalupe y San Luis Gonzaga, Congregación Mariana, Academia Miguel de Cervantes Saavedra, and Sociedad de San Vicente de Paul de Señores. Other organizations of men and women sent letters of protest from different rural areas of Jalisco, such as Ahualulco, Amatitán, Arandas, Autlán, Ayo el Chico, Capilla de Guadalupe, Ciudad Guzmán, Colotlán, Encarnación, Hostotipaquillo, Jocotepec, Juanacatlán, Río Grande, Hacienda de San Andrés, San Gabriel, El Teúl, San Juan de los Lagos, San Miguel el Alto, Tala, Tequila, Tlajomulco, Tuxpan, Zapotiltic, Zapopan, and La Barca. Dávila Garibi and Chávez Hayhoe, *Colección de documentos*, 16–288.
128. Dávila Garibi, *Memoria histórica*, 26.
129. Dávila Garibi, *Memoria histórica*, 29–31.
130. Dávila Garibi, *Memoria histórica*, 35.
131. Dávila Garibi, *Memoria histórica*, 37.
132. Dávila Garibi, *Memoria histórica*, 55–56.
133. Curley, *Citizens and Believers*.
134. Dávila Garibi, *Memoria histórica*, 60.
135. Barbosa Guzmán, *La iglesia y el gobierno civil*, 6, 220–21.
136. Dávila Garibi, *Memoria histórica*, 446–49.
137. González Flores, *La cuestión religiosa en Jalisco*, 461.
138. Dávila Garibi and Chávez Hayhoe, *Colección de documentos*, 289–96.
139. Dávila Garibi, *Memoria histórica*, 66.
140. González Flores, *La cuestión religiosa en Jalisco*, 376, 461.
141. Tamayo Rodríguez, *La conformación del Estado moderno*, 2, 90–91.
142. This vote of support was signed by the following schoolteachers: Eufrosina F. de Saucedo, Ma. de Álvarez, Francisca C. de Gutiérrez, Carmen Hernández Cambre, María Guadalupe Padilla, Rosalina Gutiérrez, María de la Luz González, Sara Saucedo, Ana and Beatriz Quintero, Adelina Álvarez; and other women who did not specify their profession, such as Isabel Fernández, Ana María Gómez, Julia Flores Vda. de González, María Catalina Casillas, Rosa Alcalde de Gómez, Agripina González, Juana G. C. de Medina, María Donaciana Rodríguez, Epifania Rodríguez, Bernardina González, Guadalupe Arriola de González, Rosario Arriola de Rubio, María Arriola de Jiménez, Guadalupe Padilla, Guadalupe G. de Lozano, Bernardina Sucedo, María Pérez, Josefina Larios, Refugio Pérez, María Panduro, Teodoro Enríquez de Panduro, and Esther

Pérez, among other women. There were approximately 140 women in all. Dávila Garibi and Chávez Hayhoe, *Colección de documentos*, 374.

143. Dávila Garibi and Chávez Hayhoe, *Colección de documentos*, 374; Salazar, *Las pugnas de la gleba*, 243–45.
144. Document 233, years 1918–19, AMG.
145. Bantjes, "Burning Saints, Molding Minds," 276–77.
146. The U.S. American Evelyn Trent Roy was the wife of Manabendra Nath Roy. M. N. Roy was a Hindu nationalist who arrived in Mexico due to the strong surveillance of the British and American secret services of the anti-imperialist movement in India. According to Barry Carr, M. N. Roy played a very important role in the foundation of the Communist Party and the development of KOMINTERN policy regarding colonial issues in the 1920s. The Roys arrived in Mexico in June 1917 and contacted the recently reestablished Partido Socialista Mexicano. Spenser, *Los primeros tropiezos*; Taibo, *Bolshevikis*, 68–71; Carr, *Marxism & Communism*, 19; Martínez Verdugo, "De la anarquía al comunismo," 24–31; Tuñón Pablos, *Mujeres que se organizan*, 25–26; document 1192, year 1918–19, AHM. Elena Torres, Estela Carrasco, and María del Refugio García published *La mujer*. These women participated in the foundation of the Panamerican League to improve the conditions of women in Baltimore.
147. Macias, *Against All Odds*, 70–80. For a more in-depth discussion of the modern woman, see chapter 1.
148. Dávila Garibi and Chávez Hayhoe, *Colección de documentos*, 107.
149. Alonso, *Thread of Blood*, 85.
150. Popo, "Mujeres icono-plastas," *La lucha: Periódico de combate; Semanario católico*, Guadalajara, November 28, 1918, 1, FE/BPEJ.
151. Popo, "Mujeres icono-plastas," *La lucha: Periódico de combate; Semanario católico*, Guadalajara, November 28, 1918, 1, FE/BPEJ.
152. Jacinta Curiel, unrecorded interview by the author, Guadalajara, August 25, 1998.
153. Among these students were Guadalupe and Isabel Martínez, Angelina Cedano, Beatriz and Ana María Quintero, Adelina Álvarez, Sara Saucedo, Ignacia Hernández, Rafaela Quintero, Josefina Ramos, Inés Ramírez, María Vizcaíno, Edmundo and Miguel S. Rojas, Nicolasa M. Guzmán, Pascual López, Petronio Hernández, and Francisco García. Due to the fact that the archives of the Escuela Iconoclasta were not preserved, the exact date of its foundation and how many children attended are not known. Salazar, *Las pugnas de la gleba*, 215–16.
154. Document 1107, year 1919, AMG.
155. Document 1107, year 1919, AMG.
156. Document 1107, year 1919, AMG.

157. T-2-919, T-10 bis "D," file no. 7079, 1919, AHJ, FT.
158. Medina Carrillo and Figueroa Mendoza, *Luis C. Medina*, 55.
159. Salazar, *México*, 210–20.
160. Samuel Ruiz de Cabañas and Atala Apodaca adopted a girl named Carmen Ruiz de Cabañas Apodaca. File no. XI/481.5/103, box 61, year 1956, ASDN, OP, DACH.
161. Mejía Núñez, "Faldas en el periodismo tapatío," 180; *Las mujeres en la revolución mexicana*, 43, INEHRM.
162. García Alcaraz, "Historia de la cultura escolar," 176.
163. Atala Apodaca, file 1397, November 25, 1924, AHJ, DE, EMJ.
164. Atala Apodaca, file 1397, April 29, 1926, and September 18, 1926, AHJ, DE, EMJ.
165. Atala Apodaca, file 1397, August 17, 1927, AHJ, DE, EMJ.
166. Ibarra Ibarra, "Ser maestro en Jalisco, 1910–1943," 24–25; Mendieta Alatorre, *La mujer en la revolución mexicana*, 88.
167. Rocha Islas, *Los rostros de la rebeldía*, 25.
168. Servín, *La oposición política*, 51.
169. Servín, *La oposición política*, 52.
170. "Partido Popular Manifiesto," *El informador*, Guadalajara, March 2, 1948, 8, HDEI.
171. Apodaca obtained 782 votes. Number 22, from January 27, 1958, to September 5, Act dated July 24, 1958, ACEJ, LAS.
172. Atala Apodaca, file 1397, July 1, 1947, AHJ, DE, EMJ.
173. Atala Apodaca, file 1397, February 3, 1954, AHJ, DE, EMJ.
174. Atala Apodaca, file 1397, August 22, 1956, and December 31, 1956, AHJ, DE, EMJ.
175. Atala Apodaca, file 1397, August 28, 1956, AHJ, DE, EMJ.
176. Book 219, Decree no. 7160, El Congreso del Estado otorga la insignia, sheet 3, ACEJ.
177. Atala Apodaca personal file, D/112/17404, ASDN, DACH, AVR.
178. Decree of the Founding of the Legión de Honor, February 8, 1949, http://www.sedena.gob.mx/leg_hon/legion/legion.pdf.
179. Personal Correspondence, series 6, General Correspondence, boxes 26, 34, AHUG, PALJGZH.
180. General Correspondence, box 26, letter dated 1971, AHUG, PALJGZH.
181. "Esquela," *El informador*, Guadalajara, September 1, 1977, 10-A, HDEI.

4. María Arcelia Díaz

1. T-9-922, box T-41 bis "A," file no. 8656, 1922, AHJ, FT.
2. Antonio Bustillos Carrillo, "Biografías de María A. Díaz," Guadalajara, undated, ACFOMAD; Hernández, *La mujer mexicana*, 41.

3. A debate evolved about the role of women in the domestic sphere as housewives and mothers regarding what ought to be considered "women's work" and why it was necessary to grant a family salary to the qualified worker, who was seen as the head of the household. See Fernández Aceves, "Once We Were Corn Grinders"; Fowler-Salamini, "Gender, Work, and Class Consciousness"; Gauss, "Masculine Bonds and Modern Mothers"; Porter, *Working Women in Mexico City*; Ramos Escandón, *Presencia y transparencia*; Ramos Escandón, *La industria textil*; Ramos Escandón, "Mujeres positivas"; Ramos Escandón, *La diferenciación de género*; Ramos Escandón, *Industrialización, género y trabajo*.
4. Fernández y Fernández, *Mujeres que honran la patria*; Hernández, *La mujer mexicana*.
5. Spivak Chakravorty, "¿Puede hablar el subalterno?"
6. Anonymous, "María A. Díaz," *La luz*, Guadalajara, 1964, 3, ACFOMAD.
7. In the early twentieth century, there were five textile factories in the Guadalajara region: La Escoba (1841–1907), La Prosperidad Jalisciense o Atemajac (1841), La Experiencia (1851), Rio Blanco (1866–1928) and Río Grande (1896). Gabayet, *Obreros somos*, 97–99.
8. Hernández, *La mujer mexicana*, 41; Keremitsis, "María Arcelia Díaz."
9. Anonymous, "María A. Díaz," *La luz*, Guadalajara, 1964, 3, ACFOMAD; Antonio Bustillos Carrillo, "Biografías de María A. Díaz," Guadalajara, undated, ACFOMAD; Arriola, "Obreras textiles," 41.
10. Anonymous, "María A. Díaz," *La luz*, Guadalajara, 1964, 3, ACFOMAD.
11. Martínez, *Lectura y lectores*; Speckman Guerra, "Las posibles lecturas," 70.
12. Maynes, *Taking the Hard Road*; Maynes, Pierce, and Laslett, *Telling Stories*; Lyons, "La experiencia lectora y escritora"; Hoggart, *Uses of Literacy*.
13. Keremitsis, "María Arcelia Díaz," 1.
14. Hernández, *La mujer mexicana*, 41.
15. Act of defunction number 5823, record 125, November 30, 1939, ARCEJ, LDG; María Guadalupe Martínez Villanueva, widow of Hernández Loza, recorded interview by the author, Guadalajara, August 15, 1996.
16. According to Jeffrey Bortz, the owners of the textile factories in Amatlán complained of the political culture of the so-called agitators, who were not locals, because they held meetings during the workday. Bortz, "'Without Any More Law,'" 281.
17. Bortz, *Revolution within the Revolution*.
18. Knight, "Working Class and the Mexican Revolution"; Lear, *Workers, Neighbors, and Citizens*; Porter, *From Angel to Office Worker*, 8.
19. Keremitsis, "María Arcelia Díaz," 2.
20. T-1–911, box T-bis "B," 1911–13, file no. 5891, AHJ, FT.

21. T-1-913, box T-bis "B," 1911–13, file no. 5894, AHJ, FT.
22. T-1-914, box T-bis "C," 1914, file no. 5911, AHJ, FT.
23. T-1-914, box T-bis "C," file no. 5906, AHJ, FT.
24. T-1-916, box T-bis "D," file no. 5925, AHJ, FT; T-1-917, box T-19 bis "J," file no. 7846, AHJ, FT; T-8-917, box T-38 bis "O," file no. 8586, AHJ, FT; T-1-917, box T-bis "D," file no. 5929, AHJ, FT; T-8-917, box T-38 bis "O," file no. 8588, AHJ, FT; T-1-917, box T-19 bis "D," file no. 5930, AHJ, FT; T-2-917, box T-10 bis "D," file no. 7071, AHJ, FT; T-9-917, T-9-918 box T-40 bis, file no. 8641, 8642, 8645, and 8646, AHJ, FT; T-1-917, box T-bis "D," file no. 5940, AHJ, FT; T-2-917, box T-10 bis "B," file no. 7067, AHJ, FT; T-8-917, box T-38 bis "O," file no. 8586, AHJ, FT.
25. T-1-917, box T-bis "D," file no. 5940, AHJ, FT; T-2-917, box T-10 bis "B," file no. 7067, AHJ, FT.
26. T-2-918, Caja T-10 bis "D," file no. 7077, AHJ, FT.
27. Keremitsis, "María Arcelia Díaz," 4.
28. María Guadalupe Martínez Villanueva, widow of Hernández Loza, recorded interview by the author, Guadalajara, August 15, 1996.
29. For a more in-depth discussion on Guadalupe Martínez Villanueva, see chapter 5 of this book.
30. Scott, "El problema de la invisibilidad," 38–65.
31. El Grupo Acción belonged to the Federación de Agrupaciones Obreras de Jalisco, a member of the CROM. It included blacksmiths, carpenters, tortilla makers, peasants, loaders, bakers, shoemakers, tailors, shawl makers, butchers, mechanics, construction workers, barbers, salespeople, ceramicists, street sweepers, textile workers, jewelry designers, and typesetters. Tamayo Rodríguez, *La conformación del Estado*, 2, 245–50.
32. After the Adolfo de la Huerta rebellion (1923–24), Zuno radicalized his labor policies. See Moreno Ochoa, *Semblanzas revolucionarias*; Tamayo Rodríguez, *Los movimientos sociales*, 4, 34–47.
33. Tamayo Rodríguez, *Los movimientos sociales*, 4, 38, 43.
34. Written speech by María Guadalupe Martínez, n.d., APGM.
35. Arroyo Alejandre, "Ires y venires en el occidente," 21–56.
36. Daniel Smith states that the definition of women's work has been problematic throughout history and that different categories of what is female labor can enlighten us regarding the cultural constructs underlying this concept. Nancy Folbre and Marjorie Abel have argued that the definition of "work" as salaried work in the labor market has devalued the uncompensated labor of women in the home. See Smith Scott, "How a Half-Million Iowa Women Suddenly Went to Work," 27–43; Folbre, "Unproductive Housewife," 463–84; Folbre and Abel, "Women's Work and Women's Households," 463–84.

37. In 1919, the Confederación Católica del Trabajo was established to struggle against the Bolsheviks and aid the working class. In 1920, it became the Confederación Católica del Trabajo de la Arquidiócesis. That same year, the CCT created the Secretariado Popular with the following commissions: labor conflicts and judicial issues, census of workers and the employment offices, labor union, agrarian labor unions, and mutual aid societies. See "Se acaba de establecer el Secretariado Popular de la CCT," *El obrero*, Guadalajara, May 15, 1920, 1, FE/BPEJ; "La Confederación Católica del Trabajo de la Arquidiócesis," *El obrero*, Guadalajara, February 14, 1920, 1, FE/BPEJ; Barbosa Guzmán, *La iglesia y el gobierno civil*, 6, 243, 45.
38. T-2–923 ZAP/571, box T-14, AHJ, FT.
39. Keremitsis, "María Arcelia Díaz," 4.
40. T-9–922, box T-41 bis "A," file no. 8656, AHJ, FT.
41. T-2–922, GUA/469, box T-13 bis "B," AHJ, FT; T-9–922, GUA/375, box T-41 bis "A," file no. 873, AHJ, FT; Sindicato de Trabajadores de La Experiencia, *Cien años de actividad*, 128–29.
42. T-7–922 GUA/168, box T-31, file no. 756, AHJ, FT; T-2–922 ZAP/441, box T-13 bis "C," file no. 7164, AHJ, FT; T-2–922 GUA/524, box T-13 bis "C," file no. 70, AHJ, FT; T-2–922, box T-13 bis "C," file no. 7166, AHJ, FT.
43. Ana María Hernández Lucas, recorded interview by the author, Guadalajara, August 17, 1996; Laura Rosales, recorded interview by the author, Guadalajara, August 15, 1996; Keremitsis, "María Arcelia Díaz."
44. T-2–923 ZAP/554, box T-14, file no. 374, AHJ, FT; T-7–923, box T-34 bis "B," file no. 8325, AHJ, FT.
45. T-2–923 ZAP/554, box T-14, file no. 374, AHJ, FT; T-7–923, box T-34 bis "B," file no. 8235, AHJ, FT.
46. T-9–925, box T-75, file no. 1608, AHJ, FT; T-1–924, box T-71, file no. 1504, AHJ, FT; T-6–924, box T-71, file no. 1493, AHJ, FT; T-4–924, box T-71, file no. 1494, AHJ, FT; T-2–924, box T-57, file no. 1254, AHJ, FT.
47. T-7–925, box T-78, file no. 1682, AHJ, FT; T-2–925, box T-78, file no. 1675, AHJ, FT; T-8–927, box T-103, file no. 2415, AHJ, FT.
48. T-1–924, box T-73, 1531, AHJ, FT; T-1–925, box T-54, 1925, AHJ, FT; T-7–925, box T-73, file no. 1532, AHJ, FT.
49. T-1–924, box T-73, 1531, AHJ, FT; T-1–925, box T-54, AHJ, FT; T-7–925, box T-73, file no. 1532, AHJ, FT.
50. Fowler-Salamini, "'La Negra Moya.'"
51. Keremitsis, "María Arcelia Díaz."
52. T-1–925 JAL/587, AHJ, FT.

53. T-7–925, box T-78, file no. 1682, AHJ, FT; T-1–924, box T-73, file no. 1531, AHJ, FT; T-1–925, box T-54, AHJ, FT; T-6–925, box T-22, file no. 8150, AHJ, FT; T-7–925, box T-73, file no. 1532, AHJ, FT; T-2–925, box T-78, file no. 1675, AHJ, FT; T-2–925 ZAP/142, box T-15 bis "A," file no. 415, AHJ, FT; T-8–925, box T-75, file no. 1597, AHJ, FT.
54. Keremitsis, "María Arcelia Díaz," 9; Hernández, *La mujer mexicana*, 42.
55. T-7–925 ZAP/141, box T-35 bis "A," file no. 661, AHJ, FT.
56. María Díaz, "Centro Evolucionista de Mujeres," *El sol*, Guadalajara, September 15, 1926, FE/BPEJ; T-1–926, box T-97, file no. 2222, AHJ, FT.
57. T-9–927, box T-104, file no. 2470, AHJ, FT.
58. María Díaz, "Reflexiones sobre la mujer," *El jalisciense*, Guadalajara, May 24, 1933, 3, 6, FE/BPEJ.
59. María Díaz, "Reflexiones sobre la mujer," *El jalisciense*, Guadalajara, May 24, 1933, 3, 6, FE/BPEJ.
60. María Díaz, "Reflexiones sobre la mujer," *El jalisciense*, Guadalajara, May 24, 1933, 3, 6, FE/BPEJ.
61. María Díaz, "María Díaz dice," *Femina roja*, Guadalajara, November 20, 1934, 1–2, AHJ.
62. Dorantes, Castillo Ramírez, and Tuñón Pablos, *Irene Robledo García*, 58–60.
63. Consuelo Ruiz, "Tesis Instinto de Lucha," Guadalajara, 1933, APGM.
64. In 1931 and 1933, editions 1 and 2 of the National Congress of Women Workers and Peasants (Congreso Nacional de Obreras y Campesinas) were held in Mexico City; the 3rd edition was organized in Guadalajara. In these congresses, there was deep division between the communists and those affiliated with the Partido Nacional Revolucionario. Despite these differences, proposals were made to improve the social, civil, and political conditions of Mexican women. See Barragán and Rosales, "Congresos Nacionales de Obreras y Campesinas"; Porter, *From Angel to Office Worker*, 11–13.
65. Hernández, *La mujer mexicana*, 42.
66. "Agradece la presencia del CFO en la inauguración del Centro de Capacitación Femenina María A. Díaz," 1941, ACFOMAD.
67. "María A. Díaz murió anoche: La noticia causó duelo en los centros revolucionarios tapatíos," *Las noticias*, Guadalajara, November 29, 1939, 1, FE/BPEJ.
68. "María A. Díaz murió anoche: La noticia causó duelo en los centros revolucionarios tapatíos," *Las noticias*, Guadalajara, November 29, 1939, 1, FE/BPEJ.
69. "El cadáver de María A. Díaz fue velado anoche en la FTJ," *Las noticias*, Guadalajara, November 30, 1939, FE/BPEJ. Among the political associations that were present were Acción Femenina, the state and municipal committees of the Partido de la Revolución Mexicana, veterans of the Revolution and of the Vanguardia Revolucionaria de Mujeres; eleven labor unions paid their respects, including

female workers of the nixtamal industry, workers from the shoe industry, city bus drivers, employees at the hospice, shoe shiners, open-air performance employees, and actors. The teacher and student organizations in attendance were as follows: the Sociedad Fraternal de Maestros, teachers and students of the Escuela Nocturna Obrera, the Federación de Estudiantes Socialistas de Occidente and elementary schoolchildren. Also in attendance were the directors of the Hospicio Cabañas, the Departamento de Asistencia Social, and thirteen professors and professionals of great renown in Guadalajara.

70. Hernández, *La mujer mexicana*, 153.
71. "El sepelio de María A. Díaz: Fue una nota imponente de duelo de los sindicatos obreros y de los grupos feministas," *Las noticias*, Guadalajara, December 1, 1939, FE/BPEJ.
72. "El sepelio de María A. Díaz: Fue una nota imponente de duelo de los sindicatos obreros y de los grupos feministas," *Las noticias*, Guadalajara, December 1, 1939, FE/BPEJ.
73. "El sepelio de María A. Díaz: Fue una nota imponente de duelo de los sindicatos obreros y de los grupos feministas," *Las noticias*, Guadalajara, December 1, 1939, FE/BPEJ.
74. For a more in-depth discussion of state funerals, see Ben-Amos, "El centro sagrado del poder," 49–74.
75. Connerton, *How Societies Remember*, 39. For Hirsch and Smith, "Feminism and Cultural Memory," 5; Young, "Toward a Received History."
76. Ma. de Jesús S. de Preciado, "Al heroísmo infatigable de la hermana y maestra," 1939, APGM.
77. Hernández, *La mujer mexicana*, 153.
78. Hernández, *La mujer mexicana*, 5.
79. "Homenaje a la memoria de la compañera María A. Díaz," 1940, APGM.
80. Bunk, "Remembering Emiliano Zapata," 457–90.
81. "Marcha María Arcelia Díaz," Guadalajara, 1940, APGM.
82. Víctores Prieto, "Himno Obrero," Guadalajara, 1940, APGM.
83. Magdalena Velasco de la Mora, "Sobre las enseñanzas de María A. Díaz a sus discípulas del CFO," Guadalajara, 1941, ACFOMAD.
84. Joaquín Cano, "Discursos para conmemorar el aniversario de la muerte de María A. Díaz," Guadalajara, 1941–44, ACFOMAD.
85. Josefina Gorjón de C., "Semblanza sobre María A. Díaz," Guadalajara, 1949, ACFOMAC.
86. "Celebración del XI Aniversario de la muerte de María A. Díaz," Guadalajara, 1950, ACFOMAC.

87. "Rompiendo cadenas," *Jalisco ceteme*, Guadalajara, August 15, 1957, APGM; "Atención a la niñez, programa de Lupita M. de Hernández Loza," *Jalisco ceteme*, Guadalajara, June 15, 1958, APGM; "La Profa. Lupita Martínez de Hernández Loza terminó brillante su primera campaña," *Jalisco ceteme*, Guadalajara, June 15, 1958, APGM; María S. López de B., "Orientación cívica de la mujer," *Jalisco ceteme*, Guadalajara, August 15, 1957, APGM; María Guadalupe Martínez de Hernández Loza, "CIUDADANÍA: Así pensamos las mujeres," *Jalisco ceteme*, Guadalajara, August 15, 1957, APGM; María Guadalupe Martínez de Hernández Loza, "Homenaje de la mujer cetemista a la Constitución: Discurso de la profesora Lupita Martínez de Hernández Loza en Congreso," *Jalisco ceteme*, Guadalajara, August 15, 1957, APGM; Carmen Mejía, "Página para la mujer: Régimen de la madre para la Lactancia," *Jalisco ceteme*, Guadalajara, August 15, 1957, APGM; Amalia Mendoza Trujillo, "La mujer Obrera opina," *Jalisco ceteme*, Guadalajara, August 15, 1957, APGM.

88. Guadalupe Martínez de Hernández Loza, *Círculo Feminista de Occidente "María A. Díaz,"* 1939–74 (Guadalajara: CTM, 1974), APMGM.

89. Vaughan, *Estado, educación*; Vaughan, *La política cultural*; Fernández Aceves, "La cultura cívica," 54–63; Fiol Matta, "'Raras' por mandato," 118–37; Schell, *Church and State Education*.

90. Cano, "Revolución, feminismo,"; Lau Jaiven, "Expresiones políticas femeninas," 93–124; Macías, *Contra viento y marea*; Ramos Escandón, "Mujer y poder"; Tuñón Pablos, *Mujeres que se organizan*; Enriqueta Tuñón Pablos, *¡Por fin . . . !*

91. Fernández Aceves, "Political Mobilization"; Fowler-Salamini, "'La Negra Moya.'"

92. Franco, *Las conspiradoras*, 11.

5. María Guadalupe Martínez Villanueva

1. Denis Rodríguez and Pedro Mellado, "Cierra Lupita Martínez largo capítulo del PRI," *Mural*, Guadalajara, January 12, 2002, section A, 1, section B, 6; José Díaz Bentacourt and Ignacio Pérez Vega, "Falleció Lupita Martínez, viuda del desaparecido ex líder cetemista Heliodoro Hernández Loza," *Público*, Guadalajara, January 12, 2002; Leticia Castro, "Es la más homenajeada: Despiden en Guadalajara a Guadalupe Martínez Villanueva, ex lideresa vitalicia del Círculo Feminista de Occidente," *Mural*, Guadalajara, January 13, 2002, section A, 1, section B, 5; "Miles en Jalisco despiden a Lupita Martínez de Hernández Loza," *El informador*, Guadalajara, January 13, 2002, section B, 2; Sonia Serrano Iñiguez, "Rinden homenajes a Guadalupe Martínez," *Público*, Guadalajara, January 13, 2002, 14; Carlos Alberto Almaral, "Rinden último tributo a Doña Lupita Martínez: Reconocimiento de la clase política y sindical," *El occidental*, Guadalajara, January 13, 2002, section A, 20.

2. Pansters, *Citizens of the Pyramid*, 26–27; Pansters, *Política y poder en Puebla*, 273; Medina Núñez, "Fuerzas políticas y procesos electorales"; Romero, "La conformación del caciquismo"; Tamayo Rodríguez, *Los movimientos sociales, 1917–1929*, 4; Tamayo Rodríguez, "Movimiento obrero y lucha sindical," 131–58; Murià, *Historia de Jalisco*; Castro Palmeros, Villa Michel, and Venegas Pacheco, "Indicios de la historia"; Tamayo Rodríguez, *La conformación del Estado moderno*, 2; Tamayo Rodríguez, "Los obreros"; Romero, *La consolidación del estado*; Romero, *El Partido Nacional Revolucionario*; Hurtado, *Familias, política y parentesco*.
3. Meyer, "Los caciques," 26–27; Sotelo, "Arqueología de la ilegalidad," 48–51.
4. Chassen-López, "Patron of Progress."
5. Fowler-Salamini, "'La Negra Moya.'"
6. Fowler-Salamini, "Caciquismo, sindicalismo," 221–22.
7. Fowler-Salamini, "Caciquismo, sindicalismo," 223.
8. The story of the life and political career of Guadalupe Martínez is based on the following interviews: María Guadalupe Martínez Villanueva widow of Hernández Loza, recorded interview by the author, Guadalajara, August 15, 1996; July 10, 1997; July 29, 1998; August 3, 1998; August 4, 1998; February 22, 2000; and the biographical album fashioned by Dolores Martínez, "Una mujer y su destino," 1975, 2 volumes.
9. For an in-depth discussion of Atala Apodaca, see chapter 3 of this book.
10. Dolores Martínez, "Una mujer y su destino," manuscript, 1975, vol. 1, 21, vol. 2, 264, APGM.
11. Dolores Martínez, unrecorded interview by the author, Guadalajara, August 15, 2001.
12. Martínez, "Una mujer y su destino," vol. 2, 289, APGM; Fernández Aceves, "Las mujeres graduadas," 120.
13. Martínez, "Una mujer y su destino," vol. 2, 35–38, APGM; Fernández Aceves, "Political Mobilization of Women in Revolutionary Guadalajara, 1910–1940," 201.
14. Letter sent by Magdalena Velasco de la Mora to the executive committee of the CFOMAD, November 26, 1941, ACFOMAD.
15. Barragán and Rosales, "Congresos Nacionales de Obreras y Campesinas," 24–44.
16. Tuñón Pablos, *Mujeres que se organizan*, 35.
17. "Las sesiones de ayer estuvieron llenas de incidentes sin que se pudiera hacer nada útil," *El jalisciense*, Guadalajara, September 14, 1934, 1, 6, FE/BPEJ; "Surgió el alboroto a causa del registro de unas credenciales de obreras de La Experiencia," *El jalisciense*, Guadalajara, September 15, 1934, 1, 5–6, FE/BPEJ; Ríos Cárdenas, *La mujer mexicana es ciudadana*, 188; Tuñón Pablos, *Mujeres que se organizan*, 48.
18. T-1-930, T-153, file no. 3898, AHJ, FT.

19. Ana María Hernández Lucas, recorded interviews by the author, Guadalajara, August 17, 1996, August 8, 1998, and May 25, 2002.
20. Fernández Aceves, "Once We Were Corn Grinders," 81–101.
21. In the manifestation in favor of socialist education promoted by the PNR, COJ, CFO, and the Universidad de Guadalajara, more than fifteen thousand workers were mobilized. Present were all the women's organizations affiliated with the COJ and the CFO. T-1-934, box T-9, file no. 6629, AHJ, FT; *El jalisciense*, November 21, 1934, FE/BPEJ; *Las noticias*, November 21, 1934, FE/BPEJ; Fernández Aceves, "Political Mobilization of Women," 266.
22. Series 066/49, 1941, AHJ, SGGASBG, FTPS.
23. Tamayo Rodríguez, "Movimiento obrero y lucha sindical," 149; Tamayo Rodríguez, "Los obreros," 81.
24. Tamayo Rodríguez, "Los obreros," 82; Tamayo Rodríguez, "Movimiento obrero y lucha sindical," 149; Romero, *La consolidación del estado*, 5, 111, 15.
25. Arias, "La industria en perspectiva," 85–93; Tamayo Rodríguez, "Los obreros," 73–76.
26. Tamayo Rodríguez, "Movimiento obrero y lucha sindical," 149–50; Romero, "La conformación del caciquismo," 297–99.
27. Tamayo Rodríguez, "Movimiento obrero y lucha sindical"; Tamayo Rodríguez, "Los obreros"; Romero, "La conformación del caciquismo."
28. Hurtado, *Familias, política y parentesco*, 117.
29. Agapito Isaac, unrecorded interview by the author, Guadalajara, March 15, 2002; "Catarino Isaac se va una época de dirigencia obrera," *El occidental*, Guadalajara, May 15, 1994, 2; José Díaz Betancourt, "Murió el líder sindical Catarino Isaac Estrada," *Público*, Guadalajara, May 15, 1994, 6.
30. Ana María Hernández Lucas, recorded interview by the author, Guadalajara, August 8, 1998.
31. Ana María Hernández Lucas, recorded interview by the author, Guadalajara, August 17, 1996.
32. Círculo Feminista de Occidente "María A. Díaz," 1947, BPEJ. The schoolteachers who submitted proposals were Guadalupe Martínez, Magdalena Carillo Hernández, María Correa Ramos, María Guadalupe Villalpando, Dolores Martínez, Amalia Mendoza, Aurea Castañeda, Margarita Martínez, Estela Ruiz Sánchez, Ma. Del Carmen Granillo, María Del Refugio Villavicencio, Isabel Siordia Orozco, Doctor Irene Robledo García, Eloisa Ruiz, Ramona Aguilar, María Socorro Rodríguez, Petra Esqueda, María Porfiria L. Vargas, Lorenza Razo, and Candelaria Sánchez. Participating here were two sisters of Guadalupe Martínez: Dolores and Margarita.
33 Círculo Feminista de Occidente, "María A. Díaz," 1947, 13-5, BPEJ.

34. María Guadalupe Martínez Villanueva, recorded interview by the author, Guadalajara, August 15, 1996. The original quote in Spanish: "El proveedor de la casa."
35. The newspaper *Jalisco ceteme* published a series of articles on motherhood, such as, for example, "Régimen de la madre para la lactancia," "Los niños no son juguetes de piedra," "Orientación cívica de la mujer," *Jalisco ceteme*, Guadalajara, August 15, 1957, 6; "Deberes de la mujer dentro del hogar," "Decálogo de los deberes sociales," *Jalisco ceteme*, Guadalajara, October 15, 1957, 6; "La mujer y el hogar," *Jalisco ceteme*, Guadalajara, November 15, 1957, December 6 and 15, 1957, 6; "Los tres defectos que entorpecen la buena marcha de un hogar," *Jalisco ceteme*, January 15, 1958, 6; "Nuestros hijos," *Jalisco ceteme*, February 15, 1958, 6; "También son niños mexicanos los débiles mentales," "Nuestros hijos," *Jalisco ceteme*, March 15, 1958, 4, APGM.
36. Ana María Hernández Lucas, recorded interview by the author, Guadalajara, May 25, 2002.
37. Ana María Hernández Lucas, recorded interview by the author, Guadalajara, May 25, 2002.
38. Otilia Contreras, unrecorded interview by Alejandra de Lira, Guadalajara, February 22, 2002; María Ríos Mora, unrecorded interview by the author, Guadalajara, May 22, 2002.
39. Hurtado, *Familias, política y parentesco*, 108–18.
40. Sánchez Susarrey, "Mecanismos de negociación y concertación política."
41. "Figuras Cetemistas: Juan Ramírez," *Jalisco ceteme*, Guadalajara, October 15, 1957, 4, APGM.
42. Heliodoro Hernández Loza, "Nuestra Tribuna," *Jalisco ceteme*, Guadalajara, October 15, 1957, 5, APGM.
43. Jesús Ruiz, "Primera Conferencia de la Prensa Obrera," *Jalisco ceteme*, Guadalajara, May 15, 1959, 5, APGM; "Conceptos que enaltecen," *Jalisco ceteme*, Guadalajara, August 15, 1959, 2, APGM.
44. "Sigue con su labor cultural el cuadro artístico del SUTAJ," *Jalisco ceteme*, Guadalajara, August 16, 1958, APGM; "FTJ y SUTAJ fomentan las artes entre obreros," *Jalisco ceteme*, Guadalajara, October 15, 1959, 3, APGM; Rebeca Escalante, "Actividades del Círculo Feminista de Occidente María A. Díaz," *Jalisco ceteme*, Guadalajara, November 15, 1959, 5, APGM; "Reconocimiento y elogios merecidos a los integrantes de la banda del SUTAJ," *Jalisco ceteme*, December 15, 1959, 5, APGM.
45. "El problema de la Celanese... Elementos comunistas y falsos líderes engañan a trabajadores demagogicamente," *Jalisco ceteme*, Guadalajara, May 1, 1959, 1, 3–4; "Revisión de contrato en Celanese Mexicana," *Jalisco ceteme*, Guadalajara,

May 15, 1959, 5; "Declaró la CROC graves inexactitudes: El Sindicato Celanese actuó con legalidad y respeto a la justicia," *Jalisco ceteme*, Guadalajara, June 15, 1960, 1, 3, APGM.

46. Rebeca Escalante, "Actividades del Círculo Feminista de Occidente María A. Díaz," *Jalisco ceteme*, Guadalajara, July 15, 1959, 3, APGM.
47. "¿Qué es un líder?," *Jalisco ceteme*, Guadalajara, July 15, 1958, 3, APGM.
48. Heliodoro Hernández Loza, "Nuestra Tribuna," *Jalisco ceteme*, Guadalajara, November 15, 1957, 1, 7, APGM.
49. See *El informador* and *El occidental* during the 1950s.
50. "Editorial: Los ataques a la CTM," *Jalisco ceteme*, Guadalajara, March 15, 1960, 5, 7; "Editorial: La CTM y la extrema Izquierda," *Jalisco ceteme*, Guadalajara, July 15, 1960, 5, 7; "Editorial: Autocrítica," *Jalisco ceteme*, Guadalajara, September 30, 1960, 4, 11; "Editorial: 1961; Año de la CTM," *Jalisco ceteme*, Guadalajara, January 30, 1961, 4, 9, APGM.
51. Craske, "Gender, Politics, and Legislation," 20; Rodríguez, *Women in Contemporary Mexican Politics*, 101.
52. "Editorial," *Jalisco ceteme*, Guadalajara, August 15, 1957, 1, 5, APGM.
53. "Editorial: Presencia de la mujer trabajadora en la política Mexicana," *Jalisco ceteme*, Guadalajara, February 15, 1958, 5.
54. Martínez, "Una mujer y su destino," vol. 1, 184, APGM.
55. Martínez, "Una mujer y su destino," vol. 1, 185, APGM.
56. Martínez, "Una mujer y su destino," vol. 1, 185, APGM.
57. Martínez, "Una mujer y su destino," vol. 2, 48, APGM.
58. Martínez, "Una mujer y su destino," vol. 2, 51, APGM.
59. Martínez, "Una mujer y su destino," vol. 2, 55, APGM.
60. Martínez, "Una mujer y su destino," vol. 2, 55, APGM.
61. Carey, *Plaza of Sacrifices*, 269–92; Cano, "Las feministas en campaña"; Olcott, *Revolutionary Women*.
62. Lau Jaiven, *La nueva ola del feminismo en México*, 21; Olcott, *International Women's Year*.

6. María Guadalupe Urzúa Flores

1. "Tiene la palabra el diputado Armando Pérez Oliva," year 1, vol. 11, no. 76, December 7, 2004, ACEJ, LAS.
2. *Diario oficial de la federación*, February 12, 1947, 3–4; Tuñón Pablos, *¡Por fin . . . !*, 75.
3. Lerdo de Tejada C. and Godina, *El lobbying en México*.
4. Castillo Gómez, "Cultura escrita y sociedad," 11.

5. John, *Analysing Public Policy*; Larason Schneider and Ingram, *Policy Design for Democracy*; Parsons, *Las políticas públicas*.
6. Knight and Panster, *Caciquismo in Twentieth-Century Mexico*; Fernández Aceves, "Engendering Caciquismo," 204–5.
7. Joseph and Nugent, *Everyday Forms of State Formation*; Olcott, *Revolutionary Women*; Vaughan, *Cultural Politics in Revolution*; Vaughan, Cano, and Olcott, *Sex in Revolution*; Vaughan and Lewis, *Eagle and the Virgin*.
8. See the different journalism articles in *El informador* regarding the public works advocated by García Barragán.
9. Chassen-López, "Patron of Progress"; Fowler-Salamini, "Caciquismo, sindicalismo"; Fernández Aceves, "Engendering Caciquismo."
10. Personal Section, 12.1, CMGUF-BCCG-CO; Roderic Ai Camp points out that she was born in 1922. See Camp, "Women and Political Leadership in Mexico," 578–79.
11. Manuel Urzúa, unrecorded interview by the author, Ajijic, Jalisco, April 24, 2008.
12. Asociación de Maestros Egresados de la Escuela Normal de Jalisco, *La Escuela Normal de Jalisco*, 4.
13. Méndez Zárate, "La reforma agraria en San Martín de Hidalgo."
14. "Fue asesinado anoche ex-diputado Alfonso Ceballos," *El informador*, March 12, 1950, 1–2, HDEI; Gobierno del Estado de Jalisco, *Cronología política*.
15. Alonso, *El rito electoral en Jalisco, 1940–1992*, 28; de la Peña Topete, "Populism, Regional Power," 203.
16. Manuel Urzúa, unrecorded interview by the author, Ajijic, Jalisco, April 24, 2008.
17. Vaughan, "Modernizing Patriarchy," 197.
18. Vaughan, "Modernizing Patriarchy," 200.
19. "Acta de cabildo," February 8, 1928, pp. 40–40v, 1927–34, AHSMH, LC, cited in Méndez Zárate, "La reforma agraria en San Martín de Hidalgo, Jalisco 1915–1935." I interviewed two men in San Martín Hidalgo. According to Tomás García Tadeo, Urzúa Flores's aunt Julia was raped, while Francisco Francillard Chalves defined the incident as attempted rape. Tomás García Tadeo, recorded interview by the author in San Martín Hidalgo, Jalisco, December 8, 2006. Francisco Francillard Chalves, recorded interview by the author in Tepehuaje, Jalisco, April 18, 2008.
20. Smith, "Civilizing Process and the History of Sexuality," 79–80.
21. Friedrich, *Princess of Naranja*.
22. María Guadalupe Urzúa Flores, unrecorded interview by the author, San Martín Hidalgo, Jalisco, December 7, 2002.
23. Pepe Camacho, manuscript of the biography of Guadalupe Urzúa, unpublished.

24. Certificado de escuela primaria superior para niñas, Zacoalco de Torres, June 15, 1931, CMGUF-BCCG-CO. Civera Cerecedo, *La escuela*.
25. Camp, "Women and Political Leadership in Mexico," 578.
26. 1.2.8 Varios, box 4, file 94, 1931, CMGUF-BCCG-CO.
27. Bakhtin, *Rabelais and His World*; Brophy, "Carnival and Citizenship," 873–904.
28. María Guadalupe Urzúa Flores, unrecorded interview by the author, San Martín Hidalgo, December 7, 2002.
29. Vaughan, "Cultural Approaches," 194, 97, 200.
30. Vaughan, "Cultural Approaches," 300.
31. Gómez Ortega, "Las primeras diputadas en Jalisco, 1955–1965," 62.
32. "Vecinos de Autlán aportan $8,000 para el camino," *El informador*, Guadalajara, August 25, 1930, 1; "Tonaya," *El informador*, Guadalajara, August 13, 1931, 3.
33. Fulwider, "Driving the Nation," 6, 20–21.
34. Camp, "Women and Political Leadership in Mexico," 579.
35. Cano, *Se llamaba Elena Arizmendi*, 22.
36. Fernández Aceves, "Voto femenino," 696–710.
37. Carey, "'Selling Is More of a Habit Than Using,'" 70.
38. Carey, "'Selling Is More of a Habit Than Using,'" 63, 69.
39. Kapelusz-Poppi, "Physician Activists," 36.
40. Kapelusz-Poppi, "Physician Activists," 36.
41. Kapelusz-Poppi, "Physician Activists," 46.
42. Kapelusz-Poppi, "Physician Activists," 45–46.
43. Kapelusz-Poppi, "Physician Activists," 46.
44. Quijano, "La medicina en México de 1940–2000," 215–16.
45. Camp, "Women and Political Leadership in Mexico," 438; Hospital file, 1940s, CMGUF-BCCG-CO.
46. Hospital file, 1940s, letter dated June 2, 1941, CMGUF-BCCG-CO.
47. Guadalupe Urzúa's papers are found in the personal archive of Jesús Camacho Barreto, without classification, June 19, 1945.
48. Civera Cerecedo, *La escuela*; Gómez Nashiki, "El movimiento estudiantil mexicano," 194.
49. 2.11.4.4 Hospital, box 121, file 4409, CMGUF-BCCG-CO.
50. 2.11.4.4 Hospital, box 121, file 4409, CMGUF-BCCG-CO.
51. Cano, "Ciudadanía y sufragio femenino," 185.
52. In 1954, Aurora Jiménez Palacios became the first congresswoman representing the new state of Baja California (1952). The next group of congresswomen were elected in 1955 and were from Chiapas, Estado de México, Jalisco, and Nuevo León.
53. Hernández Rodríguez, *El centro dividido*, 41.

54. Molyneux, "Mobilization without Emancipation?," 283–84.
55. Kaplan, "Female Consciousness and Collective Action," 545; Kaplan, *Red City, Blue Period*, 107; Roth Wood, *Revolution in the Street*, 228.
56. Carpeta sufragio femenino, 1953, APMGUF.
57. Carpeta sufragio femenino, April 30, 1953, CMGUF-BCCG-CO.
58. Arreola Ayala, *La justicia electoral en México*; Tuñón Pablos, *¡Por fin . . . !*; González Compeán and Lomelí, *El partido de la revolución*.
59. Fernández Aceves, "Voto femenino"; Gómez Ortega, "Primeras presidentas municipales y regidoras."
60. For a deep discussion about Concha Michel and her agrarian land reform proposal, see Olcott, *Revolutionary Women*, 93–94. For a gender perspective of Mexican agrarian reform, see Deere and León, *Género, propiedad y empoderamiento*.
61. 2.1 Acción femenina, box 19, file 597, Carpeta Plan de Trabajo, 1953–56, CMGUF-BCCG-CO.
62. 2.14.5 Mujeres PRI, box 142, file 5110, Carpeta sufragio femenino, 1953, CMGUF-BCCG-CO.
63. 2.2 Confederación Nacional Campesina, box 28, files 833–840, ejidos, 1950s, CMGUF-BCCG-CO.
64. "Sufragio efectivo," *El informador*, Guadalajara, July 6, 1955, 4, HDEI; "Editorial: La dictadura del poder ejecutivo," *El informador*, Guadalajara, March 16, 1955, 4, HDEI; "Editorial: Sin representación nacional," *El informador*, Guadalajara, March 2, 1955, 4, HDEI; "Editorial: El momento político," *El informador*, Guadalajara, February 28, 1955, 4, HDEI; "Editorial: Elecciones de diputados," *El informador*, Guadalajara, February 1, 1955, 4, HDEI; "Editorial: En camino del fracaso," *El informador*, Guadalajara, January 19, 1955, 4, HDEI; "Editorial: Elecciones 'limpias,'" *El informador*, Guadalajara, January 7, 1955, 4, HDEI.
65. Castañeda Jiménez, *Marcelino García Barragán*; Rivera Morán, "La cultura política."
66. Periodo ordinario, Legislatura XLIII, Año Legislativo I (1955), ACU, DDHCD; "El caso de Autlán," *El informador*, Guadalajara, April 12, 1955, 3, HDEI; Por Lussa, "Charlas de sobremesa," *El informador*, Guadalajara, June 27, 1955, 4, HDEI; "Comentarios del día," *El informador*, Guadalajara, June 27, 1955, 4, HDEI; "Editorial ¿Qué pasa en Autlán?," *El informador*, Guadalajara, June 27, 1955, 4, HDEI; "Mujeres de Autlán al Gobernador C. Lic. Agustín Yáñez," *El informador*, Guadalajara, June 25, 1955, 3, HDEI.
67. Legislatura XLIII, Año Legislativo I, periodo ordinario, Diario no. 6, August 24, 1955, ACU, DDHCD.
68. Fernández Aceves, "Voto femenino."
69. "Programa de mejoras," *El informador*, February 8, 1956, HDEI; "Inauguración de un centro escolar en Juchitlán, Jalisco," *El informador*, February 15, 1956,

HDEI; "Entregó al Patronato un Hospital Regional," *El informador*, June 1, 1956, 3, HDEI; "Terminaron la perforación de un pozo en San Martín Hidalgo," *El informador*, August 15, 1956, 4, HDEI; "Hacen falta maestros," *El informador*, September 20, 1956, 1, HDEI; "Visita a Tecolotlán," *El informador*, December 2, 1956, HDEI; "Los problemas del agro," *El informador*, July 17, 1957, HDEI.
70. "Oración," *El informador*, July 25, 1957, 4, HDEI.
71. 3.10 Revistas, box 192, file 5893, *Mujeres expression femenina*, 1977, CMGUF-BCCG-CO.
72. Gómez Ortega, "Las primeras diputadas en Jalisco"; Ai Camp, *Biografías de políticos mexicanos*, 578; Sánchez Susarrey, "Mecanismos de negociación y concertación política," 233; Camp, "Women and Political Leadership in Mexico," 438.
73. González Compeán and Lomelí, *El partido de la revolución*.
74. Ponencia, 1957, CMGUF-BCCG-CO. Hernández Rodríguez, *El centro dividido*, 30.
75. Hernández Rodríguez, *El centro dividido*, 30.
76. *El informador*, Mariana Moreno de Pelayo's published letter, January 5, 1955, 7, HDEI.
77. Hernández Rodríguez, *El centro dividido*, 27–28.
78. "Soy soldado de corazón y político de ocasión," *El informador*, Guadalajara, July 17, 1942, 6, HDEI.
79. Hernández Rodríguez, *El centro dividido*, 41.
80. Hurtado, *Familias, política y parentesco*, 84–85; Servín, *Ruptura y oposición*, 165–325; Servín, *La oposición política*, 51–61; Servín, "El movimiento henriquista," 65–82.
81. Torres González, *La fuerza de la ironía*, 165.
82. Zárate Hernández, "Caciques and Leaders in the Era of Democracy," 279.
83. Hernández Rodríguez, *El centro dividido*, 30.
84. Hurtado, *Familias, política y parentesco*, 85.
85. María Guadalupe Urzúa Flores, unrecorded interview by the author, San Martín Hidalgo, December 7, 2002.
86. Urzúa proposed as candidates for the municipal presidency Juan Pulido Zepeda (1957–59), Alfonso Gutiérrez Zepeda (1961), José F. Guerrero (1962–64), and José Raymundo López Barba (1968–70). Francisco Guerrero Santos broke away from *Lupismo* and joined another faction. J. Jesús Camacho Barreto, recorded interview by the author, San Martín Hidalgo, December 12, 2006.
87. Sánchez Susarrey, "Mecanismos de negociación y concertación política," 215–17.

Epilogue
1. Freeman, *Room at a Time*.
2. Molyneux, "Twentieth-Century State Formations," 68.
3. Ginzburg, *Threads and Traces*, 1, 9.

BIBLIOGRAPHY

Manuscripts and Archives

ACEJ. Archivo del Congreso del Estado de Jalisco
ACFOMAD. Archives of the Círculo Feminista de Occidente María A. Díaz
ACU. Archivo del Congreso de la Unión
AE. Archivo Escolar
AEC. Archivo Elías Calles
AHAG. Archivo Histórico de la Arquidiócesis de Guadalajara
AHGE-SER. Archivo Histórico Genaro Estrada de la Secretaría de Relaciones Exteriores
AHJ. Archivo Histórico de Jalisco
AHSMH. Archivo Histórico de San Martín Hidalgo
AHUG. Archivo Histórico de la Universidad de Guadalajara
AMG. Archivo Municipal de Guadalajara
APBMV. Archivo Personal Belén Martínez Villanueva
APGM. Archivo Personal Guadalupe Martínez
APJEC. Archivo del Primer Jefe del Ejército Constitucionalista, 1889–1920
ARCEJ. Archivo del Registro Civil del Estado de Jalisco
ASDN. Archivo de la Secretaría de la Defensa Nacional
AVR. Archivo de Veteranos de la Revolución
BCC-CO. Biblioteca Carmen Castañeda-CIESAS Occidente
CEHM-CARSO. Centro de Estudios de Historia de México Grupo CARSO
CGC. Colección Gustavo Casasola
CIRMC. Colección Independencia y Revolución en la Memoria Ciudadana
CMGUF-BCCG-CO. Colección María Guadalupe Urzúa Flores at the Biblioteca Carmen Castañeda García, CIESAS Occidente
DACH. Departamento de Archivo de Correspondencia e Historia
DDHCD. Diario de Debates de la H. Cámara de Diputados
DE. Departamento Escolar
DEP. Departamento de Educación Pública

EMJ. Expedientes de Maestros Jubilados
FAPECFT. Fideicomiso Archivos Plutarco Elías Calles y Fernando Torreblanca
FE/BPEJ. Fondos Especiales-Biblioteca Pública del Estado de Jalisco
FF. Fondo Fomento
FMH. Fondo Memoria Histórica
FRHN/UNAM. Fondos Reservados de la Hemeroteca Nacional / Universidad Nacional Autónoma de México
FSG. Fondo Soledad González
FT. Fondo de Trabajo
GS. Gobierno Section
HDBNE. Hemeroteca Digital de la Biblioteca Nacional de España
HDEI. Hemeroteca Digital *El informador*
HNDM/UNAM. Hemeroteca Nacional Digital de México/UNAM
LAS. Libro de Actas de Sesiones
LC. Libro de Cabildo 1927–1934
LC. U.S. Library of Congress
LDG. Libro de Defunciones de Guadalajara, 1939
LEPN. Libro de Exámenes Profesionales de la Normal
OP. Operaciones Militares
OS. Obispos Series
PALJGZH. Personal Archive Lic. José Guadalupe Zuno Hernández
REB. Relación de Expedientes dados de baja por renuncias, jubilaciones, abandono de empleo y fallecimiento
SGGASBG, FTPS. Secretaría General de Gobierno de la administración de Silvano Barba González, Fondo Trabajo y Previsión Social

Published Works

Accampo, Elinor A. "Gender, Social Policy, and the Formation of the Third Republic: An Introduction." In *Gender and the Politics of Social Reform in France, 1870–1914*, edited by Elinor A. Accampo, Rachel G. Fuchs, and Mary Lynn Stewart, 1–27. Baltimore: Johns Hopkins University Press, 1995.

Aguirre, Amado. *Mis memorias de campaña*. Mexico: Comisión Nacional para las Celebraciones del 175 Aniversario de la Independencia Nacional y 75 Aniversario de la Revolución Mexicana, 1985.

Aldana Rendón, Mario Alfonso. *Del reyismo al nuevo orden constitucional, 1910–1917*. Vol. 1 of *Jalisco desde la revolución*, edited by Mario Alfonso Aldana Rendón. Jalisco: Independencia y Revolución. Colección Conmemorativa. Guadalajara: Gobierno del Estado de Jalisco, Universidad de Guadalajara, 1987.

———. *Manuel M. Diéguez y la revolución mexicana*. Guadalajara: El Colegio de Jalisco, 2006.

———. "Masonería y revolución en Jalisco." *Estudios jaliscienses*, no. 58 (2004): 15–28.

Alonso, Ana María. *Thread of Blood: Colonialism, Revolution, and Gender on Mexico's Northern Frontier*. Tucson: University of Arizona Press, 1995.

Alonso, Jorge. *El rito electoral en Jalisco, 1940–1992*. Guadalajara: Centro de Investigaciones y Estudios Superiores en Antropología Social, El Colegio de Jalisco, 1993.

Álvarez Lázaro, Pedro F. *Cien años de educación en España: En torno a la creación del Ministerio de Instrucción Pública y Bellas Artes*. Madrid: Ministerio de Educación, 2001.

Alvarez, Sonia. *Engendering Democracy in Brazil: Women's Movements in Transition Politics*. Princeton: Princeton University Press, 1990.

Anderson, Robert D. *European Universities from the Enlightenment to 1914*. Oxford: Oxford University Press, 2004.

Apodaca, Laura. *Educación de las jóvenes: Conferencia leída en el Teatro Degollado por la señorita profa. Laura Apodaca, directora de la Escuela Normal para Señoritas del Estado de Jalisco*. Guadalajara: s.e., 1914.

Arias, Patricia. "La industria en perspectiva." In *Guadalajara, la gran ciudad de la pequeña industria*, edited by Patricia Arias, 85–93. Zamora: El Colegio de Michoacán, 1985.

Arreola Ayala, Álvaro. *La justicia electoral en México: Breve recuento histórico*. Mexico: Tribunal Electoral del Poder Judicial de la Federación, 2008.

Arrom, Silvia Marina. "Las Señoras de la Caridad: pioneras olvidadas de la asistencia social en México, 1863–1910." *Historia Mexicana*, no. 226 (2007): 445–90.

———. "Mexican Laywomen Spearhead a Catholic Revival: The Ladies of Charity, 1863–1910." In *Religious Culture in Modern Mexico*, edited by Martin A. Nesvig, 50–77. Lanham MD: Rowman & Littlefield, 2007.

———. "The Mobilization of Catholic Women in Jalisco: The Ladies of Charity, 1863–1912." V Coloquio Internacional Historia de Mujeres y de Género en México, Oaxaca, REDMUGEN, March 18–20, 2010.

———. *La Güera Rodríguez: The Life and Legends of a Mexican Independence Heroine*. Okland: University of California Press, 2021.

Arroyo Alejandre, Jesús. "Ires y venires en el occidente." In *La gran ciudad de la pequeña industria*, edited by Patricia Arias, 21–56. Zamora: El Colegio de Michoacán, 1988.

Asociación de Egresados de la Escuela Normal de Jalisco. *La Escuela Normal de Jalisco: Galería de generaciones de maestros egresados de ella, 1894–1958*. Guadalajara: n.p., 1958.

Bakhtin, Mikhail. *Rabelais and His World*. Bloomington: Indiana University Press, 1984.

Banner, Lois W. "Biography as History." *American Historical Review* 114, no. 3 (2009): 579–86. https://doi.org/10.1086/ahr.114.3.579.

Bantjes, Adrian Alexander. "Burning Saints, Molding Minds: Iconoclasm, Civic Ritual, and Failed Cultural Revolution." In *Rituals of Rule, Rituals of Resistance: Public Celebration and Popular Culture in Mexico*, edited by William H. Beezley, Cheril English Martin, and French E. William, 261–84. Wilmington: SR Books, 1994.

———. "Saints, Sinners, and State Formation: Local Religion and Cultural Revolution in México." In *The Eagle and the Virgin: Nation and Cultural Revolution in Mexico, 1920–1940*, edited by Mary Kay Vaughan and Steve Lewis, 137–216. Durham NC: Duke University Press, 2006.

Barbosa Guzmán, Francisco. *La iglesia y el gobierno civil: Jalisco desde la revolución*. Vol. 6 of *Jalisco desde la revolución*, edited by Mario Alfonso Aldana Rendón. Mexico: Universidad de Guadalajara, Gobierno del Estado de Jalisco, 1988.

Barlow, Tani E., Madeleine Yue Dong, Uta G. Poiger, Priti Ramamurthy, Lynn M. Thomas, and Alys Eve Weinbaum. "The Modern Girl around the World: A Research Agenda and Preliminary Findings." *Gender & History* 17, no. 2 (2005): 245–94.

Barragán, Leticia, and Amanda Rosales. "Congresos Nacionales de Obreras y Campesinas." *Historia Obrera* 5 (1975): 24–44.

Barrancos, Dora. "Maestras, librepensadoras y feministas en la Argentina, 1900–1912." In *Historia de los intelectuales en América Latina*, edited by Carlos Altamirano, 465–91. Madrid: Katz Editores, 2008.

Bartra, Roger *Caciquismo y poder político en el México rural*. Mexico: Siglo XXI Editores, 1986.

Batliwala, Srilatha. "The Meaning of Women's Empowerment: New Concepts from Action." In *Population Policies Reconsidered: Health, Empowerment and Rights*, edited by Gita Sen, Adrienne Germain, and Lincoln C. Chen, 127–38. Boston: Harvard University Press, 1994.

Chris Bayly, Sven Beckert, Matthew Connelly, Isabel Hofmeyr, Wendy Kozol, and Patricia Seed. "AHR Conversation: On Transnational History." *American Historical Review* 111, no. 5 (2006): 1441–64. https://doi.org/10.1086/ahr.111.5.1441.

Bazant, Mílada, ed. *Biografía: modelos, métodos y enfoques*. Toluca: El Colegio Mexiquense, 2013.

———. *Caminos docentes: Entre injertos, abonos y venenos; Clemente Antonio Neve (1828–1905)*. Toluca: El Colegio Mexiquense, 2021.

———. *Laura Méndez de Cuenca: Mexican Feminist, 1853–1928*. Tucson: University of Arizona Press, 2018.

Ben-Amos, Avner. "El centro sagrado del poder: París y los funerales de Estado republicanos." *Culturales* 3, no. 6 (2007): 49–74.

Besse, Susan K. *Restructuring Patriarchy: The Modernization of Gender Inequality in Brazil, 1914–1940*. Chapel Hill: University of North Carolina Press, 1996.

Bortz, Jeffrey. *Revolution within the Revolution: Cotton Textile Workers and the Mexican Labor Regime, 1910–1923*. Stanford: Stanford University Press, 2008.

———. "'Without Any More Law Than Their Own Caprice': Cotton Textile Workers and the Challenge to Factory Authority during the Mexican Revolution." *International Review of Social History* 42, no. 2 (1997): 253–88.

Boylan, Kristina. "Género, fe y nación: El activismo de las mujeres católicas, 1917–1940." In *Género, poder y política en el México posrevolucionario*, edited by Gabriela Cano, Mary Kay Vaughan, and Jocelyn Olcott, 309–46. Mexico: Fondo de Cultura Económica, 2009.

———. "Mexican Catholic Women's Activism, 1929–1940." PhD diss, University of Oxford, 2001.

Brading, David A., ed. *Caudillos y campesinos en la revolución mexicana*. Mexico: FCE, 1995.

Britton, John A. *Educación y radicalismo en México*. 2 vols. Mexico: SepSetentas, 1976.

———. "Teacher Unionization and the Corporate State in Mexico, 1931–1945." *Hispanic American Historical Review* 59, no. 4 (1979): 649–90.

Brophy, James M. "Carnival and Citizenship: The Politics of Carnival Culture in the Prussian Rhineland, 1823–1848." *Journal of Social History* 30, no. 4 (Summer 1997): 873–904.

Brunk, Samuel. "Remembering Emiliano Zapata: Three Moments in the Posthumous Career of the Martyr of Chinameca." *Hispanic American Historical Review* 78, no. 3 (1998): 457–90.

Brush, Lisa. "Love, Toil, and Trouble: Motherhood and Feminist Politics." *Signs: Journal of Culture and Society* 21, no. 2 (1996): 429–54.

Buchenau, Jürgen. *Plutarco Elías Calles and the Mexican Revolution*. Lanham: Rowman & Littlefield, 2007.

Burton, James. "Resistance and Accommodations: The Working People of Guadalajara, Mexico, 1910–1926." PhD diss, Florida State University, 1995.

Buve, Raymond. "Caciquismo, un principio de ejercicio de poder durante varios siglos." *Relaciones: Estudios de historia y sociedad* 24, no. 96 (2003): 17–39.

Calhoun, Craig, ed. Introduction to *Habermas and the Public Sphere*, 1–50. Boston: Massachusetts Institute of Technology, 1996.

Camacho Becerra, Juan Arturo. "Síntomas de la vanguardia." *Estudios jaliscienses*, no. 38 (1999): 48–67.

Camberos Vizcaíno, Vicente. *Francisco el grande: Monseñor Francisco Orozco y Jiménez*. Mexico: Editorial Jus, 1966.

Camp, Roderic Ai. *Biografías de políticos mexicanos, 1935–1985*. Mexico: FCE, 1992.

———. "Women and Political Leadership in Mexico: A Comparative Study of Female and Male Political Elites." *Journal of Politics* 41, no. 2 (1979): 417–41.

Canning, Kathleen. *Gender History in Practice: Historical Perspectives on Bodies, Class & Citizenship*. Ithaca: Cornell University Press, 2006.

Cano, Gabriela. "Adelina Zendejas: Arquitecta de su memoria." *Debate feminista* 4, no. 8 (1993): 387–413.

———. "Ciudadanía y sufragio femenino: El discurso igualitario de Lázaro Cárdenas." In *Miradas feministas sobre las mexicanas del siglo XX*, edited by Marta Lamas, 151–90. Mexico: FCE, 2007.

———. "Unconcealable Realities of Desire: Amelio Robles's (Transgender) Masculinity in the Mexican Revolution." In *Sex in Revolution: Gender, Politics, and Power in Modern Mexico*, edited by Mary Kay Vaughan, Jocelyn Olcott, and Gabriela Cano, 35–56. Durham: Duke University Press, 2006.

———. "Las feministas en campaña." *Debate feminista* 2, no. 4 (1991): 269–92.

———. "México 1923: Primer Congreso Feminista Panamericano." *Debate feminista* 1, no. 1 (1990): 303–18.

———. "Revolución, feminismo y ciudadanía en México, 1915–1940." In *Historia de las mujeres: El siglo XX. La nueva mujer*, edited by Georges Duby and Michelle Perrot, 301–11. Madrid: Taurus, 1993.

———. *Se llamaba Elena Arizmendi*. Mexico: Tusquets Editores, 2010.

Cárdenas Ayala, Elisa. *El derrumbe: Jalisco, microcosmos de la revolución mexicana*. Vol. 6. Mexico: Tusquets Editores, 2010.

———. *El horizonte democrático: Jalisco del liberalismo juarista a la revolución*. Vol. 1 of *Jalisco: Independencia y Revolución*, edited by María Alicia Peredo Merlo. Colección Conmemorativa. Zapopan: El Colegio de Jalisco, 2010.

Cárdenas García, Nicolás, and Enrique Guerra Manzo, eds. *Integrados y marginados en el México posrevolucionario: Los juegos de poder local y sus nexos con la política nacional*. Mexico: UAM-Xochimilco, Miguel Ángel Porrúa, 2009.

Cárdenas Ríos, María. *La mujer mexicana es ciudadana: Historia con fisonomía de una novela de costumbres*. Mexico: A. del Bosque Impresor, 1940.

Carey, Elaine. *Plaza of Sacrifices: Gender, Power, and Terror in 1968 Mexico*. Albuquerque: University of New Mexico Press, 2005.

———. "'Selling Is More of a Habit Than Using' Narcotraficante Lola La Chata and Her Threat to Civilization, 1930–1960." *Journal of Women's History* 21, no. 2 (Summer 2009): 62–89.

Carr, Barry. *Marxism & Communism in Twentieth-Century Mexico*. Lincoln: University of Nebraska Press, 1992.

Casasola, Gustavo. *Historia gráfica de la revolución mexicana: Edición conmemorativa*. Vol. 3. Mexico: Editorial Trillas, 1960.

Castañeda Jiménez, Héctor C. *Marcelino García Barragán: Una vida al servicio de México*. Guadalajara: UNED, 1987.

Castillo Gómez, Antonio. "Cultura escrita y Sociedad." *Cultura escrita & sociedad*, no. 1 (2005): 10–13.

Castro Palmeros, Margarita, Adriana Villa Michel, and Silvia Venegas Pacheco. "Indicios de la historia de las relaciones laborales en Jalisco, 1900–1937." In *IV Concurso sobre derecho laboral Manuel M. Diéguez*, 209–503. Guadalajara: UNED, 1982.

Ceballos Ramírez, Manuel. *El catolicismo social: Un tercero en discordia; Rerum Novarum, la "cuestión social" y la movilización de los católicos mexicanos, 1891–1911*. Mexico: El Colegio de México, 1991.

Cejudo Ramos, Elizabeth. *El gobierno no pueda más que dios: Género, ciudadanía y conflicto iglesia-estado en el Sonora revolucionario*. Hermosillo: Universidad de Sonora, 2021.

Chassen-López, Francie. *Mujer y poder en el siglo XIX: La vida extraordinaria de Juana Catarina Romero, cacica de Tehuantepec*. Mexico: Penguin Random House and Editorial Taurus, 2020.

———. "A Patron of Progress: Juana Catarina Romero, the Nineteenth-Century Cacica of Tehunatepec." *Hispanic American Historical Review* 88, no. 3 (2008): 393–426.

Chavoya Peña, María Luisa. *Poder sindical en Jalisco: La sección 47 del SNTE*. Guadalajara: Universidad de Guadalajara, 1995.

Civera Cerecedo, Alicia. *La escuela como opción de vida: La formación de maestros normalistas rurales en México, 1921–1945*. Toluca: El Colegio Mexiquense, A. C., 2008.

———. "La historiografía del magisterio en México, 1911–1970." In *Historiografía de la educación en México*, edited by Luz Elena Galván Lafarga, Susana Quintanilla Osorio, and Clara Inés Ramírez González, 231–58. Mexico: COMIE, 2003.

———. "Mujeres, cultura escrita y escuela en el Estado de México durante la primera mitad del siglo XX." *Cuadernos Interculturales* 7, no. 12 (2009): 161–78.

Cockcroft, James. *Precursores intelectuales de la revolución mexicana*. Mexico: Secretaría de Educación Pública, Siglo XXI Editores, 1985.

Comisión Nacional para la Celebración del Sesquicentenario de la Proclamación de la Independencia Nacional y del Cincuentenario de la Revolución Mexicana. *Diario de los debates del Congreso Constituyente, 1916–1917*. Mexico: Talleres Gráficos de la Nación, 1960.

Connerton, Paul. *How Societies Remember*. New York: Cambridge University Press, 1989.

Córdova, Arnaldo. *La ideología de la revolución mexicana: La formación del nuevo régimen*. Mexico: Ediciones Era, 1981.

Cortés Cuesta, Myrna Elizabeth. "Modernidad y representaciones sociales" BA thesis, Universidad de Guadalajara, 1999.

Craske, Nikki. "Gender, Politics, and Legislation." In *Gender in Latin America*, edited by Sylvia H. Chant, 19–45. New York: Rutgers University Press, 2003.

Cumberland, Charles C. *Mexican Revolution: Genesis under Madero*. Austin: Texas University Press, 1952.

Curley, Robert. "'Avanza el desierto': Espacio público y suicido político en el imaginario cristero." In *Los guachos y los mochos: Once ensayos cristeros*, edited by Julia Preciado Zamora and Servando Ortoll, 45–60. Morelia: Red Utopía, A. C., jitanjáfora, Morelia Editorial, 2009.

———. *Citizens and Believers: Religion and Politics in Revolutionary Jalisco, 1900–1930*. Alburquerque: University of New Mexico Press, 2018.

Dávila Garibi, Ignacio. *Memoria histórica de las labores de la Asociación de Damas Católicas de Guadalajara durante la ausencia de su meritísimo fundador, Illmo. y Rmo. Sr. Dr. y Mtro. D. Francisco Orozco Jiménez, o sea del 19 de mayo de 1914 que partió de la ciudad episcopal, al 14 de octubre de 1919 que volvió de su destierro*. Guadalajara: Tipografía de M. Iguiniz, 1920.

Dávila Garibi, Ignacio J., and Salvador Chávez Hayhoe. *Colección de documentos relativos a la cuestión religiosa en Jalisco, 1913–1919*. Guadalajara: Tipografía J. M. Yguíniz, 1920.

de Grazia, Victoria. *How Fascism Ruled Women: Italy, 1922–1945*. Berkeley: University of California Press, 1992.

de la Peña Topete, Guillermo. "Poder local, poder regional: Perspectivas socio-antropológicas." In *Poder local, poder regional*, edited by Jorge Padua and Alan Vanneph, 27–56. Mexico: El Colegio de México, CEMCA, 1986.

———. "Populism, Regional Power, and Political Mediation: Southern Jalisco, 1900–1980." In *Mexico's Regions: Comparative History and Development*, edited by Eric Van Young, 191–223. San Diego: University of California, 1992.

de los Reyes, Aurelio. *Cine y sociedad en México 1896–1930*. Mexico: UNAM, 1993.

de los Reyes, Guillermo. "El impacto de la masonería en los orígenes del discurso secular, laico y anticlerical en México." In *Secularización del estado y la sociedad*, edited by Patricia Galeana, 101–26. Mexico: Siglo XXI Editores, Senado de la República, Comisión Especial Encargada de los Festejos del Bicentenario de la Independencia y del Centenario de la Revolución Mexicana, 2010.

Deans-Smith, Susan, and Gilbert M. Joseph, eds. *A Special Issue of Hispanic American Historical Review: Mexico's New Cultural History: ¿Una Lucha Libre?* 79, no. 2 (1999).

Deere, Carmen Diana, and Magdalena León, eds. *Género, propiedad y empoderamiento: Tierra, estado y mercado en América Latina*. Mexico: UNAM, PUEG, FLACSO, 2002.

Delgado Capeans, Ricardo. *La mujer en la vida moderna*. Madrid: Bruno del Amo, 1920.

Delgado Criado, Benaventura. *Historia de la educación en España y América: La educación en la España contemporánea*. Madrid: Ediciones Morata S. L., 1994.

Domínguez Prats, Pilar. "Intelectuales españolas en el exilio de México: Margarita Nelken y Maltilde de la Torre." Paper presented at the VIII Congreso Internacional de Historia de América, Las Palmas de Gran Canaria, 1998.

Dorantes, Alma, María Gracia Castillo, and Julia Tuñón Pablos. *Irene Robledo García*. Guadalajara: Universidad de Guadalajara, Instituto Nacional de Antropología e Historia, 1995.

Dore, Elizabeth. "One Step Forward, Two Steps Back: Gender and the State in the Long Nineteenth Century." In *Hidden Histories of Gender and the State in Latin America*, edited by Elizabeth Dore and Maxine Molyneux, 3–32. Durham NC: Duke University Press, 2000.

Dore, Elizabeth, and Maxine Molyneux. *Hidden Histories of Gender and the State in Latin America*. Durham NC: Duke University Press, 2000.

Duby, Georges, and Michelle Perrot, eds. *Historia de las mujeres*. 5 vols. Madrid: Taurus, 1992.

Duffy, Eamon. *Saints & Sinners: A History of the Popes*. New Haven CT: Yale University Press, 1997.

Elias, Norbert. *Conocimiento y poder*. Translated by Julia Varela. Madrid: La Piqueta, 1994.

———. *El proceso de la civilización: Investigaciones sociogenéticas y psicogenéticas*. Mexico: FCE, 1989.

Enríquez Vargas, Ana Isabel. "La cultura política de las organizaciones obreras y las percepciones de género en la Guadalajara revolucionaria a través del *Boletín militar*, 1914–1916." BA thesis, Universidad de Guadalajara, 2011.

Falcón, Romana. *Política y caciquismo en San Luis Potosí, 1918–1939*. Mexico: El Colegio de México, 1984.

Fallaw, Ben. *Cárdenas Compromised: The Failure of Reform in Postrevolutionary Yucatán*. Durham NC: Duke University Press, 2001.

Fauré, Christine. *Enciclopedia histórica y política de las mujeres Europa y América*. Madrid: Akal, 2010.

Fernández Aceves, María Teresa. "La cultura cívica de las mujeres en Guadalajara." In *Entre imaginarios y utopías: Historias de maestras*, edited by Luz Elena Galván and Oresta López, 347–63. México: CIESAS, UNAM-PUEG, COLSAN, 2008.

———. "Engendering Caciquismo: Guadalupe Martínez and Heliodoro Hernández Loza and the Politics of Organized Labor in Jalisco." In *Caudillo and Cacique in Twentieth-Century Mexico*, edited by Alan Knight and Wil Pansters, 201–224. London: ILAS, 2005.

———. "José Guadalupe Zuno Hernández and the Revolutionary Process in Jalisco, 1920s." In *Governors of the Mexican Revolution: Portraits of Courage, Corruption, and Conflict*, edited by William Beezley and Jürgen Buchenau, 95–108. Lanham MD: Rowman Littlefield, 2008.

———. "Las mujeres graduadas en la Universidad de Guadalajara, 1925–1933." In *Historia social de la Universidad de Guadalajara*, edited by Carmen Castañeda, 97–122. Guadalajara: Universidad de Guadalajara, CIESAS, 1995.

———. "Once We Were Corn Grinders: Women and Labor in the Tortilla Industry of Guadalajara, 1920–1940." *International Labor and Working-Class History* 63 (2003): 81–101.

———. "The Political Mobilization of Women in Revolutionary Guadalajara, 1910–1940." PhD diss., University of Illinois-Chicago, 2000.

———. "Voto femenino." In *Jalisco en el mundo contemporáneo: Aportaciones para una enciclopedia de época; Tomo II; Derecho, economía y política*, edited by Héctor Raúl Solís Gadea y Karla Alejandra Planter Pérez, 696–710. Guadalajara: Editorial Rayuela, Universidad de Guadalajara, COECYT-JAL, 2010.

Fernández y Fernández, Aurora. *Mujeres que honran la patria*. Mexico: Imprenta Zavala, 1958.

Fiol Matta, Licia. "'RARAS' POR MANDATO: LA MAESTRA, LO QUEER Y EL ESTADO EN GABRIELA MISTRAL." *Debate feminista* 29 (2004): 118–37.

Folbre, Nancy. "The Unproductive Housewife: Her Evolution in Nineteenth-Century Economic Thought." *Signs: Journal of Culture and Society* 16, no. 3 (1991): 463–84.

Folbre, Nancy, and Marjorie Abel. "Women's Work and Women's Households: Gender Bias in the U.S. Census." *Social Research* 56, no. 3 (1989): 545–69.

Fowler-Salamini, Heather. "Algunas reflexiones sobre las feministas revolucionarias y su interrelación con las izquierdas mexicanas: Una prosopografía." *Revista de historia, sociedad y cultura*, no. 34 (2019): 177–202.

———. "Caciquismo, sindicalismo y género en la agroindustria cafetalera de Córdoba, Veracruz, 1925–1945." In *Integrados y marginados en el México posrevolucionario: Los juegos de poder local y sus nexos con la política nacional*, edited by Nicolás Cárdenas García and Enrique Guerra Manzo, 393–426. Mexico: UAM-Xochimilco, Miguel Ángel Porrúa, 2009.

———. "Gender, Work, and Working-Class Women's Culture in the Veracruz Coffee Export Industry, 1920–1945." *International Labor and Working-Class History* 63 (2003): 102–21.

———. "Género y la Revolución Mexicana de 1910." In *Los historiadores y la historia para el siglo XXI: Homenaje a Eric J. Hobsbawm*, edited by Gumersindo Vera Hernández, 369–400. Mexico: CONACULTA-INAH, 2007.

———. "'La Negra Moya': Alma, leyenda y liderazgo de las desmanchadoras de café de Veracruz en el México postrevolucionario." In *Mujeres en Veracruz:*

Fragmentos de una historia, edited by Fernanda Núñez, 46–64. Xalapa: Estado de Veracruz, 2010.

Fowler-Salamini, Heather, and Mary K. Vaughan. *Women of the Mexican Countryside, 1850–1990: Creating Spaces, Shaping Transitions*. Tucson: University of Arizona Press, 1994.

Franco, Jean. *Las conspiradoras: La representación de la mujer en México; Versión actualizada*. Mexico: El Colegio de México, FCE, 1994.

Fraser, Nancy. "Repensar el ámbito público: Una contribución a la crítica de la democracia realmente existente." *Debate feminista* 7 (1993): 23–58.

Freeman, Jo. *A Room at a Time: How Women Entered Party Politics*. Lanham MD: Rowman & Littlefield, 2000.

Friedrich, Paul. *The Princes of Naranja: An Essay in Anthrohistorical Method*. Austin: University of Texas Press, 1986.

———. *Rebelión agraria en una aldea mexicana*. Mexico: FCE, 1981.

Fulwider, Benjamin. "Driving the Nation: Road Transportation and the Postrevolutionary Mexican State, 1925–1960." PhD diss., Georgetown University, 2009.

Gabayet, Luisa. *Obreros somos: Diferenciación social y formación de la clase obrera en Jalisco*. Guadalajara: El Colegio de Jalisco, CIESAS, 1988.

Gallegos, José Ignacio. *Apuntes para la historia de la persecución religiosa en Durango de 1926 a 1929*. Mexico: Editorial Jus, 1965.

Galván, Luz Elena, and Oresta López. *Entre imaginarios y utopías: Historias de maestras* Mexico: CIESAS, UNAM-PUEG, COLSAN, 2008.

García Alcaraz, María Guadalupe. "Historia de la cultura escolar: Sujetos y prácticas, tiempos y espacios en dos escuelas particulares de Guadalajara en el siglo XX." PhD diss., Universidad Autónoma de Aguascalientes, 2002.

———. "Poder, educación y religión: Municipio, gobierno del Estado, Arzobispado y esculas primarias en Guadalajara., 1867–1914." MA thesis, Instituto de Investigaciones Dr. José Ma. Luis Mora, 1993.

Gauss, Susan. "Masculine Bonds and Modern Mothers: The Rationalization of Gender in the Textile Industry in Puebla, 1940–1952." *International Labor and Working-Class History* 63 (2003): 63–80.

Ginzburg, Carlo. *El hilo y las huellas: Lo verdadero, lo falso, lo ficticio*. Mexico: FCE, 2010.

———. *Threads and Traces: True, False, Fictive*. Los Angeles: University of California Press, 2012.

Gobierno del Estado de Jalisco. *Cronología política del estado de Jalisco, 1530–1988*. Guadalajara: n.p., 1988.

Gómez Nashiki, Antonio. "El movimiento estudiantil mexicano: Notas históricas de las organizaciones políticas, 1910–1971." *Revista mexicana de investigación educativa* 8, no. 17 (2003): 187–220.

Gómez Ortega, Ileana Cristina. "Las primeras diputadas en Jalisco, 1955–1965." BA thesis, Universidad de Guadalajara, 2007.

———. "Primeras presidentas municipales y regidoras en Jalisco, 1947–1977." MA thesis, CIESAS Occidente, 2010.

Gómez-Ferrer, Guadalupe, Gabriela Cano, Dora Barrancos, and Asunción Lavrin, eds. *Historia de las mujeres en España y América Latina: Del siglo XX a los umbrales del XXI*. Vol. 4, edited by Isabel Morant. Madrid: Cátedra, 2006.

González Castillejo, María José. *La nueva historia: Mujer, vida cotidiana y esfera pública en Málaga (1931–1936)*. Málaga: Universidad de Málaga, 1991.

González Compeán, Miguel, and Leonardo Lomelí, eds. *El partido de la revolución: Institución y conflicto (1928–1999)*. Mexico: FCE, 2000.

González Flores, Anacleto. *La cuestión religiosa en Jalisco: Breve estudio filosófico-histórico de la persecución de los católicos en Jalisco*. Guadalajara: Asociación Católica de la Juventud Mexicana, 1920.

González Navarro, Moisés. *Cristeros y agraristas en Jalisco*. Vol. 1. Mexico: El Colegio de México, Centro de Estudios Históricos, 2000.

———. *Cristeros y agraristas en Jalisco*. Vol. 2. Mexico: El Colegio de México, Centro de Estudios Históricos, 2000.

———. *Masones y cristeros en Jalisco*. Mexico: El Colegio de México, 2000.

Gran Logia Femenina de Chile. *Mujeres con mandil: Una historia femenina de la masonería en Chile, 1953–2003*. Santiago de Chile: Ediciones de la Gran Logia Femenina de Chile, 2003.

Gruening, Ernest. *Mexico and Its Heritage*. New York: Century, 1928.

Guerra, François-Xavier. *México: Del antiguo régimen a la revolución*. Vol. 2. Mexico: Fondo de Cultura Económica, 1988.

Hanson, Randall S. "The Day of Ideals: Catholic Social Action in the Age of the Mexican Revolution, 1867—1929." PhD diss., Indiana University, 1994.

Hernández, Ana María. *La mujer mexicana en la industria textil*. Mexico: Tip. Moderna, 1940.

Hernández, Sonia. *For a Just and Better World: Engendering Anarchism in the Mexican Borderlands, 1900–1938*. Champaign: University of Illinois Press, 2021.

Hernández Rodríguez, Rogelio. *El centro dividido: La nueva autonomía de los gobernadores*. Mexico: El Colegio de México, 2004.

Herrera, Alfonso, Carlos Guzmán, and Manuel Navarro Angulo. *Belén de Sárraga*. Mexico: s.e., 1928.

Hirsch, Marianne, and Valerie Smith. "Feminism and Cultural Memory: An Introduction." *Signs: Journal of Culture and Society* 28, no. 1 (2002): 1–19.

Hoggart, Richard. *The Uses of Literacy: Aspects of Working-Class Life with Special References to Publications and Entertainments*. London: Chatto and Windus, 1957.

Hurtado, Javier. *Familias, política y parentesco: Jalisco, 1919–1991*. Guadalajara: Fondo de Cultura Económica, Universidad de Guadalajara, 1993.

Ibarra Ibarra, Sonia. "Atala Apodaca." *La tarea: Revista de educación y cultura de la sección 47 del SNTE*, no. 8 (1996): 1–3.

———. *Educadores jaliscienses: Antología*. Zapopan: El Colegio de Jalisco, SEP-Educación Jalisco, 1994.

———. "Ser maestro en Jalisco, 1910–1943: Nuevas perspectivas del maestro jalisciense." MA thesis, Instituto Superior de Investigación y Docencia para el Magisterio, 1999.

Instituto Nacional de Estadística Geografía e Informática. *Estadísticas históricas de México*. Mexico: INEGI, 2000.

———. *Estados Unidos Mexicanos: Cien años de censos de población*. Aguascalientes: INEGI, 1996.

Instituto Nacional de Estudios Históricos de la Revolución Mexicana, Instituto de Investigaciones Legislativas de la H. Cámara de Diputados. *Las mujeres en la revolución mexicana, 1884–1920*. Mexico: Cámara de Diputados, LV Legislatura, Instituto Nacional de Estudios Históricos de la Revolución Mexicana, 1993.

John, Peter. *Analysing Public Policy*. London: Continuum International, 2002.

Johnson-Odim, Cheryl, and Margaret Strobel. *Expanding the Boundaries of Women's History: Essays on Women in the Third World*. Bloomington: Journal of Women's History, Indiana University Press, 1992.

Joseph, Gilbert. "El caciquismo y la revolución: Carrillo Puerto en Yucatán." In *Caudillos y campesinos en la revolución mexicana*, edited by David A. Brading, 239–76. Mexico: FCE, 1985.

———. *Revolution from Without: Yucatán, México, and the United States*. Durham NC: Duke University Press, 1983.

Joseph, Gilbert, and Daniel Nugent, eds. *Everyday Forms of State Formation: Revolution and the Negotiation of Rule in Modern México*. Durham NC: Duke University Press, 1994.

Junco, Alfonso. *La sra. Belén de Sárraga desfanatizando*. Mexico: Acción y Fe, 1923.

Kabeer, Naila. *Realidades trastocadas: Las jerarquías de género en el pensamiento del desarrollo*. Mexico: Paidós, 1998.

Kapelusz-Poppi, Ana María. "Physician Activists and the Development of Rural Health Postrevolutionary Mexico." *Radical History Review* 80, no. 1 (2001): 35–50.

Kaplan, Temma. "Female Consciousness and Collective Action: The Case of Barcelona, 1910–1918." *Signs: Journal of Culture and Society* 7, no. 3 (1982): 545–66.

———. *Red City, Blue Period: Social Movements in Picasso's Barcelona*. Berkeley: University of California Press, 1992.

Katz, Friedrich. *The Life and Times of Pancho Villa*. Stanford: Stanford University Press, 1998.

Kellogg, Susan. *Weaving the Past: A History of Latin America's Indigenous Women from the Prehispanic Period to the Present*. Oxford: Oxford University Press, 2005.

Keremitsis, Dawn. "La doble jornada de la mujer en Guadalajara, 1910–1940." *Encuentro*, no. 1 (1984): 41–64.

Keremitsis, Dawn. "María Arcelia Díaz (1896–1939): Union Leader, Feminist, and Defender of Revolutionary Legislation." Paper presented at the Latin American Studies Association, Guadalajara, Mexico, April 17, 1997.

Knight, Alan. "Cárdenas, Caciquismo, and the Tezcaltipoca Tendency." XXI Congreso de LASA, Chicago, September 1998.

———. "Cultura política y caciquismo." *Letras libres* 24 (2000): 16–20.

———. *The Mexican Revolution*. 2 vols. Cambridge: Cambridge University Press, 1986.

———. "The Mexican Revolution: Bourgeois? Nationalist? Or Just a 'Great Rebellion'?" *Bulletin of Latin American Research* 4, no. 2 (1985): 1–37.

———. "Popular Culture and the Revolutionary State in México, 1910–1940." *Hispanic American Historical Review* 74, no. 3 (1994): 343–444.

———. "Revolutionary Project, Recalcitrant People." In *The Revolutionary Process in Mexico: Essays on Political and Social Change, 1880–1940*, edited by Jaime E. Rodríguez, 227–64. Los Angeles: University of California, 1990.

———. "The Working Class and the Mexican Revolution, 1900–1920." *Journal of Latin American Studies* 16, no. 1 (1984): 51–79.

Knight, Alan, and Wil G. Pansters, eds. *Caciquismo in Twentieth-Century Mexico*. London: ILAS, 2005.

Koven, Seth, and Sonya Michel. *Mothers of a New World: Maternalist Politics and the Origins of Welfare States*. New York: Routledge, 1993.

Ladd-Taylor, Molly. *Mother-Work: Women, Child Welfare, and the State, 1890–1930*. Urbana: University of Illinois, 1994.

Larason Schneider, Anne, and Helen Ingram. *Policy Design for Democracy*. Lawrence: University of Kansas, 1997.

Lau Jaiven, Ana. "Expresiones políticas femeninas en el México del siglo XX: El Ateneo Mexicano de Mujeres y la Alianza de Mujeres en México, 1934–1953." In *Orden social e identidad de género: México Siglos XIX y XX*, edited by María Teresa Fernández Aceves, Carmen Ramos Escandón, and Susie S. Porter, 93–124. Guadalajara: Universidad de Guadalajara, CIESAS.

———. *La nueva ola del feminismo en México*. Mexico: Planeta, 1987.

———. "Una vida singular: Juana Belén Gutiérrez viuda de Mendoza." *Sólo historia*, no. 8 (2000): 9–14.

Lau Jaiven, Ana, and Elsie McPhail Fanger, eds. *Rupturas y continuidades: Historia y biografías de mujeres*. Mexico: UAM-Xochimilco, 2018.

Lau Jaiven, Ana, and Carmen Ramos Escandón. *Mujeres y revolución, 1900–1917*. Mexico: INERHM, INAH, 1993.

Lear, John. *Workers, Neighbors, and Citizens: The Revolution in Mexico City*. Lincoln: University of Nebraska Press, 2001.

Lerdo de Tejada C., Sebastián, and Antonio Godina. *El lobbying en México*. Mexico: Miguel Ángel Porrúa, 2004.

Lomnitz-Adler, Claudio. *Las salidas del laberinto: Cultura e ideología en el espacio nacional mexicano*. Mexico: Joaquín Mortiz, 1995.

Lyons, Martyn. "La experiencia lectora y escritora de las mujeres trabajadoras en la Europa del siglo XIX." *Cultura escrita & sociedad*, no. 1 (2005): 158–76.

Macias, Anna. *Against All Odds: The Feminist Movement in Mexico to 1940*. Westport CT: Greenwood, 1982.

———. *Contra viento y marea: El movimiento feminista en México hasta 1940*. Mexico: CIESAS, UNAM-PUEG, 2002.

———. "Felipe Carrillo Puerto y la liberación de las mujeres en México." In *Las mujeres latinoamericanas: Perspectivas históricas*, edited by Asunción Lavrin, 329–46. Mexico: FCE, 1985.

Marino, Katherine M. *Feminism for the Americas: The Making of an International Human Rights Movement*. Chapel Hill: University of North Carolina Press, 2019.

Márquez Carpet, S. J. *Las grandes encíclicas sociales*. Madrid: Editorial Apostolado de la Prensa, S. A., 1958.

Martínez Assad, Carlos, ed. *Estadistas, caciques y caudillos*. Mexico: UNAM-IIS, 1988.

Martínez, Jesús A. *Lectura y lectores en el Madrid del siglo XIX*. Madrid: Consejo Superior de Investigaciones Científicas, 1991.

Martínez Moreno, Carlos Francisco. "Masones en defensa de la República y de la Constitución Mexicana: Dos sociedades patrióticas paramasónicos en el siglo XIX." In *Secularización del estado y la sociedad*, edited by Patricia Galeana, 127–40. Mexico: Siglo XXI Editores, Senado de la República, Comisión Especial Encargada de los Festejos del Bicentenario de la Independencia y del Centenario de la Revolución Mexicana, 2010.

Martínez Moya, Armando, and Manuel Moreno Castañeda. *La escuela de la revolución*. Vol. 7 of *Jalisco desde la revolución*, edited by Mario Alfonso Aldana Rendón. Guadalajara: Gobierno del Estado de Jalisco, Universidad de Guadalajara, 1988.

Martínez Verdugo, Arnaldo. "De la anarquía al comunismo." In *Historia del comunismo en México*, edited by Arnaldo Martínez Verdugo, 15–71. Mexico: Editorial Grijalbo, 1983.

Maynes, Mary Jo. *Taking the Hard Road: Life Course in French and German Workers' Autobiographies in the Era of Industrialization*. Chapel Hill: University of North Carolina Press, 1995.

Maynes, Mary Jo, Jennifer L. Pierce, and Barbara Laslett. *Telling Stories: The Use of Personal Narratives in the Social Sciences and History*. Ithaca: Cornell University Press, 2008.

Maza, Sarah. "Stories in History: Cultural Narratives in Recent Works in European History." *American Historical Review* 101, no. 5 (1996): 1493–515.

McGee Deutsch, Sandra. "Gender and Sociopolitical Change in Twentieth-Century Latin America." *Hispanic American Historical Review* 71, no. 2 (1991): 256–396.

McLeod, Hugh. *Secularisation in Western Europe, 1848–1914*. New York: St. Martin's, 2000.

McMillan, James F. *France and Women, 1789–1914: Gender, Society, and Politics*. New York: Routledge, 2000.

Medina Carrillo, Cuauhtémoc, and Noe Figueroa Mendoza. *Luis C. Medina y el movimiento obrero*. Guadalajara: UNED, 1988.

Medina Núñez, Ignacio. "Fuerzas políticas y procesos electorales." In *Historia política, 1940–1975*, edited by Ignacio Medina and Jaime Sánchez Susarrey, 14–163. Vol. 9 of *Jalisco desde la revolución*, edited by Mario Alfonso Aldana Rendón. Guadalajara: Gobierno del Estado de Jalisco, Universidad de Guadalajara, 1987.

Mejía Núñez, María Guadalupe. "Faldas en el periodismo tapatío (primeras décadas del siglo XX)." In *Mujeres jaliscienses del siglo XIX: Cultura, religión y vida privada*, edited by Lourdes Celina Vázquez Parada and Darío Armando Flores Soria, 173–85. Guadalajara: Editorial Universitaria, Universidad de Guadalajara, 2008.

Méndez Medina, Alfredo. *La cuestión social en México: Orientaciones; Estudio presentado en la Dieta de la Confederación Nacional de los Círculos Católicos de Obreros, celebrada en Zamora los días 19–22 de enero de 1913*. Mexico: Ediciones "El Cruzado," 1913.

Méndez Zárate, Armando. "La reforma agraria en San Martín de Hidalgo, Jalisco 1915–1935." BA thesis, Universidad de Guadalajara, 2010.

Mendieta Alatorre, Ángeles. *La mujer en la revolución mexicana*. Mexico: Instituto Nacional de Estudios Históricos de la Revolución Mexicana, 1961.

Mendoza Lozano, Alicia. "Atala Apodaca, mujer jalisciense, maestra, precursora de la Revolución Mexicana de 1910." *La tarea: Revista de educación y cultura de la sección 47 del SNTE*, no. 8 (1996): 4–5.

Meyer, Jean. *La cristiada*. 3 vols. Mexico: Siglo XXI, Editores, 1973–74.

———. *La cristiada: El conflicto entre la iglesia y el estado (1926–1929)*. Vol. 2, Mexico: Siglo XXI Editores, 1974.
———. *La cristiada: La guerra de los cristeros*. Vol. 1. Mexico: Siglo XXI Editores, 1983.
Meyer, Lorenzo. "Los caciques: Ayer y hoy; ¿Y mañana?" *Letras libres*, no. 24 (2000): 26–27.
Michel Pimienta, Zenaido. *Episodios históricos de la educación en Jalisco*. Guadalajara: Talleres Vera, 1960.
Molyneux, Maxine. "Mobilization without Emancipation? Women's Interests, State, and Revolution." In *Transition and Development: Problems of Third World Socialism*, edited by Richard Fagen, Carmen Diana Deere, and José Luis Coraggio, 280–302. New York: Monthly Review Press, Center for the Study of the Americas, 1986.
———. "Twentieth-Century State Formations in Latin America." In *Hidden Histories of Gender and the State in Latin America*, edited by Elizabeth Dore and Maxine Molyneux, 33–81. Durham NC: Duke University Press, 2000.
Monroe, John Warne. "Cartes de visite from the Other World: Spiritism and the Discourse of Laïcisme in the Early Third Republic." *French Historical Studies* 26, no. 1 (2003): 119–53.
Moreno Ochoa, Angel. *Semblanzas revolucionarias, 1920–1930: Diez años de agitación política en Jalisco*. Guadalajara: Galería de Escritores Revolucionarios Jaliscienses, 1959.
Murià, José María. *Historia de Jalisco*. 4 vols. Guadalajara: Unidad Editorial del Gobierno de Jalisco, 1980.
Muriel, Josefina "Las viudas en el desarrollo de la vida novohispana." In *Viudas en la historia*, edited by Manuel Ramos Medina, 93–111. Mexico: Condumex, 2002.
Nasaw, David. "Introduction." *American Historical Review* 114, no. 3 (2009): 573–78.
Navarrete, Félix. *La masonería en la historia y en las leyes de México*. 2nd ed. Vol. 46, *Figuras y episodios de la historia de México*. Mexico: Editorial Jus, 1962.
Nervo, Amado. *La mujer moderna y su papel en la evolución actual del mundo: Homenaje de gratitud de la Asociación "Hijas de María" de la Santa Unión de los S.S.C.C.* Buenos Aires: Editorial Tor, 1919.
Ochoa, Margarita R., and Sara Vicuña Guengerich. *Cacicas: The Indigenous Women Leaders of Spanish America, 1492–1825*. Norman: University of Oklahoma, 2021.
O'Dogherty Madrazo, Laura. *De urnas y sotanas: El Partido Católico Nacional en Jalisco*. Mexico: CONACULTA, 2001.
———. "Restaurarlo todo en Cristo: Unión de Damas Católicas Mejicanas, 1920–1926." *Revista de historia moderna y contemporánea de México* 14 (1991): 129–58.
O'Malley, Ilene. *The Myth of the Revolution: Hero Cults and the Institutionalization of the Mexican State, 1920–1940*. New York: Greenwood, 1986.
Obaya, Alicia, Gloria Barredo, and Yolanda Ricardo. *Valoraciones sobre temas y problemas de la literatura cubana*. La Habana: Editorial Pueblo y Educación, 1981.

Oikión Solano, Verónica. *Cuca García (1889–1973): Por las causas de las mujeres y la revolución*. Zamora: El Colegio de Michoacán, El Colegio de San Luis, 2018.

Olcott, Jocelyn. *International Women's Year: The Greatest Consciousness-Raising Event in History*. New York: Oxford University Press, 2017.

———. *Revolutionary Women in Postrevolutionary Mexico*. Durham NC: Duke University Press, 2005.

Olivera Sedano, Alicia. *Aspectos del conflicto religioso de 1926–1929: Sus antecedentes y consecuencias*. Mexico: INAH, 1966.

Orellana Trinidad, Laura. "'La mujer del porvenir': Raíces intelectuales y alcances del pensamiento feminista de Hermila Galindo, 1915–1919." *Signos históricos* 5 (2001): 109–38.

Orozco Cano, María del Carmen. *La educación en Ciudad Guzmán*. Guadalajara: UNED, 1986.

Ortiz Albear, Natividad. *Las mujeres en la masonería*. Málaga: Universidad de Málaga, 2005.

———. "Masonería y feminismo: Clara Campoamor, feminista y masona." In *La igualdad como compromiso: Estudios de género en homenaje a la profesora Ana Díaz Medina*, edited by Esther Martínez, Ángela Figueruelo, Ma. Teresa López de la Vieja, Olga Barrios, Carmen Velayos, and Ma. Dolores Calvo, 421–34. Salamanca: Universidad de Salamanca, Centro de Estudios de la Mujer, 2007.

———. *Mujeres masonas en España: Diccionario biográfico 1868–1939*. Santa Cruz de Tenerife: Ediciones Idea, 2007.

Pansters, Wil G. *Citizens of the Pyramid. Essays on Mexican Political Culture*. Amsterdam: Thela Latin American Series, 1997.

———. *Goodbye to the Caciques? Definition, the State and the Dynamics of Caciquismo in Twentieth Century Mexico*. London: ILAS, 2005.

———. *Política y poder en Puebla: Formación y ocaso del cacicazgo avilacamachista, 1937–1987*. Mexico: FCE, 1993.

Parsons, Wayne. *Las políticas públicas*. Buenos Aires: FLACSO, Miño y Dávila, 2007.

Partido Católico Nacional. *Acción política de los católicos en los tiempos modernos*. Mexico: El Bufete J. Crespo, 1911.

———. *Programa y estatutos del Partido Católico Nacional*. Mexico: Imprenta A. Sánchez, 1912.

Pateman, Carole. "The Patriarchal Welfare." In *Democracy and the Welfare State*, edited by Amy Gutmann, 231–60. Princeton: Princeton University Press, 1988.

Pavissich, Antonio. *Mujer antigua y mujer moderna (Escenas de mañana)*. Madrid: Saturnino Calleja Fernández, n.d.

Pedersen, Susan. *Family, Dependence, and the Origins of the Welfare State: Britain and France, 1914–1945*. Nueva York: Cambridge University Press, 1995.

Peniche Rivero, Piedad. "El movimiento feminista de Elvia Carrillo Puerto y *las igualadas*: Un liderazgo cultural en Yucatán." In *Dos mujeres fuera de serie: Elvia Carillo Puerto y Felipa Poot*, edited by Piedad Peniche Rivero and Kathleen R. Martín, 15–69. Mérida: Instituto de la Cultura de Yucatán, 2007.

Pérez Ledesma, Manuel. "Por tierras de España y América: Belén Sárraga, feminista y librepensadora." In *Redes intelectuales y formación de naciones en España y América Latina: 1890–1940*, edited by Marta Casaús Arzú and Manuel Pérez Ledesma, 386–420. Madrid: Universidad Autónoma de Madrid, 2005.

Pérez-Rayón, Nora. "El anticlericalismo en México: La visión desde la sociología histórica." *Sociológica* 19, no. 55 (2004): 113–52.

Personal Narratives Group, ed. *Interpreting Women's Lives: Feminist Theory and Personal Narratives*. Bloomington: Indiana University Press, 1989.

Poniatowska, Elena. *Las soldaderas*. Mexico: Editorial Era, 1999.

Porter, Susie S. *From Angel to Office Worker: Middle-Class Identity and Female Consciousness in Mexico, 1890–1950*. Lincoln: University of Nebraska Press, 2018.

———. *Working Women in Mexico City: Public Discourses and Material Conditions, 1879–1931*. Tucson: University of Arizona Press, 2003.

Pratt, Mary Louise. "Repensar la modernidad." *Espiral, estudios sobre estado y sociedad* 5, no. 15 (1999): 47–72.

Preciado Zamora, Julia. *Por las faldas del Volcán de Colima: Cristeros, agraristas y pacíficos*. 1st ed. Mexico: CIESAS, Archivo Histórico del Municipio de Colima, 2007.

Purnell, Jennie. *The Agraristas and Cristeros of Michoacán*. Durham NC: Duke University Press, 1999.

Quijano, Manuel. "La medicina en México de 1940–2000." *Revista de la Facultad de Medicina de la UNAM* 46, no. 6 (2003): 215–16.

Raby, David L. *Educación y revolución social en México*. Mexico: SepSetentas, 1974.

Ramírez Flores, José. *La revolución maderista en Jalisco*. Colección de documentos para la historia de Jalisco. Guadalajara: Universidad de Guadalajara, Centre D'Etudes Mexicaines et Centraméricaines, 1992.

Ramírez Hurtado, Luciano. "Una feminista española en tierra azteca, Belén de Sárraga y la Convención Revolucionaria en Aguascalientes." In *Historia de mujeres en Aguascalientes. Línea Curva*, edited by Yolanda Padilla Rangel, 269–87. Aguascalientes: Gobierno de Aguascalientes, Indesol, IAM, Hábitat, 2007.

Ramos Escandón, Carmen. *Ciudadanía carente: Género y legislación en Guadalajara (1870–1917)*. Vol. 3. Guadalajara: Universidad de Guadalajara, 2013.

———. "Desafiando el orden legal y las limitaciones en las conductas de género en México: La crítica de Sofía Villa de Buentello a la legislación familiar." *La aljaba: Revista de estudios de género* 7 (2002): 1–15.

———. "Gender, Work, and Class Consciousness among Mexican Factory Workers, 1880–1910." In *Borders Crossing: Mexican and Mexican-American Workers in Transition*, edited by John Mason Hart, 71–92. Wilmington: Scholarly Resources, 1998.

———. *Industrialización, género y trabajo femenino en el sector textil mexicano: El obraje, la fábrica y la compañía industrial*. Mexico: CIESAS, 2004.

———. *La diferenciación de género en el trabajo textil en México*. San Luis Potosí: El Colegio de San Luis, 2004.

———. *La industria textil y el movimiento obrero en México*. 1st ed. Mexico: División de Ciencias Sociales y Humanidades Departamento de Filosofía-Historia Área de Cultura, 1988.

———. "Metiéndose en la *bola*: Mujeres y política en la Revolución Mexicana, o el esfuerzo por tener voz ciudadana." *Sólo historia*, no. 8 (2000): 4–8.

———. "Mujer y poder en el cardenismo: El debate por el sufragio." *Boletín virtual del Centro de Estudios de Historia de la Mujer en América Latina* 5, no. 54 (2004). http://webserver.rcp.net.pe/cemhal/articulo1.html.

———. "Mujeres mexicanas: historia e imagen: Del porfiriato a la revolución." *Revista Encuentro* 4, no. 3 (1987): 41–58.

———. "Mujeres positivas: Los retos de la modernidad en las relaciones de género y la construcción del parámetro femenino en el fin de siglo mexicano, 1880–1910." In *Modernidad, tradición y alteridad: La ciudad de México en el cambio de siglo XIX–XX*, edited by Claudia Agostoni and Elisa Speckman, 291–318. Mexico City: UNAM, 2001.

———, ed. *Presencia y transparencia: La mujer en la historia de México*. 1st ed. Mexico: Colegio de México, Programa Interdisciplinario de Estudios de la Mujer, 1987.

Ramos Palomo, María Dolores. "Belén de Sárraga: Una 'obrera' del laicismo, el feminismo y el panamericanismo en el mundo Ibérico." *Baética estudios de arte, geografía e historia*, no. 28 (2006): 599–708.

———. "Federalismo, laicismo, obrerismo, feminismo: Cuatro claves para interpretar la biografía de Belén de Sárraga." In *Discursos, realidades, utopías: La construcción del sujeto femenino en los siglos XIX–XX*, edited by María Dolores Ramos and María Teresa Vera, 125–64. Valencia: Anthropos, 2002.

———. "Mujer, asociacionismo y sociabilidad en la coyuntura de 1898." In *Sociabilidad fin de siglo: Espacios asociativos en torno a 1898*, edited by Jean-Louis Guereña and Isidro Sánchez Sánchez, 73–100. Cuenca: Universidad de Castilla-La Mancha, 1999.

———. "Radicalismo político, feminismo y modernización." In *Historia de las mujeres en España y América Latina: Del siglo XX a los umbrales del XXI*, edited by Guadalupe Gómez-Ferrer, Gabriela Cano, Dora Barrancos, and Asunción Lavrin, 31–53. Madrid: Cátedra, 2006.

———. "Un compás para trazar una sociedad igualitaria: La labor de la librepensadora Belén de Sárraga entre 1897 y 1909." *Asparkía: Investigación feminista*, no. 9 (1998): 79–94.

Reich, Peter L. *Hidden Revolution: The Catholic Church in Law and Politics since 1929*. Notre Dame IN: University of Notre Dame, 1995.

Reséndez Fuentes, Andrés. "Battleground Women: *Soldaderas* and Female Soldiers in the Mexican Revolution." *Americas* 51, no. 4 (1995): 525–53.

Ríos Cárdenas, María. *La mujer mexicana es ciudadana: Historia con fisonomía de una novela de costumbres*. Mexico: A. del Bosque Impresor, 1940.

Rius Facius, Antonio. *De don Porfirio a Plutarco: Historia de la ACJM*. Mexico: Editorial Jus, 1958.

Rivera Carbó, Ana. "La Casa del Obrero Mundial: Anarco-sindicalismo y revolución en México." PhD diss., UNAM, 2006.

Rivera Carbó, Anna. "Esther Torres: cuando el sindicalismo llevaba al futuro, 1911–1916." In *De espacios domésticos y mundos públicos: El siglo de las mujeres en México*, edited by Martha Eva, Anna Rivera Carbó, Enriqueta Tuñón Pablos, and Lilia Venegas Aguilera, 47–70. Mexico: INAH, 2010.

Rivera Morán, Gregorio. "La cultura política de los maestros de Autlán: Prácticas docentes, valopres democráticos y formas de hacer política." PhD diss., CIESAS Occidente, 2002.

Rocha Islas, Martha Eva. *El álbum de la mujer: Antología ilustrada de las mexicanas*. Vol. 4, *El porfiriato y la revolución*. Mexico: INAH, 1991.

———. "Las mujeres en la Revolución Mexicana un acercamiento a las fuentes históricas." In *Universitarias latinoamericanas: Liderazgo y desarrollo*, edited by Patricia Galena de Valdés, 49–60. Mexico: UNAM, 1990.

———. *Los rostros de la rebeldía: Veteranas de la revolución mexicana, 1910–1939*. Mexico: Secretaría de Cultura, Instituto Nacional de Estudios Históricos de las Revoluciones de México, Instituto Nacional de Antropología e Historia, 2016.

Rodríguez, Victoria Elizabeth. *Women in Contemporary Mexican Politics*. Austin: University of Texas Press, 2003.

Romero, Laura. *El Partido Nacional Revolucionario en Jalisco*. Guadalajara: Universidad de Guadalajara, 1995.

———. "La conformación del caciquismo sindical en Jalisco: El caso de Heliodoro Hernández Loza." In *Estadistas, caciques y caudillos*, edited by Carlos Martínez Assad, 293–311. Mexico: UNAM, 1998.

———. *La consolidación del estado y los conflictos políticos*. Vol. 5 of *Jalisco desde la revolución*, edited by Mario A. Aldana Rendón. Guadalajara: Gobierno del Estado de Jalisco, Universidad de Guadalajara, 1988.

Rössler, Augustin, and William H. W. Fanning. "Mujer." In *Enciclopedia Católica*. ACI-PRENSA, 1915; online ed., Kevin Knight, 1999. https://ec.aciprensa.com/wiki/Mujer.

Roth Wood, Andrew. *Revolution in the Street: Women, Workers, and Urban Protest in Veracruz*. Wilmington: Scholarly Resources, 2001.

Rubin, Jeffrey W. "Decentering the Regime: Culture and Regional Politics in Mexico." *Latin American Research Review* 31, no. 3 (1996): 85–126.

Ruiz, Ramón Eduardo. *The Challenge of Poverty and Illiteracy*. San Marino: Huntington Library, 1963.

Ryan, Mary. "Gender and Public Access: Women's Politics in 19th Century America." In *Habermas and the Public Sphere*, edited by Craig Calhoun, 260–85. Boston: Massachusetts Institute of Technology, 1996.

Salas, Elizabeth. "The Soldadera in the Mexican Revolution: War and Men's Illusions." In *Women of the Mexican Countryside, 1850–1990: Creating Spaces, Shaping Transitions*, edited by Mary Kay Vaughan and Heather Fowler-Salamini, 93–106. Tucson: University of Arizona, 1994.

———. *Soldaderas en los ejércitos mexicanos: Mitos e historia*. Mexico: Diana, 1995.

Salazar, Rosendo *Las pugnas de la gleba: Los albores del movimiento obrero en México*. Mexico: Partido Revolucionario Institucional, Comisión Nacional Editorial, 1972.

———. *México: en pensamiento y en acción*. Mexico: Editorial Avante, 1971.

Salmerón Castro, Fernando I. "Caciques: Una revisión teórica sobre el control político local." *Revista Mexicana de Ciencias Políticas y Sociales* 30, nos. 117–18 (1984): 107–41.

———. *Los límites del agrarismo*. Zamora: El Colegio de Michoacán, 1989.

Sanabria A., Enrique. *Republicanism and Anticlerical Nationalism in Spain*. New York: Palgrave Macmillan, 2009.

Sánchez Susarrey, Jaime. "Mecanismos de negociación y concertación política." In *Historia política, 1940–1975*, edited by Ignacio Medina and Jaime Sánchez Susarrey, 165–299. Vol. 9 of *Jalisco desde la revolución*, edited by Mario Alfonso Aldana Rendón. Guadalajara: Gobierno del Estado de Jalisco, Universidad de Guadalajara, 1987.

Sanfeliú Giménez, Luz. *Republicanas: Identidades de género en el blasquismo, 1895–1910*. Valencia: Universidad de Valencia, 2005.

Sárraga, Belén. *Conferencia sustentada por la eminente oradora: El domingo 4 de mayo de 1924 en el Teatro Maxim con motivo del homenaje a Felipe Carrillo Puerto, organizado por la Agrupación Socialista de la Habana. Versión taquigráfica de Ana Cañizares*. Mexico: s.e., 1924.

———. *El clericalismo en América a través de un continente*. 1st ed. Lisboa: Editorial Lux, 1914.

———. *La evolución del pensamiento y los pueblos y las congregaciones religiosas*. Mexico: Imprenta de "El Automóvil en México," 1915.

Schell, Patience A. "An Honorable Avocation for Ladies: The Work of the México City Unión De Damas Católicas Mexicanas, 1912–1926." *Journal of Women's History* 10, no. 4 (1999): 78–103.

———. *Church and State Education in Revolutionary Mexico City*. Tucson: University of Arizona Press, 2003.

———. "Las mujeres del catolicismo social, 1912–1926." In *Catolicismo social en México*, edited by Manuel Ceballos Ramírez and Alejandro Garza Rangel, 241–96. Monterrey: La Academia de Investigación Humanística, 2005.

Scott, Joan Wallach. "El problema de la invisibilidad." In *Género e historia*, edited by Carmen Ramos Escandón, 38–65. Mexico: Instituto Mora / UAM, 1992.

———. *Gender and the Politics of History*. New York: Columbia University Press, 1988.

———. *Only Paradoxes to Offer: French Feminists and the Rights of Man*. Cambridge MA: Harvard University Press, 1996.

Servín, Elisa. "El movimiento henriquista: Entre oposición electoral y la insurrección armada." In *Los matices de la rebeldía: Las oposiciones políticas y sociales*, edited by Alicia Olivera Sedano, Rina Ortiz Peralta, Elisa Servín, and Tania Hernández Vicencio, 65–82. Mexico: INAH, 2010.

———. *La oposición política: Otra cara del siglo XX mexicano*. Mexico: FCE, 2006.

———. *Ruptura y oposición: El movimiento henriquista, 1945–1954*. Mexico: Cal y Arena, 2001.

Sindicato de Trabajadores de La Experiencia. *Cien años de actividad social en la fábrica "La Experiencia 1851–1951."* Vol. 1. Jalisco: Fábrica La Experiencia, 1951.

Smith Crocco, Margaret, Petra Munro, and Kathleen Weiler. "In Search of Subjectivity." In *Pedagogies of Resistance: Women Educator Activists, 1880–1960*, edited by Margaret Smith Crocco, Petra Munro, and Kathleen Weiler, 1–17. New York: Teachers College Press, 1999.

Smith, Dennis. "The Civilizing Process and the History of Sexuality: Comparing Norbert Elias and Michel Foucault." *Theory and Society* 28, no. 1 (1999): 79–100.

Smith Scott, Daniel. "How a Half-Million Iowa Women Suddenly Went to Work: Solving a Mystery in the State Census of 1925." *Annals of Iowa* 55, no. 4 (1996): 27–43.

Smith, Stephanie J. *Gender and the Mexican Revolution: Yucatán Women and the Realities of Patriarchy*. Chapel Hill: University of North Carolina Press, 2009.

Sotelo, Greco. "Arqueología de la ilegalidad." *Letras libres*, no. 24 (2000): 48–51.

Speckman Guerra, Elisa. "Las posibles lecturas de la *República de las letras*." In *La república de las letras: Asomos a la cultura escrita del México decimonónico*, edited by Belem Clark de Lara and Elisa Speckman Guerra, 47–74. Mexico: UNAM, 2005.

Spenser, Daniela. *Los primeros tropiezos de la Internacional Comunista en México*. 1st ed. Mexico: CIESAS, 2009.

Spenser, Daniela, and Bradley A. Levison. "Linking State and Society in Discourse and Action: Political and Cultural Studies of the Cárdenas Era in Mexico." *Latin American Research Review* 34, no. 2 (Spring 1999): 227–45.

Spiegel, Gabrielle M. "Comment on a Crooked Line." *American Historical Review* 113, no. 2 (2008): 406–16.

Spivak Chakravorty, Gayatri. "¿Puede hablar el subalterno?" *Revista colombiana de antropología* 39 (2003): 297–364.

Taibo II, Paco Ignacio. *Bolsheviquis: Historia narrativa de los orígenes del comunismo en México*. Mexico: Joaquín Mortiz, 1986.

Tamayo Rodríguez, Jaime E. *La conformación del Estado moderno y los conflictos políticos, 1917–1929*. Vol. 2 of *Jalisco desde la revolución*, edited by Mario Alfonso Aldana Rendón. Guadalajara: Gobierno del Estado de Jalisco, Universidad de Guadalajara, 1988.

———. *Los movimientos sociales, 1917–1929*. Vol. 4 of *Jalisco desde la revolución*, edited by Mario Alfonso Aldana Rendón. Guadalajara: Gobierno del estado de Jalisco, Universidad de Guadalajara, 1988.

———. "Los obreros." In *Movimientos sociales, 1929–1940*, 73–97. Vol. 5 of *Jalisco desde la revolución*, edited by Mario Alfonso Aldana Rendón. Guadalajara: Gobierno del Estado de Jalisco, Universidad de Guadalajara, 1988.

———. "Movimiento obrero y lucha sindical." In *Guadalajara, la gran ciudad de la pequeña industria*, edited by Patricia Arias, 131–58. Zamora: El Colegio de Michoacán, 1985.

Téllez-Cuevas, Rodolfo. *El papel de la masonería en la política y la administración pública mexicana*. Toluca: Instituto de Administración Pública del Estado de México, 2009.

Threlkeld, Megan. *Pan American Women: U.S. Internationalists and Revolutionary Mexico*. Philadelphia: University of Pennsylvania Press, 2014.

Torres González, Gabriel. *La fuerza de la ironía: Un estudio del poder de la vida cotidiana de los trabajadores tomateros del occidente de México*. Mexico: CIESAS, Colegio de Jalisco, 1997.

Tortolero Cervantes, Yolia. *El espiritismo seduce a Francisco I. Madero*. 2nd ed. Mexico: Senado de la República, 2004.

Trueba Lara, José Luis. *Masones en México: Historia del poder oculto*. Mexico: Grijalbo, 2007.

Tuñón Pablos, Enriqueta. *¡Por fin . . . ya podemos elegir y ser electas!* Mexico: CONACULTA, INAH, Plaza y Valdes Editores, 2002.

Tuñón Pablos, Esperanza. *Mujeres que se organizan: El Frente Unico Pro Derechos de la Mujer, 1935-38*. Mexico: UNAM, Grupo Editorial Porrúa, 1992.

Ulloa, Berta. *La Constitución de 1917*. Mexico: Colegio de México, 1983.

Urzúa Orozco, Aída, and Gilberto Hernández. *Jalisco, testimonio de sus gobernantes, 1912-1939*. Guadalajara: Unidad Editorial del Gobierno de Jalisco, 1988.

Vaca, Agustín. "Devociones y trabajos de Margarita Gómez González." In *Siete historias de vida: Mujeres jaliscienses del siglo XX*, edited by Anayanci Fregoso, 90-121. Guadalajara: Editorial Universitaria, Universidad de Guadalajara, 2006.

———. *Los silencios de la historia: Las cristeras*. Guadalajara: El Colegio de Jalisco, 1998.

Vargas Reynoso, Luis Angel. "Siete meses de gobierno villista en Lagos de Moreno (1914-1915)." BA thesis, Universidad de Guadalajara, 2008.

Vasquez Montaño, Margarita. *Ethel Duffy Turner (1885-1969): Una existencia al límite, conmovida por la revolución*. Toluca: El Colegio Mexiquense, 2022.

Vaughan, Mary Kay. "Cultural Approaches to Peasant Politics in the Mexican Revolution." *Hispanic American Historical Review* 79, no. 2. (1999): 269-308.

———. *Cultural Politics in Revolution: Teachers, Peasants, and Schools in Mexico, 1930-1940*. Tucson: University of Arizona Press, 1997.

———. *Estado, clases sociales y educación en México*. 2 vols. México: Fondo de Cultura Económica, 1982.

———. "Modernizing Patriarchy: State Policies, Rural Households, and Women in Mexico, 1930-1940." In *Hidden Histories of Gender and the State in Latin America*, edited by Maxine Molyneux and Elizabeth Dore, 194-214. Durham NC: Duke University Press, 2000.

———. "Pensar la biografía." *Desacatos: Revista de ciencias sociales*, no. 50 (2016): 88-99.

———. *Portrait of a Young Painter: Pepe Zúñiga and Mexico City's Rebel Generation*. Durham NC: Duke University Press, 2015.

———. "Women School Teachers in the Mexican Revolution: The Story of Reyna's Braids." In *Expanding the Boundaries of Women's History*, edited by Cheryl Johnson-Odim and Margaret Strobel, 278-302. Bloomington: Indiana University Press, 1992.

Vaughan, Mary Kay, Gabriela Cano, and Jocelyn Olcott, eds. *Sex in Revolution: Gender, Politics, and Power in Modern Mexico*. Durham NC: Duke University Press, 2006.

Vaughan, Mary Kay, and Steve Lewis, eds. *The Eagle and the Virgin: Nation and Cultural Revolution in Mexico, 1920-1940*. Durham NC: Duke University Press, 2006.

Vázquez Leos, J. Jesús Eloy. *La masonería femenina en San Luis Potosí: Sus inicios*. San Luis Potosí: Mi Librería, 2003.

Velasco López, Octavio. "La mujer y la masonería en el Jalisco del siglo XIX: Catalina Álvarez Rivera." In *Mujeres jaliscienses del siglo XIX: Cultura, religión y vida privada*, edited by Lourdes Celina Vázquez Parada and Darío Armando Flores Soria, 110-31. Guadalajara: Editorial Universitaria, Universidad de Guadalajara, 2008.

Villegas de Magnón, Leonor. *La rebelde*. Edited by Clara Lomas. Houston: University of Houston, CONACULTA, 2004.

Vitale, Luis, and Julia Antivilo. *Belén de Sárraga: Precursora del feminismo hispanoamericano*. Santiago: Ediciones Cesoc, 2000.

Walkowitz, Judith R. *La ciudad de las pasiones terribles: Narraciones sobre peligro sexual en el Londres victoriano*. Madrid: Ediciones Cátedra, Universitat de València, Instituto de la Mujer, 1992.

Wright de Kleinhans, Laureana. *Mujeres notables mexicanas*. Mexico: Tipografía Económica, 1910.

Yankelevich, Pablo. "El Artículo 33 constitucional y las reivindicaciones sociales en el México posrevolucionario." In *Xenofobia y xenofilia en la historia de México: Siglos XIX–XX. Homenaje a Moisés González Navarro*, edited by Delia Salazar Anaya, 27–50. Mexico: SEGOB, INM, INAH, 2006.

Young, James E. "Toward a Received History of the Holocaust." *History and Theory* 36, no. 4 (1997): 21–43.

Zárate Hernández, José Eduardo. "Caciques and Leaders in the Era of Democracy." In *Caciquismo in Twentieth-Century Mexico*, edited by Alan Knight and Wil G. Pansters, 272–95. London: ILAS, 2005.

Zea, Leopoldo. *El positivismo en México: Nacimiento, apogeo y decadencia*. Sección de obras de filosofía. Mexico: Fondo de Cultura Económica, 1981.

Zuno Hernández, José Guadalupe. *Anecdotario del Centro Bohemio*. Guadalajara: s.e., 1964.

———. *Historia de la revolución en el estado de Jalisco*. Mexico: Secretaría de Gobernación, Patronato del Instituto Nacional de Estudios Históricos de la Revolución Mexicana, 1964.

———. *Reminiscencias de una vida*. Guadalajara: Biblioteca de Autores Jaliscienses Modernos, 1973.

INDEX

Academia Miguel Cervantes, 105
Ácrata, 7, 34, 218n27, 224n57
Adelitas, 7, 34
agrarian reform, 7, 32, 57, 167, 183, 185–86, 189–90, 206, 213
Agraristas, 185, 206
Aguilar, Ramona, 161, 171, 257n32
Aguirre Berlanga, Manuel (governor), 95, 104
Alatorre, Luis, 90
Alemán Valdés, Miguel (president, 1946–52), 116–18, 167, 194
Alianza, 93–94
Allende, Sebastián (governor, 1932–35), 163–65, 185
alliances: agrarian, 205; caciques, 185; Catholic Church, 27; governors, 126–27; labor, 9, 18, 123, 126–27, 148, 150, 155, 164–66; political parties, 24, 27, 148, 150, 155; president, 116; women form, 108, 126–27, 151, 164–66, 205
Alonso, Ana María, 109
Alvarado, Salvador, 67, 84, 85
Alvarez, Sonia, 13
Álvarez del Castillo, Enrique, 206
anticlerical campaigns, 2–3, 9, 14–17, 37, 46, 68, 87, 158

anticlericalism: and anarcho-syndicalism, 2, 83, 125, 158, 209; de Sárraga Hernández and, 4, 16, 46–51, 55–65, 68, 71–75, 77–80; and freethinking, 1–2, 4, 16, 46–49, 51–52, 57–60, 63–65, 75–81
antifascism, 46–48, 80
Antihuertista, 91–94, 116
antireelectionism, 89
Apodaca, Atala Anaya (1884–1977): and anticlericalism, 41, 82–83, 93, 95, 97–99, 101, 108, 114; bureaucratic and political career, 41, 96, 98–99, 100, 113–14, 117–19; and Centro Radical Femenino, 108, 110–12; civic education, 17, 40, 45, 96–98, 119, 210; family of, 86, 112, 119; as propagandist, 37, 39, 41, 83, 87, 98–100, 102, 109; and radical feminist movements, 109; secular education, 45; speeches, 99, 119; and women's rights, 39, 214
Arbitration Board, 124, 138
Argos, 41, 102–3, 213
Article 33, 61, 71
Article 115, 167
Article 123, 123, 127, 139, 154, 159
Article 130, 79

Asociación Católica de la Juventud Mexicana, ACJM (Mexican youth Catholic association), 26, 104, 233n126
Asociación de Damas Católicas de Guadalajara, ADCG (Catholic ladies association of Guadalajara), 25, 129
Asociación General Femenina (General women's association): Andalusia, 52; Valencia, 52
Asociación Librepensadora de Mujeres en Gracia, 51
Aurora Social (Justo Sierra group), 89
authoritarian, 156; accusations of, 25; men as, 8; practices, 127, 140; women as, 148–52, 169, 174–83, 202–13
Ávila Camacho, Manuel (1910–46), 167

Badillo, Basilio (governor), 69, 126
Barba González, Silvano (governor, 1939–43), 138, 185
Barreda, Gabino, 37
Bazant, Mílada, 5
biography, the study of, 4–6
Blanco, Lucio, 95
Bloque Independiente de Agrupaciones Obreras (Independent bloc of worker's associations), 134
Boletín militar, 34–35, 37, 39, 65, 93, 98, 100, 109
Bolsheviks, 70
The Book of Spirits (Kardec, 1857), 50
Bouquet, Manuel (governor), 104, 106
boycotts, 53, 64, 79, 106–7
Buve, Raymond, 11

cacicas, 6, 181–82
caciquismo: as distinct from *gestora*, 18, 181–84, 208; in practice, 74, 164–73,

179, 185, 201; in scholarly literature, 10–11, 18, 154–55, 179–82; and social class, 178, 183; and women, 10–11, 153–56, 179–82, 183, 204–8
Calleros, Enrique R. (1870–1950), 89
Calles, Plutarco Elías, 2, 68, 71–81, 114, 213
Calles Law, 79
Camacho, Arturo, 91
Camacho Barreto, Jesús, 205
camaradas, 187
Camp, Roderic Ai, 188, 208
campesinas, 34, 142, 203
Cananea Copper Company, 28
Cano, Gabriela, 196
capitalism, critique of, 22, 48, 124
Cárdenas, Elisa, 89
Cárdenas, Lázaro (1934–40), 80, 177, 189, 206
Cárdenas García, Nicolás, 11
Carranza, Salomé, 43
Carranza, Venustiano, 37, 42, 101–2, 107, 111–13, 185, 202, 213
Carrillo Puerto, Elvia, 79, 81, 112, 145, 150, 208
Carrillo Puerto, Felipe, 72–74, 79
Carvia, Ana, 52
Casa Amiga de la Obrera (Friendly house for women workers), 127
Casa del Obrero Mundial, COM (Worldwide house for workers), 18, 34, 122, 158
Castellanos Tapia, Luis, 99
Castillo Ledón, Amalia, 208
Castro, Sofía, 133
Catholic: charity, 23, 26, 56, 130; education, 14, 27, 44–46, 65, 71, 85, 98–99, 130; militants, 22, 24, 27, 70, 103, 106; protest, 60, 70, 101–3, 105–6;

resistance, 68, 98–99, 103–6; schools, 26, 104, 233n126; Workers' Congress, 107
Catholic Church: critique of, 56–57; and feminists, 110, 210; hierarchical society model, 21, 24; identity, 104, 107; influence on gender roles, 9, 87; and labor, 23, 25, 68, 73, 75, 107, 120, 125, 132; and modernity, 56, 81; opposition to revolutionary state, 21, 24, 27, 74, 91, 126, 233n126; and Orozco y Jiménez, 21, 24–27, 30, 91–92, 98, 104–8; and revolutionary leaders, 29–31, 73–80, 83, 91; and the state, 9–10, 71–74, 82, 120–21, 127, 135; and women, 9–10, 15, 21, 34–35, 40, 43–44, 81–83, 103; women's impact on social policies of, 25, 213
Catholic clergy, 16, 26, 29, 35, 96, 98, 100; de Sárraga Hernández critiques, 46, 53, 56–57, 65, 67, 71, 76, 78
Catholic education, 10, 20, 65, 114
Catholic lay organizations, 23
Catholic Normal School (Normal Católica, 1902–14), 30
Catholic organizations: of women, 9, 21–26, 35, 40, 45, 65, 79, 104–9; of workers, 23, 107, 125, 132
Catholic social action: and hierarchical society model, 22; ideology, 83; and labor, 23–25, 68, 73, 75, 107, 120, 125, 132; lay organizations, 23; opposition to revolutionary state, 22, 27; and Orozco y Jiménez, 21, 24–27, 30, 91–92, 98, 104–8; women's impact on social policies, 21
Catholic Workers' Society of the Holy Family and Our Lady of Guadalupe, 23

Ceballos, Alfonso G., 183, 185–86
centers: Our Lady of Guadalupe (Sociedad de Obreros Católicos de la Sagrada Familia y Nuestra Señora de Guadalupe), 23, 106; Sacred Heart of Jesus, 27, 106
Centro Bohemio (Bohemian center), 91, 95–96, 99, 101, 113–14
Centro de Capacitación Femenina María A. Díaz, 138–39
Centro Evolucionista de Mujeres, CEM (Women's evolutionist center), 134
Centro Instructivo Obrero Republicano de Madrid (Republican workers' educational center of Madrid), 48
Centro Radical Femenino, CRF (Women's radical center), 17, 40, 108–12, 125
Chakravorty Spivak, Gayatri, 17, 121
Chassen-López, Francie, 5–6, 154
Chávez Hayhoe, Salvador, 105
children: Catholicism and, 27, 98, 105, 158; and Masonry, 51; and patriotism, 90, 197; and social programs, 30, 32, 36, 99–102, 126–29, 168, 189, 200; and women, 128–29, 167, 197, 200; and workers, 110, 119, 170, 172
child welfare, 8
Chumacero, Blas, 146
cinema, 9, 25
Círculo de Estudios Sociales León XIII, 25
Círculo Feminista de Occidente, CFO (Western feminist circle, 1927–2002), 17, 111, 121, 134–38, 158–61, 166–67, 211
Círculo Feminista de Occidente María Arcelia Díaz, CFOMAD (María Arcelia Díaz Western feminist circle), 138–52

Círculo Liberal Fénix (Phoenix liberal circle), 89
Círculo Liberal Josefa Ortiz de Domínguez, CLJOD (Josefa Ortiz de Domínguez liberal circle), 41, 97–113
citizenship: Catholic, 14; defined, 14, 16, 17, 88, 105; and gender, 3–4, 8, 12–14, 16; male liberal, 86, 94, 213; women and, 2, 4, 8, 12, 14, 176, 177, 180
civic education, 40, 98, 200, 213
civil code, 34, 84
class: classlessness, 196; conflict, 141, 144; consciousness, 141; identity, 213; and race, 200. *See also* middle class; skilled labor class; working class
clericalism, 1, 35, 45, 56–57, 64, 68, 74, 81
clerical reform, 22
clientelism, 12, 164
Club Femenil Antireeleccionista Leona Vicario, CFALV (Leona Vicario Femenine antireelectionist club), 89
Club Liberal Benito Juárez, 99
Club Sara Pérez de Madero, 89
Club Valentín Gómez Farías, 89
Collegio Pio-Latino-Americano Pontificio, 22
Comité Agrario Regional (Regional agrarian committee), 190
Comité Campesino (Peasant committee) of Jalisco of the Partido de la Revolución Mexicana (PRM), 190
Comité Colimense Pro Constitución (Colima committee for constitution), 79
Comité Coordinador Feminino para la Defensa de la Patria (Women's coordinating committee for the defense of the fatherland), 80–81
Comité de Mujeres por la Defensa de la Patria, 81
compadrazgo (fictive kin), 165
Compañía Hidroeléctrica de Chapala, 132
Compañía Industrial de Guadalajara, 121, 132
Confederación Católica del Trabajo, CCT (Catholic labor confederation), 129–30
Confederación de Agrupaciones Obreras Libertarias de Jalisco, CAOLJ (Jalisco confederation of libertarian labor associations), 126–27
Confederación de Partidos Liberales de Jalisco, CPLJ (Jalisco confederation of liberal parties), 69
Confederación de Trabajadores de México, CTM (Workers' confederation of Mexico), 116, 146, 155, 165, 173–80, 206
Confederación Ferrocarrilera (Railway confederation), 71
Confederación Nacional Campesina, CNC (National peasants' confederation), 190, 192, 198–211
Confederación Nacional Católica del Trabajo, CNCT (National Catholic labor confederation), 130
Confederación Nacional de Organizaciones Populares, CNOP (People's national confederation of organizations), 206
Confederación Obrera de Jalisco, COJ (Jalisco labor confederation), 127, 134, 136, 160–67
Confederación Regional Obrera Mexicana, CROM (Mexican regional labor confederation), 74, 81, 120, 126–27, 131, 142, 154, 233

Confederación Revolucionaria Obrera y Campesina, CROC (Revolutionary confederation of workers and peasants), 169
Congreso de Mujeres de la Raza, 79
Congreso Nacional de Mujeres (First national women's congress, 1953), 196
Consejo Feminista Mexicano, CFM (Mexican feminist council), 108, 125
Constitution (1857), 28, 61, 69, 158
Constitution (1917), 12, 32, 68, 71, 79, 109, 154, 208. *See also* Article 33; Article 115; Article 123; Article 130
Constitution (Jalisco), 167
Constitutionalists, 20–21, 27–32, 36–37, 39, 97, 100, 113, 209
consumption, 3, 39, 44, 134
Coracero, Silvestre, 185, 188
corn grinders, 162–65
Corona, Ramón, 118
corporatist politics: in labor movement, 180, 213, 214; of Martínez Villanueva, 164–74; and state formation, 89, 180–81, 207; and women's activism, 180, 188, 209
corruption, 39, 161–67, 174, 179
Cortés, J. Concepción, 91
councilwomen, 197–98
Cristero War (or Cristiada, 1926–29), 79–80, 83, 114, 185, 202
Cultural Department, 117–18
cultural history, new, 7
cultural memory, 140
Curiel, Jacinta (1906–2002), 110
Curley, Robert, 104

Dávila Garibi, Ignacio, 105
de Baducci, Blanca, 94
de Buen, Odón (1863–1945), 48

Decree 1913, 105–8
Decree 1927, 106
Degollado Theater, 1, 20, 35. *See also* teatros: Degollado
de Gorjón, Josefina C., 142
de Jesús S. de Preciado, María, 140
de la Barra, Francisco León (president), 68, 123
de la Cueva, Amado, 101, 126
Dénizard Rivail, Hippolyte Léon (1804–95), 50
Departamento Agrario (Agrarian department), 202
Departamento de Agricultura y Ganadería (Department of agriculture and livestock), 185
Departamento de Enseñanza Primaria y Normal (Department of primary and normal education, Jalisco), 114
Department of Education, 114, 119, 139. *See also* Secretaría de Educación Pública
Department of Labor, 169. *See also* Labor Department
deputies: federal, 24, 165, 169, 171, 177, 198, 201–4, 212; state, 63, 114, 138, 161, 171, 176, 198, 201
Deraismes, Marie (1828–94), 52
de Sárraga Hernández, Belén (1872–1950): and anticlericalism, 4, 16, 46–49, 51, 55, 57, 60, 63–65, 68, 71, 75, 77–80; and education, 56, 59, 62, 65; and fascism, 80; and freethinking, 46–52, 55, 57–60, 63–65, 68, 75, 77, 79–81; and Masonry, 49–52, 63, 66, 70, 83, 87–88, 103, 209, 211; and Republicanism, 55, 65; and sexual difference, 45–47; and Spiritism, 4, 46–51, 57–63, 83, 90, 209, 211

determinist vision, 44
Díaz, J. Merced, 121
Díaz, Juan, 205
Díaz, María Arcelia (1896–1939): advocacy for workers' rights, 121, 133, 136, 211; bureaucratic and political career, 130–34, 138, 151; and the Círculo Feminista de Occidente, 17, 111, 121, 134–38, 158–61, 211; labor rights, 130, 136, 144; literacy campaigns, 136, 162; "Marcha María Arcelia Díaz," 141; unionization efforts, 17, 122, 134; and women's education, 136, 144, 211; and women's politics, 121, 133, 136, 148, 150; and women's suffrage, 137
Díaz, Porfirio, 8, 37, 57, 158, 209
Diéguez, Manuel M. (general), 27–32, 82, 91, 95–107, 113–14, 124, 158, 185
Dirección de Bienes Nacionales (National assets department), 193
Dirección de Epidemiología (Epidemiology department), 195
Dirección General de Educación of Jalisco (General department of education), 114
Dirección General de Educación Primaria y Especial of Jalisco (General department of primary and special education), 114
discipline, 31, 85, 139–40, 145, 154, 159–62, 165–67, 172–76
discourse: Catholic, 104; CTM, 149, 155, 174; maternalistic, 195; revolutionary, 123; speech, 47; state, 71, 73–74, 123, 127, 149; theory of, 5, 151; women in, 2, 16, 44, 51, 104, 169, 195, 213; women's, 14–17, 39, 44, 47, 103, 144, 169, 175–76
division of labor, 13, 197

divorce, 15, 57, 74, 79, 84, 178
domesticity, 8, 11–14, 45, 181, 184, 186, 189, 208
domestic workers, 19, 106, 134, 212
Domingo Soler, Amalia (1835–1909), 51, 60
Domínguez, Belisario, 93
Dore, Elizabeth, 83, 212

Echeverría Álvarez, Luis (president), 206
education: civic, 40, 98, 117–19, 200, 213; historiography on, 9, 86; impact on women's mobilization, 9, 16, 20, 21, 35–36, 144, 148, 171, 209–11; public, 30, 36, 102, 136, 148; rationalist, 20, 48, 74; secular, 45, 49, 52–53, 57, 211, 213; women's access to, 16, 20, 37, 42–43, 49, 51, 86–87, 99
educational policies: feminist advocacy and, 35–36, 148, 162, 210; and labor, 9, 86, 119, 148, 165, 171–72, 181; and social reforms, 20, 30, 34, 41, 119, 162, 190, 200
eight-hour workday, 148
ejidatarios, 185, 190, 204–5
El abogado cristiano (Episcopal Methodist Church), 63, 67–68
El Batán (paper factory), 132
El clericalismo en América (Belén de Sárraga, 1914), 54, 56–57
El correo de Jalisco, 27, 64
El Derecho Humano (Mixed Masonic Order), 52
elections: federal, 138, 169, 175, 201, 203, 206; Jalisco (1912), 24, 63; municipal, 28, 138, 161; popular, 138, 161, 212; state, 63, 138
Elías, Norbert, 3

employment, 10, 123, 127–30, 136, 164, 176
equal pay for equal work, 19, 127, 136, 212
Escuela Federal José Clemente Orozco, 117
Escuela Moderna, 48–49
Escuela Nacional Preparatoria (National preparatory school), 36
Escuela Urbana 64, 117
essentialism (essentialist perspective), 43–44
Estrada, Roque, 89
Estrada García, Elisa, 111
experience, as analytical category, 5, 10, 18

fanaticism, 34, 51, 57, 67–68, 90, 98, 109, 197
fatherland, 17, 26, 34, 71, 76, 90, 158, 180. See also *patria*
Federación Anticlerical Mexicana, FAM (Mexican anticlerical federation), 67
Federación de Agrupaciones Obreras de Jalisco, FAOJ (Jalisco federation of workers' associations), 120, 131
Federación de Partidos del Pueblo (Federation of people's parties), 205
Federación de Trabajadores de Jalisco, FTJ (Jalisco federation of workers), 111, 138, 153
Federación Estudiantil Universitaria (University student federation), 72
Federación Malagueña de Sociedades Obreras, FMSO (Málaga federation of workers' societies), 53, 79
Federación Nacional de Escuelas Técnicas (National federation of technical schools), 193–94

Federation of Freethinkers of Brussels, 1, 47
female consciousness, defined, 13, 196–97
Fémina roja (CFO newspaper), 136, 160, 213
feminine action, 161, 190, 191, 200
femininity, 2, 16, 34, 37, 62, 66, 70, 132, 136, 191, 209
feminism: impact on labor rights, 121, 125, 138, 140, 150, 156, 159, 212; impact on state formation, 97, 119, 168; local, 144, 156, 158; transnational, 1, 4, 14–16, 18–19, 36, 125, 135
Ferrer Guardia, Francisco, 48–49
Ferrero Balaguer, Emilio, 49
Fillipi, Ernesto (Monsignor), 70
Flores, Gerardo (father of Guadalupe Urzúa Flores), 184
Flores Magón, Teresa, 81
Flores Magón brothers, 40, 41, 71, 122
Flores Monroy, Rosario, 184
Fourier, Charles (1772–1837), 52
Fowler-Salamini, Heather, 7–8, 133, 154
Franco, Jean, 6, 151
freethinkers: and feminism, 46–47, 51–53; International Congress of, 53, 55; and labor movement, 53, 57, 59, 63, 67
French Revolution, 36, 49, 65, 86
Frente Único Pro Derechos de la Mujer, FUPDM (United front for the rights of women), 162–63
Friedrich, Paul, 187
Fulwider, Benjamin, 190

Galindo, Daniel, 20, 36–37
Galindo, Hermila, 42–43, 45, 62, 81, 84, 112, 145, 150

Index   297

García Barragán, Marcelino (general, 1895–1979), 170, 183, 190, 201–5
García Ruiz, Ramón, 119
García Tadeo, Tomás, 205
gender order, 45, 47, 62, 66, 83, 109, 155, 214; in biographical studies, 6
gender politics: and caciquismo, 10–11, 153–56, 171–73, 179–82, 204–8; citizenship, 3–4, 8, 12–14, 16; and feminism, 6, 14–16, 18, 43–44, 47, 62, 213; impact of Mexican Revolution, 7–10, 34, 42, 86, 89–91, 102–3, 119; invisibility, 125–26, 150–51; and labor force, 127–30; and labor movement, 31–32, 34, 150–52, 154–55, 171, 180; policies, 8, 21, 66, 82–84, 119, 200, 210, 212; of representation, 34–35, 47, 66, 103; and social change, 12, 179; and social movements, 13, 104, 179; and women, 37, 42, 47, 62, 82–86, 150–51, 189–91, 196–97
gender studies, Mexican Revolution in, 1–4, 6–9, 16–17
gestora (advocate), 181–84, 191, 198, 207–8. See also *cacicas*
Gil Preciado, Juan, 206
Gollaz, Francisco, 69
González, Soledad, 72
González Luna, Efraín, 201
González Luna, Javier, 174
Great Liberal Convention, 90
Guadalupan Workers Organization (Operarios Guadalupanos), 23
Guerra Manzo, Enrique, 11
Guevara, Aurelia (1864–1956), 88, 117
Gutiérrez, Rosalina, 108

Hacienda y Crédito Público (Ministry of finance and public credit), 193

Henríquez Guzmán, Miguel (general), 205
Hernández, Ana María (federal labor inspector), 138–41
Hernández, Eusebio Adolfo, 73
Hernández, Felisa, 48
Hernández, Leonardo, 73
Hernández, Sonia, 14
Hernández Cambre, Carmen, 108, 110
Hernández Cambre, María Trinidad, 108, 125
Hernández Loza, Heliodoro (1898–1990), 154–55, 161–66, 168–74, 179
Hernández Lucas, Ana María (Anita Hernández), 161–62, 165–66, 169–71
Hernández Rodríguez, Rogelio, 204
Hidalgo theater (Colima), 79
Hidalgo y Costilla, Miguel (1753–1811), 73, 95, 100, 117
Hill, Benjamín, 95
Huerta, Victoriano, 17, 20, 27
Huertistas, 29, 39, 68, 91, 93, 95, 101; Antihuertista, 103, 209, 212
Hugo, Victor (1802–85), 21
Hurtado, Javier, 170
hygiene, 21, 35, 42, 90, 167, 168, 189, 195

Iconoclasta (CRF newspaper), 108, 110
identity: anticlerical, 109; Catholic, 104, 107; labor, 166; masculine, 173–74; political, 13, 45; and women, 19–20, 82, 209–10
Independent Party, 89
Institución Libre de Enseñanza (Free institution of teaching, 1876), 36
Instituto Colón, 114
Instituto Nacional de Ayuda a la Madre Soltera (National welfare institute for single mothers), 138

Instituto San José (Saint Joseph institute), 36
intermediary, women as, 10–11, 153–56, 179–82, 183, 204, 206–8. See also *cacicas*; *gestora*
Isaac, Catarino (1910–94), 165–66
Iturbe, Ramón F. (general), 101, 116

Jacobins, 68, 73, 109
Jiménez, Aurora, 177, 261n52
Juárez, Benito (1858–72), 27, 66–67, 73, 76, 94–96, 118, 158, 184
Juárez, María, 131, 142
Junco, Alfonso, 71
Junta Central de Conciliación y Arbitraje, 176
Junta de Mejores Cívicas y Materiales (Board of civic and material improvements), 195
Junta Diocesana de Acción Católica Social, IDACS (Catholic social action diocese board), 25
Junta Revolucionaria Constitucionalista, 93

Kapelusz-Poppi, Ana María, 192
Kaplan, Temma, 13, 196–97
Kardec, Allan, 50
Katz, Friedrich, 29
Krause, Karl Christian Friedrich (1781–1832), 49
Krausism, 49

La antorcha valenciana, 51
labor: and cultural memory, 140–50; María Arcelia Díaz and, 137, 141, 156, 163, 167, 169, 175, 177; organized movement, 16, 130, 136, 144, 153, 173; political engagement of women

leaders, 171; reform, 23–25, 28–32; ritual, 140, 152; social policies, 171, 173; unionization efforts, 173
Labor Department, 31, 123, 130, 132–34, 141, 159
labor force, 127–29, 156, 164
La Buena Nueva (Spiritist center), 49
La conciencia libre (1896–1907), 51, 55
La cuestión social en México (Méndez Medina), 24
La Enciclopedia Católica (1907–15), 43
La Escoba (textile factory), 121–22, 157
La Experiencia (textile factory), 111, 120, 125, 129–32, 144
La mujer en la vida moderna (Delgado Capeans, 1920), 43
La mujer mexicana en la industria textil (Ana María Hernández), 141
La mujer moderna y su papel en la evolución actual del mundo (Nervo, 1919), 43
land reform, 181, 184, 206
La sra. Belén de Sárraga desfanatizando (*Madame Sárraga Defanaticizing*; Junco), 71
Lazos León, Florinda, 145
legislation: labor, 19, 31–32, 83, 105, 126–27; Sunday rest, 127, 162
Ley Protectora del Obrero Mexicano (Protective law of the Mexican Worker), 31
liberalism, 21, 26, 63, 70, 111, 209
Liga Amigos del Pueblo, LAP (Friends of the people league), 41, 90–91, 94–99
Liga Anticlerical (Cuba), 72
Liga de Comunidades Agrarias, 126, 191
Liga de las Clases Productoras (League of the working classes), 89

Liga de Mujeres Ibéricas e Hispanoamericans (League of Ibero-American women), 79
Liga de Mujeres 10 de Mayo de la Colonia Francisco Villa (Mexico City), 138–39
Liga Nacional Defensora de la Libertad Religiosa, LNDLR (National defense of religious freedom league), 173n76, 236
Liga Protectora de la Obrera, LPO (Women workers' protective league), 125
literacy campaigns: María Arcelia Díaz and, 17, 122, 135, 139, 162, 166; and feminists, 122, 135; Martínez Villanueva and, 173; role in labor movements, 76, 162, 166, 211; Urzúa Flores and, 191, 200; and women, 16, 83–85, 162, 166–67, 210–11
López, J. Trinidad, 186
López Cotilla Medal, Manuel, 118
López de Ayala, Ángeles (1856–1926), 51
López Portillo y Rojas (governor), 25, 27
Luna, Florencio, 91
lupistas, 205–8

Maderismo, 23, 88–89, 103, 158
Madero, Francisco I., 2, 17, 24; assassination of, 23, 27, 28; on women, 57–68, 90–91; women's support of, 57, 72, 73, 88–89, 95–96, 100, 209, 212–13
maquiladora industry, women in, 176–77
Marino, Katherine M., 1, 14, 209
Martin, Georges (1844–1916), 52
Martínez, David, 157–58
Martínez, Dolores, 149, 151, 168
Martínez, Jesús A., 122
Martínez Villanueva, María Guadalupe (1906–2002): *cacicazgo*, 169–73; corporatist politics, 166, 171, 179; discourses, 175–79; educational and labor policies, 18, 166, 171–72, 175; family of, 157–58; feminism, 159, 162, 164; music, 173, 175; policies, 18, 166–67; political career, 161; role in the CFO-FTJ alliance, 158, 166, 171, 179; and sports, 173; unionization, 158, 161–62, 165; women's mobilization, 158–60, 163, 179; women's suffrage, 137, 156, 163, 167, 169, 175, 177
masculinity: and civic duties, 9, 36; heads of the family, 32, 250n32; and ideas, 20, 70; and identity, 173–74; and labor, 171; and the military, 34; norms of, 34; patriarchal, 44; representations, 34–35, 37, 65–66, 70, 171, 209; virility, 34, 65, 75; and women, 2, 16, 34, 37, 62, 65–66, 70, 96
Masonic Lodge (Universal Rite of Gonzalo Lecuona), 71, 112
Masonry, 49–52, 63, 66, 70, 83, 87–88, 103, 209. See also de Sárraga Hernández, Belén
Masons, 24, 28, 51–53, 59, 63, 67–70, 88, 107
maternalism: intersection with feminist movements, 135, 144; in policy, 10, 13, 17, 18, 151, 155, 167–69; as political identity, 155, 180; in public sphere, 8, 10, 13. See also motherhood
Maximilian (1864–67), 23
May Day, 162
McGee Deutsch, Sandra, 8
Medina, Luis C., 131

Mella, Julio Antonio, 72
memory: acts of, 45, 81, 119, 138–51, 175, 207; studies of, 5
Méndez de Cuenca, Laura (1853–1928), 87
Mendoza, Amalia (1965–67), 161, 171
Mexican Consulate, San Francisco, 71
Mexican Legion of Honor, 118
Mexican miracle (1940–70), 179–81
Mexican Revolution (1910–17), 6, 7
microhistory, 5–6
middle class, 12–13, 34, 47–49, 125, 150, 163, 171, 184–86
minimum wage, 31–32, 111, 123–24, 127, 133–34, 148, 159, 165
Ministry of National Defense, 99
Mistral, Gabriela, 15, 78, 145
modernity, 4, 15–17, 56, 81, 85
modern women: discursive and visual representation of, 4, 9, 20, 39–42, 52, 109, 119, 213–14; in feminist discourse, 20, 52, 70, 84–85; moderate path, 20, 43–44; politicized, 130–38; and revolution, 41–42, 84–85, 87, 109, 119
Molyneux, Maxine, 10, 12, 13, 83, 212
Monroe, Warne, 50
Morales, Carmen, 135
morality: Catholic, 109, 130, 159; national, 49–50, 59; as subject (education), 99; of women, 8, 84–85, 135, 159, 191
Mora y del Río, José (archbishop), 68, 79
motherhood, 8, 13, 51, 155, 169, 180; role in political identity, 155, 164, 169, 180; scientific, 144; single, 127. See also maternalism
mother-work, concept of, 13
Moya, Eufrosina (1907–69), 130, 133

Mujer (Fanning), 43–44
Mujer (Rössler), 43–44
Mujer antigua y mujer moderna (Pavissich, 1920), 43
Mujeres de la Raza (Women's congress race), 79
Mujer Moderna (*Semanario ilustrado la mujer moderna*). See *Semanario ilustrado la mujer moderna*
Mújica, Francisco, 73
Municipal Board of Conciliation and Arbitration, 133
municipal government, 111, 114, 167, 185, 205, 206; and education, 168, 189; independence of, 24, 31, 32; president of, 28, 99, 104, 117, 131, 168, 186, 198, 206–8; social programs, 194; and women, 167, 171, 177, 181, 184, 197–98, 206–8, 212. See also Ceballos, Alfonso G.; Hernández Loza, Heliodoro; López, J. Trinidad; Municipal Board of Conciliation and Arbitration; Zuno Hernández, José Guadalupe
Municipal Pantheon, 139, 142
music, 64, 107, 141, 173, 175, 188
musicians, 102, 184

Nacional de Mujeres (First national women's congress, 1953), 196–200
National Catholic Congress, 23
National Confederation of Catholic Worker Organizations, 24
National Congress of the Federación Mexicana de Organizaciones Femeninas (Mexican federation of women's organizations), First, 175
National Congress of Women Workers and Peasants, 142

National Congress of Women Workers and Peasants, Second (1933, Mexico City), 159, 162, 253n64
National Congress of Women Workers and Peasants, Third (1934, Guadalajara), 137
National Female Assembly of the Extraordinary Congress of the Federación Obrera Femenil (affiliated with the CTM), 178
nationalism, 28, 94
Navarro, Luis, 26
Nelken, Margarita, 80–81
Normal School (Escuela Normal para Profesores), 20, 41, 168; Atala Apodaca and, 86, 88, 97–100, 108, 110, 112; María Arcelia Díaz and, 125, 134; Martínez Villanueva and, 156, 158; Practical School Annex of, 30, 88; Urzúa Flores and, 184, 188, 194
Normal School for Women, 20, 97

Obregón, Alvaro (president), 2, 39, 68, 71, 100, 108, 113, 126
O'Dogherty, Laura, 26
Olachea, Agustín (general), 93, 116
Olcott, Jocelyn, 12, 14
O'Malley, Ilene, 7–8
Ordorica, María Victoria, 89
Orozco y Jiménez, Francisco (archbishop, 1913–36), 21, 24–27, 30, 91–92, 98, 104–8
Ortega, Aurelio, 88, 117

pacifism, 46
Padilla, María Guadalupe, 108
Panduro, María, 108
Partido Católico Nacional, PCN (National Catholic Party), 23–27, 41, 58–59, 63–65, 68, 88, 107, 124
Partido Comunista Mexicano, PCM (Mexican Communist Party), 116
Partido Constitucional Progresista, PCP (Constitutional progressive party), 24, 59, 67
Partido de la Revolución Mexicana, PRM (Party of the Mexican Revolution), 137, 138, 151, 155, 168, 177, 190–91, 214
Partido Democrático (Democratic party), 107
Partido Liberal Jalisciense (Jaliscan liberal party), 112
Partido Nacional Revolucionario, PNR (National revolutionary party), 107, 137
Partido Popular, PP (People's Party), 74, 116, 175, 214
Partido Popular Socialista (Socialist popular party), 74, 175
Partido Revolucionario Institucional, PRI (Institutional revolutionary party), 116, 118, 138, 149–56, 161, 167–83, 191–92, 196–208
patria, 20, 80. *See also* fatherland
patria potestad, 178
patriarchy: defined, 8; and family, 32, 179, 182, 189, 205; and labor, 170, 213; modernization of, 17, 181, 184, 186, 189, 208, 210, 213; peasants and, 84; political activism and, 8, 37; and political family, 81, 152, 164–65, 170, 210; in scholarly literature, 8, 10, 45, 155; and the state, 17, 84, 210, 214; and women, 44, 50, 97, 210, 213–14
Pedersen, Susan, 30
Philippines, 51–52
pictorial representation, 39
Pineda Flores, Carlos, 201

Pino Suárez, José María, 23, 91, 100
Pi y Margall, Francisco (1824–1901), 48, 53, 60, 65–66
politics, impact on women, 10, 62, 84, 97, 119, 135–36, 211–12
Portillo y Rojas, José López (governor), 25, 27
Pratt, Mary Louise, 4, 20
Presbyterians, 59, 68
priests, 56, 74, 76, 77, 79, 96, 120
progressives: advocacy for women's rights, 76–77, 125, 166; defeat of, 63; involvement in revolutionary movements, 37, 63, 98, 116, 129, 164, 166, 187; role in anticlerical campaigns, 56, 111–12
propagandists, 7, 37, 39, 72, 83, 89
public sphere: Catholic Church on women in, 103; labor and, 128; Madero on women in, 90; politics in, 116; women in, 8, 13–18, 32, 44, 137, 158; women redefine, 62, 84, 181–82, 188, 210
Puritan lodge of Valencia, 51

race (*raza*), 6, 17, 20, 37, 186
race formations, 200
radical feminist movements: impact on women's rights, 4, 13–17, 34, 42–44, 48, 90, 121, 135; and labor movement, 14, 108–12, 125
Ramos, María Dolores, 49
Ramos Escandón, Carmen, 8
Redón, Aldana, 88
Reds, 69, 73, 125, 130, 132
regidoras (female members of the city council), 138, 156, 171, 176–77
Rendón, Guadalupe, 142
Rendón, J. Merced, 121

Republican, Spanish, 47–55
Republican League of Portuguese Women (1909), 55
Republican mother, 87–88
Rerum Novarum (1891), 22, 40
Reyes, Bernardo (general), 89
Reyismo, 40, 41
rights, individual, 31, 105, 109, 148
Río Blanco (textile factory), 122, 129, 132–33
Rizal, José (1861–96), 52
Robledo García, Irene (1890–1988), 30, 40–41, 95, 136
Robles, Jovita, 162
Robles Gil, Emeterio (governor), 64
Rodríguez, Emilio (1882–1962), 72
Ropero de los Pobres (Poor people's wardrobe), 26
Rosales, Laura, 134, 171
Roy, Manabendra Nath, 108
Ruiz, Consuelo, 136
Ruiz Cabañas, Samuel, 100, 102, 112
Ruiz Cortines, Adolfo, 149, 177–78, 196, 204–6, 213
Rumbos nuevos, 55, 74–81, 213
rural politics: and educational reforms, 200; Urzúa Flores and, 188, 198–204, 206; women in, 8, 184, 189, 191, 198–204, 206

Salazar, Rosendo, 112
Sánchez Susarrey, Jaime, 206
Sanfeliú Giménez, Luz, 52
San Martín Hidalgo (Jalisco, Mexico), 181, 183–86, 188–91, 193–98, 201–7
Santa María, Refugio, 162
Santa Zita Conference, 105–6
Schell, Patience, 26

schools: Academia Comercial "Vizcarra," 188; Benito Juárez, 3; breakfast programs, 30; Colegio de San Nicolás, 192; Josefa Ortiz de Domínguez, 188; Juan Palomar, 170; Quetzalcóaltl, 113. *See also* Catholic: schools; education; Normal School

Scott, Joan, 3, 6, 12, 42, 47, 125

Secretaría de Educación Pública, SEP (Secretariat of public education), 67, 145, 189

Secretaría de Industria (Ministry of industry), 127

Secretaría de la Defensa Nacional (National defense ministry), 114, 118, 205

Secretaría de Salud (Health ministry), 192–94

secularization, 83, 212

segregation of women, 128–29, 177

Semanario ilustrado la mujer moderna (Galindo), 42, 85

Servín, Elisa, 116

Severidad lodge, 51

sexual difference, 12, 46–47, 96

sexuality, 132, 188–89, 191

Sierra, Justo, 20, 89

Silva Romero, Francisco, 169, 170

Sindicato de Obreras Escogedoras de Café de Córdoba, 154

Sindicato de Trabajadores de Molinos de Nixtamal y Similares, STMNS (Union of cornmeal mill and similar workers), 165

Sindicato Libertario de Obreros de Río Blanco, 133

Sindicato Progresista Libertario Obreros del Batán (1925), 132

Sindicato Único de Trabajadores Automovilistas de Jalisco, SUTAJ (Sole labor union of the automobile workers of Jalisco), 140, 153

Siqueiros, David Alfaro, 91, 126

Sirgo, Fernando, 73

Sivón, Nicolás, 98

skilled labor class, 86, 123, 193

Smith, Stephanie, 84

socialist educational project (1934–40), 136, 162, 167

social question, the, 22, 40, 44, 83

social reform: impact of feminist movements, 44, 137; intersection with labor and educational policies, 28, 31, 121, 133, 136, 144, 211; role of key activists, 23, 28, 31, 44, 59, 210

social volunteerism, 153

Some Passages from the Life of María Arcelia Díaz (1979), 148

Sor Juana Inés de la Cruz, 9

Spanish Civil War (1936–39), 80

speech: Laura Apodaca offers, 35, 37, 42, 94–96, 99; de Sárraga Hernández offers, 51, 59–63; María Arcelia Díaz offers, 20–21, 142; Martínez Villanueva, 175–78; men offer, 20, 93, 106, 144, 187; public, 1, 20, 148, 182, 188; women offer, 14, 144

Spiritism, 4, 46–51, 57–63, 83, 90, 209, 211

sports, 96–97, 136, 165, 171, 173, 175, 200

state formation, 4, 9, 183; new state formation (1920–40), 6, 16; postrevolutionary (1917–40), 18, 181

strikes, 28, 99, 111, 122–24, 127, 151, 158, 161–63

subaltern, 6–7, 17, 121, 150, 183, 211

subjectivity, 5, 211

suffrage: impact on women, 156, 169, 175, 177, 183, 184, 212, 214; male, 12; municipal, 181, 198; in scholarly literature, 1, 12; as secondary concern for women, 45, 46, 53, 81; women favor, 42, 137, 163, 167, 208. *See also* vote
suffragette, 46

Talleres Gráficos (Printers' workshops), 112
teachers: Catholic, 25, 41, 105, 130; in scholarly literature, 9; and social programs, 30; women as, 31, 37–41, 69, 88, 96–99, 102, 117, 158; and workers, 25, 40–41, 110, 136, 140, 145, 159–61
teatros: Degollado (Guadalajara), 20, 69, 87, 94–97, 110–11; Hidalgo (Colima), 79; Maxim (Havana), 72; Obrero (Mexico City), 69; Principal (Guadalajara), 41, 97, 99, 112; Xicoténcatl (Mexico City), 59
temperance, 21, 94
temporalities, 3
textile factories, 121–22, 157; workers, 121–22. *See also* La Escoba; Río Blanco
Threlkeld, Megan, 14
"To Kardec" (Belén de Sárraga), 49–50
Topete, Everardo (1935–39), 185
Torres, Elena, 112
tributes, 72, 73, 87, 139–49, 177

Unión de Obreros Libertarios de Atemajac (1924), 132
unionization: María Arcelia Díaz and, 17, 122, 134, 136, 211; impact on labor rights, 158, 161–62, 165, 177, 211;
modernization, 31, 161, 211; rural politics, 28
Unión Libertaria de Obreros de Río Blanco (1924), 132–33
Unión Obrera de La Experiencia, UOLE (La experiencia labor union), 1, 120, 131, 133
Unión Profesional de Empleadas de Comercio (Professional union of catholic female employees), 105, 130
Unión Profesional de Maestras del Sagrado Corazón de Jesús y de la Asunción, 130
upper class, 25–26, 34, 121
Urzúa, Manuel (nephew of Guadalupe Urzúa), 184
Urzúa Flores, María Guadalupe (1912–2004): family of, 184, 186; as *gestora*, 181–83; music, 184; political career, 183–84, 189, 202; public works, 189–92; in rural politics, 185, 188, 194, 197–98, 200, 205–8; and San Martín Hidalgo hospital, 192–95; women's suffrage, 181, 183–84, 196–98, 208

Valadez Ramírez, Antonio (governor), 120
Valencia, Felipe, 97
Vargas Trejo, Florita, 89–90
Vasconcelos, José, 78
Vaughan, Mary Kay, 5, 7, 8, 59
Velasco de Alemán, Beatriz, 194
Velásquez, Fidel, 146, 155, 174
veterans, 69, 114–16, 118
Villa, Francisco, 29–30, 39, 100
Villanueva, María, 157
Villistas, 21, 29–30, 39, 41, 57, 82, 91, 100
Virgin of Guadalupe, 9, 82–83, 109

vote, 76, 80, 108, 132, 171, 175–78, 196. *See also* suffrage

wages, 111, 134. *See also* equal pay for equal work
Walkowitz, Judith, 50
women: and Catholic Church, 16, 34, 43–44, 83; and Catholic rights, 79, 93, 105; Catholic vision of, 21, 25–26; and citizenship, 8, 12–14, 16, 84, 86; and consumption, 39, 42, 44; contribution to educational reform, 83–84, 102, 136, 211; contribution to labor reform, 135–36, 150; education of, 10, 34–37, 42–44, 62, 87, 99, 135–36, 144; as elected officials, 165, 167, 169–70, 180–81, 196, 198, 201–2; emancipation of, 1, 108, 136, 142, 144, 159, 179, 213; and fashion, 20, 35, 39–44; and feminist congresses, 67, 81, 85, 159, 162; and feminist movements, 10, 42–43, 136; impact of, 83–84, 101–2, 135, 211–12; impact on state formation, 97, 119, 150, 168; and labor, 84, 135, 150, 167–68, 211; and politics, 10, 62, 84, 97, 119, 135–36, 211–12; representation of, 9–10; and revolutionary leaders, 34, 85, 96, 98; rights, 15, 34, 42–43, 87, 121, 135, 150, 209
Women's Day (March 8), 80
working class: and Catholics, 26, 107; the Centro Radical Femenino, 112; cross-class relations, 49; and education, 73; gender relations, 166–77; organizations, 158, 163–64; and revolutionary leaders, 29–30, 36; rural, 86; and transnational feminism, 15; and women, 36, 52–53, 81, 88–89, 99, 121–22, 130–34, 144
Wright de Kleinhans, Laureana (1846–96), 87

Yáñez, Agustín, 69, 198

Zapatistas, 21, 57
Zárate, José Eduardo, 205
Zuno Hernández, José Guadalupe (1923–26), 69, 91, 112, 114, 126

In the Confluencias series:

The Sonoran Dynasty in Mexico: Revolution, Reform, and Repression
By Jürgen Buchenau

Freethinkers and Labor Leaders: Women, Social Change, and Politics in Modern Mexico
By María Teresa Fernández Aceves
Translated by Tanya Huntington

The Enlightened Patrolman: Early Law Enforcement in Mexico City
By Nicole von Germeten

Men of God: Mendicant Orders in Colonial Mexico
By Asunción Lavrin

Strength from the Waters: A History of Indigenous Mobilization in Northwest Mexico
By James V. Mestaz

Informal Metropolis: Life on the Edge of Mexico City, 1940–1976
By David Yee

To order or obtain more information on these or other University of Nebraska Press titles, visit nebraskapress.unl.edu.

www.ingramcontent.com/pod-product-compliance
Lightning Source LLC
Chambersburg PA
CBHW021345300426
44114CB00012B/1085